Alan Bishop is Professor of English at McMaster University, Hamilton, Ontario. He has edited several volumes of Vera Brittain's writings, including *Chronicle of Youth*, her diary of the First World War.

Mark Bostridge won the Gladstone Memorial Prize at Oxford University. His books include *Vera Brittain: A Life*, shortlisted for the Whitbread Biography Award, the NCR Non-Fiction Prize, and the Fawcett Prize; *Lives for Sale*, a collection of biographers' tales; and *Florence Nightingale: The Making of an Icon*, published in autumn 2008.

Letters From A Lost Generation

First World War Letters of Vera Brittain and Four Friends: Roland Leighton, Edward Brittain, Victor Richardson, Geoffrey Thurlow

Edited by Alan Bishop and Mark Bostridge

virago

VIRAGO

First published in Great Britain by Little, Brown and Company in 1998
This edition published by Virago Press in 2008

Photographic Acknowledgements: McMaster University Library: illustrations
1, 3, 4, 6, 10, 12, 13, 15; Shirley Williams: illustrations 2, 5, 7, 8, 9, 14, 16, 17;
Paul Berry: illustration 11.

A CIP catalogue record for this book is
available from the British Library

ISBN 978-1-84408-570-5

Typeset in Bembo by M Rules
Printed and bound in Great Britain by
Clays Ltd, St Ives plc

Papers used by Virago are natural, renewable and recyclable
products made from wood grown in sustainable forests and certified
in accordance with the rules of the Forest Stewardship Council.

Mixed Sources
Product group from well-managed
forests and other controlled sources
www.fsc.org Cert no. SGS-COC-004081
© 1996 Forest Stewardship Council

FSC

Virago
An imprint of
Little, Brown Book Group
100 Victoria Embankment
London EC4Y 0DY

An Hachette Livre Company
www.hachettelivre.co.uk

www.virago.co.uk

In memory of Paul Berry (1919–1999)

and for

Mark Walton and Iza Bishop

CONTENTS

ILLUSTRATIONS

A NOTE TO THE TEXT

The letters from which this book has been composed are in the Vera Brittain Archive of the William Ready Division of Archives and Research Collections, McMaster University Library, Hamilton, Ontario. They preserve, to an extraordinary and perhaps unique extent, two major correspondences of the First World War, and one side of three others.

To Vera Brittain, who later drew on the letters in writing *Testament of Youth* (1933), we owe their preservation. Her brother Edward and fiancé Roland both sent back to her, for safe-keeping, the letters she wrote them (64 and 142 respectively); and she carefully stored the letters they, and Victor Richardson and Geoffrey Thurlow, wrote her (Edward 136; Roland 108; Victor 35; Geoffrey 22). Geoffrey's letters to Edward (41) came into her possession after the latter's death. These sets appear to be complete, apart from Edward's final letter or letters to Vera, and her letters to Edward between June 1917 and June 1918.

In addition, some letters by Roland and Victor to Edward (8 each), by Edward to Roland (1) and Geoffrey (1), and by Vera to Geoffrey (2), have survived. The Brittain Archive also holds extensive related correspondences or communications, including telegrams, Field Service and other postcards, letters of condolence, and family letters – notably those between Vera and Edward and their parents (Vera's letters to her mother partially replace those missing from her correspondence with Edward).

The editors' main task in preparing the text has been to abridge the many (often very long) letters so as to lay bare the vivid and moving personal stories they tell, against the historical background of a cataclysm that destroyed four of the five writers. In general, it has been necessary to reduce the letters considerably in number and length. Vera's letters have been reduced more than the four men's, and some episodes detailed in *Testament of Youth* or *Chronicle of Youth* (her diary of the period) are minimally represented.

The selected letters, or excerpts from letters, are chronologically arranged. We have attempted to retain what is significant, personally and historically, in their content, and what is characteristic, idiosyncratic, in their writing.

Omissions within letters are indicated by the conventional three stops. Where multiple stops and asterisks were used as punctuation by the writers (especially Roland and Vera), these have been standardised at five. Punctuation has not been altered generally unless confusing or disturbingly incorrect. However, Vera Brittain frequently has dashes where full-stops are normal – presumably a result of rapid writing: these have been rendered as stops unless clearly intended as dashes.

Misspellings and other obvious minor errors have been corrected silently; but idiosyncratic variants like 'alright' and 'temporally' have been retained. Missing or obviously erroneous words have been replaced, within square brackets. Addresses and salutations have been standardised, once established; but significant changes in them are shown. Paragraphing has been imposed occasionally where a systematically larger gap between sentences suggested that the writer intended an economical alternative to conventional paragraphing.

We have avoided interpolations except to give necessary bridging information. Biographical and chronological information relating to the main figures will be found before the Introduction; brief explanatory notes, keyed to pagination, will be found after the letters; and, before the Index, a selective bibliography.

We hope that, in our editorial principles and all our editorial decisions, we have done justice to letters we love and admire.

Acknowledgements

We gratefully acknowledge the efficient and cheerful assistance given by the staff of the William Ready Division of Archives and Research Collections, McMaster University Library – especially by Carl Spadoni, Renu Barrett, Margaret Foley, Kathleen Garay, and Eden McLean.

Paul Berry, Senior Literary Executor for the Vera Brittain Estate, has encouraged and watched over this project with all his customary kindness and good sense. We are very grateful to David Leighton for his permission to publish Roland Leighton's letters and poems, and letters by Marie and Robert Leighton; and to Shiona Robotham for her kindness in permitting use of Victor Richardson's letters.

Among others who have offered advice and support, we would like to mention: Robin Baird-Smith, Charles Bostridge, Lyndall Gordon, David Goudge, Margaret Howatson, Andrew Lownie, Boaz ben Manasseh, David Mullooly, Richard Neustadt, Pamela Norris, Peter Parker, Marion Shaw, Katie and Scott Thomson, Mark Walton, Rebecca Williams, and Shirley Williams. The editors also acknowledge, with gratitude, the guidance and enthusiasm of Lennie Goodings and Sarah White at Little, Brown.

Alan Bishop
Mark Bostridge

April 1998

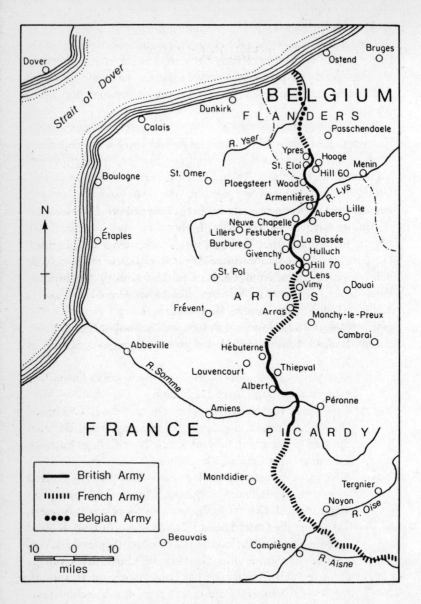

The Western Front in December 1915

CHRONOLOGY

1893   Birth of Vera Mary Brittain (29 December) at Newcastle-under-Lyme, north Staffordshire.

1895   Birth of Geoffrey Robert Youngman Thurlow at Chingford, Essex (5 March); birth of Victor Richardson at Hove, west Sussex (18 March); birth of Roland Aubrey Leighton in London (27 March); birth of Edward Harold Brittain at Macclesfield, Cheshire (30 November).

1908   Geoffrey Thurlow goes to Chigwell School in Essex.

1909   Roland, Edward and Victor go to Uppingham School in Rutland.

1911   Vera leaves St Monica's School at Kingswood in Surrey and returns home to Buxton, Derbyshire.

1913   Vera meets Roland at the Uppingham School 'Old Boys' (June); Vera rejects a proposal of marriage from Bertram Spafford (September); Edward sits the New College Entrance Examination at Oxford (December).

1914   Vera wins a Somerville College exhibition (March); Roland stays with the Brittains at Buxton (April); the Uppingham School Speech Day (11 July); the outbreak of war (4 August); Vera passes the Oxford Senior Examination (August); Roland is acting recruitment officer at Lowestoft (September); Vera goes up to Somerville, Geoffrey to University College, Oxford; Roland enlists as a second lieutenant in the 4th Norfolks (October); Edward is gazetted as a second lieutenant in the 10th Sherwood Foresters, Victor in the 4th Royal Sussex Regiment (November); Vera and Roland meet in London (December).

1915   Geoffrey leaves Oxford and enlists as a second lieutenant in
       the 10th Sherwood Foresters; Vera begins her second term at
       Oxford; Victor catches cerebro-spinal meningitis while in
       camp at Horsham, and is removed to hospital in Brighton for
       seven weeks (January); Roland visits Vera in Buxton before
       leaving for the Front with the 7th Worcesters (March); Vera
       begins her third term at Oxford (April); Vera takes Pass Mods.
       before going down from Oxford in order to nurse as a VAD
       at the Devonshire Hospital in Buxton (June); Roland on
       leave in England (August); Geoffrey goes to the Front with
       the 10th Sherwood Foresters; Vera starts nursing at the 1st
       London General Hospital, Camberwell (November); Roland
       is wounded while leading an expedition to repair the barbed
       wire in front of trenches at Hébuterne, and dies at the
       Casualty Clearing Station at Louvencourt (23 December); at
       the Grand Hotel in Brighton, Vera learns of Roland's death
       while waiting for him to come home on leave (26
       December).

1916   Edward departs for the Front with the 11th Sherwood
       Foresters; Geoffrey suffers shell shock and a face wound
       during heavy bombardment at Ypres (February); Vera visits
       Geoffrey in hospital at Fishmongers' Hall in London
       (February–March); Edward returns to England on leave
       (June); Edward is injured on the first day of the Battle of the
       Somme (1 July) leading the first wave of his company's
       attack, and is sent to the 1st London General in Camberwell;
       Geoffrey returns to France; Edward is awarded the Military
       Cross (August); Vera travels to Malta to nurse at St George's
       Hospital; Victor transfers to the 9th King's Royal Rifles, and
       leaves for France (September).

1917   Victor is badly wounded during an attack at Arras (9 April),
       and arrives in England for specialist treatment at the 2nd
       London General Hospital in Chelsea (19 April), where he is
       visited by Edward; Geoffrey is killed in action at Monchy-le-
       Preux in an attack on the Scarpe (23 April); Vera receives two
       cables from England, the first tells her that Victor's sight is
       now gone, the second informs her of Geoffrey's death (1
       May); Vera arrives back in England (28 May); Victor dies in

hospital (9 June) and is buried at Hove; Edward returns to the Front (30 June); Vera begins nursing at the 24th General at Étaples (August); Edward is posted, with the 11th Sherwood Foresters, to the Italian Front in northern Italy.

1918   Vera and Edward on leave together in London (January); Vera nurses at Étaples during Ludendorff's great offensive (March–April); she is forced to break her VAD contract to return home to care for her parents (end of April); Edward is killed in action during a counter-attack against the Austrian offensive on the Asiago Plateau (15 June); Vera and her father receive the telegram containing the news of Edward's death (22 June); Vera's first book, *Verses of a V.A.D.*, which includes elegies to Roland, Edward, Victor and Geoffrey, is published by Erskine Macdonald (August); Vera is working as a VAD at Queen Alexandra's Hospital on Millbank when the Armistice is declared (11 November).

BIOGRAPHICAL NOTES

Correspondents and other individuals referred to frequently throughout the text:

Vera:
: Vera Brittain (1893–1970). Educated at St Monica's School, Kingswood, and Somerville College, Oxford (1914–15, 1919–21); served as a VAD in London, Malta and France, 1914–19; postwar career as a writer, feminist and pacifist. Her most famous book is *Testament of Youth* (1933).

Roland:
: Roland Leighton (1895–1915). Educated at Uppingham School, Rutland; served as a second lieutenant in the 4th Norfolk and 7th Worcestershire regiments, 1914–15; died of wounds near Hébuterne, 1915, and buried at Louvencourt.

Edward:
: Edward Brittain (1895–1918). Educated at Uppingham School, Rutland; served as a second lieutenant and captain in the 10th and 11th Sherwood Foresters, 1914–18; awarded the MC in 1916; killed in action on the Asiago Plateau in 1918, and buried at Granezza.

Victor (Tar/Tah):
: Victor Richardson (1895–1917). Educated at Uppingham School, Rutland; served as a second lieutenant in the 4th Royal Sussex Regiment and the 9th King's Royal Rifle Corps, 1914–17, died

in London of wounds received in the Battle of Arras, 1917, and buried at Hove; awarded the MC posthumously.

Geoffrey: Geoffrey Thurlow (1895–1917). Educated at Chigwell School, Essex, and University College Oxford; served as a second lieutenant in the 10th Sherwood Foresters, 1915–17; killed in action at Monchy-le-Preux, 1917; buried in an unmarked grave.

Mr Brittain: Thomas Arthur Brittain (1864–1935). Father of Vera and Edward Brittain. Director of paper mills, Brittains Ltd, 1890–1915.

Mrs Brittain: Edith Brittain (1868–1948), née Bervon. Mother of Vera and Edward Brittain.

Mrs Leighton: Marie Connor Leighton (*c.* 1865–1941). Mother of Roland Leighton. Writer of serial stories for the Northcliffe Press, and the author of some eighty books, including *Convict 99* (co-written with her husband Robert, 1898), and *Boy of My Heart* (1916), a memoir of Roland (published anonymously).

Mr Leighton: Robert Leighton (1858–1934). Father of Roland Leighton. In 1896 he became the first literary editor of the *Daily Mail*. Author of popular adventure books for boys.

INTRODUCTION

'Nothing in the papers, not the most vivid & heartbreaking descriptions, have made me realise war like your letters.' This was Vera Brittain writing to Roland Leighton, her future fiancé, on 17 April 1915, little more than a fortnight after he had arrived on the Western Front; and her judgement might appropriately be extended to the other letters which make up this present collection. They were written in the years 1913 to 1918 between Vera Brittain and the four young men – Roland Leighton, Vera's younger brother Edward, and their two close friends, Victor Richardson and Geoffrey Thurlow – who were killed in the course of the First World War. Taken together, this correspondence presents a remarkable and profoundly moving portrait of five young people caught up in the cataclysm of total war, writing and responding to one another's reactions and to the tumultuous events as they occurred.

Few collections of First World War letters span the duration of the conflict, or present both sides of the correspondence. Fewer still contain both male and female perspectives. Furthermore, the broader picture which these letters provide allows us to see and understand the war from a variety of points of view: that of the young officer in the trenches, of the volunteer nurse in military hospitals at home and abroad, and here and there, too, are glimpses of what life was like for the civilian population on the home front. *Letters From a Lost Generation* offers important historical testimony, then; but it also tells a powerful story of idealism, disillusionment, and personal tragedy representative of the common experience of thousands of people throughout Britain at this time. Perhaps best of all, the letters convey the uncertainty, confusion, and almost unbearable suspense of wartime.

Only a small proportion of the 560 or so letters from which this selection has been made have ever been published before, though they formed the backbone of *Testament of Youth* (1933), Vera Brittain's bestselling account of her First World War experiences. When she began to write the book in 1929, she was determined to quote freely from the personal letters which survived in her own and in her mother Edith's possession, but inevitably she was in the end prevented from being as frank and open in her use of them as she had hoped, by the restrictions of copyright. In the cases of Victor Richardson and Geoffrey Thurlow, for example, she was forced to rely heavily on paraphrase.

This current edition deliberately includes only the passages we consider to be of the greatest interest and significance and complete letters, therefore, have in many instances not been printed. It has also been our intention that the main focus throughout should be on the four men. While Vera Brittain remains, of course, pivotal to the drama that unfolds, it is also true that her war experiences have become increasingly familiar in the past twenty years as *Testament of Youth* has confirmed its position as a much loved and valued contribution to the literature of the First World War. In order to keep this book to a manageable length, we have sacrificed much extraneous information relating to Vera Brittain's time at Oxford, together with a lot of repetitive detail about her period as a nurse. Those seeking a more comprehensive account of these aspects of her life are referred to *Chronicle of Youth: Vera Brittain's War Diary 1913–1917* (Gollancz, 1981) edited by Alan Bishop, to *Vera Brittain: A Life* (Chatto & Windus, 1995) by Paul Berry and Mark Bostridge, as well as to *Testament of Youth* itself.

Vera Brittain's own letters as a young woman bear many of the stylistic hallmarks of someone born to be a writer. These qualities are perhaps most strikingly evident in the correspondence of 1915 between Vera and Roland Leighton, which poignantly demonstrates all the difficulties, constraints, and misunderstandings which could arise in a love affair during wartime. To a great extent, though, *Letters From a Lost Generation* is a portrait of four public school boys, Roland, Edward, Victor, and Geoffrey, who went almost straight from school to the dreadful fate that awaited them as infantry subalterns on the battlefields of France, Belgium and Italy. Their voices as they emerge in their letters to Vera Brittain, and to each other, are often eloquent, rarely resentful or questioning, occasionally dulled by grief, or by the sheer monotony of army routine, sometimes immature, but then expanding suddenly with passages of vivid and startling immediacy.

Three of the men were educated at Uppingham School in Rutland. Roland Leighton, Edward Brittain and Victor Richardson all arrived at The Lodge, one of Uppingham's school houses, in 1909. By the time they left the school in the summer of 1914 they had become firm friends, dubbed by Roland's mother, Marie Leighton, 'the Three Musketeers'; and Edward's connection with Roland would in some ways be further strengthened by the beginnings of Roland's relationship with Vera, though it is also clear that Edward was at first mildly jealous of his sister's involvement with his close friend.

In the early years of the century, Uppingham was still living off the reputation it had gained during the period of its most famous headmaster, Edward Thring. Between 1853 and his death in 1887, Thring had transformed Uppingham from an obscure county grammar into a major public school embodying the 'muscular Christian' ideal. Since Thring's day, however, there had been a marked decline in standards, and some of the worst aspects of public school athleticism, militarism and morality had appeared. The artist C.R.W. Nevinson, who was at the school shortly before Roland, Edward, and Victor, remembered in his autobiography, *Paint and Prejudice* (1937), that Uppingham had nonetheless been considered one of the best of the public schools.

Since then I have often wondered what the worst was like. No qualms of mine gave me an inkling of the horrors I was to undergo . . . I was kicked, hounded, caned, flogged, hair-brushed, morning, noon and night. The more I suffered, the less I cared. The longer I stayed, the harder I grew.

This toughening-up process was no doubt considered a formative element in the boys' development, but Nevinson's memories also throw interesting light on another characteristic central to the public school ideal of the age. As a result of R.B. Haldane's Army Reforms of 1907, Officers' Training Corps (OTC) had been introduced into public schools as a gesture towards national preparedness for war. At Uppingham the introduction of the cadet corps was an idea that fell on fertile ground. Nevinson recalled the mood of 'appalling jingoism' that had prevailed at Uppingham during the South African War, and the Uppingham OTC was very largely to determine the school's ethos in the years immediately preceding the outbreak of world war. Regardless of whether a boy belonged to the corps or not, the atmosphere of militarism was pervasive. No one, for instance, was allowed to take part in any inter-house athletic or sporting contest, or win a school prize, without having first passed a shooting test.

The OTC provided the institutional mechanism for public school militarism. But a more complex web of cultural ideas and assumptions, some taken from the classics, some from popular fiction, some even developed through competitive sports on the playing fields, was instilled by schoolmasters in their pupils, and contributed to the generation of 1914's overwhelming willingness to march off in search of glory. Traditions of chivalry, the values of self-sacrifice, fair play, selfless patriotism, honour, duty – 'heroism in the abstract' – all played their part in fostering illusions about the nature of warfare. For some there was additionally the matter of the school's honour. As Geoffrey Thurlow, who had attended Chigwell School in Essex, a minor public school foundation dating back to the seventeenth century, wrote in one of his final letters from France as he waited for the action in which he would be killed: 'I only hope I don't fail at the critical moment as truly I am a horrible coward: wish I could do well especially for the School's sake.'

The young Vera Brittain stood in awe of the public school ideal. 'For girls', she lamented in her diary during her visit to Uppingham for the school Speech Day in July 1914, 'there is nothing equivalent to public school for boys – these fine traditions & unwritten laws that turn out so many splendid characters have been withheld from them – to their detriment.' Without doubt, the most splendid of these characters, in Vera's eyes, was Roland Leighton, and it is Roland who dominates the first half of this book, and whose memory makes its presence felt throughout the second half, after his death.

Roland was very definitely the leader of the Uppingham triumvirate, living up to his Uppingham nickname of 'Monseigneur'.

At school he was a brilliant prizeman, Captain of his house and Colour-Sergeant of the OTC, among other school offices he held, and when war broke out, he was the first of the three to get to the front. As befits the member of a literary household (both his parents were professional writers, and Roland himself was a poet), Roland's letters are the most self-consciously literary of the collection, and in their finer passages, written once he was out in France, he juxtaposes pastoral scenes with elements of the destructive force of war, to strikingly ironic effect. His letters also trace most clearly the sad path which led from idealism to disillusionment. In September 1914, while still in England, he writes to Vera that the war 'is to me a very fascinating thing – something, if often horrible, yet very ennobling, and very beautiful . . .' And yet, after barely a week in the trenches, he has been forced to realise that 'There is nothing glorious in trench warfare. It is all a waiting and a waiting and taking of petty advantages – and those who can wait longest win. And it is all for nothing – for an empty name, for an ideal perhaps – after all.'

After Edward's death, Vera Brittain found it difficult to come to any certain conclusions about the character of the younger brother who had been her closest companion since childhood, and whose Military Cross had made him a family hero. 'It is, and always has been, difficult to estimate what manner of person Edward really was at the close of his Uppingham years,' she wrote in *Testament of Youth*, 'and it becomes harder as time marches on.' The strong core of self-containment which made him difficult to know in person is a quality also reflected in many of his letters. 'Immaculate of the trenches', as he was known by his fellow officers because of his immaculate attire even in the worst conditions of active service, often appears orderly and controlled when writing to his beloved sister. Sometimes his guard drops, and a humorous side to his personality is revealed. After 1 July 1916, when he distinguished himself in action on the first day of the Battle of the Somme, he comes into his own, and a new note of authority is discernible.

There are few clues to be found in Edward's letters to Vera, or in hers to him, which might offer a solution to the mystery surrounding Edward's death in action on the Asiago Plateau in northern Italy in June 1918 (one of the major gaps in the correspondence is the apparent disappearance of Vera's letters to Edward for the final year of his life). In 1934, the year following the publication of *Testament of Youth*, Vera made the discovery that, shortly before the action in which he was killed, Edward had been faced with an enquiry and, in all probability, a courtmartial when his battalion came out of the line, because of his homosexual involvement with men in his company. It remains a possibility that, faced with the disgrace of a courtmartial, Edward went into battle deliberately seeking to be killed.

Some readers might be tempted to deduce from the evidence of the ardent quality of some of Geoffrey Thurlow's letters to Edward (the other side of the correspondence does not survive), especially from the closing tag of many of them ('Him that thou knowest thine'), that their relationship may have gone beyond the bounds of chaste friendship. It is, however, important to emphasise that sentiments that appear overtly homosexual to modern sensibilities may, in the context of their time, have been nothing of the kind. Edward and Geoffrey had quickly befriended one another while training together in England in 1915, and their friendship had remained unbroken when Geoffrey was sent out to France ahead of Edward with the 10th Sherwood Foresters in October 1915.

Born in Chingford, Essex, the youngest child of elderly parents, a retired printer and his wife, Geoffrey had attended the nearby Chigwell School where he became Head of School in his final year. 'He was a boy of the highest sense of duty and remarkable singleness of purpose,' *The Chigwellian* recorded after his death, 'and for these qualities, as well as for his tact . . . and his charm of manner, he stands out prominently from among the many excellent Heads of School whom we have known.' A 'non-militarist at heart', Geoffrey had not rushed to enlist in the first months of the war, but had gone up to University College, Oxford, in the autumn of 1914. After only a term, he had felt compelled to put aside his personal objections to the war for patriotism's sake, and volunteer.

Geoffrey's obsession with failing, his lack of confidence, and his fear that he would be unable to show courage in battle are the constant refrain of his letters. But there is also a wonderfully humorous side to what he writes, and his lively vignettes, amounting almost to a stream of consciousness, possess a texture wholly unlike any of the other letters in the book.

Geoffrey's concern that he would prove too 'windy' contrasts with the attempts of Victor Richardson, the last of the Uppingham three, to convince himself and others that he could take on the mantle of the warrior, and become a military hero. Overshadowed at Uppingham by Roland and Edward, Victor was less academically promising than either of his two friends, though he won a place at Cambridge, and had an ambition to be a doctor. He also came from a more ordinary and less affluent background: his father was a popular but poorly paid junior partner in a well-established dental practice in Hove.

Possessed of enormous sweetness of character, Victor was known by his friends to be completely dependable and trustworthy, as Roland's names for him, 'Father Confessor' or 'the Brighton Block', imply. But that sweetness was accompanied by characteristics of self-effacement and self-deprecation which could clearly be a source of irritation.

The idea of a lost generation – that the postwar decline of Britain could be blamed on the fact that the best men, the noblest, strongest, and most cultivated, had been killed between 1914 and 1918 – became a powerful national myth in the inter-war years, and Vera Brittain was its most prominent spokeswoman. The emotive appeal of the myth has ensured that it has never quite been overthrown, despite an impressive array of statistics to counter its central contention; and reading these letters it is not difficult to understand why.

Vera Brittain returned to her own personal recollections of the 'lost generation' in the last article of any significance that she wrote towards the end of her life. In 1968 she was the only woman contributor to a volume of essays entitled *Promise of Greatness*, published to commemorate the fiftieth anniversary of the Armistice. Despite her promise to Edward that she would return to Uppingham if he was killed, she had never revisited the school, and so had never seen the names of 'the Three Musketeers' inscribed in gold lettering on the list of 447 old boys commemorated on the school war memorial. 'There are too many ghosts [there] for me,' she had explained to Maurice Richardson, Victor's younger brother. Nevertheless, in an article about her war service she invoked the memory of Uppingham in the summer of 1914 as a symbol of a vanished world of prewar innocence:

What does the date, August 4, 1914, immediately bring back to me? ...
The huge figures of the war casualties and the cost of war expenditure
vanish in a phantasmagoria of human scenes and sounds. I think,
instead, of names, places, and individuals, and hear, above all, the echo
of a boy's laughing voice on a school playing field in that golden
summer.

And gradually the voice becomes one of many: the sound of the
Uppingham School choir marching up the chapel for the Speech Day
Service in July 1914, and singing the Commemoration hymn ... There
was a thrilling, a poignant quality in those boys' voices, as though they
were singing their own requiem – as indeed many of them were.

As we approach the eightieth anniversary of the Armistice, the last
major anniversary of the First World War to be commemorated
while there are participants still living, the voices heard in these letters strike a deep chord. Each one of their stories is imbued with a
strong element of tragedy and a sense of promise unfulfilled; but they
are emblematic too of their generation, haunted by grief and loss,
and singled out for destruction.

ONE

28 SEPTEMBER 1913 – 29 JULY 1914

The fate that held our youth within its power
   Waited its hour.
– VERA BRITTAIN, 'The War Generation: Ave'

Down the long white road we walked together,
Down between the grey hills and the heather. . . .

You seemed all brown and soft, just like a linnet,
Your errant hair had shadowed sunbeams in it,
And there shone all April
In your eyes.
                    – ROLAND LEIGHTON, 'Nachklang'

   Only a turn of head,
   A good-bye lightly said,
   And you set out to tread
   Your manlier road.
– ROLAND LEIGHTON, 'L'Envoi'

In December 1911, shortly before her eighteenth birthday, Vera Brittain completed her final term at St Monica's School in Kingswood, Surrey, and returned to her parents' home in Buxton, Derbyshire. For much of the following two years she was occupied with life as a provincial debutante, attending formal dances, assisting her mother in receiving and making calls, and playing golf and tennis. However, the ceaseless round of socialising soon palled, and Vera formed an ambition to go to university at Oxford. In the autumn of 1913 she began to study towards this end. In September of this year she also received her first proposal of marriage from a neighbouring businessman, Bertram Spafford, a man she barely knew, but rejected him immediately. Her younger brother Edward, who had been her closest companion since childhood, and was in his final year at Uppingham, was also hoping to go to Oxford. He wrote to express his amusement and sympathy at the news of the proposal.

Edward Brittain to Vera Brittain

The Lodge, Uppingham School,
28 September 1913

Dear Mrs Vera Spafford,
   Thank you very much for your letter. I can stand 4d so you needn't have bothered about the stamps but thanks v. much all the same. I think it is quite exceptionally priceless you receiving a proposal at your age. Don't be too hard on the wretched man. If he really does love you I suppose he has a right to say so, so to speak, though, as you say, I daresay the money question is not far in the background. If I were you I wouldn't be too rude because it is more his misfortune than his fault that he wants to marry you. Of course I know Father must be very annoyed, but you should point out to him that the fault is not so much with the creation as with the Creator. Plenty of people before to-day have conceived impossible unions for themselves with another, without it being any fault of theirs. I daresay it has been a good thing in a way. It is always desirable to learn a thing early and everyone needs a little practice in the gentle art of rejection of suitors. You will doubtless have to repeat the process many times in future before you find

the right man, if you ever do, as there are far too many men who consider themselves only in the marriage question. It is always 'She will suit me alright', never 'Shall I suit her alright?' as well.

I hope you have started regular work now; I want you to write and tell me what you are doing and where you are in a certain book etc. from time to time. Have you got Palgrave's Golden Treasury thing yet?

    With much love
      Your affectionate

          Edward

Edward to Vera

Uppingham, 16 November 1913

The birth certificate accompanied by an entrance form and a character certificate duly went to Oxford yesterday and I hope I shall not have to ask anyone to get me another birth certificate at any time if it is so dreadfully expensive.

Please have a look at the Beethoven Concerto and a Sonata or something if you have time before the holidays: in my spare moments of which there are few just now I continue my course of self-instruction on the piano. I forget if I ever told you that I won my House Fives with a small fellow called Addington who is a coming Fives player: we got 12/6 each which was rather useful though I expect he has spent his on grub by this time; mine is intact, waiting in store for an evil day. I haven't done nearly as much reading as I ought to have done for the Exam. but I haven't any time. Can you tell me anything about the History of Europe or the World between A.D. 100 and 1066 because I know nothing, or tell me of a book which puts it shortly. I only know that Charlemagne was crowned in 800 but what he was doing there I haven't the faintest.

Edward to Vera

Uppingham, 7 December 1913

This must be short as I have a bad cold (don't tell Ma it is bad) and I want to lie up before chapel this afternoon; I have got a bit of a headache too as the result of doing too much work but it is nothing and I shall be quite alright in a day or two. Unfortunately we now have to start doing ordinary exams. but I shall just do them badly. I think I might have done much worse in the Papers; the Unseens were the only things really rather above me but there were 200 people up for about 30 scholarships and 20 Exhibitions, so I don't expect to get anything. We met most of the O.U.'s [Old Uppinghamians] at Oxford and they were very nice to us. . .

Oxford is heaven on earth except for the climate which gave me this cold. I went to have a look at Somerville; it seems quite nice though I couldn't see much of it at night. I drink to next year when I expect we shall enjoy ourselves there.

Edward to Vera

Uppingham, 25 March 1914

Many thousand congratulations on your Exhibition. Why would you not believe me before when I told you that the *average* woman of to-day is not clever? If, as you say, you did partly the wrong work it shows that you must have been far superior to the majority for them to give you an Exhibition. . . I feel quite out of it myself not being able to get anything; the only chance is either that next year's scholarships should take place a week earlier or that 10 days would not put me out of it or that New College should offer an Exhibition. I can't get that Music Schol. at Balliol either because it is not until 1916. However you at any rate have saved the family reputation and I heartily congratulate you once more; it will be most useful to you all the time you are up at Oxford as Scholars and Exhibitioners form a higher class of their own and it will also be a great satisfaction to feel that you have succeeded in earning something. I wish I could.

Having won an exhibition to Somerville College, Vera had still to pass the Oxford Senior Local examination in July before a place at the university was definitely hers. For a short time that spring, though, her attention was distracted from her studies by the arrival at Melrose of Edward's school-friend Roland Leighton, who had come to spend a few days with the Brittains over the Easter holidays. Roland had recently been awarded a scholarship to Merton College, Oxford, the crowning achievement of a glittering school career. At Uppingham he was the captain of his house, The Lodge, captain in classics, praepositor (prefect), editor of the school maga-zine, president of the Union Society, and Colour-Sergeant of Uppingham's Officers' Training Corps. Vera was wary of him at first, but by the time she left for a short holiday in the Lake District, she had begun to find him stim-ulating company; and he, for his part, found it difficult to hide his disappointment that he would be spending his last days in Buxton without her.

Roland to Vera

Melrose, The Park, Buxton, 22 April 1914

Dear Vera,

– Edward has commanded me to address you in this way. I hope you do not object – Here is The Story of an African Farm, but such a wretched little edition after all, that I feel it is hardly worth sending you. I find it is the only one not out of print now. Please forgive it & me. The spirit was willing, but the publishers unaccommodating. When you have read it let me know what you think of it, and whether you agree with me that Lyndall is rather like you – only sadder perhaps and not so charmingly controversial.

I am so very sorry that you had to go away just as I was learn-ing to renounce the Quiet Voice and had begun to feel less shy. It sounds very selfish of me to say this; but I have enjoyed my visit to you (as you put it) immensely. Now that the greater attraction has taken herself off I shall be free to devote myself to the neglected Edward. Not that he seems to mind very much.

I am very disappointed about that book. I hope you do not mind. Meanwhile – till Speech Day.

Yours very sincerely

Roland Leighton (or Aubrey if you prefer it.)

Vera to Roland

Melrose, Buxton, 25 April 1914

Dear Roland –

...Thank you so very much for the 'Story of an African Farm', I am delighted with it. I cannot think why you should despise the edition, as it pleases me, for though the ornate bindings look very elegant in my bookcase, the plainer ones are the kind I *use*. I have not begun it yet as the 'Mill on the Floss' is still unfinished, having been somewhat neglected while I was away. When I have read it I will write and tell you what I think of it. Probably I shall be unable to see any resemblance to myself in Lyndall, but doubtless that will be owing to my lack of skill in *self*-criticism.

I too was very sorry to go away on Tuesday, though I have had such a delightful time that I need not complain . . . . . I have motored round all the Lakes except Westwater, and have never in my life seen anything so lovely – 'Earth has not anything to show more fair.'

I hear you & Edward managed still to live quite comfortably in spite of my departure, and that you were dragged off somewhat unwillingly to a dutiful inspection of our magnificent Manchester – once seen, always avoided! . . .

I shall make every effort to come to Speech Day, & shall look out most carefully for the Quiet Voice, especially if you are well laden with prizes as the result of the occasion. The Quiet Voice, you perceive, is intensely symbolic, – at least to me.

Once again many thanks for the book.

Yours very sincerely

Vera M. Brittain

Vera to Roland

Buxton, 3 May 1914

I promised to tell you what I thought of 'The Story of an African Farm'. I have nearly finished it & it has impressed me very much; it is the kind of book that makes an incident in the story of our 'soul's years'. Some books are like that though I have not come across many; others that have similarly made me, so to speak, stop short are Merejhkowski's 'Forerunner', that I told you about, & Olive Schreiner's 'Woman & Labour'. Mrs Humphry Ward's 'Robert Elsmere' did so too, also Wordsworth's poetry. I wish you would read the two former; the 'Forerunner' illustrates strikingly the contrast between convention & insight, between progress and tradition. 'Woman & Labour' is very much an expanded version of Lyndall's remarks on the position of women.

I think I *am* a little like Lyndall, and would probably be more so in her circumstances, uncovered by the thin veneer of polite social intercourse. But how you should think me like her, & why you see any resemblance, I cannot imagine. The book is so wonderful because it is so like life; nothing is nicely wound up, and everything left in the unsatisfactory state things are always left in this world. I am very glad you gave it to me.

Vera to Roland

Buxton, 24 May 1914

Edward informs me that you seem to be somewhat depressed and suggests that a letter from an entirely unexpected quarter might lighten the gloom for a moment or so. I cannot imagine a few commonplace lines serving any such purpose, but as I am subject to the complaint myself I am most willing to try and remove it from someone else, even though the attempt should be ineffectual. . . .

I am coming to Speech Day right enough; in fact if I can summon up enough courage to face your confessedly merciless criticism of feminine attire, I may even wear a new frock for the occasion!

I hope your 'Sallust before Sunrise' is progressing favourably . . . . . Do keep your essay on 'To have gained one's ideal is to have failed' because it is one of my fundamental principles, and as Edward says it is your motto, we might agree on the subject.

Roland to Vera

Uppingham, 30 May 1914

I have been told several times that among the foremost of my many vices stands an infinite capacity for leaving letters unanswered for an unpardonable length of time. Please forgive my having lived up to my reputation once again.

It was too bad of Edward to trouble you with exaggerated bulletins on my melancholic condition, as he seems to have done. But when the outcome is so charming a letter, how can I pretend to regret his having called in the dea ex machina? Thank you very much indeed for what was certainly not 'a few commonplace lines'. As a matter of fact my depression was more apparent than real, and has been succeeded by the careless, Omar Khayhamesque, make-the-best-of-your-last-term feeling, diluted a little perhaps with the sadness of conscious failure and the still sadder disillusionment of success. I suppose I shall become very sorry to leave this place by the time the end of July is here. At present I do not feel particularly depressed by the prospect. Edward will feel it much more than I shall, I think, if only because his life here has been less egoistic and self-centred.

I have a confession to make. I have not yet read more than about ninety pages of 'The Forerunner'. I took it out of the library a day or two before I came back here, and after keeping it nearly three weeks I had to send it back without having had time to read more than one or two pages since the beginning of the term. I am going to send for it again soon when I have less work to do than at present. I promise that whatever happens I will read it before Speech Day comes – and you and the new frock.

Vera to Roland

Buxton, 22 June 1914

Perhaps Edward has told you I have been very busy this week taking part in some amateur theatricals; I simply glory in acting of all kinds – both off the stage as well as on it – and have enjoyed myself thoroughly. We did 'Raffles' in the Opera House, not much of a play from a literary standpoint but excellent from that of the audience. It is very much of a man's show, and I had not much to do except try to look nice, and as the make up was very judicious I think I managed that alright.

Edward tells me you are going to carry off half the prizes in the school on Speech Day, so perhaps it is just as well I am coming – if only to make *sure* that the Quiet Voice is not in evidence. You will need someone to help you carry the books; if I gave you my assistance it would really be the crowning point to a most effective proceeding.

————

Edward to Edith Brittain

Uppingham, 5 July 1914

I have discovered that it is my special prerogative to be 2nd or 3rd in everything I do. It is apparent in my position in the House, the School, the Orchestra, & other things and strangely uniform . . . I am much troubled that I have only 3 weeks more here; I cannot bear the thought of leaving nor could I really bear to stay; most quixotic and paradoxical. But I shall not forget Uppingham.

Speech Day was one of the high points of the Uppingham school year. The weather that July was especially fine and cloudless, and a large body of parents and old boys had assembled. A service in the chapel opened the proceedings, followed by the review of the Officers' Training Corps on the school's playing field during which 350 boys, among them Roland, Edward and their mutual friend Victor Richardson, stood to attention for inspection. At midday the prize ceremony was held in the Memorial Hall, presided over by the headmaster, the Reverend McKenzie. The climax of his speech struck an ominous and prophetic note: 'Be a man – useful to your country; whoever cannot be that is better dead.' Roland collected a record number of seven prizes, watched proudly by Vera, who had come to Uppingham with her mother. She wrote of Roland in her diary that 'He seems even in a short acquaintance to share both my faults and my talents and my ideas in a way that I have never found anyone else to yet.'

Roland to Vera

Uppingham, 15 July 1914

I cannot tell you how much I enjoyed the two days you were here. They stand out as an oasis in an otherwise commonplace and uninteresting term. One result has been to make me still less sorry to leave this place and these people. Edward indeed somewhat distressed me yesterday by saying that he did not like the effect that talking with you had upon me. It made me too isolated and exclusive. He implied that in his opinion the more friendly I became with you the more I should drift apart from him. I hope he does not really think this. Please do not mention to him, of course, that I told you what he said.

You will let me know how you have got on in your exam., won't you? I suppose I shall not see you again until October at Oxford – unless you happen to be anywhere in the neighbourhood of Lowestoft. I am sorry that you and my mother have not yet met each other after all. Would it be quite impossible for Edward to bring you with him when he comes? I suppose so. It is a great pity.

Vera to Roland

Buxton, 17 July 1914

I know you keep all deep feelings to yourself – so much so that certain of your friends do not credit you with having some of them at all. Probably you would not do otherwise even if you could, but may not such reticence be laid aside a little just in poetry? But here I am criticising unasked as usual.

I am sorry Edward thinks as he does about the effect talking with me has on you. It must be partly the effect of the general depression he is suffering from. Why he imagines I should assist you to drift away from him, or that you should drift away from him without my assistance, I cannot think. He and I have always been great friends, and I do not think there is a greater difference between you & him than there is between him & me. But I do not believe for a moment you will drop him, unless the sentiments expressed in the second verse of your 'L'Envoi' poem, which he set to music, are insincere. . .

I wish I *could* have met Mrs. Leighton; I should like to run the gauntlet of her criticism even though it were unflattering – But I don't think I ought to accompany Edward to Lowestoft – not for any conventional reason, but because I am quite sure one of us at a time would be quite enough for your mother. As she has never seen me, there is no guarantee that she would like me; she might detest me; I know one or two women who do.

. . . I am afraid that after all you will not see me at Oxford in October, at all events not this October, for I am determined I will go in the end. The results do not come out till the end of August but I do not need to be told them. I wish I had not been given an Exhibition now as it is far more annoying to have one and be made to give it up than never to have had it. It will be a case of what Olive Schreiner calls 'a striving & a striving & an ending in nothing'.

Roland to Vera

> *Uppingham, 29 July 1914*
> *5.15 a.m.*

Thank you for your letter, as also for the one before which I have not yet acknowledged. I am at present terribly rushed in an endeavour to get all my books etc packed and to say goodbye to everyone before going off to Camp with Edward and Richardson at 8.55. I can therefore only write a few hurried lines before I dress.

I am so sorry if what you say about your Latin in the Exam. is really true. But I shall not give up hoping to see you at Oxford this October until I know for certain that you have not passed. You are probably taking much too black a view after all. I am afraid I can imagine very well what you must feel like. Depression and defiance mixed. But please don't be too melancholy and depressed, will you? Olive Schreiner and her 'striving and striving and ending in nothing . . . . . and no one knew what it had lived and worked for' is too needlessly dispiriting – at least for the present occasion. If you were not able to come up in October after all it would be terribly disappointing: but you are coming.

Less than a week after Roland wrote his letter, Britain declared war on Germany. The international situation, which had been worsening all summer, suddenly reached crisis point when, on 4 August, Germany invaded Belgium as a preliminary to its attack on France. The British had previously been divided about being drawn into what many regarded as a 'Balkan quarrel', and many had been reluctant even to act in support of France; but Germany's act of aggression against 'gallant little Belgium', in flagrant violation of international treaty, removed most doubts. Britain was the only Allied power to declare war on Germany, rather than the other way round, and there was much idealistic talk of this being 'a war to end war', and of 'making the world safe for democracy'. Men, young and old, and from all sections of society, flocked to the recruiting offices to enlist. Roland, Edward and Victor, who had been sent home early from their summer camp at Aldershot, organised by the Officers' Training Corps, were among those public schoolboys who, in the great surge of excitement, attempted to find temporary commissions in the army. None of them was to be immediately successful.

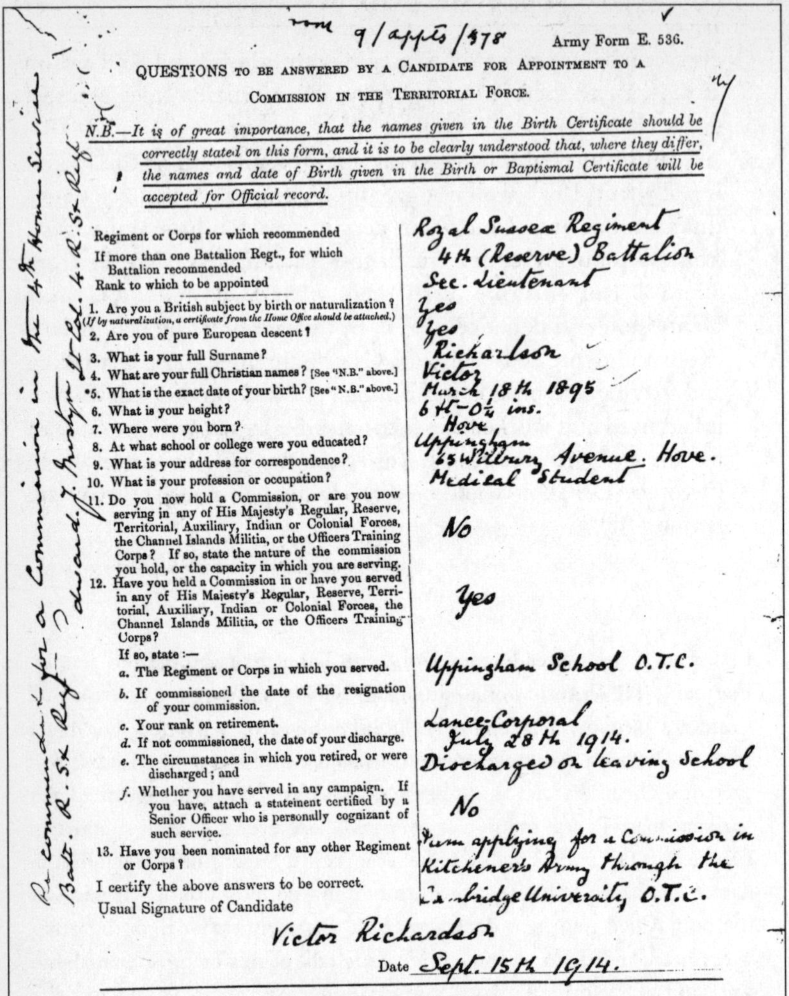

Army Form E. 536.

QUESTIONS TO BE ANSWERED BY A CANDIDATE FOR APPOINTMENT TO A
COMMISSION IN THE TERRITORIAL FORCE.

N.B.—It is of great importance, that the names given in the Birth Certificate should be correctly stated on this form, and it is to be clearly understood that, where they differ, the names and date of Birth given in the Birth or Baptismal Certificate will be accepted for Official record.

(left margin, handwritten, vertical): Recommended for a Commission in the 4th Home Service Battn. R. Sx. Regt. ... Lieut. Col. 4 R. Sx. Regt.

Regiment or Corps for which recommended
If more than one Battalion Regt. for which Battalion recommended
Rank to which to be appointed

1. Are you a British subject by birth or naturalization? (If by naturalization, a certificate from the Home Office should be attached.)
2. Are you of pure European descent?
3. What is your full Surname?
4. What are your full Christian names? [See "N.B." above.]
*5. What is the exact date of your birth? [See "N.B." above.]
6. What is your height?
7. Where were you born?
8. At what school or college were you educated?
9. What is your address for correspondence?
10. What is your profession or occupation?
11. Do you now hold a Commission, or are you now serving in any of His Majesty's Regular, Reserve, Territorial, Auxiliary, Indian or Colonial Forces, the Channel Islands Militia, or the Officers Training Corps? If so, state the nature of the commission you hold, or the capacity in which you are serving.
12. Have you held a Commission in or have you served in any of His Majesty's Regular, Reserve, Territorial, Auxiliary, Indian or Colonial Forces, the Channel Islands Militia, or the Officers Training Corps?
  If so, state:—
  a. The Regiment or Corps in which you served.
  b. If commissioned the date of the resignation of your commission.
  c. Your rank on retirement.
  d. If not commissioned, the date of your discharge.
  e. The circumstances in which you retired, or were discharged; and
  f. Whether you have served in any campaign. If you have, attach a statement certified by a Senior Officer who is personally cognizant of such service.
13. Have you been nominated for any other Regiment or Corps?

I certify the above answers to be correct.
Usual Signature of Candidate

Answers (handwritten):

Royal Sussex Regiment
4th (Reserve) Battalion
Sec. Lieutenant
Yes
Yes
Richardson
Victor
March 18th 1895
6 ft. 0½ ins.
Hove
Uppingham
55 Wilbury Avenue. Hove.
Medical Student

No

Yes

Uppingham School O.T.C.

Lance-Corporal
July 28th 1914.
Discharged on leaving School

No

Now applying for a Commission in Kitchener's Army through the Cambridge University O.T.C.

Victor Richardson

Date Sept. 15th 1914.

MEDICAL CERTIFICATE.

I certify that N. V. Richardson is fit in health for the discharge of the duties of an Officer of the Territorial Force.

Signature _____ Major, R.A.M.C.

Date 15 Sept. 1914

(stamp): SUSSEX TERRITORIAL ... No. 3 10/1820

* Does not apply to a candidate who has served as a Commissioned Officer in the Regular Army, the Territorial Force, or the British Auxiliary Forces.

(8 8 17) W 6631—80 20,000 1/13 H W V   Forms E. 536 / 25

[see over.

Application completed by Victor Richardson for a commission in the Territorial Force, September 1914

TWO

21 AUGUST 1914 – 1 APRIL 1915

. . . the black pine-trees on the mountain-side,
The river dancing down the valley blue,
And strange brown grasses swaying with the tide,
All spoke to me of you.
     – VERA BRITTAIN, 'Then and Now'

Love have I known, and dawn and gold of day-time,
And winds and songs and all the joys that are,
Known once, and as a child that tires with play-time,
Leaped from them to the elemental dust of war.
     – ROLAND LEIGHTON, 'Ploegsteert'

Roland to Vera

Heather Cliff, Lowestoft, 21 August 1914

I am feeling very chagrined and disappointed at present. I expect Edward has told you that I have been trying for a temporary commission in the Regulars. Everything looked quite promising, and the Colonel of the Norfolk Regiment whom I had to go and interview volunteered some most flattering remarks in his report on 'the suitability of the candidate'. On Tuesday it only remained for me to go up for my Medical Exam. I got on very well until they stuck up a board at the end of the room and told me to read off the letters on it. I had to be able to read at least half, but found I could not see more than the first line of large letters. The Medical Officer was extremely nice about it, and tried his best to let me through by being as lenient as he could: but it was of no use, I am afraid. . .

I had set my heart so much on getting that commission that I am most depressed at being thwarted at the last moment. I had almost settled that after the war if all went well, I should remain in the Army professionally. That of course is quite out of the question now. (Do *you* think that a military career would have suited me, I wonder? Possibly not.) I have since tried the Field Artillery and Army Service Corps, but find that they are just as particular about eyesight as the Infantry are. To make matters worse all the Territorial battalions – where wearing eye-glasses would have been permissible – have already many more officers than they want, so that I cannot get a commission of any kind now. I do not think I could go as far as trying the Légion Étrangère in the French Army, although someone did suggest it.

The war is very much of a reality down here. The harbour, bridges etc. are all guarded, and you are liable to be challenged suddenly by a sentry if you go out for a walk after dark. Tonight there is a flotilla of mine-sweepers with two cruisers anchored about a quarter of a mile out to sea immediately opposite the house. They are presumably laying mines, but they only came up after dark, and have put out all their lights so as not to be seen. Through field-glasses it is just possible to make out the black out-line of their hulls. Earlier in the evening one of the cruisers fired two shots across the bows of an ultra-inquisitive tramp steamer which she considered was coming too near.

All these external interests conspire to prevent me from doing any work – any of my work for Merton I mean. Whether I shall get to Oxford after all depends on the state of the family finances, which the war is far from improving. If I do, I shall still hope to see you there. You will soon hear for certain, n'est-ce pas?

. . . . . A dreary and egotistical letter, I am afraid. Good-night. It is getting on for 1 a.m.

Yours ever sincerely

Roland Leighton

P.S. You may be amused to hear that I am engaged in cultivating a moustache – as an experiment.

Vera to Roland

Buxton, 23 August 1914

You are constantly apologising for your letters being egotistical. Please do not. Any letters worth having are always so; one does not trouble to correspond with people unless one is interested in them personally.

On your account, I am very sorry about your failure to get a commission, as you seem so disappointed, but from another point of view, I think it is perhaps just as well, especially as you might have stayed in the Army for good. Not that I feel you are unsuited for a military career, as I know you have capabilities which would make it a success. But I think it would have been a pity, not because I under-rate the value of intelligence in military affairs but because you have certain intellectual qualities (which I think we admitted in conversation, so there is no want of discrimination in my referring to them) which the Army would have no use for at all, & on account of which you would not have received promotion any quicker than men who do not possess them. I find it is difficult to express exactly what I mean, & why I am glad you are not going into the Army; I can only refer you to Lyndall's remarks on the supreme importance of choosing a career in which all one's qualities can be made use of...

Edward is going to business now just for the time being, & is becoming very interested in it. Once I thought he would not make a good business man, but now I am coming to the conclusion that the work will suit him admirably; I think the objection to it lay rather in his surroundings than in his nature. But I feel more isolated than ever. I have been accustomed to think of Edward & I as standing together apart from our united family and relations, who carry the stamp of generations of commercial efficience and artistic inefficience – But he is so quickly developing affinities with them, I have to stand apart alone, a sort of changeling who is utterly unable to create connecting links between herself and their unimpeachable and complacent prosperity...

Lowestoft must be interesting just now. Sometimes I feel that if I could only realise the meaning of war a little more, I should find the utter disorganisation of existence at present more endurable, though when I read about the tragedy of Belgium, I have an uncomfortable feeling that I have always regarded too many things as a matter of course – But somehow I could bear better a sense of tragedy that calls for strength & endurance than the mere annoyance of interrupted work, & the well-meant efforts of various ineffectual people to be useful. On Wednesday I am going in for a First Aid exam., more to see if I know anything about it than because I think I do, & I do not really care very much whether I pass or not.

I do hope you will be able to go to Oxford just the same. But it seems impossible to expect anything from the future just now; life is so indefinite & one has to wait for each day to know what to do next. That is a great source of depression to a person like me, who am always working in the present for what I hope from the future.

Vera to Roland

Buxton, 27 August 1914

I heard this morning that I have passed my exam. after all; I thought you would like to know. I cannot understand why, as there is no getting out of the fact that my Latin Prose was distinctly bad, but as the Unseen & Vergil papers were practically correct, perhaps they had mercy on me, or perhaps the actual copy of Prose I sent up was not so bad as the rough copy I showed Edward. I am so very glad, as I do not know how I could have endured the thought of you & Edward enjoying Oxford life & myself cut off from it all for another year.

You *will* go, won't you? I am sure if you can only manage to get there they will not let you go again if they can help it; I have heard that Oxford is always ready to make concessions on behalf of talented & industrious persons suffering from impecuniosity. And one *can* manage on so little if one chooses.

Roland to Vera

Lowestoft, 28 August 1914

I am so glad – so very glad. You do not know how wretched I should have felt if you had failed. And now we shall be able all three to be at Oxford together – you and Edward and I. For, come what may, I *will* go now. I think I shall be able to manage it all right, if McKenzie gives me a leaving exhibition of even £30 a year. And I look forward to facing a hedge of chaperons and Principals with perfect equanimity, if I may be allowed to see something of you the other side. . .

Richardson is down here at present – very nice but a little dull and commonplace so far. When Edward comes on the 8th I shall be able to judge to what extent he has seceded to the ranks of commerce and respectability. It is a pity that your isolation should be increased and emphasised. I wish you were coming down here too!

Vera to Roland

Buxton, 6 September 1914

I expect you will be glad that Edward is allowed to do something definite at last; I do not know how much he has told you but I do not suppose it is much, as he had about twelve other letters to write. He goes before the nomination committee at Oxford on Friday, and as I suppose he will be regarded as a suitable candidate he will probably be given a post before very long in something.

You have no idea the domestic storms that have been necessary in order to achieve this object; I have come in for a good many because I have persistently urged from the beginning of the war that Edward ought at least to try for something. Not that I am in the slightest degree a militarist, for I suppose no enlightened person in these days regards war as anything but an insanity & a check to progress & civilization.

But it seems to me that to refrain from fighting in a cause like this because you do not approve of warfare would be about as sensible as refusing to defend yourself against the attacks of a madman because you did not consider lunacy an enlightened or desirable condition.

Of course I shall miss Edward dreadfully at Oxford, as I should have been allowed to see quite a lot of him, but after all I am merely one of thousands of women who can ill spare their only brothers. At any rate I hope it will only be for a part & not for all the time, but really I have heard so many estimates of the length of the war that I am quite without an estimate of my own. Some people talk persistently about Kitchener being at Ostend with an enormous force, & that a battle is imminent large enough to end the war in a month; others speak of it being a slow business likely to last three years. Judging by what has happened in only a month of warfare, it seems the latter condition would necessitate a return to chaos.

Edward has been already examined by the doctor, & has been found to be not only in robust health but perfect in sight, hearing etc. He managed to read all the letters on the sight test except the bottom line. The doctor has also spoken to Daddy & has, I am delighted to say, soothed him somewhat.

Roland to Vera

Lowestoft, 29 September 1914

October 9th is getting very near, but I can no longer say confidently that I am coming up to Oxford. I have been, you know, very envious of Edward and Ellinger and Richardson and all those who will have the opportunity of doing something of what now alone really counts; and I think that at last I too may have the same. I stand a good chance of a commission in the 4th Norfolks and shall know definitely in about a week's time. Anyhow I don't think in the circumstances I could easily bring myself to endure a secluded life of scholastic vegetation. It would seem a somewhat cowardly shirking of my obvious duty. In fact if I do not get to Oxford at all, as seems possible, I shall not much regret it, – except perhaps in that I shall miss the incidental pleasure of seeing you there. Of course, all being well, I could go up after everything is over. I feel, however, that I am meant to take some active part in this war. It is to me a very fascinating thing – something, if often horrible, yet very ennobling and very beautiful, something whose elemental reality raises it above the reach of all cold theorising. You will call me a militarist. You may be right.

Vera to Roland

Buxton, 1 October 1914

Edward has told me how unhappy you have been because you did not know definitely what you could do, so I am very glad to hear you have a chance of a commission at last. I never expected you would want to go to Oxford; conditions now are very different from what they were about a month ago when you wrote to me. There cannot be any question that you are doing the right thing, though even if you are unsuccessful you certainly cannot accuse yourself of cowardly shrinking when you have done your best.

I don't know whether your feelings about war are those of a militarist or not; I always call myself a non-militarist, yet the raging of these elemental forces fascinates me, horribly but powerfully, as it does you. You find beauty in it too; certainly war seems to bring out all that is noble in human nature, but against that you can say it brings out all the barbarous too. But whether it is noble or barbarous I am quite sure that had I been a boy I should have gone off to take part in it long ago; indeed I have wasted many moments regretting that I am a girl. Women get all the dreariness of war & none of its exhilaration. This, which you say is the only thing that counts at present, is the one field in which women have made no progress – perhaps never will (though Olive Schreiner thinks differently). The fact that circumstances are abnormal is no consolation for not being able to take [an] active part in them. Why cannot they have us at least in the commissariat departments? I am sure some of us would be very successful there. At present the only part women can play in war is that of a nurse, and even at small local hospitals they are not allowed under the age of twenty-four, and I think the war will hardly last until I attain that age. People say the best thing one can do is to stick consistently to one's ordinary work, but it is easier said than done. I sometimes feel that work at Oxford, which will only bear fruit in the future and lacks the stimulus of direct connection with the war, will require a restraint I am scarcely capable of. It is strange how what we both worked for should now seem worth so little. I cannot feel the same enthusiasm for Oxford when you & Edward & Maurice will not be there; though, as you say, the pleasure of meeting you would only be 'incidental', perhaps once a week; still, to begin a new kind of existence with one's friends, & to begin it alone, are very different things. But it is the best I can do at present; college life is perhaps the vegetation you call it, but it is less vegetation than my existence here; Oxford may lead to something, but Buxton never will. . .

I still hope that we may yet all be at Oxford together in spite of everything; and that things which used to count so much will

begin to count again. It would be a pity for your splendid scholarship to be wasted. Meanwhile – I can only wish you the best of
luck over your commission, & the realization of all you hope it
may bring.

———————

Roland to Vera

Lowestoft, 7 October 1914

Thank you for your charming letter. I am only sorry that circumstances compel so inadequate an answer on my part. I have
received orders to pack up my belongings and migrate to
Norwich tomorrow; and in consequence am at present very busy
and somewhat rushed. I was informed yesterday that my application for a commission had been approved by the County
Territorial Association & forwarded to the War Office, and that I
was to join my regiment without waiting to be gazetted. The
colonel commanding the battalion said that my commission was
practically a certainty, although I might not perhaps be gazetted
for another fortnight or three weeks. I shall not mind this waiting
so much now that I am to have something definitely useful to do.
Not but what I expect I shall find it rather lonely at first, as I do
not know anyone in Norwich at all. I have to billet myself in
lodgings – 22 Grove Road, Norwich.

It seems strange to think that the day after tomorrow you will
be at Oxford and beginning a new life – and alone. You will write
to me soon, and tell me your first impressions of Somerville, won't
you?

———————

Vera to Roland

Somerville College, Oxford, 18 October 1914

I am very glad to be here, and thankful to have escaped, permanently I hope, from the old aimless life and the increasingly
unsuccessful attempts to accommodate myself to unresponsive

surroundings. There is a kind of atmosphere about university life, whatever its faults, which one does not get before coming here & is scarcely likely to get after; it is a specialised rare thing, to miss which would certainly be a loss, & so I hope you will come & try it some day however inappropriate it may seem among the present conditions. . .

Of course you know Edward is here, not at New College, but training with the O.T.C. After a short & sweet wrestle with Miss Penrose as to what I might or might not do with him, I have managed to be permitted to do nearly anything. I am so glad to have him here, & have seen a great deal of him already. Another Uppinghamian named Jessop from Faircroft goes to the same Logic lectures as I do. (I am taking Logic in lieu of Maths. for Pass Mods.) I have not noticed him yet but he recognised me from seeing me at Speech Day, and is sure to try & speak to me, though Edward has informed him that a women's college must be treated as though it were in quarantine.

Edward tells me you are having a pretty strenuous time at Norwich; I should like to know all about it. I expect you are glad to have plenty more to do even if it is hard work. You were quite right in thinking that Oxford life this term would have been deadly for an undergraduate; I do not know how those there can endure not to be in khaki.

Roland to Vera

Norwich, 18 October 1914

Me voici établi – tout à fait en militaire. I may still have to wait another fortnight, I am told, before I am gazetted: but meanwhile I am doing the same work as if I were already officially on the strength of the battalion. I have to get up at 5.45 a.m. and am kept hard at work with intervals for meals until 7.30 p.m. By that time I usually feel too tired to do anything but have some dinner and get to bed. Often, however, there is a recruiting meeting or some kindred function later in the evening, which the junior officers have to attend to support the colonel. The latter I like very much.

He is a rough and ready but very capable man, with a strong sense of humour and the face of a barrister turned low comedian. The other men on the staff are all very nice, if somewhat dull. There are eight other incipient officers in the same case as myself, and two or three more coming on later, I suppose. At present however the regiment is not up to full strength, and needs in fact about 400 more recruits. Hitherto I have been chiefly occupied in putting the men through section and company drill and attending lectures on Field Engineering – digging trenches etc. On the whole I like the life immensely. To be continuously busy in this way is a great joy – especially when the busy-ness is of immediate utility. The only thing I fear is that chameleon-like I may be taking on the commonplaceness of my restricted military surroundings. I don't think, you know, that I could after all endure to adopt the Army for a permanent career. It would – in peace time at any rate – be far too narrow. It needs the enthusiasm and inspiration of actual conflict to raise it from a mere trade to an art or an ecstasy. . .

Thank you very much indeed for the offer of socks etc. I think, however, that men actually at that mysterious place conveniently known as 'the front' need them at present more than myself who stand little chance of going out there inside six months. If and when I do go, I will let you know and ask you to knit me a tie. We shall probably be stationed in Norwich until after Christmas, when we may be sent on to Colchester to take the place of the battalion of the Norfolks which is at present there waiting to go off to France. There is a bare possibility that I might be able to get transferred to this Foreign Service battalion, & so get out sooner. I have sent in an application; but am told that it is very unlikely that it will be taken any notice of.

It is Sunday evening and someone next door has begun to strum hymn tunes on a bad piano. It is 'Onward Christian Soldiers' now: but I am afraid that I am not at all in the mood for it. I am supposed to learn up all about Outposts by tomorrow; but shall be too sleepy, I expect.

Goodnight.

Roland to Vera

4th Batt. Norfolk Regt., Norwich, 16 November 1914

I have been finally posted to No. 4 Company as senior subaltern. This is known as the Business Company and contains a better-educated class of men than the others, ranging from shop-assistants to commercial travellers, bank clerks, and three solicitors. The difference in smartness and intelligence between these and the ordinary agricultural class of soldier is very marked. My company commander is usually employed on special duty, and in consequence the task of superintending the training of the men has devolved almost entirely upon me. I find it intensely interesting, and am developing quite a paternal fondness for the company as a whole. In addition to this I have been appointed Battalion Signalling Officer, and am in charge of the signalling section and despatch riders. All of which keeps me very busy.

My attempts to get to the front have for the time being failed. The adjutant here seems to have taken rather a fancy to me and has been putting himself out considerably on my behalf; but without success, I am afraid. He had hoped to get me transferred to the other battalion of the Norfolks at Colchester, which is under orders to go out to France next week. They are, however, considerably over strength as it is, and have already had to send three or four of their extra officers back into the Reserve. I have also been making inquiries as to being transferred to another (if possible Regular) regiment and getting out front-wards that way: but in any case I find that I should have to pass a second Medical Examination. The regimental doctor declares that I am practically certain to be rejected for Foreign Service on account of this confounded eyesight of mine. My only chance would be to get the special intercession of some influential person, or to show such conspicuous brilliance in a particular branch as to outweigh the defect. . .

The battalion is now up to full strength, but sadly deficient in rifles and uniform as yet. It is quite likely that we shall be ordered to migrate to Colchester soon, when the other battalion has gone off to France. I have been buying Camp Kit – a valise, sleeping-bag etc. – in anticipation: also, a revolver. I have just received a cheque for £30 as my outfit allowance; but I do not expect it will cover everything. Other people would perhaps make it do, but I, as you probably know, am a bad financier.

Today I hear that they are sending large bodies of troops to the neighbourhood of Cromer, presumably to guard against a sudden raid. We received a message from the War Office this morning asking if we were prepared to move out of Norwich, if required, at six hours' notice. It is rumoured that we shall probably be sent – if we do move – to take the place of some other more prepared battalion that has been hurried off to the coast. Personally I think the best thing we can do is to stop where we are.

The family at Lowestoft have been having quite a thrilling time. They saw the whole of the naval engagement off Yarmouth the other day, and a day or two ago nearly captured a spy.

Vera to Edith Brittain

Oxford, 18 November 1914

[Edward] has been specially recommended for one of the next commissions, & expects to go in a day or two. He came up yesterday morning to tell me about it, looking so nice in his officer uniform, & he created great interest in the minds of those working at their windows by walking up & down with me in the garden.

Vera to Roland

Oxford, 29 November 1914

Many thanks for your letter – I am glad you are getting on so well and liking your work. You have doubtless heard from Edward that he has been gazetted at last and departed from Oxford on Monday – to the 11th. Batt. Sherwood Foresters at Frensham. One of the O.T.C. people told him that his commission was so long delayed because they thought him too young, but as he is nineteen to-morrow that objection of course no longer exists. From the very little he has said about his work I gather he has been rather a success here and that they thought very well of him in the O.T.C. – so much so as to urge that he should be gazetted. Apparently for that reason he has not been sent to a new battalion but to one that has been formed for some time & is likely to go to the front comparatively soon – probably about February. In spite of the appalling weather they are still sleeping under canvas, so that on the frequent occasions when the rain pours down in the characteristic way it has in Oxford I wonder all the time how he is enjoying it:

Edward to Vera

> *11th Batt. Sherwood Foresters, Frensham,*
> *30 November–3 December 1914*

I am getting on very well indeed here now and find some of the other subalterns very decent – one with whom I am sharing a tent at present is exceptionally nice. You needn't worry about me as we are really very comfortable; the tents keep the rain out well and we sleep on camp-beds in a sleeping bag with heaps of blankets and coats on top, besides which I put on a sweater and bed-socks in addition to pyjamas. We each have a servant to make the bed etc. and attend to us in all ways. The food also is excellent and the officers' mess is a huge tent with boarded sides with two long tables down the middle. We also have an ante-room where we can write letters (though I am writing this in my tent) and see all the papers in creation. It has rained nearly all the time I've been here . . . . . (As you were).

> *Albuhera Barracks, Aldershot, Dec. 3rd 1914*

This sort of thing is likely to happen at any time; I have had no time to write till to-day since Monday and much has happened. On Saturday the Brigade Major (Colonel Hornby D.S.O.) asked me for names of people at Oxford who wanted commissions and so I supplied a few and put down Roland also for a transfer from the T.F. [Territorial Force] Reserve... The result was that he came down to Frensham on Monday night and saw Hornby and the General (Sir David Kinlock) and arranged to come to the Sherwood Foresters who had just two vacancies if he could get released from the Norfolks. I got a wire from him saying that he is coming this evening while I was on parade this afternoon and so I feel rather pleased with myself for having arranged it so well.

We marched from Frensham here yesterday (9 miles) and are really very comfortable. There are 2 subalterns to a room – though it is too late now for me to share with Roland as I am sharing with a fellow called Nelson who is really very decent – and we have fires etc. sleep on our camp beds and have quite a good time... I was Supernumerary Orderly Officer to-day which means inspecting the men's quarters and seeing to their food, and turning out the guard at 9 a.m. and 10 p.m.

To-morrow we are going a route march of 18 miles, and on Monday we are going out to billets for a week.

———————

Roland to Vera

11th Sherwood Foresters, Albuhera Barracks,
Aldershot, 8 December 1914

My transfer has not appeared in the Gazette yet, but I am told that this is, as is usual with the War Office, merely a matter of time. Meanwhile I am getting into my work here quite well, surrounded by as inane a cluster of young officers as the most commonplace mind could desire. I have, however, managed to get into the same room as Edward – which is by way of an antidote. He has at present gone away for a week with the rest of his company to a place a few miles off for purposes of Field Training.

I have just been inoculated against enteric and have been given 48 hours light duty to recover in. My arm is feeling very stiff and my head a little heavy, but otherwise it has not affected me.

I shall think of you tomorrow wrestling with Greek verbs. I do hope you will get the ones you know. All Classics seem to me incredibly far away now. I am not at all sure that I shall want to go to Oxford when this war is finished. I shall have forgotten everything, and it will all seem such a waste of time. Let me know how you get on, won't you?

Vera to Roland

Buxton, 11 December 1914

I cannot tell you how delighted I was to hear of you and Edward getting together after all. It was one of the things I always wished might have happened but thought too satisfactory to be probable. All Edward's military experiences seemed at the beginning to be going so badly – first his difficulty in getting father's consent, & then the long wait for a commission, & then Maurice getting ill so that there was no chance of their ever being together. But it really does seem to have happened for the best, as if Edward had got into an earlier battalion it would probably have filled up quicker & there would have been no vacancy for you. You must be glad to get out of the Territorial Force into the Regulars – they seem to touch the war so much closer. I can quite understand your feeling very far removed from such a life as University life and that the contemplative part is a waste of time compared with the active part you are playing at present. But of course it is not a waste of time really, and perhaps after all you will come again to see that it is not.

Roland to Vera

Aldershot, 14 December 1914

Please do not think that I have come to consider the contemplative side of life a waste of time compared with the active side. You do not know what I would not have given these last few months, – what I would not give now, – to meet with a little intellectuality around me, or to have half an hour's talk with someone with some personality and temperament. Even now in war time the Army means mental starvation. By the time this war ends I shall have become too commonplace and orthodox for you to care to talk to. Nothing would induce me now to take up the Army as a permanent career.

Edward came over for two hours last night and told me among other things that you would be twenty-one on Dec. 29th. Somehow I never consider you as fifteen months older than myself. What would you like for a birthday present? Have you got a Swinburne, or is there any other book you would like to have particularly? Do please let me know.

Vera to Roland

Buxton, 19 December 1914

I enclose a pair of bed-socks which I thought you might like now the weather is getting so cold. You ought to have had them before as I started knitting them when I came down from Oxford, but various interruptions have delayed their completion. If you despise such things, or the zeal of unoccupied relatives has provided you with enough for a war ten years long, I expect you know of someone you could pass them on to...

I am sorry you find the Army mental starvation, but glad that you do not want to stay in it permanently; I always feel there must be some special position waiting for you in the world which only you can fill adequately. The inanity of the Army type seems only too general; the specimens here are not very encouraging. It is a pity men are turned into types so easily; to me it is rather a melancholy proof of the small amount of personality which the majority of people possess. But your worst enemy would not include you in that category. Of course you will never become too orthodox & commonplace for me to care to talk to.

You know I ought to refuse to allow you to send me anything for my birthday, but judging from past experience I suppose it would be no good if I did refuse. At any rate I must insist that it is something very small. I have a Swinburne – not complete, but fairly adequate – as I could not get on without one. But I have no modern people at all except Olive Schreiner, Meredith & Ibsen. I have not in fact read very many, & can leave the choice safely to you as your tastes are so often like mine. It is a serious matter I suppose to be twenty one & responsible for one's self entirely. It seems absurd – not that I am that age, as especially among my contemporaries I often feel far more – but that you are not; you seem so old for your age that I always feel younger, & now with your recent responsibilities & anxieties I suppose you will be more so than ever. Even beside Edward at Oxford I felt a mere child; he seems to have grown up absolutely & so suddenly. Do tell me how he gets on sometime; he never says a word about himself.

Roland to Vera

Bramshill Park, Winchfield, 20 December 1914

The War Office have just written to say that they cannot sanction my transfer to this regiment. I am hoping with the help of the second in command here to get over this. I think it is only red tapeism on their part. It will, of course, be a great disappointment if this decision is final. I received the intimation an hour ago, and am going in to Aldershot tomorrow and thence to see a certain Colonel Roy at the War Office. I so hope it will be all right.

Roland to Vera

1 Titchfield Terrace, Regent's Park, London,
26 December 1914

I have come to the conclusion that a long-distance telephone is a most unsatisfactory means of communication. We did not get on at all well the other morning. I couldn't hear you and you couldn't hear me, and the result was disastrous. I am sorry.

I have moved to this place, where Mother has taken rooms for a short time for the purpose of interviewing publishers etc. I shall therefore be up in town till January 1st.

I should love to come out to lunch with you on 30th... Mother says she would like me to bring you along to see her while you are in London. How long are you going to be up here? A day only? Could you manage to come round to tea, do you think? or could you & Edward come to lunch with us instead of me with you?

Vera to Roland

Buxton, 28 December 1914

As you have again changed your address you may not have received the note Edward sent you about meeting us on Wednesday. We want you to be outside the Comedy Rest. [aurant], Haymarket at 1.50. It is a little late for lunch but I hope you will not mind as our train will not arrive till 1.25. So I am afraid we could not get to you in time to have lunch at Regent's Park, but I could easily manage tea the same day, or else lunch or tea on Thursday, whichever suits you best. I shall be in town until Saturday morning – except the Wednesday & Thursday nights, which I am spending with some relations who live just outside, at Purley. I shall have an aunt with me all the time who is chaperoning me about while I do my shopping; will it matter? She is a little talkative but very nice. You know I am most anxious to see your mother, don't you? I expect you know that I am very shy about it too. I should hate to suggest to her a pupil teacher, or under-secretary for research in Church History, or anything of that kind.

Roland to Vera

London, 28 December 1914

I feel that today I ought to be writing you something more than an inelegant letter – an illuminated address, or a birthday ode at least. But I am going to see you in two days time, and it is easier to say nice things than to write them, (and safer than either, perhaps, to think them), and, if my infant courage should fail me in the presence of your twenty one years, know that I have at least thought all the most charming things you could yourself have wished expressed.

Roland to Vera

London, 1 January 1915

Thank you, again, so very much. It has been such a delight to be with you these two days. I think I shall always remember them in their wonderful incompleteness and unreality.

When I left you I stood by the fountain in the middle of Piccadilly Circus to see the New Year in. It was a glorious night, with a full moon so brightly white as to seem blue slung like an arc-lamp directly overhead. I had that feeling of extreme loneliness one is so often conscious of in a large crowd. There was very little demonstration: two Frenchmen standing up in a cab singing the Marseillaise: a few women and some soldiers behind me holding hands and softly humming Auld Lang Syne. When 12 o'clock struck there was only a little shudder among the crowd and a distant muffled cheer, and then everyone seemed to melt away again leaving me standing there with tears in my eyes and feeling absolutely wretched.

I am glad I did not try to meet you again this morning. It would have spoilt everything after last night. All the same I don't like to feel that you are in London and yet I cannot see you – even if it is only for a day. It may be so long before we get another chance of meeting; and even now these last two days I have left unsaid most of what I had wanted to say.

★ ★ ★ ★ ★

You are a dear, you know,

R.A.L.

Vera to Roland

Buxton, 4 January 1915

I am glad your address has come at last; I wanted very much to write to you.

I tried so hard that night to think of something to say that would express what I felt. I am sorry my aunt's thanks had to do for both of us. But perhaps you understood how I could not speak.

I am glad it was London in which those two days were spent – London is the scene of all my dreams & visions, so it was a fitting stage for their unreality. It seems right too that your mother should have been part of them. I cannot tell you how pleased I am that I have met her, and that she thinks of me no longer merely as Edward's sister. Yes, I think I agree that another day might have spoilt those two, and perhaps it was best to leave things as they were. But I should have liked so much to have met you again all the same; I felt on Thursday evening that I was just beginning – that you were allowing me to begin – to know the real you a little. It has not been easy to discover, but you will let me keep what I *have* found, & not deliberately remove it again, won't you. It is little enough after all. . .

The roses you gave me have lived such a long time – a proof that I am not what you prefer me not to be. I wore them all yesterday; they were as sweet-scented as ever, & somehow their fragrance seemed to cling around me like a benediction –

I am so sorry you find Peterborough dull; I know it must be hard to go back to your old regiment after having left it. I sympathise very much; both of us now seem to be doing about the only things possible to us, and yet neither the circumstances nor the individuals that surround us are exactly what either of us would choose. But I believe you are meant for some special destiny, just as I have always felt I am, and I do not doubt that some day we shall both come into our own. Meanwhile in the present rather dreary part of your experience I expect you will have to do as I do at Oxford – live in your world without being part of it – be in things but not of them – I think it must be much easier to work as one of a like community than as an isolated individual, but I am afraid the second alternative is the only one possible to such people as you & I. After all perhaps it is better; though less enjoyable, it is finer & makes for strength.

I shall look forward to your letters when after a long & tiring day you are sometimes not too weary to write them. They were always very gladly received at Oxford last term; I too, as perhaps you know, often need cheering up, and especially at college, where so many people lack imagination even though they have intellect, and where consequently I often feel more lonely than when I am by myself. I told you the other day I had never met any class of people with which I could feel myself in sympathy. But after all I do not need a class; an individual – perhaps I mean *the* individual – is far better.

I also shall not soon forget New Year's Eve. I suppose the New Year came in while I was watching the rather blurred lights on the railway line rushing swiftly past in the darkness. Unreal as the day seemed, the impressions it has left and the remembrance of it are utterly beyond comparison with the fleeting memory of a dream. They are intensified too by the tragedy around us all, which seems now to remind me of itself with a new insistence and underlie everything like the deep & solemn accompaniment of a song.

Thank you for your letter. It seems to express just a little more of the unsaid part, & brought back to me some of Thursday's glowing incomplete unreality.

Yours ever –

V.M.B.

Edward to Vera

Aldershot, 7 January 1915

I am very glad you enjoyed yourself so much in town and liked Mrs Leighton. You might find her a little embarrassing in her own home.

Roland to Vera

Peterborough, 7 January 1915

It was such a sweet letter, and with so much to be read in it that was not written in ink. Before a week ago perhaps I could not have understood it and you not have written it. Now it is different. You say that you are just beginning to know the real me. You do not know how much it means to me to have caught a glimpse of the real you. You are nearly always acting – by force of temperament and circumstances: so am I. But I shall remember that we have met in the wings between the acts: and grease-paint and powder remain always transparent to one who has once studied the face beneath.

I am afraid this can only be a truncated and inadequate letter. There are few things I would rather do than write to you; but, instead, I am at present compelled to spend the short time available in attending the minor social functions of a provincial town that a sudden influx of Khaki has sent somewhat off its head. We are hedged in at every spare moment by invitations to dances, tea-parties and charity bazaars, and I as a newcomer have to be taken round to show myself and be gushed over.

By the way, when do you go back to Oxford, and do you go straight across country from Buxton? I was thinking that I might manage to meet you in London – our London – on your way. I could invent some excuse for getting a few hours' leave. If this would not work, would Leicester do instead? It is not very far from here. I should so like to be able to see you again.

Yours ever

R.A.L.

———————

Vera to Roland

Buxton, 10 January 1915

It is such a pleasing suggestion of yours. If only you can manage your part of the arrangement, all will be well, as mine is fixed up already. I go up to Oxford next Saturday, the 16th. I am afraid London is impossible – I only wish it had not been, but it is quite out of my way. But I can manage Leicester quite well – I always go to Oxford via either Birmingham or Leicester; both routes are equally convenient, or rather equally inconvenient, as there is a long wait at either station . . . If you can, I think the easiest way to find me would be to meet my train – I am not sure if 11.28 is the exact minute but it is the London train, so you would have no trouble finding out. There is no need for me to say how much I should like to meet you again.

Peterborough's excitement over the advent of khaki is amusing, & somehow to me is remotely suggestive of Jane Austen. Even in Buxton they have watched their best hotel converted into barracks for 1000 soldiers without the slightest sign of emotion. In fact people here, though very few of them are directly connected with the war, are evidently so depressed by it that they can scarcely be civil to one another. They have even quarrelled over looking after the wounded at our temporary hospital – a task over which I should have thought even the meanest people could have kept their unworthier feelings under control. I am longing for the week to pass and end this constant jar of being among people & surroundings about as unsuitable for me as anyone could choose. Life here has always been difficult, & the more my mind progresses the more intolerable it becomes. I suppose hereby I learn better to appreciate Oxford, whose academic narrowness can be resisted, & is accompanied by other & better things. I wish I could take some step that would set me free from this pettiness – & indeed from every kind of pettiness – for ever.

I am afraid these reflections are not very cheerful & are after all only informing you of what you know well enough. You must accept the weather as an excuse; everything is covered with dirty grey snow, the whole world looks melancholy & the trees are dripping intolerably with a dismal monotony.

I hope you will come to Leicester.

Roland to Vera

Peterborough, 13 January 1915

I have managed to get my leave for Saturday all right, though the Colonel would probably be somewhat surprised if he knew the real reason for my wanting to go to Leicester. I can catch the 7.45 a.m. train from here which arrives at about 10 o'clock or soon after. This will give me plenty of time to meet your train at 11.28...You need not leave for Oxford before 2.30 need you? and we can go and have lunch somewhere in the meantime. I hope you know your way about Leicester, because I am afraid I don't. It would be rather a fiasco if we lost ourselves & missed the train.

I have just caught the regimental cold which has made me very hoarse and inclined to the Quiet Voice. I hope it will have disappeared by Saturday.

I am looking forward so much to seeing you. If I could not have got leave I should have come without.

Vera to Roland

Oxford, 17 January 1915

All yesterday evening, when, whatever my other causes of complaint, I had at least a comfortable room to sit in & a warm fire to dream over, I was thinking about you & your long & cold journey back again, & wondering if when you finally returned you would still think it had all been worth while. I feel as though I had all the advantages and you all the discomforts of yesterday, & yet I remember that in spite of all that I again never thanked you. I was waiting for the inspiration of the moment when I finally said good-bye to find expression for what I meant to say, but then the persistence of – what I will still call temerity – surprised me into silence...

I do hope your cold is not worse – I am very afraid the journeying may have done it harm.

I do wonder how I am going to get through this eight weeks.
I told you I should feel unsettled . . . . .

Roland to Vera

Peterborough, 20 January 1915

I am so sorry not to have written to you before this, but the further development of my cold has kept me in bed for the last three
days. I don't really think the pilgrimage to Oxford had much to
do with it. It would probably have got worse without that. Not
that it matters either way: it would take much discomfort to be
adequate compensation for Saturday. 'Do I still think it was all
worth while?' Can you ask?

My return train was not due till 5.58, and so I took another
hansom and followed in your wake. I went and looked once again
at what little of Somerville is visible from the outside, and then
walked down the Corn & the High and so to Merton. I stood for
a long time looking up at the tower and wondering whether I
should ever know Oxford otherwise than as a stranger. It was just
growing dark and the charm of it all was accentuated by the twilight. The grey walls and ragged edges of stone against the sky
seemed so impersonal and unchanging – the forgotten waifs of a
dead world where tomorrow is always as yesterday. I envied you
who can live in this dream-city.

I hope that by now you feel less unsettled . . . . . or do I hope so?
Perhaps not. Yet work is the only thing to do – to work and to
wait. At least I am thinking so now.

Roland to Vera

Royal Norfolk & Suffolk Yacht Club,
Lowestoft, 22 January 1915

You will be surprised to see that I am here. So am I.

This morning we had a sudden order from the War Office for

the regiment to move down to Lowestoft at once. I and another officer have been sent on in advance to make preparations, & arrived here about six o'clock this evening. I have not had time to go home yet & probably shall not have for some time. We have to arrange billets for 1000 men before they all arrive at 12 o'clock tomorrow morning, as well as billets for the officers and suitable parade grounds etc.

As soon as I get an address I will let you know. I suppose that Heather Cliff will find me faute de mieux. It seems so strange to be back here again.

Vera to Roland

Oxford, 24 January 1915

I certainly was rather surprised to see that the postmark on your letter was 'Lowestoft'. I was quite alarmed lest you should have obtained your desired transference to some other regiment, & been sent home on leave pending your immediate departure for the front...

Do you know that the boy who was head of the Lodge – I think his name was Thomson, – when you & Edward first went to Uppingham, has been killed in action. I remember Edward was very fond of him. Sometimes I feel as though this war was claiming them all, 'the eloquent, the young, the beautiful & brave', just as the French Revolution did, but even more pitilessly & more universally. Can anything justify that?

Roland to Vera

Cliffside Hotel, Lowestoft, 31 January 1915

We have at last got more or less settled down here. A large part of the work has fallen to me in my capacity of billeting officer, and since this time last week I have scarcely had a moment to myself. It is a fault of mine that I am always selfish enough or conceited enough to believe that no one else in my department can do any-thing except myself, and in consequence I usually give myself more work to do than is really necessary. We have just been sent 1000 new rifles and 400,000 rounds of ammunition, which looks as if a raid was expected. I was up nearly all last night supervising the unpacking of them; in fact I had in all only 3½ hours sleep – though I ought not to tell you so, or you may be tempted to follow my deadly example. (Please don't: though I cannot very well scold you, can I?) You may be amused to hear that the rifles are modern Japanese ones, although no one is really supposed to know it. They are quite good weapons, if rather more compli-cated and delicate than the ordinary British rifle. But it seems rather disgraceful that we should have to be dependent on Japan in this way.

Our headquarters down here are at the far south end of the town, so that I very rarely have time to go up to Heather Cliff. In fact I might as well be at Peterborough. I am as usual discontented with the playing at soldiers that goes on here, and am off to Colchester tomorrow, if I can get the Colonel's permission, to interview a major in the 4th Suffolks (Territorials). The 4th Service Battalion of the regiment has already been at the front some time and has now asked for three more officers to be sent out. I am trying to be one of them. It will probably mean my transferring first to the Reserve Battalion and then going out from there. I shall need to be very tactful, though, in persuading both my colonel here to let me go and the other one to accept me.

I am very comfortable here, of course: but a rolling stone does not like to be forced to gather moss. I would give anything to be allowed to go to France. Doesn't Lyndall say somewhere that you can get anything you want if you only want hard enough? I feel so ashamed of myself for still being one of the 'gentlemen in England now abed'. I don't think you mean it when you say that you prefer that I should not go.

Vera to Roland

Oxford, 2 February 1915

I suppose after the implied reproach in your last letter I must wish that your mission to Colchester was successful. But it is so much easier to be brave for one's self than for other people. In consideration of your own wish to go to France, and of what I might think of you if you had not that wish, I do want you to go, but when finally I come to regarding myself I find it not so easy to make what I ought to desire agree with what I actually do. I am content to think of your departure, so long as it is always going to be, & *is* not. I know you will get what you want in the end; people who mean to always do. So that one thing will become settled, but the others will remain indefinite just the same. . .

You will let me know of any new developments as soon as they occur, won't you?

Roland to Vera

Lowestoft, 5 February 1915

No. It was no good after all. The two officers hurriedly asked for by the battalion at the front had already been sent off two days before. They had been chosen and ready for some weeks, and nothing that I could have done would have made any difference. I was informed on Sunday that the 4th Suffolks had very few officers ready to go, and I had hopes of being one of the two . . . . . I saw the Colonel of the Reserve Battalion at Colchester and he was quite willing and in fact eager to transfer me to his regiment. But he could only offer me a problematical chance of getting sent out in May; and so I am refusing the offer. If I am to be condemned to stop for any length of time with a Home Service regiment I much prefer this one. I hope not to have to stop in any such kindergartens. It is very disappointing, n'est-ce pas, not to be able to do what one wants? I should not mind so much if it were some definite and immutable disqualification that keeps me back – my eyesight, for instance – but it is always some annoying detail. I am going up to the War Office on Monday to see if there is any other Territorial regiment at the front that needs fresh officers.

Vera to Edith Brittain

Oxford, 7 February 1915

[Roland] has received promotion & is now a first lieutenant; isn't it splendid of him! It is really very excellent considering the short time he has been serving... I wish Edward could get it too, but of course he is not old enough yet.

Meanwhile Victor, who had been stationed at Horsham as a second lieutenant in the 4th Royal Sussex Regiment, fell severely ill.

Roland to Vera

Lowestoft, 8 February 1915

I had a letter yesterday to say that Richardson is very dangerously ill with cerebro-spinal meningitis at Brighton. Edward and I have arranged to go down there, although it is very doubtful whether we shall be able to see him, as he is still unconscious and must be kept quiet. I am just off to London now and am to meet with Edward at Brighton this morning.

This is all I know about it at present. I do hope that he will get through it all right; although the doctor here says that this form of meningitis is more often fatal than not.

I am feeling most distressed about him.

Vera to Roland

Oxford, 9 February 1915

Please write & tell me as soon as you can what has happened & what you & Edward have done. I am very anxious & distressed for all your sakes & can think of nothing else until I hear.

———————

Roland to Vera

Lowestoft, 10 February 1915

I met Edward at Brighton on Monday at about 3 p.m. He had already been there since 10.30, but had not been allowed by the doctors to go near Richardson. His father and his aunt are permitted to see him for a few minutes only once a day. I am thankful to say that he seems decidedly better now, although the doctors will not say definitely that the danger is passed. When he was brought over from Horsham his case seemed quite hopeless. That was last Tuesday. Since then he has been delirious most of the time, but now is beginning to be conscious, although he cannot yet realise where he is. He persists in repeating commands and seems to imagine that he is drilling men. The chief danger is that, being so weak, he may have a relapse. Personally I have hopes that he will be all right now.

———————

Vera to Roland

Oxford, 14 February 1915

I can't tell you how glad I am to learn that the news about Victor is so much better. You & Edward both seemed so despondent that I feared there was no hope at all. It really does seem wonderful that he can possibly recover; can he do so completely or will he be more liable after this to a similar attack in the future?

You certainly do seem to have had more success this time at the War Office. I expect you will get what you want as I don't

suppose there are an undue number of people who are anxious to
go to the front before they are sent. Apparently Edward does not
expect to go for quite two months and even then it may be only
to train.

Roland to Vera

Esplanade Hotel, Lowestoft, 15 February 1915

Have you forgiven me for keeping you letterless so long? It seems
to me ages since I wrote to you last.

Everything here is always the same. The same khaki-clad civilians do the same uninspiring things as complacently as ever. They
are still surprised that any one should be mad enough to want to
go from this comfort to an unknown discomfort – to a place
where men are, and do not merely play at being, soldiers. I am
writing this in front of an open casement window overlooking
the sea. The sky is cloudless, and the russet sails of the fishing
smacks flame in the sun. It is summer – but it is not war; and I
dare not look at it. It only makes me angry, angry with myself for
being here, and with the others for being content to be here.
When men whom I have once despised as effeminate are sent
back wounded from the front, when nearly everyone I know is
either going or has gone, can I think of this with anything but
rage and shame?

It must seem to you rather futile, if not ridiculous, for me never
to have anything to tell you except what I have *not* succeeded in
doing. At present all I pin any faith to is the Captain Riley I went
to see at the War Office, and a remote chance of getting into
Strathcona's Horse if Colonel Seeley, who has had me recommended to him, retains his command of the Canadian Brigade,
and if my equestrian capabilities are equal to it.

I have just been put in command of a detachment of 61 men,
on a secret mission as escort to a fleet of motor omnibuses which
are to act as a Transport and Supply Column in case of emergency. I don't really expect it will come to much; but if the
Germans do land I may find myself rushing round the country in

sole command of 60 motor vehicles filled with stores and ammunition. It would be rather an adventure, n'est-ce pas? But I hope to be safely at the front by that time. . .

Victor is getting better very slowly. . . . I gather that he is still delirious at intervals, and does not yet know what he is suffering from.

Vera to Roland

Oxford, 28 February 1915

I think it is harder now the spring days are beginning to come to keep the thought of war before one's mind – especially here, where there is always a kind of dreamy spell which makes one feel that nothing poignant & terrible can ever come near. Winter departs so early here, and during the calm & beautiful days we have had lately it seems so much more appropriate to imagine that you & Edward are actually here enjoying the spring than to think that before long you may be in the trenches fighting men you do not really hate. In the churches in Oxford, where so many of the congregation are soldiers, we are always having it impressed upon us that 'the call of our country is the call of God'. Is it? I wish I could feel sure that it was. At this time of the year it seems that everything ought to be creative, not destructive, & that we should encourage things to live & not die.

Roland to Vera

Liverpool Street Hotel, London, 12 March 1915
11.30 p.m.

I think I have succeeded at last. If all goes well, I stand a good chance of getting out to the front – either straight to Belgium or else to the Dardanelles – in about ten days time. At worst I ought to be out there in a month with a second draft. I hope to leave within the ten days.

I have been up in town since yesterday, Thursday, morning when I was telegraphed for by the War Office. Another officer of the 4th Norfolks – a Captain Chamberlin – had gone up there partly on his own business and partly on mine, and chanced to hear that there were two vacancies for officers in the 7th Worcestershire Regt. which is on the point of going off to the front. He mentioned my name to General Heath, who is in command of the South Midland Division and a friend of his, with the result that I received a telegram ordering me to report myself at the War Office at once. When I arrived here I found another telegram telling me to meet the Colonel of the 7th Worcesters (Territorials) at Maldon, Essex at 11 o'clock this morning. I have just come back about an hour ago. The colonel, who is an ex-regular himself and a very charming man, has agreed to take me on as a Supernumerary foreign service officer and promises to get me out to the front as soon as ever he can – which will probably be with the rest of his battalion in about ten days' time. I am now in process of being transferred and expect to be ordered down to Maldon on Tuesday to join my new regiment. I am going back to Lowestoft tomorrow afternoon and shall probably be up in town again on Monday to do some shopping, if for nothing else.

You come down on Monday, n'est-ce pas? Couldn't you arrange for me to meet you somewhere, either on your arrival or any time that is convenient? I couldn't go off to the front without seeing you.

Vera to Roland

Buxton, 15 March 1915

You will have received my first letter by now telling you that I went down ten days earlier because I was ill, so I did not get yours till to-day. I can hardly believe it is true; I was expecting something like it of course but it was none the less of a shock for all that. It is still difficult to realise that the moment has actually come at last when I shall have no peace of mind any more until the War is over. I cannot pretend any longer that I am glad even for your sake, but I suppose I must try to write as calmly as you do – though if it were my own life that were going to be in danger I think I could face the future with more equanimity.

If you do not go for a month I can easily arrange to see you as Edward & I are spending two days in London in a week or two. But if you go in ten days I *will* see you to say good-bye somehow even if I go to London for the day from here. I might even arrange to spend the two days in London sooner; I am writing to Edward now. Is it quite easy to get up to London from Maldon? I suppose they would give you leave.

Vera to Roland

Buxton, 16 March 1915

I am arranging to go to London on Thursday unless I hear to the contrary from you. I could manage Friday if Thursday will not suit you. Would you mind wiring if you can see me on Thursday as there is not much time & I still have to arrange to meet you. Please wire as soon as you receive this . . .

I expect you will be far too busy to have much time to spend with me, but I must see you to say goodbye; there are so many things I want to ask & hear about. I can scarcely believe you are actually going – of course I have been expecting it all the time but so long as it remained indefinite it seemed so very far ahead. And now – gladly as I would think of nothing but the honour & glory which going into action may bring you – I cannot help thinking of all else it may mean. It is all so very near.

Roland to Vera

7th Worcester Regt., Maldon, 16 March 1915
7 p.m.

Just reported myself here. Am going on leave tomorrow morning & shall be in town from then till Friday evening. When can I meet you? I shall be quite on my own & at liberty to come up to Manchester if necessary.

It was eventually arranged with Mr and Mrs Brittain that Roland should come to Buxton, and stay at Melrose, in order to say his farewells. He arrived on the afternoon of 18 March, and during a walk in a fierce snowstorm on the moors, and later, after dinner when they were left alone in the morning-room, Vera and Roland continued an intense and emotional discussion about his reasons for wanting to go to the Front, and the possibility that he might not return. It was his worship and pursuit of heroism in the abstract, Roland claimed, that really compelled him to go. Early on the wintry morning of 19 March, Vera said goodbye to him on Buxton station as he left for Maldon on the first stage of the journey, with his regiment, to France.

Roland to Vera

Maldon, 19 March 1915
10 p.m.

I have just got settled here and had some supper. I find that my company is billeted at Heybridge, a small village about a mile out from Maldon itself. I have been consigned to the tender care of the vicar's wife – a small wizened thing, with an air of being much given to all good works. There are two other officers billeted here – both of them utter fools and with atrocious manners. Everything is very dull and uninteresting. A country vicarage is not in harmony with my temperament at all, least of all now. But it will not be for long. We know nothing definite; but we probably sail on Thursday. I cannot see things in any right proportion yet, or realise that I am actually going. I am sure it is much more real to you than to me.

★ ★ ★ ★ ★

And so, it is over now – the parting. 'Only a turn of head –' And all that is left is to wait and work and hope. But I *am* coming back, dear. Let it always be 'when' and not 'if'. As yet everything is incomplete: but last night, unreal as it seems to be, must have some consummation. The day will come when we shall live our roseate poem through – as we have dreamt it.

★ ★ ★ ★ ★

If you want to give me a little present to take away, I have thought of something – a fountain pen (self-filling & with a more or less broad nib to suit my writing). I should find this very useful, but let it be quite a plain, inexpensive one.

Vera to Roland

Buxton, 21 March 1915

I am so glad you have thought of something you would like. I will send the fountain-pen to-morrow, but I had to write to you to-day, in case after all you go earlier than you expect.

Since you went I have thought many times how selfish & how wrong I was – to appear to doubt your mind's decision, which saw so clearly what it could not express in words, first because my own apprehension was temporally clouded by personal distress. You will forgive me, won't you? – for I do understand really what is driving you forward; I do know that the highest kind of courage is that which is ready, not to sacrifice itself on behalf of some obvious cause which all men can see to be right, but if necessary to die for the sake of an ideal. I do recognise that your 'heroism in the abstract' is that ideal, and therefore I would not attempt any more to interfere with your resolution even if I could. You wanted me to approve of your going. Does this admission satisfy you? More I cannot say, because I am not strong enough for the recognition of what is right to conquer the feeling of personal sadness. Because of this too I think I forgot that, whether enforced action or enforced inaction be the harder part, the actual farewell can be no less bitter to you than to people who care for you. It is strange that you referred to that poem of yours because it has been in my mind so much since you departed – 'And you set out to tread your manlier road.' It is hard that on that difficult path I can do nothing to help you face the Death you

will meet with so often. But when you are fighting the fear of it –
bravely as I know you will – I too shall be facing that fear, and can
at least be with you in spirit then.

Not immediately, but some time after you had gone, I began to
dream of all that may still be after the war – *when* you return, and
to plan out work to make me worthier of the future and to fill up
the hours until the sorrowful time is past. Hope springs anew in
the secret heart, I suppose because physical existence would be
impossible without it. I do not believe that so much that has just
begun could always remain incomplete. It would not be right for
us to be given a vision of the Promised Land only to be told we
were never to enter it. We shall dwell in it in the end, and it will
seem all the fairer because we have wandered in the desert
between then & now.

You *will* tell me when you actually leave England, won't you?
Perhaps it will be hardest of all then, but I would rather know.

Goodbye my dear, and as much love as you wish.

V.

Vera to Roland

Buxton, 22 March 1915

I do not know how to thank you – but perhaps you can imagine
a little how I felt when I opened your letter this morning, and will
not require of me to express it in words. I can never say how much
it means that you should still have thought about giving me something although you were so busy, & I told you you were not to. I
need not tell you how precious it will be to me – I shall scarcely
dare to wear that which is the visible sign of so much. How did
you know I liked amethysts best? They are so full of light & depth
that I feel as if I were looking into someone's soul. I shall look at
it so often – not that I require any outward token to make me
think of you, or to keep living the memory of Thursday night –
but I can spare no remembrance, and this will make one more...

And now I suppose, soon after you read this, you will indeed be departing – going to that land of sorrow & strife where we must trust you to Time – & whatever it is that is God. . .

It shall not be goodbye – it cannot be. I send you at our parting all that is most precious to me too – the best of love and hope.

So – till we meet again – au revoir.

V.

Roland to Vera

Maldon, 26 March 1915

I have tried so hard to find time to write to you the last two or three days, but have hardly had a moment to spare. Thank you so very much for your two charming letters and for the fountain pen. The nib, as you can see, suits me very well; and it is, and will be, an added delight to write to you with *your* pen . . . . . I am glad you like amethysts, if only because I do myself and chose it for that reason.

You must have wondered whether after all I had gone away without being able to let you know. We are still here waiting for our final orders. It would have been so much more satisfactory if we had been sent off at once. As it is, it is more than probable that we shall go on Sunday night, or rather Monday morning at about 2 a.m. We go by special trains to Southampton, where we are kept more or less in hiding until the evening. We then cross over in small steamers – about 200 men in each – under cover of the darkness. Havre is where we are to be landed (though I am not allowed to tell you this), and from there presumably we are sent up into the fighting line. I will try to send you a telegram when we get to Havre, if censors allow such things. (I have just received lengthy orders regarding censorship. I have to censor all the letters written by the 60 odd men in my platoon; while my own are inspected by my company commander, and then forwarded unfastened to one of the censors-in-chief at headquarters. He stamps all letters and sends them off.) I have not forgotten our arrangement about putting small dots – in pencil – under certain letters, that you may know where I am. Your letters to me, of course, will not be tampered with at all... You had better not send any letters out to me, though, until you know for certain that I have just got to France. I will scrawl you something to let you know as soon as I can. And you will not mind, will you, if most of my letters are only scrappy?

Have you written to Mother yet? I told her I had been to Buxton to say good-bye, and have just had a long letter from her, largely about you. I asked her what you told me to, and said that you were writing yourself also. You will won't you? You can be as frank as you like. She will understand.

It is nearly 2 o'clock and I have to get up early. But I cannot help thinking of you tonight. I have just been wondering what it will feel like to be twenty tomorrow. Shall I feel so very old? And yet we are both only children still – children who have dreamt each the dreams of a child, and meeting at the gateway of a fairer garden tremble lest after all their dreams come true.

Goodnight, dear. Love and Hope.

R.

Vera to Roland

Buxton, 28 March 1915

When your telegram came yesterday & your letter this morning I was so sorry I had not written for your birthday, even though all I could have wished for it was conveyed, though perhaps unexpressed, in the letter before. I know you knew it was not because I had forgotten or was not thinking of you all day, but I had not the least idea whether you had gone or not. I am sending you the conventional wish now – which I will not express in the conventional words since they have acquired a commonplace meaning, and could never represent my passionate desire for the wish to be fulfilled...

I have just been for a long walk with Edward. He said you had said little or nothing to him about me, but in spite of this I talked about you because I wanted to take the opportunity of finding out what he thought while I had it. I even told him a little about London & Oxford. I found it easier to talk to him than ever before. You are wrong in thinking he disapproved of what has arisen between us. He was very far from being even indifferent; he was definitely glad. I don't think you have ever realised the extent of affection & admiration he feels for you. His mind went back into the past as he talked of the days when you were at school together. He is glad that I may be the means of establishing your connection with him, and saving from loss what was wrought out between you in Uppingham days. May be he has not at all the same kind of mental and spiritual kinship with you that I have – perhaps he never will have. But still the relationship may be closer than you imagine. I know you and your mother have always said that he has either nothing in him or else he conceals very well what he has. Will you not give him the benefit of the doubt and believe that the latter alternative is the true one – as I do.

I have just written to your mother, a very inadequate sort of letter badly expressed. I hope she will really understand. Your letter at least gave me the courage to write it.

Since I last wrote I have read 'The Story of an African Farm' over again. Olive Schreiner says there that to a certain order of minds trouble & loss cause deep heart-searching and blind painful seeking into the vast problems of our existence. I think mine must be of that order, for the last few days I have done nothing but think and think until my mind is weary with watching the shadows of realities that flit before it, and wrestling through the darkness with the little light it has. But always when I think I say to myself that someday I will tell you what I have thought and with you in the future will talk about it all. Surely that day must come.

Of course I shall not mind how scrappy your letters are – I know they will be all that you can make them and when I get them whatever they are I shall be so glad. At least I am pleased the Censor will not see mine – so that I can give you a little of what perhaps you will want when you are out there –

I don't want to stop writing but I must because I am anxious for this to catch the post – ...

Goodbye – & best of love –

V.

Roland to Vera

Maldon, 30 March 1915

Your letter caught me all right. I would have told you before that I was not going off at once if I had known as much myself. But we have received our final orders now; we start tomorrow (Wednesday) evening at 6.30 from here. When exactly we shall get to France is uncertain, as troops are sometimes kept at the docks for as long as 48 hours. On the other hand we may be in France for breakfast on Thursday.

I am very glad if somewhat surprised to hear about Edward. He seemed so frigidly calm and even unsympathetic when he was here on Friday. Yes, I *will* give him credit for having emotions & hiding them. Do tell me what he said about it all.

I am terribly busy at present paying billets, issuing emergency rations etc. & have to attend an officer's meeting in a few minutes. This is just a hurried note to catch the post. Think of me tomorrow night – and after. I can hardly realise that in a very few hours I may be in a trench.

———————

Roland to Vera

Telegram, Folkestone, 1 April 1915

Just on point of crossing

Roland

———————

Vera to Roland

Buxton, 1 April 1915

So you went from Folkestone after all. I know the docks there & can picture you all preparing to start in the darkness. It was just like you to think of sending me a telegram notwithstanding all the hurry & responsibility in which you were involved.

Although you told me you might be kept 48 hours at the docks, when I went to bed last night considerably after midnight I somehow knew you had gone & wondered if you were safe on the now terrible sea . . . Think about you! Had you need to give me *that* injunction? If you had asked me to try & fix my mind on something else I might have had to make an effort. I cannot open a book without finding some subject we once discussed, or seeing some words which remind me of something you once said. The last few days I have been seized with a roaming spirit but I cannot seek solitude in any favourite place without passing some road that I went along with you, or thinking that some day we will walk there again.

How I look forward – with eagerness & yet fear too – to the first of your 'scrappy letters'. You will tell me all you have to go through, won't you – at any rate as much as Censorship will allow. Please don't keep things back with a vague idea of sparing my feelings; I am not so weak that I fear to face in imagination what you have to endure in reality. I have just been reading a letter of yours which you wrote me at the beginning of the war; you said you felt you were meant to take an active part in it, that it fascinated you because in spite of its horrors much of it was very ennobling & beautiful, & there was something elemental in it which raised it above the reach of all cold theorising.

I suppose it is that 'something elemental' which you are finding now, and that war makes plainly manifest the very heights & depths of human nature. I know how you will conquer the terror of these things, how your keen soul will discern the beauty & glory of them shining through the gloom in which they are shrouded, how fearlessly you will look down into the depths & up into the heights. Why should you hesitate to tell me of these things? I can after all read about them in the papers, only without that personal element of yours which will make them specially mine. I shall not be afraid to know and confront the real; the imagined has far greater terror for me. Let me share your hardships – perhaps your sufferings – in the only way I can.

You asked me to tell you just what Edward said but I do not know there is much more than I told you before. After all I think I talked most. He did not say much but what he did say was very decided in favour of everything. It was more his whole attitude that impressed me than any actual words I could quote. He had quite made up his mind before ever you came here that you were going to be interested in me & I in you. It pleased him very much when what he expected was just what happened, & when he began to think that what had begun as interest was continuing as something more, his satisfaction increased accordingly. I accused him of keeping up his friendship only from a sense of duty & he contradicted this very firmly – especially in your case. He said that if ever he ceased to trust you it would mean that he had first ceased to have faith in everybody else. My own feeling on this point did not need the confirmation of his agreement with it, but I was very glad to hear him say that. It is rarely he expresses so much.

Let me know soon if you got safely across to France. It seems almost irony to say 'safely', since I must think of you now, I suppose, as going from one danger to another, & yet be content to wait & hope. Well I *will* do it & thank Heaven for each danger that is past.

A. F. A. 2042
114/Gen. No./5248.

FIELD SERVICE
POST CARD

The address
only to be writ-
ten on this side.
If anything else
is added, the
post card will
be destroyed.

Miss V. M. Brittain
Somerville College

Oxford

Angleterre

NOTHING is to be written on this side except the
date and signature of the sender. Sentences not
required may be erased. If anything else is added
the post card will be destroyed.

I am quite well.

~~I have been admitted into hospital~~

{ ~~sick~~ } ~~and am going on well.~~
{ ~~wounded~~ } ~~and hope to be discharged soon.~~

~~I am being sent down to the base.~~

I have received your { letter dated April 17th
~~telegram~~ „ _____
~~parcel~~ „ _____ }

Letter follows at first opportunity.

~~I have received no letter from you~~
{ ~~lately.~~
{ ~~for a long time.~~

Signature }
only. } R.

Date April 20th 1915

[Postage must be prepaid on any letter or post card
addressed to the sender of this card.]

(25000) W1.W3497-293 1,000m. 2/15 M.R.Co.,Ltd.

Field Service Post Card sent by Roland to Vera

THREE

3 APRIL 1915 – 26 AUGUST 1915

Violets from Plug Street Wood –
Sweet, I send you oversea. . . .

(And you did not see them grow
Where his mangled body lay,
Hiding horror from the day;
Sweetest, it was better so.)
— ROLAND LEIGHTON,
'Villanelle'

One long, sweet kiss pressed close upon my lips,
   One moment's rest on your swift-beating heart,
And all was over, for the hour had come
         For us to part.
— VERA BRITTAIN,
'St. Pancras Station, August 1915'

Roland to Vera

France, 3 April 1915

My first opportunity since landing here at 1 a.m. Thursday morning. We came via Folkestone & Boulogne and are now at a place about 12 miles from the firing-line. We go on again the day after tomorrow to — which is quite near the trenches. I will write to you again tomorrow when I shall have more time. I am very rushed at present. It is all as yet unrealisable. It seems very far from death and horror and fighting. The only immediate sign of war is a sudden flare of light along the road at night and a glimpse of a French military car rushing past, or an occasional patrol of blue coated cavalry. We can hear distant reports of heavy artillery fire, but we are of course quite out of the danger zone ourselves at present.

    Till tomorrow;

R.

———

Vera to Roland

Buxton, 5 April 1915

I have had the dearest letter possible from Mrs Leighton – She is going to let me know at once anything she hears . . . She shares my desire to be in Northern France now in any capacity whatever. How I envy the women whom circumstances & opportunity have enabled to go. But these are the fortunate minority; the majority of us are all waiting, which is hardest of all, & not knowing where people are or what they are doing. I can't deny that I have been very sad since I knew you had really gone – I cannot help thinking always how precious the life is you are risking, and of the time you are giving up, which people often forget to reckon in their estimate of the country's debt to such as you, but which, as *I* know, means so much to anyone with intellect & aspiration. Yet I cannot help feeling glad you were ready to give them up too – I suppose the stuff of which heroes are made is hardly likely to be acquired by living only so as to escape reproach, & doing just what is strictly necessary & no more. After all no experience however terrible can be counted as loss, if one is not overcome by the experience, but is stronger than it, as I know you will be.

The other night I went to bed in about the most depressed frame of mind I have ever been in, & though I had not been reading or thinking of 'The Story of an African Farm' I woke up in the morning with the words so clear in my mind that I was almost saying them to myself – 'The Echoes of Despair slunk away, for the laugh of a brave strong heart is as a death-blow to them.' I felt then that I was a weak & worthless creature to let myself be crushed by sad thoughts – one can't help having them, but one can act as though one hadn't. I *will* be content to wait, but I will be able to do it better if every moment is crowded with work. . .

There is a large Hospital here, which has been extended lately to admit wounded, & I went to the Matron of it yesterday & asked if I could help there in any way. She said they had more work than they could manage satisfactorily, & she would be glad to take me on as a voluntary helper for the rest of the vac. I am going up to London to-morrow for a day or two & shall begin after that; there is still about three weeks left. I don't suppose the work I shall have to do could possibly be dignified by the name of nursing, – except in the will to do it, which is as good as if the work were ever so skilled. It will more likely consist of darning socks or washing things – chiefly the former, as apparently so many people can't do it. Strange to say that is one of the things I *can* do – you would hardly connect the art of darning with me, would you! But I can – even Mother says so!

I have also been thinking about the Long Vacation, which is more than 3 months. Of course I can still work at the Hospital – & there may, alas, be more need for workers there than ever then. But just lately an appeal has been made to all women who are willing & able to register themselves at Labour Exchanges as being ready either to train for skilled labour or undertake unskilled labour so as to take the places of men who have gone

& set others free. It provides thus for the contingency of a long war.

Roland to Vera

France, 7 April 1915
2.45 p.m.

I have only a very few minutes before the post goes out, but I must write if only two lines to thank you for your sweet letter which arrived yesterday afternoon. It is the first and only one I have received so far. I cannot tell you how much it has meant to me.

I am about 5 miles from the firing line now but have not been under fire yet or in the trenches. Will write tonight if I can.

Very much love

R.

Roland to Vera

7–9 April 1915
10.45 p.m.

I will begin this letter tonight, though I shall only be able to write a very little. In about a quarter of an hour I have to go out to visit sentries, and when I come back I shall be too sleepy to do anything but go to bed. I am writing this in the kitchen of a French farm house about 3 miles south of B[éthune], where I am billeted with three other officers. We have our meals in here and sleep on straw on the floor. The others are asleep already. The men are in barns outside. We are about five miles from the nearest part of the firing line, and just out of range of the guns, although we can of course hear the reports of the heavy artillery firing quite plainly. At night the flares sent up from the German trenches lighten the sky on two sides of us every four or five minutes. I was watching them this evening on my way back from our Battalion Headquarters. We were also warned last night to be on the look-out for German snipers, but we have not come across any yet. Two German aeroplanes passed over this afternoon at about 5.0 p.m. But so far we have seen no fighting. We stop here for four days I think and shall then probably be moved on again and into the trenches.

★ ★ ★ ★ ★

Across the miles between – good night, dear.

Thursday April 8th

I have been over here just a week, and it seems six times as long. We came over from Folkestone at about midnight last Wednesday, arriving in Boulogne soon after 1 a.m. on Thursday. The sea was perfectly still and the night brilliant with moonlight. All the men were sent below and the lights on board put out. There was not a sound the whole time beyond the swish of the water against the side. We had a destroyer as escort, that kept level with us about 300 yds off. It all seemed like a dream.

We stayed in a Rest Camp at Boulogne till Thursday afternoon and then were taken by train again to a village near Cassel. We arrived there at 1.0 a.m. in the morning after a very tiring day in the train, and then had five or six miles to march. Luckily I found a horse to ride myself, which was a great improvement on march-ing, especially as now all officers have to carry the same heavy equipment as the men in addition to revolvers, field glasses etc. As it was, when we arrived we had to find billets for the men and I did not get to bed myself till 4.45 a.m. on the Friday morning. We stayed at this place over Saturday and Sunday (Easter Sunday, in places where they have time to remember such things) and on the Monday moved on to where we are now. We had a march of 18 ½ miles, along a cobbled road for the most part of the way – the typ-ical French main road in this part of the country, very long and straight, paved with large stones, & with tall thin sentinel trees on each side. The last part of the march was done in pouring rain and through inches of mud, and by a mistake we had to stand waiting about in it all for over an hour. It was not at all pleasant at the time, and several men dropped out on the way. We all were more or less soaked to the skin when we got here, but one has to get used to that. I got my platoon in without any one missing, which was something. But it is remarkable how little anyone minds small discomforts out here.

Roland to Edward

France, 9 April 1915

Dear Teddie,

Many thanks for your letter, which arrived yesterday morning. We are now in billets at —, about 5 miles behind the firing line. We have been here since Monday when we had the devil of a march from —, 18 ½ miles further West, in rain and mud and carrying full Tommies' web equipment including pack, as well as our own field glasses, revolver etc. Tomorrow we are off again, this time actually to the trenches and we shall probably be in them on Monday or Tuesday. We can hear the heavy guns from here and at night the German flares make patches of light in the sky every few minutes. We had an alarm last night, but it fizzled out into a hoax of the Brigadier's to see if we were ready.

We are in a farm-house here and are quite comfortable. There are four officers together and we sleep on straw on the floor of what was once a kitchen. The Germans were in occupation of the whole district here a few weeks ago and have left bullet holes etc. about in various places.

Vera to Roland

Buxton, 11 April 1915

So far I have received your first two letters & the postcard from Cassel. Of course I looked it up on the map; it seems uncomfortably near the places where most of the fighting has been so far. I am glad to know that letters can mean so much, as I see by your few lines that they do. I can imagine a little what it must be to get them, as I expect in spite of the responsibility & work & concentration of mind required of you, you must at times feel very much alone. I will write as often & as fully as I can. I suppose the Censor does not see my letters. Not that I should take any notice if he did; I look upon him as an entirely impersonal element who could be quite well disregarded in anything I should want to say. . .

. . . Somerville College has been requisitioned by the War Office for the duration of the war. . . The majority of us are going into part of Oriel College – the St Mary Hall Quadrangle – which has been lent us by them. Can't you imagine the indignation of the remaining undergraduates at this feminine invasion of their hallowed precincts! Those of us who cannot be accommodated at Oriel are going into rooms in Oriel St. & district. I am to be – I had almost said 'billeted' – in rooms at a place called Micklem Hall in St Aldate's. . .

Since coming home I have heard that they are expecting a great many wounded in the summer & will probably want all the extra nurses they can get. They say they will be almost sure to need me, not merely to darn socks as I am doing now, but to do the usual probationers' work. It will mean a pretty strenuous time but I think I can manage it, & shall probably do that. It is better to do work where one is less skilled but more needed than where one is more skilled but less needed – especially as I believe that an intellectual person is able to master every experience with varying degrees of effort. This sort of skill can only be acquired by practice, but is acquired quickly. So if you *must* get wounded, try & postpone it till about August, by which time I might be efficient enough to help to look after you. Just think of that!

Roland to Vera

France, 11 April 1915

We arrived here last night at about 6.30 p.m. at — [Armentières] a large town on the border of France and Belgium. I am now actually in the firing line and am to take my platoon into the trenches this evening at 7 o'clock. The trenches run right into the town on one side and I could hear the rifle fire last night as I lay in bed. Our guns are a little way back, I think, and fire over our heads. The Germans started shelling the town again the day before yesterday but so far I have only heard & not seen the shells with the exception of one shrapnel one that burst some distance off on our right as we marched in last night. Many of the buildings in the town show signs of former bombardment, and there are bullet holes in the walls of houses in the main streets. I am billeted with another subaltern in a small house on the outskirts of the town fronting a dusty square with the grandiose name of the Place République. The Rue Victor Hugo is just round the corner. The town itself is rather cleaner than might be expected, the streets are wide, and there are tramway lines along one or two of them. It is the largest town we have yet come across, and it seems delightfully incongruous that there should be good shops and fine buildings and comfortable beds less than half an hour's walk from the trenches. We go in tonight and are to be relieved on Tuesday evening – 48 hours in all. An inexperienced regiment is not left to hold part of the line on its own at first, but is put with other more experienced men who initiate them into the mysteries of dug-outs, listening posts, etc, and what one may and may not do. After Thursday we shall probably be sent back again to the forward base – possibly to the place we have just left. . .

I wonder if I shall be afraid when I first get under fire.

Best of love
Yours always

R.

Roland to Vera

France, 12 April 1915
In the Trenches
12.30 p.m.

I am writing this sitting on the edge of my bunk in the dug-out that I am sharing with an officer of the —s. One company of this

regiment and half a company of our own men are occupying
part of a line of trenches running parallel to the German and varying from 70 to 180 yards from them. At the moment there is
practically no rifle fire on either side except for a German sniper
or two who is having a few chance shots at a traverse two or three
yards to the right of this hut. Two bullets have just skimmed along
the roof, but as this is well covered with sandbags there is no
danger inside. Our heavy artillery has been shelling a large disused
brewery behind the German lines all the morning. The shells
come straight over the trenches, and you hear first the dull boom
as they leave the muzzle of the gun, & then the scream of the shell
passing overhead, ending in a crash as it bursts. This is going on as
I write now. I have just been outside in the trench watching it all.
You dare not put your head over the front parapet of the trench
for even a second, of course, or the German snipers would 'pot'
you. But by peeping round the corner or using a periscope you
can just see the brewery (or rather the remains of it) and the
clouds of smoke from the bursting shells. The smoke is mostly
green (lyddite) but sometimes black from the larger howitzer
shells (nicknamed for this reason 'coal-boxes'), or tinged red with
the dust from the falling brickwork. But they have just ordered us
by telephone to keep under cover, because of the danger from the
fragments blown back from our own bursting shells. This is why I
am in the dug-out now. It is a wooden hut built into the rear part
of the trench, about 7 feet square and 5 feet high at the highest
point. It has two low bunks for sleeping, some shelves, a small table
& two wooden chairs. There is a window of sorts in the rear wall
and the whole is covered all round with earth and sandbags. Its
name – nearly all these dug-outs have names – is Le Château
Germaine (why, I haven't any idea). On top is a small weathercock of wood and tin stuck there out of bravado by a former
inhabitant.

The firing has stopped now & it is lunch time.

★ ★ ★ ★ ★

4 p.m. Same Day.

The guns have been at it again this afternoon and the Germans
have been shelling our communication trenches behind in return.

The continued noise is trying and has given me a headache. The artillery firing has stopped now, but some damned German keeps on sniping at the top of a small wooden post that projects a few feet to the left of our dug-out. The front parapet of the trench is about two feet higher than our roof & in consequence all his shots go harmlessly overhead, but his persistence is annoying & worthier of a better object. He takes the top of the post to be a periscope, I think.

Stray bullets are always flying overhead, especially at night; but no one minds them. After dark it is possible to look over the parapet, as, even when they send up flares, they rarely see you plainly enough to aim at. In the day time you are safe enough if you keep your head down. The dangerous part is getting in and out of the trenches. This is nearly always done just at dusk; but the Germans have the advantage over us at this point of the line in having several buildings to snipe at us from. Two men got hit last night just after they had got out – neither of them very seriously. We met them being carried off on stretchers as we were coming in. A cheerful introduction to life in the trenches, n'est-ce pas? None of our men have been touched yet, though a bullet whizzed uncomfortably near my head on the way in last night. I myself cannot yet realise that each little singing thing that flies near me holds latent in it the power of death for someone. Soon perhaps I may see death come to someone near and realise it and be afraid. I have not yet been afraid.

★ ★ ★ ★ ★

After Tea.

This letter has to be written at intervals. There is not really very much to do in the trenches, but the officers have to go round now and again to see that the men are in their right places and the sentries looking out (in the daytime through periscopes). They go round every three hours or so at night as well & so don't get much sleep. No one is allowed to take his clothes off, and so you have to scrape as much mud as possible off your boots with a bayonet, tie up each foot in a small sack to keep the mud out of your sleeping bag, & get in boots and all. You rarely have much opportunity to shave or wash properly.

We came in last night and are relieved again tomorrow night. I am learning a great deal here. The whole place is like a small town, honeycombed with passages and dug-outs (called by the men here 'bug-hutches'). These have some most amusing names written up over them e.g. Westminster Bridge, The Bridge of Size and Tiers, Ludgate Hill, Marble Arch, Dean's Yard, Southend Pier, The Junior Carlton, The Pulpit, Buckingham Palace, etc. At present the weather is very good, but when it rains the trenches become ditches full of mud. The British have held this line since the beginning of November when they turned the Germans out. There are three German graves a little further down along the trench. There is no name on them, but merely a piece of board with 'German Grave – R.I.P.' scrawled on it. And yet somebody once loved the man lying there.

On the way here we passed a clump of about thirty graves by the roadside – all of men of one regiment killed lately in these trenches. Such is war!

★ ★ ★ ★ ★

It is just getting dusk and the ration parties will be coming in to take back letters with them. This letter will have been carried under fire by the time it reaches you.

Good night, dear, and do not worry on my account. Good night and much love. I have just been kissing your photograph.

R.

Roland to Vera

France, 14 April 1915

Just returned from trenches last night. All our men came back all right, though two of the —s in our trench got wounded by a rifle grenade, and one of our subalterns (who was at Uppingham with me, by the way) was shot through the wrist this morning. It is nothing very serious, but he will probably be sent home for a time. Nothing much happened yesterday beyond some more heavy firing from our big howitzers. On the whole I was sorry to have come out last night. It is, at first at any rate, very interesting;

though in time I can imagine one would get bored with the sameness of it all. On Monday night I went out in front of the trenches with two sergeants to inspect a sap trench that we have been pushing out towards the German lines. From about 60 yards out we could hear them calling to each other. I was struck with the extremely youthful sound of their voices. We got in again all right, though they sent up a flare right over our heads as we were climbing over the parapet. . .

We are staying here till Saturday and then going on possibly to take up a line of trenches of our own.

Vera to Roland

Buxton, 15 April 1915

Your letter written on April 7th, 8th & 9th came this morning. I can't tell you how it interested & thrilled me. When I read it I felt a kind of queer exultation which was anxiety & dread at the same time. I shudder to think that even as I read you may be in danger from those very guns which you heard thundering in the distance, & yet all my fears are sometimes strangely over-ruled by a store of faith in your future – which I told your mother I felt, & which she says she feels too. You say little about yourself, but I know well enough the kind of spirit – the real courage, not of one who is indifferent to danger & fatigue, but who feels them all & still can bear them – which brings you triumphant through all the experiences, & will through many more. If only I could share them with you! I would give anything to be a man for the duration of the war, & change back again of *course* when it was over. If I with you could see the flares from the German trenches at night & hear the artillery guns firing, instead of only knowing that you see & hear these things, I think I should feel almost all the exultation & scarcely any of the dread. Perhaps it seems all very well to talk – but I should indeed welcome the physical exertion & endurance, the long marches & even nights of work after wearying days. . .

My work at the Hospital here in the Long Vacation is practically fixed up. I was there yesterday – you would have been amused if you had seen me sitting among socks, surrounded by wools of divers hues & one or two females of uncertain age. It is a splendid place, & most excellently managed; they have extended it to take in 150 wounded as well as all the usual patients; it is not full just now but expects to be crowded in the summer. I would much rather go there than to the temporary Red Cross Hospital, where the discipline is not nearly as good. If one must be under authority it is preferable to have it as strict as possible.

I am glad you have heard from Edward; I can well believe he was amusing if he wrote to you about me. Do tell me what he said; I should love to know. He seems to be enjoying himself very much just now, & never troubles himself about the future – possibly because his does not as yet hold such possibilities as yours or mine. He is having a much better time than any of us in fact; he is learning to ride, & has opportunities for tennis & innumerable concerts. I suppose it is all part of his usual luck; life always seems to go so well for him, helped by his temperament, or lack of it, that sometimes I wonder if it is not compensation for what is to come. 'A short life & a gay one!' You know he is Battalion Scout Officer, don't you? Isn't that a rather dangerous job? As far as I can make out he seems to be rather good at it. . .

Several more men I know have gone to the front recently; the 6th Sherwood Foresters (T.F.) went out just before you did, though I only knew the other day. Among them are a good many I used to play tennis with & meet at dances. I don't know any of them well enough to correspond with but Daddy got a letter from one to-day which he seems to treasure very much. They are somewhere in the Neuve Chapelle region, which I suppose is not far from you. Isn't it terrible to think that all that engagement & those dreadful losses were the result of a mistake – I am afraid since hearing about the despatches concerning Neuve Chapelle, which were published to-day, a good deal of the exultation has gone out & the dread come in. Soon, I suppose, they will try to take Lille again, in which engagement your regiment will be involved, & then . . . . . ?

Vera to Roland

Buxton, 17 April 1915

Nothing in the papers, not the most vivid & heart-rending descriptions, have made me realise war like your letters. Yet sometimes I feel that what I am reading is all a thrilling & terrible dream & that I shall wake & find things as they were. That cannot be; things will never be as they were, but if Heaven is kind perhaps one day I shall wake & find you with me again. Sometimes even your existence seems a dream too, and I have to look at your letters & the things you have given me to make myself feel it is real . . . The presence of danger seems to make your gift shine out but the more brilliantly. You did not need to tell me you had not been afraid – your letter told me that very plainly, I think you will always be more afraid of fear than of the actual present dangers which terrify many people who were quite unmoved before they came to them. I can realise too how thin grows the barrier between life & death in those trenches out there. When I read about the ever-present dangers from snipers & bullets & German trenches 80 yards away, as well as the possibility of actual engagements, it seems hard to believe that anyone can escape. If ever you are tempted to hold your life too cheaply don't forget that you have left behind one or two people who do not, but who may hold theirs so if you fling yours away. How can you say 'Don't worry on my account'? You don't really want me not to & I don't believe I want not to either; after all, any number of weary apprehensive nights & days is not too high a price to pay for the happenings that have led to my being able to feel the anxiety I do. . .

Kingsley's idea that 'Men must work & women must weep', however untrue it ought to be, seems in one sense fairly correct just at present. I certainly try to do as much as possible of the former, & very rarely have an inclination towards the latter – but I do feel like it a little when you tell me you have been kissing my photograph. I envy the photograph; it is more fortunate than its original. *She* never seems quite to have got past your reserve or been able to know you properly. I suppose it is the nearness of death which breaks down the reserves & conventions which in the midst of elemental things are seen to matter so little after all.

I never thought I should ever say to anyone the sort of things I write to you. At ordinary times one little knows how deeply one can be moved.

Vera to Edward

> *Buxton, 18 April 1915*

I really must write to-day & tell you about some most thrilling letters I have had from R. all about what it is like out there ...

... I feel I should give anything to be there with him. I quite envy you; don't you feel you wouldn't miss it for anything! Somehow it seems as if to die out there wouldn't be so very hard as it would anywhere else. But with what a sort of diabolical skill does the game of life & death seem to be organised out there! I can hardly believe that *he* is really experiencing it all, or that it is not a dream.

Vera to Roland

> *Buxton, 20 April 1915*

The name of your wounded subaltern (2nd Lieutenant Armstrong, wasn't it?) was in the casualty list this morning. I am glad you told me about him, or I should have thought your regiment had been in some sort of action, & have been alarmed. I always glance rapidly down the list for 'Worcester Regt. (T.F.)' before looking at any names. I wish it had been you. Doesn't that sound horrid? But then your desire would have been fulfilled for you in a fairly satisfactory way, & it would have meant a little respite from anxiety for me. But I don't really want you to be invalided home till I go down from Oxford, when I could be with you a little if you wanted me.

I don't know why I persist in writing to you as if you were going to be wounded; it is scarcely tactful. But ever since you went out I have had a sort of certainty you will be, & before long, though perhaps it is because you said you wanted to be. You wished to go to the front, & now in spite of many obstacles, you are there. You always seem to have got what you wanted, & I think you always will.

There has been a great deal of feeling in England over the death of 2nd Lieut. Gladstone M.P. whose name appeared in the casualties last week. He seems to have been one of those people who had a queer premonition of their fate; he wrote to a friend of his just before going into the firing-line 'You ought to be glad & proud that I am going into the trenches; it is not the length of existence that counts but what is done in that existence.'

I mention his death because it seems to be one of the kind that not only could but ought to have been avoided. He had been less than a week in the trenches when in the day-time he got up on the parapet of his trench to try & locate a sniper, & was immediately shot. Is it necessary for people to do that? Surely even heroism does not require people to expose themselves to such an obviously certain death when doing so seems so useless to anyone. A brother of a man who has been at the front ever since the war began & has never even been scratched says his brother tells him that the longer a man has been in the trenches the more careful he becomes, & that though death can be guarded against only to a certain extent, people can help themselves quite considerably with regard to it. He said the reason why so many young officers get killed a very short time after they go out is that they act rashly & take unnecessary risks (as this Gladstone seems to have done) before experience has taught them just what they may & may not do.

Don't laugh if I say – Do be careful, remembering it is for our sakes as well as yours. I hate to think of you wandering about in front of the trenches only 60 yards from the Germans & in full view of their fire. I suppose these things must be, & so – my apprehension sleeps not. (But don't on this account not tell me. I will be quite as wakeful if you don't.)

Roland to Vera

France, 20–21 April 1915

Your two last letters came one last night and one the night before, and I read them by candlelight sitting on the little wooden bench outside my dug-out. I am sitting there now writing this, while the sun shines on the paper and a bee is humming round and round the bed of primroses in front of me. War and primroses! At the moment it does not seem as if there could be such a thing as war. Our trenches are in the middle of a vast wood of tall straight trees – at least the support and reserve trenches are inside the wood, the fire trenches on the front edge. We have held the whole of this wood since the beginning of November and it is all a maze of small paths and isolated huts and breastworks. My own dug-out is in the second line, about 180 to 200 yards behind the fire trenches on the wood-edge. Hence the possibility of having primroses planted in front, behind the shelter of the breastwork. Half my platoon is in this support line and half in the fire trenches, so that I have to divide my time equally between them, except that of course I have my meals and sleep (when I have the time) down here, where there is cover from view, if not altogether from fire. As a matter of fact the wood is all exposed to shell-fire; and two of our men since yesterday morning have been hit by snipers as far back as in the third line. One bullet whistled past my head as I was shaving this morning just round the corner. Yesterday afternoon we were shelled for some time; and had our first man killed – shot through the head.

The portion of the line we are holding here is one of the best known, and much too strong now to be retaken by the Germans. It is probable that they will keep us here for some time – perhaps as long as two months. We are to be relieved by the 8th Worcesters every four days, have four days' rest in billets a few miles back, and then come in again for another four days. We are to go out to billets tomorrow Wednesday morning.

It is very nice sitting here now. At times I can quite forget danger and war and death, and think only of the beauty of life, and love – and you. Everything is in such grim contrast here. I went up yesterday morning to my fire trench, through the sunlit wood, and found the body of a dead British soldier hidden in the under-growth a few yards from the path. He must have been shot there during the wood fighting in the early part of the war and lain for-gotten all this time. The ground was slightly marshy and the body had sunk down into it so that only the toes of his boots stuck up above the soil. His cap and equipment were just by the side, half-buried and rotting away. I am having a mound of earth thrown over him, to add one more to the other little graves in the wood.

You do not mind my telling you these gruesome things, do you? You asked me to tell you everything. It is of such things that my new life is made.

Wednesday 21st

I had no opportunity to finish this yesterday.

We are going out of the trenches this afternoon at 4.0 o'clock. It is now 11.30 a.m. I shall be glad of the rest, as it has been a tiring four days here. I was up nearly all last night mending the barbed wire entanglements in front of our trenches, and this morning can hardly keep my eyes open. There is nothing glorious in trench warfare. It is all a waiting and a waiting and taking of petty advan-tages – and those who can wait longest win. And it is all for nothing – for an empty name, for an ideal perhaps – after all.

When it is all finished and I am with her again the original shall not envy the photograph. The barrier which She seems to have found was not of reserve but rather of reverence. But may it not perhaps be better that such sweet sacrilege should be an anticipa-tion rather than a memory?

R.

––––––

Vera to Roland

Buxton, 23 April 1915

As we left the Hospital we stopped for a few moments to talk to one of the wounded soldiers – a little elderly man who had been at Neuve Chapelle. His appearance made a great impression on me; he did not look unnerved, or even painfully ill – but very, very sad.

Back to Oxford to-morrow. . .

Vera to Roland

Micklem Hall, Brewer Street, St Aldate's,
Oxford, 25 April 1915

I received your letter dated April 20th this morning. Yes, tell me all the gruesome things you see – I know that even war will not blunt your sensibilities, & that you suffer because of these things as much as I should if seeing them, – as I do when hearing of them. I want your new life to be mine to as great an extent as is possible, & this is the only way it can – Women are no longer the sheltered & protected darlings of man's playtime, fit only for the nursery & the drawing-room – at least, no woman that *you* are interested in could ever be just that. Somehow I feel it makes me stronger to realise what horrors there are. I shudder & grow cold when I hear about them, & then feel that next time I shall bear it, not more callously, yet in some way better – . . .

I am wondering just how ever I am going to stand the next eight weeks – not because of the discomfort of my surroundings but because of their pleasantness. I remember once at the beginning of the war you described college as 'a secluded life of scholastic vegetation.' That is just what it is. It is, for me at least, too soft a job . . . I want physical endurance; I should welcome the most wearying kinds of bodily toil. To sit at my table & do a Latin prose feels not only a physical but a mental impossibility. Perhaps I *am* doing just what I ought – perhaps it *is* the best way to prepare for a future in which I am beginning to think it may be more eminently desirable & glorious to earn my own living than even I thought before. But just at present this sort of work is becoming impossible. Instead of doing it, I sit dreaming over it, thinking of you among barbed-wire entanglements at night, & of you suffering from the horrors of war & yet keeping your essential personality – as I see you are in your letters – untouched by them all. I think of the dead man in your regiment & how you might have been he. And all this is doing no one any good. Two people who finished their exam. last term have gone down to nurse. If it hadn't been for pass Mods. I would have done the same; as it is I have to stop here & finish that, else the two last terms & my father's money & the college's are all thrown away, & if I came back here it would be beginning 3 years all over again.

But, as you know, I am going to nurse in the Long [Vacation], & if the war shows no signs of ending I am not sure that I shall come up again till it is over, but stay & nurse more. Suffering myself makes me want nothing so much as to do all I can to alleviate the sufferings of other people. The terrible things you mention & describe fill me, when the first horror is over, with a sort of infinite pity I have never felt before. I don't know whether it is you or sorrow that has aroused this softer feeling – perhaps both. Sorrow, & the higher joy that is not mere happiness, & you, all seem to be the same thing just now. Is it really all for nothing, – for an empty name – an ideal? Last time I saw you it was I who said that & you who denied it. Was I really right, & will the issue really not be worth one of the lives that have been sacrificed for it? Or did we need this gigantic catastrophe to wake up all that was dead within us? You can judge best of us two now. In the light of all that you have seen, tell me what you really think. *Is* it an ideal for which you personally are fighting, & is it one which justifies all the blood that has been & is to be shed?

I suppose you know that a most terrible battle is raging just about 10 miles north of you – & may possibly spread south. I saw in the paper to-day that as long as the Germans hold Menin, they can extend the battle by pouring in as many troops as they wish between Ypres & Armentières. Is there any chance of this? The paper calls this second battle of Ypres the most important conflict of the war & the Germans are getting the best of it. They say the victory of the British at Hill 60 was nothing to the immense advantage the Germans have gained the last few days. They are making a second desperate fight for Calais, are pouring in thousands of troops through Belgium, & are using asphyxiating bombs – another international law broken. All the Allies have fallen back. If this is to go on it seems the war must be interminable. Even the papers admit a decisive victory to the enemy so it must be a tremendous one. Surely, surely it is a worthy ideal – to fight that you may save your country's freedom from falling into the hands of this terrible & ruthless foe! It is awful to think that the very progress of civilization has made this war what it is – particularly intellectual progress, without a corresponding moral progress. Just to think that we have got to the stage of motors, aeroplanes, telephones & 17 inch shells, & yet have not passed the stage of killing one another.

At the end of your letter you seem to imply that you think I meant a kind of faint reproach when I spoke of a barrier between us. I meant nothing of the sort; no one could realise more clearly than I that for everything to be left off – I pray temporally – in the middle was hard, but better so. Of course I know that reverence & reserve are incomplete without one another – before I met you I have let people know how they appeared to me because they seemed to imagine it was unnecessary to use more than a very slight amount of either one or the other. These qualities have a very strong influence in me, & for that very reason their presence in you is the last thing I could wish removed. But what you call sacrilege is only sacrilege when it comes too soon – at the right time it is the culminating point of the very reverence we both admire. My letter was a passionate regret aroused by the emotion in yours; not however a regret because anything we did ought to have been done differently, but because the progress of a very precious thing has to stop awhile with its culminating point still unreached. It is not unnatural surely to know a thing is right & yet regret that it has to be.

You speak of 'anticipation' – it is very sweet to think that such a thing may be again, & that you in spite of everything have hope enough to look forward. Now you are in the midst of it all, do you still feel you will come through to the end? I always am thinking how you said 'I *am* coming back,' & that one day our dreams will come true.

Roland to Edward

Flanders, 27 April 1915

Am writing this in the trenches somewhere in Flanders, sitting on a plank outside a dug-out. There is nothing much doing at present, it being just after lunch when the snipers usually cease from sniping and our gunners have not yet begun to drop their afternoon shells into the German trenches. The latter are anything from 50 to 250 yards away at this part of the line. We are holding the front edge of a wood – a wood very famous in the history of the war – and our support and reserve trenches are hidden away inside. Half of my platoon is in the fire trench and half back in the second line. I have spent the morning in building a new traverse, and at present what with being very tired and sitting in a July sun I am feeling almost too sleepy to write. I didn't go to bed at all last night but went out instead with an R.E. [Royal Engineers] Captain to inspect wire entanglements etc. in front of our position (and incidentally nearly came to a bad end by being mistaken for Germans and fired at by one of our own men. Luckily the damned fool was in too much of a funk to fire straight!) Nearly everything in the way of work is done at nighttime and we rest during the day. We have 4 days in and 4 days in billets a mile or so back. We came in on Sunday night and are due to go out again the day after tomorrow. Our position here is very strong, and in consequence life tends to become somewhat monotonous in time. The snipers are a chronic nuisance, but we do not get shelled very often, which is a distinct advantage. We have been here 10 days and have had only 1 killed and 6 wounded (none seriously). Armstrong got a bullet through his left wrist & has been sent home – lucky devil! They have stopped all leave other than sick leave now, so that I may be stuck out here for an indefinite period. As far as I can see, the war may last another two years if it goes on at the same rate as at present.

I seem to have kept you in disgraceful ignorance of my movements lately. Folkestone, Boulogne, Cassel, Steenwerek, Armentières, and — are my meanderings to date, and we seem stuck where we are now until this part of the line advances. It is all very interesting here and I am enjoying it immensely. My only fear is that, being a rolling stone, I may find it monotonous in time if we stay here always on the same job.

When are you coming out to join me? In time for us to go down Unter den Linden arm in arm?

Let me know any news of Tar if you can. He hasn't answered my last letter.

Roland to Vera

Flanders, 29 April 1915

I never remember having written a letter at this time of the morning before. It is just after dawn and everything is very still. From where I am sitting I can see the sun on the clover field just behind the trenches and a stretch of white road beyond. There are birds singing in the wood on our left, and small curls of blue wood-smoke from the men's fires climbing up through the trees. One of our Machine Guns has been firing single shots every few minutes with a cold and lazy regularity that seems singularly in harmony. Everyone else except the sentries is asleep.

I am the officer on duty from 3.30 a.m. till 8.0 a.m., when I shall go to sleep again until about half past ten. Meanwhile I have to keep awake, walk up and down the line every hour to visit all the sentries, and give any orders that may be necessary. As a matter of fact we are usually awake most of the night and go to sleep at odd times during the day. When you are never allowed to take your clothes off, it ceases to be any trouble to go to bed, or to get up.

We have left our trenches in the wood, and have been since 6 p.m. last night holding another piece of the line about a mile and a half further to the South. We came at a few hours' notice to relieve a Regular Brigade which is being sent on to Hill 60. These are more the conventional type of trenches here – one long ditch, as it were, with a high sandbag parapet and dug-outs in the front wall. There is much less room of course than when there was a large wood behind to walk about in. Also, there are no primroses or violets here, but only sandbags and boarding and yellow slag. Which is perhaps as it should be.

★ ★ ★ ★ ★

7.30 a.m.

Have just come back from my rounds. A French biplane went up a few minutes ago and is circling round and round over the German lines. They have got two anti-aircraft guns and a Maxim trying to hit him. It is a marvellous sight. Every minute there is a muffled report like the pop of a drawn cork magnified, and a fluffy ball of cotton wool appears suddenly in the air beside him. He is turning again now, the white balls floating all around him. You think how pretty it all is – white bird, white puffs of smoke, and the brilliant blue of the sky. It is hard to realise that there is danger up there, and daring, and the calculating courage that is true heroism.

. . . . . He is out of range now.

★ ★ ★ ★ ★

Midday

I have just read your letter, written on the 25th. I cannot answer it now – not as I should like. For one thing I have a lot of men's letters to censor before the post goes – prosaic and unimaginative most of them, but a few make me feel like a Father Confessor –, and also two other officers are sitting by me chattering inanities. I will write again this evening, or tomorrow morning early, when I can do so alone.

I am taking care of myself as much as I can, and don't put my head over the parapet. Only yesterday a man in the regiment we relieved was shot through the head through doing that. He died while being carried out. An officer who saw it happen gave me some gruesome details which I will not repeat. All I myself saw were the splashes of blood all the way along the plank flooring of the trench down which they carried him. It was his own fault, though, poor devil.

Roland to Vera

Flanders, 1–3 May 1915

Yesterday we got rushed off suddenly to occupy a line of support trenches, and had to stay in them till 3.30 a.m. this morning. We are to hold them again this evening, I believe; which, with nothing more inspiring to do than sit still in the rain for the most part of the night, does not sound inviting. Still, at the worst it is good practice, and you can listen to the undulating roar of a distant artillery bombardment from the direction of Ypres not with equanimity but with a certain tremulous gratitude that it is no nearer. Someone is getting hell, but it isn't you – yet.

This morning I took a digging party of 50 men about 2 miles the other side of our wood (we are not actually in it any longer, but we keep in the neighbourhood). They had to deepen a support trench on the slope of a hill behind our line. We were out of range of rifle fire but all the buildings near had suffered badly from the shells. It was a glorious morning and from where we were on the hill we could see the country for miles around. It looked rather like the clear cut landscape in a child's painting book. The basis was deep green with an occasional flame-coloured patch in the valley where a red-roofed farm house had escaped the guns. Just below the horizon and again immediately at our feet was a brilliant yellow mustard field. I left the men digging and went to look at some of the houses near. All the windows were without glass and the rooms a mass of debris – bricks, tiles, plaster, rafters, a picture or two, and even clothing buried among the rest. There were shell holes through most of the walls and often no walls at all. One large château had been left with only the outside walls standing at all. I enclose a rather pathetic souvenir that I found among the rubbish in the ruins of one of the rooms – some pages from a child's exercise book. Soon after I came back to the trench a German howitzer battery that had caught sight of us sent over 38 3.5" shells, which fortuitously hit nearby, though they were all within thirty or forty yards of us. Luckily you can always hear this sort coming and we had time to crouch down in the bottom of the trench, which is the safest place in these circumstances. When the shell hits the ground it makes a circular depression like a pudding basin about a yard and a half across by 18 inches deep, burying itself deep down at the bottom. The explosion blows a cloud of earth and splinters of shell into the air, so that when they fire a salvo (all four guns together) the effect is rather terrifying and you wonder if the next one will come a yard or two nearer and burst right in the trench on top of you. I do not mind rifle fire so much, but to be under heavy shell fire is a most nerve-racking job.

Vera to Roland

Oxford, 1 May 1915

I was up at 3.45 this morning for the famous May Morning ceremony . . . as the clock struck four all the people turned towards the tower & became absolutely silent. Then immediately after, as the sun was rising, the choristers on the top of Magdalen tower sang the May Morning Latin hymn, turning towards the sun . . . I could quite easily have wept at the beauty & pain of it. I couldn't help thinking how different everything is from what we pictured it would be, & how you had meant to be here, & how you would have loved it if you had been. . .

The battle in the Ypres district seems altogether rather a sad affair. We have stopped the German advance & the fury of it has died down for the present, but it seems to have cost us a great deal, to get back a few, not nearly all, of the trenches etc. they took from us. The casualty lists are long, especially among Territorial Regiments. They seem to be bearing all the strain that Kitchener's Army was meant for in the spring. The 'Times' is depressing & talks about the war lasting well into next year. It certainly doesn't look like ending soon when the enemy are still capable of such terrific onslaughts. It would be so much easier to work & hope if one hadn't to do it indefinitely. But I suppose it is weak to want things to be easy. When I read your letters & find how you never complain of anything by so much as a word, dear, although I know you shrink from horror & ugliness just as much as I do, I feel I am not being one little bit brave.

I hear Mother is sending you out some socks for your men. I

am glad you are giving us some faint idea at last of things you want. I do feel such pleasure in sending them.

Goodbye for the present – very best of love –

V.

P.S. Those green envelopes which don't have to be censored are a very pleasing idea. Not that your *letters* ever suffered much from over-'reserve'! But it makes it easier to write to people, doesn't it, when your letters are not going beneath the eyes of someone intermediate, though impersonal.

Vera to Roland

Oxford, 7 May 1915

It is horrible to think of you under shell fire, & in support trenches. I suppose you really are very near the vast chaos that was Ypres – if not actually in it. I wonder, if all this ever ends – sometimes I feel as if nothing but the end of the world could finish it – & you are still left to us, if you will be very different. I suppose you are bound to be – people, especially those whose sensibilities are fine & keen, can't go through this sort of thing & remain the same. Your letters, certainly, don't seem to illustrate you as fundamentally altering, but they do show you to me as becoming very much more all I have known you to be. It seems so characteristic of you to be facing death one moment, & seeing so clearly the beauty of the world, & life, & love, in the next. I am glad my letters arrive so soon after I write them. I like to think of you receiving & reading them, & wonder what you feel when you see my writing on the envelope, and if it is anything like *I* feel when I see yours. Sometimes, in my nightmare moments, I think that perhaps one day he will not read the words meant only for him, into which I have put so much of all that is me...

My great object at present is to get this term over ... I don't think another term here while the war is in its present condition (and you in yours) would be tolerable. *And* – if I have to bear still more, it will be in action, not in scholastic seclusion, that I shall

have to find the necessary strength – if indeed I *could* ever find
it... This at least I know – that if at any time I have to face the loss
of *you*, dear, nothing I have done before will be possible for a very
long time to come. Every letter makes me realise how near you
are to that great Fact .....

———————

Roland to Vera

In the Trenches, Flanders, 9 May 1915
6.30 a.m.

One of my men has just been killed – the first. I have been taking
the things out of his pockets and tying them round in his handkerchief to be sent back somewhere to someone who will see
more than a torn letter, and a pencil, and a knife and a piece of
shell. He was shot through the left temple while firing over the
parapet. I did not actually see it – thank Heaven. I only found him
lying very still at the bottom of the trench with a tiny stream of
red trickling down his cheek onto his coat. He has just been carried away. I cannot help thinking how ridiculous it was that so
small a thing should make such a change. He could have walked
down the trench himself an hour ago. I was talking to him only a
few minutes before .....

I do not quite know how I felt at the moment. It was not
anger (– even now I have no feeling of animosity against the
man who shot him –) only a great pity, and a sudden feeling of
impotence .....

It is cruel of me to tell you this. Why should you have the
horrors of war brought any nearer to you? And you have more
time to think of them than I. At least, try not to remember: as I
do.

★ ★ ★ ★ ★

11 a.m.

A glorious summer day, which helps one to forget many things.
Today we have been instructed to 'give a demonstration of
frightfulness', i.e. to make ourselves as generally objectionable as

possible. We began at 4.30 a.m. by exploding 1600 lbs. of guncotton under a German trench, and are progressing favourably with the help of machine guns, rifle grenades, and trench mortars. They have been shelling us a little. I hope they will not take to using any of their poisonous gas; although we have just been served out with respirators and goggles as a protection.

I should so like to write you a really long letter as an adequate recompense for letters that help me to live, in an atmosphere where the commonplace is perhaps more a thing to be feared than the terrible. But you will understand.

Vera to Roland

Oxford, 11 May 1915

Last Friday was the sort of day that made one begin to wonder if it was possible for the world to continue – horror piled on horror till by the time night came, I should think the whole of England was full of despair. First one opened the Times & read of Allies' reverses both in Flanders & Galicia, Germans poisoning wells & using gases, war-clouds rising between China & Japan, possible intervention of America on the wrong side, & a long casualty list of about 200 officers. Then at midday I saw on the placards of the ultimatum having been sent to China, & at tea time read that a man I know had been killed in action. As a finale to all this, last thing at night the sinking of the Lusitania was announced with its loss of 1500 lives. It was the sort of day that contained about as much as you would want to think about for a year under ordinary circumstances.

Mrs Leighton seemed a little anxious because she had not heard from you for some time, but said she supposed we couldn't expect many letters now you were in the thick of the actual fighting, as she thinks you are.

Tell me honestly, are you? It won't make it any easier, dear, if you try not to let me know. Are you anywhere near the gas area? I suppose the Censor will allow you to tell me this. He has never objected to anything you have put so far. I suppose we are now in the midst of just what has been prophesied for the Spring all along. How much darker, I wonder, will it have to get before the dawn comes? At any rate it gives one practice in how to suffer & steel one's self against shocks, – if that is any comfort.

I hear that when Edward goes out it will almost certainly be to the Dardanelles. I hope it may not be soon. I wish he had not to go there, as it takes so long for news & letters to come. It must be terribly hot too, & I believe is much stricken with smallpox & cholera – though of course it has not as yet the accumulation of war horrors that there is in Flanders. . .

I approached the Principal here the other day on the subject of provisional notice for a year – in case of Red Cross work. She told me I needn't take any steps at all with regard to college until 3 months before the beginning of next term, which means about the middle of July. I hope by that time enough will have happened to clear up my indecision.

———————

Edward to Vera

Maidstone, 13 May 1915

We came here on Sunday and go to Wrotham by train every morning – 10 miles away – march up a hill for about 4 miles and dig trenches which are almost an improvement on those at the front. The country up there is more beautiful than any inland country I have met with in England and the trenches extend or will do when completely finished for 90 miles . . . It is awfully boring for the officers having to watch the men dig and to measure as they go along; occasionally I dig myself but am not really allowed to, as we are supposed to superintend. We are only here for a fortnight, then I think back to Sandgate for a fortnight and then to a camp near Guildford. We are still very short of rifles and I don't know when we shall go out; it is quite likely that we shall go to the Dardanelles. I want to transfer to the Field Artillery but it is very difficult.

———————

Roland to Edward

Flanders, 13 May 1915

Dear Edward,

I was so glad to get your letter – a very charming one, may I say, if tinged with ennui somewhat and more still with the 'lacrimae rerum'... I needn't tell you how much I should like you to be over here after all for many reasons. But I don't know about the Artillery. They say that it takes 5 years to make a gunner, but that's all balls. When you first mentioned it I thought that you'd probably get out quicker where you are, but I've been talking to one or two Artillery officers about it and they are more hopeful. The Regular R.F.A. [Royal Field Artillery] is the thing to get into, I gather. They are hard up for officers in the Regulars now and will allow Territorials (and Kitchener's Army too, I suppose) to transfer if recommended by a Brigadier or greater nut and able to pass the Medical Exam. . . Anyhow it's worth trying, and the Gunners have a topping time over here compared to a damned footslogger. Of course when they do get it they get it Hell – Germans rushing on towards the guns 100 yds away, and your horses half mad, and the trees broken, and two men and a boy left out of your battery to get away with. I was talking to a Canadian Artillery Officer yesterday who was in that recent show at St Julien near Ypres, and they seem to have had perfect Hades.

I don't quite know how you are to manage to work your transfer, though. You won't be able to do it by going straight at it – at least, I think not. As one who has had many experiences, and many disappointments, and ultimate success, in trying to get round Red Tape and Army Orders I can only advise you to get hold of somebody at Whitehall or elsewhere who actually knows of a job for you. It is absolutely useless writing to the War Office: practically useless writing to an individual unless he knows you already... Of course I am in a way at the wrong end of the string here, inasmuch as you will need some training in England first. But I might come across an opening in the Infantry somewhere...

Personally I am going on much as usual – alternately about 4 or 5 days in the trenches & 4 days rest in billets. Nothing much doing where we are. On Sunday we had a Divisional order to be 'frightful' to distract the attention of our friends opposite from what the French were up to further to the South. We began at 4.0 a.m. by exploding 1600 lbs of guncotton under part of their trench, & continued at intervals with rapid fire, Machine Guns, trench howitzers, rifle grenades, artillery shelling etc. until evening. There was a devil of a noise but nothing much else, and beyond knocking down a bit of parapet and barely missing my dug-out with a diminutive shell of sorts they seemed quite docile about it.

To me this War seems still to be a long job & in a sense only just beginning. The French have been doing remarkably well, though, these last two or three days. Someone will have to get a move on soon; I don't look forward to stopping where we are during the hot weather. The whole country is a muck-heap. (E.g. three days ago while digging a machine gun emplacement just to the front of my bit of trench we had to cut through 3 dead bodies to get there.)

Perhaps everything will end suddenly. Qui sait? As far as I can see there is still a large percentage of the English population that hasn't yet realised that there's a war on at all.

However –

I was very pleased to hear both from you & from the Old Block himself that he is getting on so well now. I suppose the Royal Sussex will not see him again, will they? I wish I could have seen him before I came away. So you think you may be amused – again? (Why again?) Tah the confirmed bachelor and a hospital nurse! Well, after all – yes, it *is* all very amusing. Et tu, Brute?

———

Vera to Roland

Oxford, 13 May 1915

Your letter written on the 9th arrived this morning. Do my letters really help you to live? I wish they could do more & ensure your life. Your description of that man's death made me feel a little as you say you did when you saw him lying dead. . .

Why was it cruel of you to tell me about it? It would be much more cruel if you didn't, when I asked you to. I should feel very hurt indeed if you were to try to shield me from things, instead of letting me share them, as I am ready to do. I wouldn't think of denying that horror & death & war are terrible things & made me suffer too, but there is something which even while it is impotent is yet stronger than they, & claims your frankness. It is easier to say 'forget' than to do so, but I would rather be unable to forget than be given nothing to remember. Perhaps when it is all over & the beautiful things in life come back, it may be possible to forget the sorrows they replace. But till then – I will be satisfied if I am called upon to remember.

Even if it is making us both very sad, that is all we can expect at present. I always think of the sorrow I saw in the face of the little private I met at the Hospital, who had been in Neuve Chapelle, & wonder, if ever I see you again, if you will wear that kind of look. Your expression was sad & serious enough before, too; as if you felt the griefs and responsibilities of the world more than most people. Perhaps you did – & do. I am glad you sent your private's few belongings home. It was like you to think of that. War seems either to make people quite callous, or more sensitive. I would rather you were one of the latter, though I suppose it makes it harder for you – now.

I see by the casualty list to-day that a Major Dore of your regiment has been wounded. Is that a result of your outburst of frightfulness? And do such instructions portend a taking of the offensive?

You never seem to go into billets now or to get any sleep. Do you have to stay in the trenches all the time, & aren't there enough people for you to exchange with? . . . I keep reading names in the paper where trenches have been lost or re-taken & wonder if that is where you are. I found an excellent map of Ypres & district (about 20 mile radius) in the Times. It is now on my wall & I look up all the names.

I notice in your last two or three letters you have seemed a little distressed because you think my letters are more frequent than yours. Please don't be. I wish I could make you realise how unspeakably precious your letters are, & then you would know that you don't need to apologise for their shortness. You don't want me, do you, to deprive myself of the joy of writing as much as I do, just because you can't answer as often, or to the same extent?

If I have more time to think, I also have more time to write – which just now is better than thinking. And when you tell me my letters help you to live, I mean to write more & more. . . I know you think – so much – even when you can't write, & that you do write as often as you are able, – and there is nothing better I would ask. Sometimes I rather suspect you write to me when you are tired out with work & want to sleep, when a little rest would do you much more good than writing to me. I don't like to think you do that. It is for me a great deal you must take care of yourself.

Is the commonplace more to be feared than the terrible even in Flanders? It certainly is here. One rises to the occasion when a sudden call is made upon one's endurance; it is the long long hours of suspense & depression that lie on one's mind as a kind of dull heaviness & at times make one nearly mad. That is another reason why you mustn't shrink from telling me the dreadful things you yourself experience; I can bear them better than the burden of every day.

I have just had a letter from one of my great friends at school, whose brother, who is in the Buffs, was wounded near St Julien on the 3rd & is now in hospital in London. There are only 3 officers, including him, left of his battalion & only 159 men out of 5000. North of Ypres must indeed have been hell. This man hadn't slept or had his clothes off for 24 days before being wounded. They had to hold their trenches while under shell fire without a single gun to help them, and watched the Germans forming to attack them without being able to do anything. Their trenches were taken & as he was lying wounded he saw the Germans bayoneting his men & several of his friends, who were wounded . . . He is a very nice boy; I wonder how he will be affected by this awful experience. He also got a whiff of the poisonous gas, & says it half blinded & made him sick for hours. I do hope, whatever else happens to you, you won't have to suffer from that. It is such an unsporting & diabolical method of warfare. I suppose we shall have to stoop to the same methods if nothing else will stop them. Is there any antidote at all to the poison? . . .

I do hate to think of you seeing that man dead, & feeling as you must have felt about it. I think I would rather it had been me that had seen it & felt it. You are after all so inappropriately placed in your present surroundings – & yet so splendid. I should love to see you in the trenches looking thoroughly dirty & untidy, since I have only been permitted so far a vision of absolute immaculateness. I wonder if I should even recognise you. It is an aggravation to me that though I can often visualise the faces of perfectly uninteresting people whom I don't care for at all, I can never quite see yours in my imagination. But one more look – if only. . . . .

Goodbye again, & ever so much love –

V.

Roland to Vera

In Billets, Flanders, 14–15 May 1915

I am so sorry, dear, to have kept you without a letter for some time. Your own letter of May 11th came just an hour ago; and such a sad, disappointed letter, too. It made me feel such a beast to have been the cause of it: but you know that I always write as often as I can, and let everyone else except Mother wait. . .

Everything is still all right, dear, so far. We are still holding the same part of the line that we have had since leaving the wood. I have seen no real fighting – in the open, I mean – yet, but only the kind that consists in sitting quiet in your sandbag-padded ditch perhaps for months and taking an occasional shot at a more or less docile and usually invisible enemy who is content to do the same under the same conditions 100 or so yards away. At night he sends up flares every ten or fifteen minutes to make sure that you have not so far forgotten yourself as to come out to cut his wire entanglements or throw grenades into his trench. If you have any similar suspicions you fire off a flare or two in his direction now and again. The whole thing is a most static performance. Now and then a man gets killed, usually through exposing himself unnecessarily: occasionally the enemy's artillery shell your trenches – which is unpleasant –, and your gunners proceed to do the same to him . . . . . It is not until one side decides to make an attack that there is any real fighting. Then reserve troops are brought up to strengthen the line where the attack is to be launched from; the artillery begin a bombardment of the enemy's trenches, ending in an infantry assault across the open. Perhaps our line of trenches is taken and you sweep on again to the next; perhaps you are beaten back. The whole time you are under fire, and what, if on a large scale, becomes a battle may last for hours or intermittently for days.

There is a great difference between being really in action like this and sitting in trenches in comparative safety – which is as far as I have got so far. They are of course merely successive stages, not different varieties of warfare. All trench fighting must come ultimately to the climax of an action in the open or neither side would gain any ground. It is beyond human endurance for troops to fight in the open indefinitely: they must occupy some kind of fortified position in order to keep hold of the ground they have gained or still retain.

During the winter months both sides have more or less hibernated in trenches. The real fighting has now begun and both Allies and Germans are trying to advance. The whole line cannot advance at once. All that can be done is to try to break through at one or two points. Hence our great struggle at Ypres and that of the French, to the South. Between these two points the aim of the Allies is to hold the line in sufficient force to prevent the Germans withdrawing any troops to send to support the two critical points to North & South. It is on a portion of this more or less quiescent front that I am at present . . . . .

Saturday Morning 10.30 a.m.

I am writing this sitting under a lilac tree in the garden. It is the same house – a disused school – that we were in when billeted in the town before, about three weeks ago. The sunshine and the smell of the lilac remind me of May in a St John's Wood garden – and it hurts.

There was some heavy artillery firing somewhere not far off which kept me awake for some time last night. Ypres again, I am afraid; though it sounded nearer. It is perfect Hell up there now. It is appalling to see the number of wounded that are brought back by endless ambulance columns. The casualty lists in the papers must be longer than ever. And then – what infuriates me more than most things – to read of London going mad with unreasoning anti-German fury just because the Lusitania goes down and something a little nearer than Flanders comes home to them. [Why] not all this before?

R.

Vera to Roland

Oxford, 16 May 1915

I have been reading the last day or two about all the fighting last Sunday on the ridges north of Lille, 20 miles south of Ypres. Consequently I am waiting most anxiously for a letter, to see if you were in it or not. The loss of life seems to have been terrible, & the result not worth it, which is worst of all. I had a long letter from Edward on Friday; he seemed very anxious about you & to be afraid you were in the thick of it. He seems to be getting rather impatient with the Sherwood Foresters, so I am sure *you* would have been long ago; you would never have been content there even if your transfer had been effected. They never get given any rifles & never seem any nearer going out... I hope Edward will get his transfer, in which case he would be more likely to go to France. I don't want him to go to the Dardanelles...

Time is heavy-footed, but it is nearly half-term. I have given provisional notice for this place, in case I want to go down for a year & nurse, as I told you I might. In any case I cannot give my work the attention it deserves... They have taken to putting war telegrams on a board in front of the Town Hall here, which is only a few yards from this house. I purposely pass it often & look – It is a better way of getting information than the 'Times', which makes me cold to read it, it has been so depressing lately. Yesterday it published the longest list of casualties since the war began. It also said that we might have to give up everything in the world before our object can be achieved. I expect – judging by the casualty lists – that some people have given up everything in the world already, at least everything that counts. I suppose I may.

Two girls here have had their brothers wounded but the majority are quite indifferent. Someone is laughing uproariously downstairs. I can't let your letter be spoilt by the kind of feeling that gives me, so I will stop. I will write again very soon, possibly to-morrow, to make up for this inadequate sort of letter, which is rather swamped in its expression by the thoughts of you in my mind.

Roland to Vera

In the Trenches, Flanders, 17 May 1915

We are not in the actual fire trenches this time but taking our turn of being in reserve in a ruined farm just behind. There is not really much farm left – four or five battered walls and none of the original roof – and every now and then the Germans drop a shell on it and knock down a bit more. They have not touched it very recently, though, and it is more or less safe. There are three officers and a half company in this farm and the remainder in another about a quarter of a mile to our left. I am writing this in the officers' hut at the back – a little shed made of planking and corrugated iron. It is rather more luxurious than might be expected and actually has four wooden chairs and two small tables and an old shell-case full of apple-blossom on one of them! There is an apple-tree that I can see from the window now, standing in the middle of a field yellow with buttercups. It is raining slightly and for the moment is very still. You could walk across the field and think you are in England, except that English fields are not pitted here and there with shell holes and the trees haven't usually got telephone wires looped from one to another in unexpected places.

I have had a most interesting afternoon. I went along with Captain Chamberlin (who was in the Norfolks with me & largely instrumental in getting me out here) to the trenches of the — Regt. a little farther down the line. They are Regulars and take turns with a regular battalion of Edward's present regiment in holding this section. Their trenches are the most interesting I have yet seen anywhere. I cannot go into technical details; but at one point they hold a forward barricade 40 yards from the Germans and just in front of a ruined house. From here they had sapped out and made a mine a little time back. A few days ago they heard the Germans mining towards them on a slightly higher level. Two officers and two men went down their own tunnel and found the Germans just breaking in to a small gallery on the right. They had a fight down there in a space barely large enough to crawl along, and succeeded at last in driving the Germans back a few yards and firing our mine, which blew up the German one above it. The explosion made a large crater in the ground about half way between the two lines of trenches. The following night the Germans crept back out to this hole, set up a row of iron plates on the front edge and began firing at the British parapet, killing the —s senior major. Another small party of 5 men and an officer crept nearer and began throwing bombs into our trench, but the whole lot were routed by bombs and grenades and fled, leaving a revolver and five Mauser rifles which I saw through a periscope lying out in the open about 10 yards or so the other side of our parapet. A few bold men of the —s are going to try to get these souvenirs tonight, though if the Germans happen to send a flare up they will be lying by the side of the rifles, I am afraid. Yesterday an Engineer officer & two men went down the mine tunnel to explore, before it was properly free of gas. They were all three overcome by the fumes: and a third man went down, brought up the officer and one man, and on going down for the third time was himself asphyxiated. The two who were brought up have recovered, but the others had to be left down in the mine embedded in the clay. This afternoon when I got there they had just let a canary down in a cage to make sure that the air was pure enough, and then with some difficulty they brought up what looked like a long rigid mass of clay – the remains of a man who deserved the V.C. if ever anyone did.

It was all rather gruesome to see – the mine and the way they had to haul the men up with ropes – but it was intensely interesting. In the front barricade you cannot talk above a whisper because if the Germans hear you they send a bomb or two or a rifle grenade over on top of you. But one learns that here too in the perhaps monotonous round of trench warfare there is latent the opportunity for heroism – and in this case a heroism the more real because without glamour and even without light.

★ ★ ★ ★ ★

. . . I am just off to give my platoon an impromptu lecture on asphyxiating gases. We have been served out with goggles and respirators now. The latter are soaked in a chemical that neutralises the chlorine or bromine in the gas and makes it quite harmless. No gas has been used in this part of the line yet, but we are quite prepared for it if it comes.

***

Vera to Roland

Oxford, 18 May 1915

Have you read any of the War Sonnets of Rupert Brooke – the most promising poet of the younger generation, who enlisted in the Navy when the war broke out, & died at Lemnos a few weeks ago – to the great grief of Literature & the whole world. I must quote one or two because I know you will like them. Somehow I feel that Rupert Brooke must have been rather like you. It is not yet possible to buy his poems in print, though of course there is a greater demand for them than there probably would ever have been if he had not died so tragically. Throughout them all there is a strangely prophetic note of his coming fate – which he seems to see with sad & grave foreboding, & yet to regard it with courage & hope too.

Roland to Edward

Flanders, 19 May 1915

Trench only 40 yards from the Deutcher at this point, and they chuck rifle grenades etc. if you talk above a whisper . . .

No, the wood we were in a little time ago was only Ploegsteert, not Ypres (correct English pronunciation by the way is Plug Street!). We may be going up to latter portion of Hades soon, though. First New Army just turned up, looking very smart & church parade-like. This will wear off very soon: but they're a damned fine looking crowd. Mostly Scots regiments – no one's round this part of the world. They haven't been shoved in any trenches yet, but we've got their gunners behind us now. (Incidentally an order has just come round from G.O.C. regarding the artillery sending shells into our own trenches!) . . .

Affectionately

Monseigneur

———

Vera to Roland

Oxford, 21 May 1915

I don't think I have ever read anything quite so terrible as the official report on the German outrages in Belgium. It is in the weekly Times I have sent you to-day . . . their treatment of the women and children is worst of all. If ever they get over here I shall go about with a revolver – not for them, but for myself. I don't know how any man can read it and not enlist. It makes me feel I could do anything to the German soldiers if only I had the power, & I want to say to you & everyone else at the front I know, 'Once you get hold of them do your very worst.' The worst you could do to them wouldn't make them suffer as much as they made the Belgian women & children suffer. Somehow I think it must be a sort of encouragement when you are in the trenches to read accounts like that. It is the only justification you need for what you are doing.

———

Roland to Vera

In Billets, Flanders, 22 May 1915
3 p.m.

I am in a field behind a farm house, perched on top of a large iron roller – you see them in England sometimes with a horse drawing them and the driver sitting in a little seat behind. I have just sent my servant into the nearest town to buy oranges and bits of looking-glass to make periscopes with. Everyone else has gone to sleep, as most of them were out digging trenches nearly all last night. I've had quite a lot of sleep lately myself and so prefer to sit out here in the sun and write letters – which is probably what I should have done in any case. Everything is very quiet now. There is a lark singing overhead and one of our mountain guns firing at intervals far away on the right. I am feeling very lazy – rather like a fat bumble-bee in fact; and rather pleased with the world, except that my pipe has gone out and I've left the matches in the house, and this seat's rather uncomfortable, and there's a war on. It is very nice sometimes to be a person of moods. . .

I am very fond of the sonnets. Three of them I had read before, but not the last one. There is a grave a few yards away from where I am sitting – a private of the Somerset Light Infantry killed in December: which makes the two poems on 'The Dead' more real than ever. There is also a Major of the 19th Hussars buried near here (we put a new fence round the grave the last time we were out of the trenches). I cannot help thinking of the two together and of the greater value of the one. What a pity it is that the same little piece of lead takes away as easily a brilliant life and one that is merely vegetation. The democracy of war! . . .

★ ★ ★ ★ ★

I must be off to practise throwing hand-grenades and other unpleasantly explosive things of the kind, and to instruct my platoon in how to use them. The men are supposed to rest when in billets, but you have to parade them now & again to prevent them getting too lazy. They are inclined to prefer flirtation with a rather pretty girl in the cottage across the road to rifle-cleaning and similar more necessary occupations. Which, I suppose, is natural, but not to be encouraged too much.

———————

Vera to Roland

Oxford, 23 May 1915

Oxford is a little desecrated this week-end with Whitsuntide trippers . . . I feel that nothing would relieve my feelings better than physically & verbally to 'go for' some of the young men. They are lounging down the street smoking cigarettes with a vacant expression in their eyes & a self-satisfied smile on their faces, twirling Japanese umbrellas in their hands & poking at the passers-by with them. I can scarcely bear to look at them and think that you and such as you are enduring toil and weariness & risking death that they may remain safe, and that your task is made all the harder & heavier because the hero of the Japanese umbrella refrains from relinquishing it for a bayonet. No one has the right to lounge now-a-days, not even an American. . .

The other night I had a queer sort of half-dream in which I thought you came here to see me while I thought you were still in Flanders, and you hadn't told me you were coming because you wanted me to see how I should take the surprise. I wonder how I should! I only wish dreams were prophetic . . . I wonder if to confess the need of someone's personal presence is to confess a human weakness too. Often I think perhaps it is, & that the highest of all human relationship is expressed in a sentence in Waldo's letter to Lyndall – 'Sometimes such a sudden gladness seizes me when I remember that somewhere in the world you are living and working.' But to me it seems possible to feel that & the personal need as well.

———————

Edward to Vera

Maidstone, 23 May 1915

. . . Heavy Artillery is very important in this war, and, moreover, if I can only get into some part of the Artillery, I might be able to get up higher when I have learnt the work. However they may not have a vacancy or something may go wrong; transfer is very difficult, but I am very fed up with this Battalion. . . We have finished our trench-digging at Wrotham. It is part of an huge line of trenches from the sea to Reading in a semicircle – the last main defence of London which we shall never abandon in the event of a raid whatever the cost, because our women and children are behind. A very big raid is quite on the cards.

Vera to Roland

Oxford, 26 May 1915

I have some sad news for you to-day; at least, if you haven't heard it before it will come as rather a shock, I am afraid. R. P. Garrod, who was with you at Uppingham, is dead; he was killed in action (in the artillery engagement, I suppose) near Festubert, the day you wrote to me. I have cut out & enclosed all I could find in the 'Times' about him. I had never spoken to him, but I often heard Edward mention him; and because he was connected so much with you & Edward at school I feel his death almost as a personal loss. I can see him now playing the 'cello at Speech Day last summer, less than a year ago. I expect he little dreamed of his own fate when he heard the headmaster say 'If a man can't serve his country he's better dead.' . . .

I am longing to begin nursing; the only way to support suffering one's self is by alleviating even if it is only a little & indirectly, the sufferings of this unhappy stricken world. I shall not come back here till the war is over. I am anxious to play my small part in what is only another division of the same strife that you are in now, the only field at present where 'that immortal garland is to be won, not without dust & heat.' . . .

Have you really kept all the letters I have written since you went out? That adds to the feeling of sweet responsibility which writing to you gives me. I thought you would be bound to throw them away now, as I didn't think you would have anywhere to keep them. I'm sorry your case is full, but am not concluding that that means you want me to stop writing. You will have to adopt a selective process & weed out all but the nicest. I don't suppose you have time to reread them as I do yours. All I have had from you this term live apart from everything else in the big purse you carried for me in London.

Edward has now gone to Martinique Barracks, Bordon, Hants. . . A battery (the 132nd) of the Royal Garrison Artillery is being formed here in Oxford . . . he has written applying for a vacancy, & enquiring if it has a reasonable chance of soon going to the front, where *he* seems to be agitating to get now.

———————

Vera to Roland

Oxford, 30 May 1915

I went with a few other Somerville people to give an entertainment to the wounded soldiers at Somerville. I expect our performance was something like the one you saw at the Red Cross Hospital – it was a mixture of singing, dancing, & more or less elementary acting. I had some of the singing to do. The majority of wounded at Somerville are not very bad cases; most of them were able to sit in the garden, where we gave the entertainment, and those not quite so well sat in the windows of the rooms all round. But of course most of them were cripples & bandaged in various ways, and I don't know when anything has made me feel so sad as the combination of the music, the lovely garden on a glorious afternoon, and these fine specimens of humanity with their once strong bodies broken & helpless. One feels at such times that no cause is great enough to excuse the wrong that made them like that. . . Most of the men were Tommies; I saw two or three who could not have been more than sixteen, if that; they looked mere schoolboys. There were a few officers too; three of them were sitting a little apart from the men talking to visitors who had come to see them, and I saw one or two more hobbling about the garden in pyjamas & long overcoats. One was a tall, thin, cheerful-looking boy who reminded me very much of Edward from a distance. In fact from the impression he gave me I could almost picture Edward limping along supported on one of those padded crutches – as indeed he may one day. . .

A more than usually heated conflict is going on in the papers about the war in general and conscription in particular. Lord Northcliffe's papers seem to be attacking anyone in authority, especially Lord Kitchener, and the rest of the press is attacking Lord Northcliffe. If the subjects of their controversy were not so immense and terrible it would be quite amusing, but as it is it seems a dreadful state of affairs that the authorities are quarrelling among themselves at home while men who are in their hands are dying for them abroad. One begins to doubt the advisability even of the freedom of the Press, when it alone has the power to make & unmake ministers at almost a moment's notice. Everything is looking very dark just now – unless the Coalition Government & the entrance of Italy into the war may grow into rays of light in time. What do you think about conscription yourself? I think men at the front must surely know more about it than the squabblers in the Cabinet. Edward is very much against it; he says it would to a great extent destroy the morale of our army, which is the chief factor in rendering it superior to other armies in general. Personally, I become intensely irritated when I see the hero of the Japanese umbrella stalking along the street, but at the same time I cannot imagine him any use as a soldier, especially under compulsion, or having any but a deteriorating effect upon any army he went into.

Roland to Vera

Flanders, 31 May 1915

I was very sorry to hear of Garrod's death and, although sorry, perhaps still more amazed at the nearness of it all. Yes, I think he is the first Uppinghamian of my year to fall. I had known him before, too. He was at the same Preparatory School in London with me, and we always used to walk home together and were rivals for a long time. It is part of the irony of life, too, that one could not easily find anyone less of a born soldier than he. A scholar, and a musician, and above all a peace-lover. I have just written to his mother; but there is so little that one can say.

Vera to Roland

Oxford, 2 June 1915

There was a Zeppelin raid on London at last, in the early hours of yesterday morning. Most people there are said not to have known about it till they read it in the papers at breakfast, but that may only be a journalistic remark. It is all rather mysterious as, quite sensibly, it is not allowed to be published what part of London the bombs fell on. There were 5 deaths & a good many serious injuries, & several fires. People here tried to telephone through to their relations & were not allowed; owing to the secrecy preserved several wild rumours got about, one actually to the effect that Liverpool St. Station was burnt down! When I think of the appearance of Liverpool St. I can't help feeling that if it *had* happened, things might have been worse. However, the paper explicitly stated this morning that no public building was damaged. I have several friends in London & have heard nothing alarming from them yet, so I don't think anything really disastrous can have occurred.

Roland to Vera

In the Trenches, Flanders, 3 June 1915

April, May, June – my third month out here. I wonder if I shall still be Somewhere in Flanders when July comes, and memories of Speech Day 1914, and all that I had hoped of Oxford. Do you remember the Sunday that we walked up and down Fairfield Garden together and wouldn't come in out of the rain? And I couldn't keep the tears out of my eyes afterwards when Sterndale-Bennett played Karg Elert's Clair de Lune in the chapel. You were sitting at the back near the door and I couldn't see you without looking round, I remember. It all seems so very far away now. I sometimes think I must have exchanged my life for someone else's. . .

★ ★ ★ ★ ★

The Prime Minister, of all persons, was responsible for the abrupt ending of my last letter. He was brought along to have an informal look at us, and it was arranged that he should see the men while they were having a bath in the vats I told you of before. We only had about half an hour's notice and had to rush off and make arrangements for the 'accidental' visit. I and two other subalterns being at the moment in a mischievous mood decided to have a bath at the same time, and successfully timed it so that we all three welcomed Asquith dressed only in an identity disc. . . He looked old and rather haggard, I thought.

The men of Kitchener's Army whom we had to instruct went out again early yesterday morning. They were quite a fine lot of men, though the officers seemed rather too old – both 2nd Lieuts. I met were over 30 & had come to be instructed by subalterns 10 years younger. I cannot help thinking that enthusiasm is more valuable than experience in a war like this.

Vera to Roland

Oxford, 4–5 June 1915

In the 'Times' I have sent you to-day there is an account of the Battle of Festubert, in which Garrod fell. Several regiments &

individuals are mentioned; the London Regt. is not but I don't doubt it deserves it equally with the others. If you hear any details about how he died you will let me know them, won't you? Some people would say it is morbid to want to know details, but I don't think it is a bit; a closer knowledge removes that horrible impersonality which fills you almost with despair, making you feel that he who has fallen is a mere name, a mere unit, among multitudes that perish. It is *this* feeling that is morbid, because not even the least important officer or man is a mere name & unit: each one typifies & reproduces in himself the sacrifice & heroism of the whole, so giving it & us the 'gifts more rare than gold'.

. . . I think the sacrifice of people like Garrod is greater, just because they are not born soldiers, than that of men who go keenly into war glorying in the excitement of battle. Perhaps this sounds like a truism – but I do feel strongly what the value must have been to him of all the things he had worked for & gave up. Olive Schreiner again seems so applicable to him – 'A striving & a striving & an ending in nothing, & no one knew what it had lived and worked for.' I wonder if it *has* ended in nothing after all. What wouldn't one give to know!

Roland to Vera

Flanders, 4 June 1915

Our time in the trenches is not up until tomorrow night, but my company has been withdrawn into a farm-house or two just behind the line. I have got one farm more or less to myself. The extraordinary part of it is that the farmer & his wife are still living here, although shells fall round about every day & it is well in front of all our guns. They do not seem to mind, though. Unlike many of the farmers here they are not suspected of being spies in league with the Germans. Many are known to be (we have been in three such farms); and I can never understand why all civilians are not cleared out of this area altogether. The farmer's wife here is very attentive, has cleaned all the coal and some of the dirt out of my bedroom, given me her best chair, and insists on sending my servant in with little bowls of fresh milk every two hours. I don't know if she expects me to wash in it or what.

I went to my first funeral this morning at our little cemetery on the road up to the trenches. A shell fell among a group of our signallers two days ago, killing one outright and badly wounding two or three others. One of them, a young lance corporal in my company, died of his wounds early this morning, and we buried him at 12.30, sewn up in his blanket, and hurriedly, because the grave and the little cluster of men round it were open to view and formed a distant target for the German shells. It was all very simple; no firing party, no flag-covered coffin, no flowers. The man had been recommended for the D.C.M. for laying a telephone wire under fire a week or two ago. It is such a pity that he could not live to wear it.

Which reminds me (because this man sang at it) that I got up a concert for the company two or three days ago while we were in billets at Nieppe. I managed to borrow a piano, and the men sat in the open on forms. There were quite a lot of good singers to be found in the battalion, and it was a great success. I could not help thinking of the last occasion when I had done this sort of thing, as President of the Union Society at Uppingham. You would have been amused to see me on an improvised stage of planks singing a duet with a French girl to the strenuous accompaniment of a somewhat heavy handed corporal at the piano.

Roland to Vera

Flanders, 5 June 1915

We had a man-hunt late last night or rather early this morning, trying to find a sniper who was firing somewhere just behind our lines. Probably a civilian from one of these pro-German farms, I should think. He had six shots at an artillery officer in the morning, & two at our signalling officer, three at me, and several at odd ration parties during the evening. We sent out search parties to poke around in the ditches and long grass where the report of the rifle seemed to come from, but we had to give it up at 2.0 a.m. as it was getting light already. I wish we could have found him. It would have given me much pleasure to have caught him red-handed and shot him on the spot. . .

★ ★ ★ ★ ★

I have been looking through your letters this morning. I don't think I can carry them all about with me, as apart from any question of room there is always a good risk of their getting lost, which I could never forgive myself. There is only one person to whom I could trust them. May I send them to you to keep for me until you can give them back to me again yourself some day, and levy for such sweet guardianship what price you will? I wish I could keep them always with me; but that is impossible, I am afraid. They have meant so very much to me that I do not like to give them up – even to you.

Roland to Vera

In Billets, Flanders, 6 June 1915

I am in a large farm now, with tall poplar trees all round. They have been shelling it a good bit today and we had to send all the men out into a hollow in the field behind in case any shells fall in the actual buildings. No damage has been done.

I went to mass this morning in a very small chapel in the village near. The parish church is all in ruins – shells again. The curé was an old dear and grew quite eloquent on the subject of the war. The congregation was an interesting study – mostly women and old, gnarled, sunburned farm labourers, all with the stolidity of the typical Flemish peasant and the black, square-cut, Sunday clothes that looked as though they had been made for their great-great grandfathers.

There are rumours that we are going to be moved to a different line of trenches, though not out of our divisional area. This will not mean Ypres; only a little change of scene.

Vera to Roland

Oxford, 8 June 1915

Of course you may send me my – or rather your – letters. You had better send them as soon as you can after you get this, as I go down in a fortnight's time, & it would be a pity for them to be lost when you are taking these precautions to prevent just that. I am proud that you care so much for them, though I don't see myself why you should; they have often made me angry by their inadequacy. I would say 'Why not just destroy them' – only that seems rather an absurd thing to say when you appear to care for them as if they were really worth something... You won't really be giving them back in a sense – you will only be returning the medium through which my spirit has to reach to yours, and the spirit itself you will keep when its outward form is in my possession. It will be queer getting my own letters back – I almost think it will hurt rather seeing them again. I don't think I shall be able to bring myself to read them – not at least without pain. They cost so much more than paper & ink.

You are a rash person to say I can levy what price I will. You must have discovered ere now my well-known capacity for doing the unexpected. You don't know what you mayn't be letting yourself in for! However I won't charge you a war-tax on them, & if I want any payment for my services I will demand it when I put them back into your hands again.

Roland to Vera

Flanders, 13 June 1915

It is just beginning to get light. I have not been to bed yet tonight but as we have to stand to arms at 3 o'clock every morning it is not worth while turning in now until 4 o'clock when I can sleep on until breakfast. The Germans have been very quiet all night – out mending their wire most of the time to judge by the sound. We have been out in front too, listening for possible patrols and seeing what little there is to be seen. There is a field of tall grass now between the two lines and it is very hard to see anyone lying down even a yard or so away. This has disadvantages – e.g. you come unexpectedly upon odorous and unburied remains of long deceased Germans; which, without going into further details, is decidedly unpleasant...

Everything much as usual. We have been shelled a bit lately – both in our last farm (I had my suspicions of the lady of the house) and in my sector of trench two days ago. Three of the company wounded and one knocked down and bruised, by one of the heavy shells at the farm. The next one that came killed or wounded 12 civilians – mostly children playing in the road. It's not so bad when you know you're in for it, but it gets on your nerves rather wondering whether the next one is going to drop on your farm or not. You can hear the crooning whistle of each shell passing overhead; or rather you hear it coming and sincerely hope that it *will* pass overhead and not condescend to take any notice of your existence. I am getting quite expert now in the nuances of shell sounds.

Roland to Vera

Flanders, 14 June 1915

I am writing this in a field opposite the estaminet where I am billeted. It is afternoon, and hot, even in the shadow of a wild-rose hedge. It is very quiet except for an occasional shell overhead from our own artillery behind. I am feeling somewhat ennuyé and very far from bellicose at the moment. One never seems to get much forrader; and I never was a very patient individual, as you may have found out by now – too ardent an admirer of the meteoric, with an innate abhorrence of gathering moss.

I have just been investigating the viscera of a new kind of hand-grenade with discretion and a penknife. They are very fascinating toys. which reminds me that we have had an epidemic of mine explosions in this part of the world the last few days. Ours seem to have gone off where they were intended to, and the Germans' where they were not, and none of them in my trench – which is very satisfying on the whole...

Would you like to send me a rattle? Don't laugh; although it sounds so suddenly infantile. I want a loud wooden one (not too large) like an old watchman's rattle, to call the attention of respirator-swathed men to the fact that I should like to give an order if I could only speak intelligibly through a smoke-helmet. Then I proceed to required gesticulations. It's for gas attacks, of course. . .

P.S. It is possible that I may be able to get 6 days' leave in the near future.

Vera to Roland

Oxford, 15 June 1915

I begin nursing almost at once after going down – on Sunday June 27th. It is getting very near now. I have just come back from going all over Somerville – the Hospital Somerville, I mean. It simply makes me feel that I want to start this minute. I should get just to love the men, I know. I am told they nearly all want to talk to you, & tell you all about it; some nurses haven't the patience to listen but it wouldn't be a question of patience with me; I should love to hear. . .

Edward came here on Saturday & stayed till Sunday evening. We talked about you & Richardson & the war most of the time . . . Edward thinks he has got his transfer into the Artillery, though not yet quite certain . . . He is almost more keen about it than I have ever seen him over anything, except perhaps music; of course he doesn't like his battalion, but doubtless you know why & all about it. I expect he will go out towards the autumn – unless he gets into a more or less prepared battalion, & I don't suppose he will as he will have to learn Artillery work from the beginning. A few weeks one way or the other doesn't seem to make much difference now – the war will be so long that the last people who go to the front will have as much of it as they care about. At least that is how I feel just now. I don't see what can end anything so tremendous. Anyhow I hope he won't go to the Dardanelles. It is a regular death trap just now. Nearly all the

Manchester Regiments are out there – Territorials that is – with the result that there is someone dead or wounded every day almost that I know quite well. Yesterday I saw the name of a man among the killed with whom I have done a considerable amount of amateur acting – & there was another the other day with whom I have often played tennis, & met out. I feel as if I shall soon have no acquaintances left, to say nothing of friends... I told you people at college had on the whole very little direct connection with the war, but only to-day a girl I know quite well went home because her brother has just been killed in the Dardanelles. He also was in a Lancashire Regiment . . . . . I feel as if I were standing on a lonely & dismal shore, watching the tide gradually surround & cut me off, & I am almost sure that it will not turn before it has reached me.

———————

Vera to Roland

Oxford, 19 June 1915

When, oh when, is 'the near future'? In this case it is perhaps just as well you put the most important part of your letter in the postscript, otherwise I might not have taken in the rest, and would have forgotten to send you your rattle...

Sometimes I have felt that I could forgive the future everything if it would let me see you once again. (I don't think I should really; I think I should forgive it still less, but still that is sometimes what I have thought.) At other times I feel I couldn't bear to see you again till the war is over; that though I am out to face hard things there is just one I couldn't endure, and that is to live over again the early morning of March 19th on Buxton railway station. But now the possibility of having to do so begins to arise, I know that it is more than worth while – even this. One is willing to pay the bitterness of death for the sweetness of life.

———————

Roland to Vera

Flanders, 22 June 1915

It is such a long time since I wrote to you last. We have just taken over some fresh trenches and so I have been busier than usual these last few days. We are about 300 yards from the German line here – a nice safe distance as regards rifle grenades and such like annoyances, but liable to be shelled much more. There are trees, hedges, and growing corn which prevent one side seeing very much of the other. So much so that the other afternoon I crawled with two men up to within about 70 yards of their trenches, completely hidden in the long grass. . .

Did you ever come across J. S. Martin at Uppingham . . . I see that he was killed out here a few weeks ago. He was in the R[oyal] Irish Rifles and, though not intellectually brilliant, one of the most charming persons I have known. I came back from Camp with him the many years ago that make last year, when War was a newly discovered toy which both of us hungered to play with. I was growing to have quite an affection for him. The second of my year now.

Roland to Vera

Flanders, 26 June 1915

We are being sent down South in the next few days, presumably to where Garrod was, or somewhere in that part of the world. In consequence all leave has been cancelled – at least for the present.

I will write you a proper letter as soon as I can.

On 27 June Vera started work as an auxiliary VAD nurse at the Devonshire Hospital in Buxton, a short walk from Melrose. It was the beginning of a nursing career which was to last, with interruptions, for the next four years.

Vera to Roland

Buxton, 28 June 1915

I can honestly say I love nursing, even after only two days. It is surprising how things that would be horrid or dull if one had to do
them at home quite cease to be so when one is in hospital. Even
dusting a ward is an inspiration. It does not make me half so tired
as I thought it would either...

The majority of cases are those of people who have got
rheumatism resulting from wounds. Very few come straight from
the trenches, it is too far, but go to another hospital first. One man
in my ward had six operations before coming & is still almost
helpless...

I have various things to do, all of which belong to the kind of
work which is called probationers' work. Another nurse & I have
three wards to look after between us. Generally I do two & she
does one, as she has other work like massage to do which does not
come within my sphere. I have to take the men their breakfasts
(they are nearly all in bed for breakfast), prepare the tables for the
doctor, with hot water etc, tidy up & dust the wards & make the
beds. These latter are not made in the ordinary way but in a particular method you have to learn how to do, & are called medical
beds. Not every sick person has a medical bed, but cases of
rheumatism always do. Then I have various other jobs during the
morning, such as going round with the doctor to see the patients,
bandaging limbs, helping semi-helpless people to get up & put
their clothes on (I had extreme difficulty this morning in putting
on a man's sock for him!), waiting on the nurses while they do
massage etc, taking round milk at lunch time, preparing dinner, &
in general being at the beck & call of the nurse who is over
me...

We had a letter from Edward this evening. He is rather
depressed about his transfer; he says at this rate he won't get it till
about 3 months after he is out, which would be a lot of good. If
he stays with his present regiment he says he is going out in 2
months' time, probably to Malta & the Dardanelles – that dreadful death-trap. I wish my Father wouldn't make things worse by
continually railing against things as they are at present, swearing at

the government, conjuring up horrors & saying his life will be
ruined if Edward is killed. Every horror he conjures up has a
double import for me, because I connect it both with you &
Edward too. . .

The papers are very pessimistic. I suppose our fortunes have
reached about the lowest ebb that they have touched ever since
the war began.

Roland to Vera

France, 2 July 1915

I am writing this in front of a little window in the roof, looking
out over red tiles overgrown with tufts of moss across a valley of
grey-green corn fields to a wooded ridge in the distance. It is all
very still in the sun. Farther to the right and hidden behind the
gable of the roof are what look like pyramids, black and pointed
against the sky. They are slag-heaps, and far from picturesque at
close quarters. This is a colliery district, and the road from here to
the next village is dotted with squat miners' cottages. The miners
themselves come back from work along this road – the road to
Paris, they tell us with awe – small, rather bent men most of them,
in light blue overalls and blue skull caps with coal-blacked faces
and hands. The nearest mines are two miles off, but many of the
men live in our village here. I am billeted in a house on top of the
hill – quite comfortable, and with a real bed to sleep in. The pro-
prietor amuses himself with a little farming, while Madame is the
sage-femme of the village and announces it on an unnecessarily
large brass plate on the door. She spends a large part of the time
chasing Marie-Louise aged 4, whose ideas of discipline are somewhat lax. We have been here two days now and probably stay here
for another week, though everything, as usual, is uncertain. Before
this we did six days marching in stages, the marching during the
evening when it was cooler, putting up each night at a different
town or village and resting during the day. It has been quite a
change and good practice for men who have got somewhat fat
and lazy through 3 months of trench work. Where we go to next,

I don't know. We are at present about 10 miles from the firing
line – farther than I've been for a long time – and are said to have
been brought down South here to be used as a flying column and
rushed off wherever we may be wanted. At present we are merely
resting. . . . .

. . . . . A company of Turcos has just gone by along the road,
singing a weird chant punctuated with hand clapping. They all
look very negroid, but are wellbuilt men and march well. They
have French officers, wearing an apologetic expression and singularly useless looking swords.

Vera to Roland

Buxton, 3 July 1915

I am sorry you are moving towards Festubert, and into – I can't
say the danger zone, for you have been there all the time, but into
that region where the danger is most acute. I expected that when
the time came you would go to Ypres; it is a surprise your being
sent to the other extreme. I am very disappointed about your
leave & could be still more so, only I won't let myself think too
much about it. I had hoped that before you went into the actual
thick of the fighting, I should see you once again, & learn to
realise you tangibly as intensely as I do intangibly. The friends of
almost everyone I know seem to have been back just lately either
wounded or on leave . . . Perhaps after all it is a compliment paid
to us by Fate – for I always think that the people who are given
the most strain on their endurance are usually those who are
capable of enduring most . . . . .

Nursing is going on well – I like it more & more. The chief
things it spoils are my shoes & my hands! . . . I like all my patients
immensely – particularly a sandy-haired lance-corporal from the
Devon Regiment. He is quite helpless; I have to get him up
every day & bandage his leg. He was wounded in four places,
each bad; he has been on his back for many months & is likely to
be on it many more, but he is always cheerful & everything is
always right for him. It is really a pleasure to look after him. I

would rather look after Tommies than officers – except one officer. Sometimes I try to imagine he is you – only he is very thin,
which does not aid the fancy! They are all most amusing about
the tea in the morning, they call it 'khaki-water' (with some justice) and have a different exhibition of wit over it every day. I
have to be very solemn & dignified & act as if I were at least 10
years older than those boys of my own age (fortunately the
nurse's dress helps the illusion) but it is usually very difficult to
keep my face straight.

Vera to Roland

                                                Buxton, 10 July 1915

Speech Day! – divided from us by just a year of cataclysms. We
thought then that nothing would prevent our being together at
Oxford but the remote chance of my failing in a small & annoying exam; we didn't dream that a European War would do the
trick! How utterly amazed we should have been if someone had
told us that in a year's time you would be an officer in the fighting line and I should have voluntarily renounced for the time
being the place I was striving so hard to gain at Oxford, to take up
work which I should then have thought the very last kind of
thing I would go in for. . .

   I had a most extraordinary dream the night before last – or
rather, yesterday morning. It was very agonizing too, but fortunately ended better than it began. I thought I was in a vague sort
of room, a schoolroom of some kind it seemed, or an office, but
all very indefinite . . . I knew I was in very great suspense & was
waiting for news of some kind. I had not been there long when
another vague person came up to the table & said 'He is dead; he
has died of wounds in France.' Somehow or other I knew that it
was you they were talking about – & that I had been waiting to
hear information about you, but I was aware too that these
people did not know you personally & had never even come
across your name before . . . I shuddered all over with the
kind of shock one gets when something happens that one has

half-expected, & which is almost worse than the entirely un-expected. I felt as if the ground under my feet were unsteady & went very chill & sick . . . . . it was something [like] the feeling I had when we said goodbye at the station, only more so. And I said to the vague person 'How do you know; are you sure?' and he answered, 'Yes, it is written down on this paper – the name is here,' and he handed me a piece of paper folded. I unfolded it hastily & there written in unfamiliar but quite ordinary hand-writing I saw the name 'Donald Neale.' (It was written down & spelt just like that; how the name came into my head I cannot tell at all, as I have known nobody of that name either in life or literature.)

Vera to Roland

Buxton, 18 July 1915

Whence this long silence, dear? I know of course that there is some good reason for it – I am almost afraid to know what. I am so sorry I have not written for so long. I have been extremely busy, but that is not the reason as I am never too busy to write to you. But I have been waiting to get a letter before writing again – expecting to get one every day, every post in fact. I have such a dread of writing a letter & getting it officially returned unread by the person for whom it was intended – I think that is the most horrible way of learning about casualties that there is. But I cannot wait any longer now, as if you have not written just because you have too much to do, you must be wondering what has become of me & my correspondence. . . If there is nothing wrong, you'll forgive this selfish anxiety, won't you? As a day or two ago I picked up the 'Times' & saw 'Heavy fighting between Arras & Armentières'. . .

Goodbye, dear. A Field Service postcard is all I ask.

Roland to Vera

France, 18–21 July 1915

Your letters to me are like an interrupted conversation; and I remember afterwards in odd moments what you said, and wonder sometimes if you get tired of talking to a phantom in the void who does not answer or show that he has understood.

Yes, I too thought about Speech Day . . . so much . . .

This letter is bound to be scrappy, I am afraid, as it has to be written at odd moments. We are back again now at B[urbure] where we were for some little time a week ago or more (the mining village I sent a postcard of). We were down farther to the South for 4 days (when I last wrote you an inadequate epistle with the postcard) just at the junction of the French & British lines. I went up to the trenches and through our lines to the French, passing a sentry in khaki on one side of a small traverse and another in sky-blue two yards further on. There is no dividing line except just the change of uniform. I went along some of the French trenches just for curiosity and found everybody very enthusiastic and loquacious and unshaven. I had quite a long talk with two or three of the men. They seemed less inclined to grumble than ours, more resigned to the inevitable perhaps, as men who had well counted the cost of such a war, conscious that they were fighting on French soil still for their national existence.

Monday 19th

Am writing this in the train. We left Burbure this morning and the battalion is going South again – but much more so, to a district where no British troops have yet been. There are French soldiers at all the stations, who cheer us as we pass. It is a glorious day & very hot.

Later

Just arrived in billets, very hot and dusty after a few miles' march from the station. Sleepy little village full of very povertystruck inhabitants, mostly old women, who have never seen khaki before.

Very picturesque country round here. The sky was wonderful as we came along an hour ago – deep blue with mackerel spots of light gold clouds in the west meshed like gold chain-armour on a blue ground, and below on the horizon a long bar of cloud so dark as to look purple against the sun. Why are sunsets more beautiful usually than sunrise?

July 21st 6.30 p.m.

A very long interval, I am afraid, dear. I had to rush off without finishing this letter on Monday night & was too sleepy when I came back. Since then I have been having a very interesting time. I was wakened at 1.30 a.m. the same night by an orderly with a note from headquarters ordering me to pack up my things and take a party of 50 men off to report to the Headquarters of the VIIth Army Corps at M— at 8.0 a.m. This place is about 3 miles from where I was in the last paragraph. On arrival I found a very charming Château which the headquarters were to move into that evening (yesterday). My job was to help the Camp Commandant get everything ready. I had a very busy day yesterday as a sort of Assistant Chamberlain of the Household, and the same today. This morning another 50 men arrived for me, and I have risen to being temporarily attached to the Staff of the VIIth Corps here as Officer Commanding the Headquarters Company. I, the Camp Commandant (a very charming and dandified Major) and the General's A.D.C. are the only officers here out of 16 who haven't got 'red hats'. I have been given a small room in the Château, and am getting quite used to meeting Generals and Staff Colonels round every corner. There are five generals in the house now, and heaps of people hanging around with enigmatical appellations such as 'The D.D.M.S.' (Deputy Director of Medical Services), 'The A.P.M.' (Assistant Provost Marshal) or 'The I.O.M.' (Inspector of Ordnance Machinery). It is somewhat embarrassing to be told by someone that he is 'a G.S.O.3'!

I don't know how long I am to stop here, I'm sure, but temporary Staff appointments are decidedly interesting.

———————

Vera to Roland

Buxton, 21 July 1915

Mother enquired yesterday why we had heard nothing of you for so long. I told her, quoting from your letter 'He says he's been leading too peripatetic an existence lately for letter writing.' Mother's sole comment was 'What words he does use! Whatever does it mean?'

Dear pedantic soul, I was so relieved to hear from you. When you are marching about I expect the time goes quickly without your realising it, and when I am at the Hospital I have not much time to think about being anxious, only in the times between when I have leisure to be selfish, I do begin to wonder & surmise.

———————

Roland to Vera

VIIth Corps Headquarters, France, 23 July 1915

I am so very sorry to have made you anxious about me, but I hope you have got a letter by now. The difficulty is not so much to find time to write as to get letters sent off. When we are on the move as we have been so much lately the postal service is temporarily stopped and we cannot either send or receive any letters for perhaps a week. Hinc illae lacrimae.

I am not quite so rushed now as I have been the last two days. The Corps is getting settled down in its new quarters now and there is less organisation to do. I have not given so many orders to so many different persons, about everything from the disposition of a general's furniture to the amount of food required for odd numbers of men and horses, in my life before. It sounds easy enough to tell people to do things, but I don't think anything is more tiring.

My C.O. came round yesterday and wanted to have me back again with the Battalion. The Camp Commandant wants to keep me here. So I at present don't quite know what is going to happen. I prefer this to wandering over France doing nothing in particular, but on the other hand don't want to miss any real fighting.

Vera to Roland

Buxton, 24 July 1915

I think Edward is coming here for a fairly long leave in a week or two – possibly the last. Mother wants him & me to have a snap-shot taken together – *I* say as a typical example of 'two people (one at any rate for the first time in her life) who-are-doing-just-what-other-people-think-they-ought!' If we have it done you shall have one. My uniform suits me rather better now than in that photo. I sent you. It has grown to me more & I to it. I no longer feel strange or uncomfortable in it and I don't think it is really unbecoming.

Vera to Roland

Buxton, 28 July 1915

I am hoping that you will get an early chance of leave for convenience sake as well as for all the other things too, as I really don't know what I may be doing in the fairly near future . . . This present Hospital is of course only a temporary affair – though the temporariness may be either long or short according as things turn out. It is not really a Military Hospital, but a civilian Hospital with a military side; it affords however a very satisfactory combination of usefulness to other people with training for myself while I am seeing about other things to do. I am at present very necessary where I am but they expect to be much slacker after the autumn has begun – of course the Hospitals are everywhere but an over-flow Hospital more so than most. . .

I heard a day or two ago that there is a faint chance of my get-ting into a large London Hospital as a V.A.D. The Hospital is an immense place at Camberwell (No 1. London General); it has been established I think since the beginning of the War but has recently been greatly extended & contains over a thousand beds. They have to make a necessary increase in the nursing staff & want more V.A.Ds. . . I should love to go there as they get all the wounded straight from the trenches and the V.A.Ds have all the minor dressing to do. Fully trained nurses are rather scarce just now, and it is counted that two V.A.Ds take the place of one trained nurse (though I don't think they do really, I had no idea what a capable person a trained nurse was till I went to the Hospital). This Camberwell place is of course a Government affair, so you have to sign on for 6 months & get paid at the immense rate of £20 a year, but you get your board and lodging free as well.

Vera to Roland

Buxton, 29 July 1915

I am sending you this afternoon the poems of your brother-spirit, Rupert Brooke. I think you will love them all, as I do; not the War Sonnets only, though they are perhaps the most beautiful.

We have heard definitely from Edward that he is coming here to-morrow, for, I suppose, the last time . . . He seems to be taking his 6 days' leave as soon as possible, so I suppose he is anxious to get it over – as indeed, I certainly am. I almost wish he could go without my seeing him again. Every time I see him I feel he is more indispensable, & it doesn't do to feel that people are indispensable now-a-days, though I am guilty of it with regard to more than one person . . . . . There are some things I feel about his going that I would feel about no one else's, and which indeed no one could understand unless they had all their life been very fond of one particular brother or sister. But it is like flinging a large piece of one's Past into Limbo, not knowing if one will ever get it back. . .

One consolation at any rate is that I think he realises what he is in for as well as anyone *can* know who has not been out there. You can picture to yourself how coolly he has studied the question of the worst horrors of war, in stories, newspaper articles, and official reports like that on the Germans in Belgium. He has also talked to several wounded back from the Front, all of whom seem to have been of rather a depressing nature with a great horror of going back. When I spoke to him at Oxford I realised he had fully taken in all that they had told him and was ready to face what might be . . .

Do you ever see the Times History of the War? There is an excellent account of the battle of Neuve Chapelle in this week's number though I can hardly bear to read about it, for the thought that you or Edward might get mixed up in a similar barbarous and sanguinary business. It all seems so wicked too – just a pure orgy of slaughter, of terrible and impersonal death, with nothing in the purpose and certainly nothing in the result to justify the perpetration of anything so horrible. War does bring to light the fundamental contradictions of human nature in a state of semi-civilization such as ours. It is quite impossible to understand how we can be such strong individualists, so insistent on the rights and claims of every human soul, and yet at the same time countenance (& if we are English, even take quite calmly) this wholesale murder, which if it were applied to animals or birds or indeed anything except men would fill us with a sickness and repulsion greater than we could endure. I suppose it makes matters worse to have such thoughts, but when you think how easily that pile of disfigured dead is heaped up in a few minutes by a sharp Artillery fire, and yet what an immense and permanent difference each single unit thus shamefully cut off makes to a whole circle of individuals, you feel that if you are not mad already, the sooner you become so and lose the power to realise, the better. It is no wonder that so many women laugh with such bitterness at the criminal folly of men. It is only because these immense catastrophes are run entirely by men that they are allowed to happen.

———————

Roland to Vera

France, 30 July 1915

I have been back with the Battalion again a day now. My little experience with Corps Headquarters was most interesting, though short lived. We are going into the trenches in about 3 days time, which was chiefly why I and the 100 men I had with me were recalled. Also two of the officers in my Company are away – one with a badly sprained ankle and the other, I am afraid, dying of appendicitis in a military hospital a few miles away. The other sub-alterns left were all new & inexperienced so that the assistance of myself was much needed. I am at present acting junior captain and second in command of the company.

While I was at Corps Headquarters I didn't have any real Staff work to do or much chance of showing that Roland Leighton has any more ability than the average subaltern. I think they were very pleased with me, though, as the A.D.M.S. asked the General specially whether I could not be kept there permanently, instead of being relieved by some other officer from another of the battalions in the Corps when a fresh 100 men came in. The General said that this was impossible in the circumstances, but that if he got together a permanent Headquarters Company, as he intended to do soon, he would offer me the command of it. At any rate, I have learnt a lot about how an Army Corps is run, if nothing else. I enjoyed myself very much, and found all the officers there very nice indeed and not so wooden by a long way as one is inclined to picture the Staff as being. I got a glimpse of civilisation one afternoon by motoring in to Amiens to do some shopping. It was filled with French officers and very gay and unwarlike. The sight of English officers, hitherto a rarity, interested them very much. I went to look at the cathedral, but found it all banked up outside with sandbags.

Roland to Vera

France, 2 August 1915

Dear Child – I have always liked this name for you, though I ought not to call you 'child', ought I? – thank you so much for Rupert Brooke. It came this morning, and I have just read it straight through. It makes me feel as if I want to sit down and write things myself instead of doing what I have to do here. It stirs up the old forgotten things, and makes me so, so angry and impatient with most of the soul-less nonentities one finds around one here. I used to talk of the Beauty of War; but it is only War in the abstract that is beautiful. Modern warfare is merely a trade, and it is only a matter of taste whether one is a soldier or a greengrocer, as far as I can see. Sometimes by dint of an opportunity a single man may rise from the sordidness to a deed of beauty: but that is all.

———

Vera to Roland

Buxton, 3 August 1915

I am sorry you have left the Corps Headquarters. It was such a relief – even if only for a short time – to feel that you were safe. But I hope very much that the General will form his permanent Headquarters Company very soon and that you will go back. It would be a fine appointment. . .

Edward came here on Saturday & goes again on Thursday. He keeps telling the family most cheerfully that the 9th Sherwood Foresters had three last leaves, and the same thing may happen to him, but he told me privately that it is his opinion that they really are going in about a fortnight . . . . . Mentally I said good-bye to him in New College Chapel an hour or so before he went back to Aldershot, and I would have been glad not to have to do it again.

All the same it is very hard to realise that it *is* the last time. His attitude towards home & all of us is – as you can perhaps imagine – so exactly the same as it has always been. . . He talks mostly about music & books, with an interest that is quite unimpaired & not the least assumed. In town the day he came here he bought several new books to read & quite a lot of music to learn & try over while he was at home. And yet he isn't the least in the dark about what the Front means – or the least afraid of facing the reality. He had a long talk with one of my patients at the Hospital and the man – an absolutely straightforward & candid person – said to me afterwards that he thought he would be some good at the front and at any rate seemed to know well enough what he was in for. But he is very cheerful and unapprehensive, and the Future – near or far, doesn't appear to trouble him very much. Although on Sunday night when we went for a walk together he became suddenly very serious as he told me a few things he wanted done if he should die. . . I only know I don't understand him at all. Perhaps I never shall now.

He is about the last of all my friends & acquaintances to go. When he is gone all I care for will be at the front – except your Mother. War or the Country or whatever name you like to call it will have taken almost all that makes my existence worth while – my work, my future and the people I love best.

Isn't it queer that to-morrow is War's first birthday! I wonder how many people there were who on last August 4th thought the War would not be over by that time next year . . . And here we are after a year's fighting further from the end than we were at the beginning! (That sounds like a paradox, but indeed when we began there seemed to be many more reasons for hoping for a speedy conclusion than there are now.)

———

Vera to Roland

Buxton, 5 August 1915

Do you remember the hilly road over the moorland, where we went along during a walk one Sunday, the first time you came here? Yesterday evening about 9.0 Edward & I went a long way up that road . . . We talked for a long time and very seriously; a good deal of it was about you. I don't think I shall ever forget it.

I don't know why, but somehow I think that Edward in his heart has a kind of haunting feeling he will not come back. He does not exactly say so, but he said he had achieved scarcely anything as yet, and he did not see that his life was very much good to anyone; he wasn't even sure if it was much good to himself. As for me, I don't know what I think about it all any more than I did when you went; my mind is in a turmoil; I only know I feel very alone. He wanted Rupert Brooke's poems to take out with him, so I gave him the book . . .

My efforts to move don't seem to be attended with very great success . . . I seem to have spent my time bombarding Devonshire House with letters for the last week, without very much effect. Apparently whenever one wants to change the conditions of one's work a little, the difficulties are great . . . Edward said that it was the same thing when he was trying to get a commission; every possible obstacle was placed in his path.

Vera to Roland

Buxton, 8 August 1915

I am so glad you liked Rupert Brooke. I too read the book straight through & then wanted to 'write things myself' very badly indeed. How very like me you are in one or two ways – though if you weren't so strong a feminist I should hesitate to put that, thinking you might regard it as anything but a compliment, and immediately correct me in a Quiet-Voice-on-paper sort of style! . . .

Why shouldn't you call me 'Dear Child'? I like the name from you; I have always liked it when Edward used it, but from you it seems to mean more still. We are, after all, as you said in a letter a little while ago, only children still in years, but the childhood has been rather buried of late and been superseded by other things which in the normal course of events we ought never to have known or realised until we were at least past thirty. It is Europe's fault, not ours, that we have grown to a precocious bitterness, and learnt that glamour fades, and that behind that glamour (which we ought not to have penetrated for some years to come) grim realities lie, – as when, for instance, I say that the more intimate you become with a nurse's duties, the harder it is to see the beauty in them, and you say that warfare is merely a trade and it is only a matter of taste whether one is a soldier or a greengrocer. But don't despair – dear child! Even War must end sometime, and perhaps if we are alive in three or four years' time, we may recover the hidden childhood again, and find that after all the dust & ashes which covered it haven't spoilt it much. . .

Sometimes I wonder how it is we have borne as we have the events of the last year. We are such a nation of grumblers, and I know that I and so many other people were annoyed by such little discomforts, and complained so bitterly because we were separated from friends for quite a short time, when both we & they were perfectly safe. From a personal point of view I can only say it is because things have developed gradually & I have worked by degrees up to a pitch where I am able to face them. I don't know what it must have been for those whose most beloved people were in the Regular Army and who had to face the consternation and amazement of an utterly unprecedented War, and lose the dearest and best at the same time.

Edward's going, deeply as I have felt it, has not made anything like the impression that yours did; it has simply intensified feelings that you in departing aroused, nearly five months ago. Of course there are reasons for this, not to be gone into or examined too closely – yet. But, putting these other reasons aside, I know it is partly that he has been gradually getting nearer & nearer the end of his training for some time past, and it is in the natural order of events that his departure comes. Whereas your memorable letter – 'I think I have succeeded at last' – came like a bombshell, which I did not in the least expect.

Roland to Vera

France, 15 August 1915

I am coming home on leave on Wednesday – in three days time. I did not know definitely till this morning & only had time to scribble a very hurried few lines to Mother, telling her to let you know too. I don't know whether this will reach you in time, as posts are variable & unreliable. I will telegraph as soon as I reach civilisation or know definitely when or where I am likely to arrive. I am afraid it is no good your trying to communicate with me at all until I get to England. I will leave my arrangements about what I am going to do when I get there until later. Consult Mother on the subject.

I cannot realise that I really am coming at last, dear.

Very much love –
Till Wednesday

R.

Roland to Vera

Telegram, Lowestoft, 19 August 1915

Arriving Liverpool St 11.30 tomorrow will meet you st pancras first class ladies waiting room as soon as I can get across there

Roland's leave lasted for just under a week, during which he and Vera agreed to become unofficially engaged 'for three years or the duration of the War'. After spending the first night at Buxton, they travelled down to Lowestoft to be with his family. In some ways it was an unsatisfactory time for both of them, getting used to each other again after so many months of separation. They enjoyed only one true moment of intimacy as they sat alone on a cliff path, the afternoon before their departure. Silently drawing Vera closer to him, Roland rested his head on her shoulder for a while, and then kissed her. As Vera had to report for duty, back at the Devonshire, on 24 August and Roland was not returning to France until the end of the week, they had agreed that he should see her off at St Pancras. At the station, on 23 August, he kissed her goodbye and then, almost furtively, wiped his eyes with his handkerchief. 'I hadn't realized until then that this quiet & self-contained person was suffering so much,' Vera wrote in her diary. As the train began to move she had time to kiss him and murmur 'Goodbye'. She stood by the door and watched him walk back through the crowd. 'But he never turned again. What I could see of his face was set and pale.'

Roland to Vera

London, 23 August 1915
7.0 p.m.

I could not look back dear child – I should have cried if I had. I am writing this in a stationary taxi drawn up in a corner of Russell Square. The driver thinks I am a little mad, I think, to hire him and then only sit inside without wanting to go anywhere at all . . . I don't know what I want to do and don't care for anything, except to get you back again; and that I cannot do – yet. How far it seems, sweet heart, till we may live our roseate poem through, as we have dreamed it so long.

I cannot write for the pain of it.

[Goodnight, dear Child, good night.]

———————

Vera to Roland

Buxton, 23 August 1915
Midnight (et après)

When I arrived I found no one in the house but servants, one of whom informed me that Father had an overnight wire from Edward this morning to say he was going to France to-night. Father & Mother at once rushed off to Farnham on the chance of catching the regiment before it left, but even so they may have been too late. He has gone off even more suddenly than you did. . .

My thoughts keep racing feveredly from you to Edward & from Edward to you. So I must do something & writing to you is the only thing I am capable of doing at the moment. How it has all happened at once! . . .

I am trying to recall the warmth and strength of your hands as they held mine on the cliff at Lowestoft last night – so essentially You. It is all such a dream. Often as I have come home by the late train I have seen the moonlight shining over the mountains, but it has never looked quite the same as it did to-night. It is getting so late.

Vera to Roland

Buxton, 24 August 1915

Apparently Edward is not going out with the battalion. They have 8 supernumerary officers and the Division has suddenly refused to have more than 30 going out with each battalion. So they have had to eliminate 8 who are to be sent to Lichfield and to be held as drafts for the 11th though while at Lichfield they will be attached to the 13th. . . Apparently he is very depressed about it all and has mad ideas of trying again for the Artillery. Write to him and find out for yourself about it. He is at Bordon till Monday. Tell me honestly, does this eliminating him mean he is not much good or that the Colonel doesn't like him – or is it just luck? I want to know really what you think. It is all very annoying – he has been rather unlucky all through and the Battalion seems unsatisfactory. I am sure he's not a bad officer – he is too keen for that.

Roland to Vera

The Howard Hotel, London, 24 August 1915

In a way I am glad that I am going back tomorrow. If I cannot be with you I prefer to be as far away as possible. How much would I not give to be able to hold you and kiss you again even for a moment! And not being able to, I feel an insane desire to rush back to France before I need, and leave all to memory as all that matters is already left.

I have just written to your Father. It is entirely informative – not interrogative, and merely a brief & slightly formal notification of what the world is pleased to call our engagement. I should prefer that the world knew nothing about it; but that unfortunately is impossible.

Roland to Vera

Telegram, Brixton, 26 August 1915

Till we may live our roseate poem through

Roland to Vera

In Billets, France, 26 August 1915
2.30 p.m.

I got back here at about 11.30 a.m. this morning after a rather tiring journey by train and motor. I found your long letter waiting for me. It was so strange in a way to read something that you had written before you saw me and when my coming back at all was only problematical. And now it seems to count for so little that I did come back after all, so little that I saw and talked with what was no longer a dream but a reality, and found in My Lady of the Letters a flesh and blood Princess. Did we dream it after all, dearest? No; for if we had it would not have hurt so much. I am feeling very weary and very very triste – rather like (as is said of Lyndall) 'a child whom a long day's play has saddened'. And it is all so unreal – even the moon and the sea last night. All is unreal but the memory and the pain and the insatiable longing for Something which one has loved.

There is sunshine on the trees in the garden and a bird is singing behind the hedge. I feel as if someone had uprooted my heart to see how it was growing.

<u>Violets</u> — April 1915

Violets from Plug Street Wood,
Sweet, I send you oversea.
(It is strange they should be blue,
Blue, when his soaked blood was red,
For they grew around his head;
It is strange they should be blue.)
Violets from Plug Street Wood
Think what they have meant to me —
Life and Hope and Love + You
(And you did not see them grow
Where his mangled body lay;
Hiding horror from the day;
Sweetest, it was better so.)

Violets from oversea,
To your dear, far, forgetting land
These I send in memory,
Knowing You will understand.

R.A.L.

FOUR

27 AUGUST 1915 – 26 DECEMBER 1915

Give me, God of Battles, a field of death,
A Hell of Fire, a strong man's agony. . .
         – ROLAND LEIGHTON, 'Ploegsteert'

    The twilight shades are falling
      Across a summer sea,
    And you have gone your way again
      Without a word to me.
       – VERA BRITTAIN, 'A Farewell'

    The sunshine on the long white road
    That ribboned down the hill,
    The velvet clematis that clung
    Around your window-sill
    Are waiting for you still.
          – ROLAND LEIGHTON,
            'Hédeauville'

Roland to Vera

France, 27 August 1915

I have just written to Edward. I don't quite know what to make of it, except that his C.O. probably dislikes him and has taken this opportunity of showing it. In the letter he wrote to me which arrived during my absence he says that the C.O. is a perfect beast and 'I know he loathes me and I loathe him'. I don't for a moment think that there is any question of Edward's not being a competent officer. But it seems to have been all so unexpected. And to be sent back to Lichfield instead of to France must have infuriated him to desperation. . . I am so very sorry about it. I do hope he will not get too depressed and disheartened.

I am still very much so myself, I am afraid, and much more than 'depressed because Vera has gone'. I cannot take an interest in anything out here for its own sake. There doesn't seem anything worth living for. It is hard that one should have to pay for everything in the way of pleasure: but perhaps the gods will count this as part-payment for Next Time. And yet was it not worth all the pain in the world, dearest?

I am very glad that neither you nor Mother were at Victoria to see me off. It was very sad. The men were boisterously cheerful in a manner that deceived no one; the officers walked up and down the platform or stood in little groups, all very quiet and self restrained. There were not very many women there, but there was a look in their eyes that made one turn one's face away in reverence. 'It would be so much better if they would not come,' I overheard one weather-beaten major saying. 'It only makes it harder.' They stood very still as the train moved out, each as unconscious of the rest as if she were in a separate world. Only one actually cried – a young girl of about twenty. I thought of you, and I turned my face away again. It hurt so.

———

Vera to Roland

Buxton, 27 August 1915

It seems to me that things are still more unfinished, still more 'left off in the middle' than they were before. The world, of course, won't think so – but *we* learnt in those few days that the farther you go, the farther you see there is to go. I thought when I saw you off in March that nothing in the world could make me feel more deeply than I did then. I was mistaken.

I thought then that if you had kissed me once and we had had even that much of fulfilment, I should be more resigned to whatever cruel thing fate had in store for me. There again I was wrong. Resignation is a thing of the devil; it can't come until one has abandoned the hope that hurts so. So now, because you have kissed me, instead of being resigned, I feel an insane impatience quite unlike anything I have known before 'to be able to hold you & kiss you again even for a moment.' So much so that last night, looking out at the dark earth lying silent beneath the midnight stars, I said in my mind 'Oh Roland! Why ever did you exist! And why do I exist! What have we poor mortals done that we should have to suffer so much pain.' . . .

My hospital work has lost the little glamour it ever had. I think that glamour didn't belong to the work at all, but arose from my suddenly getting the thought in between my prosaic duties 'Perhaps I shall hear to-day that he is coming back.' But now in the midst of those prosaic duties instead there comes the thought of you saying 'I don't *want* to go back to the Front' – and I wonder if you are finding it as dreary now as I am finding this. Or worse still, just when I have to do the dullest and most practical things, there comes the remembered sensation of the half-bitter, half-sweet thrill of your arm around me, and then I have to clench my hand very tight to keep down – not tears – but the fierce desire to throw everything violently about the room.

And yet all the time I have the feeling that I shall see you again very soon, much sooner than I think. Reason of course says no to this, but intuition keeps saying yes. But after all it may only be due to the thought that another 5 months without seeing you is so impossible.

Roland to Vera

Bois de Warnimont, France, 28 August 1915

I have brought the Company out woodcutting for the R.E. [Royal Engineers] this morning, and am writing this sitting on a tree trunk in a clearing. It is a glorious morning – very hot outside; but in this world of green and brown it is a sheer delight. The wood is about 3 miles long and covers two little hills and a valley between. Someone has just begun to whistle part of the Overture to 'William Tell', and it sounds so appropriate here among the aisles of trees with the ring of axes as a background. And this is war!

I ought not to be sitting down writing this now really. I am supposed to be walking round seeing that the men do their work properly. Before I began this I did a little wood chopping myself, just because I felt a childish desire to & greatly to the amusement of the men, I expect.

Vera to Roland

Buxton, 29 August 1915

No, somehow 'the memory and the pain and the insatiable longing for Something which one has loved' doesn't sound as if you were forgetting quite as soon as one might have supposed you would, even though 'each picture flies'.

For my part, I find you still elusive, still intangible, and truly in that way it seems to count for so little that you did come back at all. When I get your letters I feel as though I know and understand you much better than when I meet & see the actual you. You yourself always puzzle me. Reverence – reserve – indifference – in their actual manifestation they are so alike, and the more full of emotion you are, the more alike they become. If there weren't a few physical signs to help me, if the expression you resolutely drive away from your mouth didn't sometimes betray itself in your eyes, I should never know you at all. Sometimes I wonder why it is that two women, neither of them ordinary, should love you so. When you begin to try & find reasons for it, it all seems so illogical. And yet the Fact is now a part of my entire existence, and has long been inseparable from hers.

Vera to Roland

Buxton, 30 August 1915

Your little Villanelle is just perfect. I did not say much before, because, like you, I suffer from a reticence which only letters can break through . . . . . it is far & away better than the poem 'Into Battle' of poor Julian Grenfell's, which the 'Times' printed after he had died of wounds. . .

★ ★ ★ ★ ★

We don't know quite what to make of the Edward business. Apparently all the people he is left with have been in the battalion a shorter time than he or are in some way inferior (Thurlow is among them) and others have been taken out some of whom were his juniors both in age and time-seniority. Poor Mother is worrying herself that he may have done something disgraceful . . . of course everyone is liable to sudden temptations and those not always the least immaculate . . . Mother had a letter in which he said 'I don't think I shall soon get over being left behind. If only they had made up their minds about this officer business six weeks ago I could have been in the Artillery by now.' It was, as you doubtless know, his own Division which refused to let him go into the Artillery on the ground that they couldn't spare him at that stage. If he hasn't done anything wrong, I really think they have treated him rather badly . . . . . Edward told me his C.O. was not in the social sense of the word quite a gentleman, & it is quite possible that Edward may have been gently but firmly snobbish in a very aggravating sort of way. I have never seen him snobbish, but I can quite imagine he might be so to someone he disliked. . .

I wonder if I shall ever feel your arm round me again, and your queer bristly head against my shoulder. Even if there is a Heaven, those sort of things don't happen there, do they? And somehow a Heaven without those things would seem a very inadequate sort of place now. It was the sweetest hour of my life. And it belonged only to you,

> 'And no one else remembers
> Except the moon and I.'

Vera to Roland

Buxton, 31 August 1915

Mother says she doesn't know how two people dare to be engaged who have only been together for short times at long intervals. Six days is the longest I have ever been with you . . .

I keep trying in quiet moments to recall your face to my mind. I wonder why it is so difficult, my dear one, when I can remember ordinary & uninteresting people quite well . . .

When I do manage to revisualize you it is only in sudden flashes which are tantalising by their transitoriness. I don't know why, but I can remember you best of all as you were on that Sunday night when you came down looking so sleepy and dusted off Mrs Leighton & I to bed!

Edward to Roland

Martinique Barracks, Bordon, 1 September 1915

Dear Tonius,

Many thanks for your letter of condolence . . . It has been an understood thing for some months now in the Aldershot Centre at any rate that a battalion should take out 8 supernumerary subalterns and so the list of our officers going abroad (which of course included me) published on the Saturday I met you in town contained 38 officers. However on the following Monday a Divisional Order arrived to the effect that no more than 30 officers were to go. Now I am not not by any means among the 8 junior subalterns, nor am I – as far as I, most other officers, and the men who know me well can see – among the 8 most incompetent. However the Orderly Room Hymn of Hate has been swelling loudly against me for some time and I was left behind. . .

Incidentally all the officers and men were of the opinion that the C.O. has made an awful mess of the battalion. About six new officers arrived within the last fortnight 3 in the last three days; the consequence is that 2 Company Commanders, 3 Seconds in Command of Companies, and about 6 Platoon Commanders don't know their men in the very least. It is the officers who, though young, have been with the battalion longest and who know their men best, who have been left behind . . . he pays no regard to the well-known suggestion in infantry training . . . that it is essential for officers and N.C.O.s to have a thorough knowledge of their men before going on active service.

★ ★ ★ ★ ★

I took a pathetic farewell of my platoon on Liphook Station and I know they were genuinely sorry that I couldn't come with them . . . we haven't heard anything further of them yet. The unfortunate 8 with 60 crocks have been cleaning up barracks . . . I expect we shall go to Lichfield to-morrow. . . If things are not satisfactory I shall try for the Artillery again as probably being the quickest and most satisfactory way of getting out in the end. Don't you think so? After the treatment accorded to me by the 11th I have no very great wish even to join them again unless the C.O. gets killed in the meantime.

I suppose it is no good being depressed and I suppose the future will disclose something good in the end. As you say the difficulties the Triumvirate has had in trying to do that most ordinary thing which men call fighting for your country have been most gigantic – difficulties in getting a commission, delay caused by illness, and my insuperable difficulties in trying to get out.

Hoping to join you some day.

Ever yours

Edward

Roland to Vera

France, 1 September 1915

It is not good for autocratic persons always to get what they want from other people. I should of course love a letter each day: but only on condition that you really have time to write it. It hurt me to hear of your going to sleep with all your clothes on the other night out of sheer weariness. Please promise that you will never stop up late when you are tired just for the purpose of writing to spoiled and selfish autocrats. You know, dear, I would rather not get a letter for weeks than that you should not get enough sleep. I believe you work yourself too hard as it is at that wretched hospital. . .

I too will try to write to you every day if I can. If I can't you will know that I have been too busy, and forgive me.

This afternoon we are going to practise-attack – possibly but not at all probably in preparation for a real one. I am gradually getting back my old interest in what happens out here. I will not say 'Out of sight, out of mind'; though you may think so. But it is perhaps easier to forget out here – to forget not what one has known & has felt, but the pain that accompanies the memory. . .

Would you like to send me some papers again? – Punch or something more or less literary such as The Nation, Saturday Review or Spectator, or anything attractive you may come across yourself.

Vera to Roland

Buxton, 1 September 1915

When I think of Woman's position in general & my own in particular, everything seems intolerable. I have been impressed in this home of mine with the disadvantages of being born a woman until they have eaten like iron into my very soul – from the scorn that is showered on my determination to be independent to such remarks as Father's when he had taught Edward to drive his motor & I said I wanted to learn. 'You can go & smash up someone else's machine if you like, but you're not going to have mine.' I have just been reading Lyndall's oration to Waldo and it has not made me any less angry. Just not having you to talk to makes not having you all the harder. However bitter I was you would not be angry but you would understand in your quiet and trust-inspiring way, as you did the other day when I said things which I suppose this Early Victorianism of a world would be shocked to think I thought, let alone said to you.

I am afraid that if ever our separated paths do join together, you will find an amount of bitterness & cynicism to eliminate which even you don't suspect, before I shall ever begin to be a 'pleasant companion', as the world would say. But to me you, in this respect most of all, have been on oasis in the desert. A man who could see from a woman's point of view was something to me quite undreamed of. And you interested me first when I first realised you could, after you had talked to me in the wood about your Mother.

★ ★ ★ ★ ★

. . . This letter is angry & cold. Life now I have had & lost you again is so empty & dull & depressing; often in the last few days as I have finished my work at the Hospital I have said to myself in utter despondency 'How weary I am' – which I never dreamed of doing before.

Roland to Vera

France, 2–3 September 1915

I . . . didn't at all want to get up at 6.0 a.m. this morning to take the company out to dig trenches in the rain. I have just come back again, and am impatiently waiting for 3 o'clock, which brings the post and, so often that even the post office must know them by now, square letters with a certain pointed and rather masculine handwriting which Mother said was slightly cynical. I hope one does come today, if it is only an empty envelope with nothing inside. It makes such a difference, dear. I do wonder if I am like my letters in the same way in which you are like yours. We both seem less reserved in letters, more like our real selves. In fact you pretend to understand my letters better than myself, don't you? Am I such a fearsome person in real life after all?

It is nearly letter time now. Meanwhile I am munching bull's eyes with a delightfully infantile enjoyment.

Vera to Roland

Buxton, 3 September 1915

Our correspondence appears to be something like our conversation – I always do the most talking. I cannot tell why I do at all; I think it must be you that makes me talk, for in ordinary everyday life to ordinary everyday people I really do very little. Even your Mother, though I love her, complained, as I told you, that she got nothing out of me.

It is such autumn here to-day – very cold, with almost wintry gleams of sun. The summer seems to have come and gone without my having noticed it. It was the one time of the year when I used to take life quite lightly – and this year I have had to take it more seriously than I ever thought to take anything . . . Thoughts & feelings like those of the last year, & more particularly of the last few weeks, destroy the first phase of one's youth – its careless, happy freshness. The first thing I noticed about you the other day was that that had gone – if indeed you ever really had it. And I am afraid that all the compensation in the world will not bring it back to either of us ever . . .

★ ★ ★ ★ ★

It was such a surprise to me this morning to see in the 'Times' the death of a cousin of mine from wounds received in the Dardanelles. I didn't even know he was out. These casualties in Gallipoli are really terrible. So little seems to be accomplished for the loss of so much. At the present rate of advance – about ½ a mile in six months –, it will take 28 years to get through, by which time all the men of this generation & the next will have been annihilated. Shall *we* see 'the morning break'?

Roland to Vera

France, 4 September 1915

It is raining now, and I have just had to beat a hasty retreat from the orchard where I was in the course of having a bath – an unusual thing in England at 11.45 a.m., but I have to get one when I can out here. I usually amuse other people rather with my washings, which are unnecessarily prolonged and elaborate. As it was the rain caught me in the last stage when I was crouching in a wooden tub and receiving the somewhat icy contents of an inverted bucket in the small of the back.

We go into the trenches tomorrow, and holding the unenviable office of Mess President I shall have to be busy this afternoon making arrangements for the feeding of six somewhat particular officers during 12 days of isolation. I have discovered incidentally that I could make quite a good cook! You will have to give me lessons.

★ ★ ★ ★ ★

Your letter [of 1 September] has just arrived. How very icy and cynical it is! I wish you could have talked the letter to me instead of writing it. I should love you when you were really angry, I know. As it is I do sympathise very much, sweetest. Oh damn, I know it . . . . .

Vera to Roland

Buxton, 4 September 1915

It is a good thing the Front helps you to forget. Perhaps if I went away from here and did work a little different from what I was doing – before – I might forget a little too – forget at any rate the painful side of memory, as you can... But it will not be possible to forget you, Roland, ever, except perhaps in death. For then - about which we both admitted we could come to no conclusion – one may be obliged to forget, even against one's will. I never can understand the Nirvana ideal – which you sometimes rather rejoice in, don't you? I would rather suffer aeons of pain than be nothing...

★ ★ ★ ★ ★

Edward is here for the week-end. The camp or whatever it is at Lichfield seems to be a kind of depôt of officers – there are over 100 of them, all waiting to be sent out as drafts to wherever they are needed .....

You were a little annoyed, weren't you, because I called you autocratic. But, autocratic or not, you don't value yourself sufficiently in some ways.

Vera to Roland

Buxton, 5 September 1915

Is it really only a fortnight ago to-night since we walked home across the heath in the darkness?

> *'I shall remember miraculous things you said*
> *My whole life through.'*

But just as when, too deeply moved to look, I felt you near me in the train, in the garden, on the cliff beside the sea, & could not believe you have ever really been to the Front, so now, with miles and days and events between us, I find it hard to realise it was not in a dream you held my hand. Yet we did dream it true once. Shall we ever, I wonder, again? ...

My physical energy in my Hospital work is returning – perhaps due to the autumn exhilaration of the weather – but I cannot say that my interest is. . .

I wonder if you, wounded, would display that tragic patience which sears one's heart more than all the groans & complaints. But I must be practical, & therefore try, I suppose, to keep you out of my thoughts . . . . .

Roland to Vera

France, 6 September 1915

Please forgive my not writing yesterday, but it was our day of coming back into the trenches and I had no opportunity at all. Today even I am too busy to do more than scribble a few lines. It will certainly have to be you who do all the talking for the time being – which you declare is the case anyhow. Perhaps you are right. England & you seem very far away today. I suppose it is because I always live for the present, and my present consists now of walking along miles (or what seem miles) of trenches mostly very muddy and dilapidated and intermittently giving Sunday instructions to unshaven and mud-bespattered followers with a view to the aforesaid ditches becoming ultimately more inhabitable. I know of nothing more melancholy & depressing than an old trench, disused and overgrown with grass, with dug-outs fallen in or wrecked by shells, and here and there a forgotten grave and a rusty bayonet. Of such is the glorious panoply of war!

Excuse this melancholy tone. It is only temporary; and you yourself are as much given to moods as I. Please try not to be depressed, dearest, and bitter and as cynical as when you wrote of the 'kind condescension of a person with a Quiet Voice towards Someone he is supposed to love!'

Roland to Vera

France, 7 September 1915

I hope it is not a sign of too volatile a temperament to be much affected by one's immediate surroundings. I am very much so. The places I happen to be in, the clothes I am wearing, whether the day is wet or fine; these are the things that regulate my moods. There are some people who would say that, not being a woman, I have no business to have moods: but let that pass. This afternoon is glowing with the languorous warmth of the dying Summer; the sun is a shield of burnished gold in a sea of turquoise; the bees are in the clover that overhangs the trench – and my superficial, beauty-loving self is condescending to be very conscious of the joy of living. It is a pity to kill people on a day like this. In a way, I suppose, it is a pity to kill people on any kind of day, but opinions – even my own – differ on this subject. Like Waldo I love to sit in the sun, and like him I have no Lyndall to sit with. But it was the last verse of his poem: it is only the first of mine.

> *'For, hand in hand just as we used to do,*
> *We two shall live our passionate poem through*
> *On some serene tomorrow.'*

★ ★ ★ ★ ★

I wonder sometimes which I am born to be, a man of action with lapses into the artistic, or an artist with military sympathies. Mother has asked me once or twice lately whether I should like to go into the Regular Army as a profession. I say no because I foresee the atrophy of my artistic side. On the other hand a literary life would give no scope for the adventurous & administrative facet of my temperament. What am I to do? . . .

7.0 p.m.

I have missed today's post, sworn in most un-drawingroom fashion at one of my sergeants for leaving undone the things that he ought to have done, have had to give away some of my men to do unnecessary work for the Engineers, and assisted by the anticipation of having to wander round muddy trenches on a cold night for an indefinite period, am not in a fitting state of mind to write any more of a letter to you. I am apt to be cynical when annoyed and should afterwards repent having been bitter towards Someone who has enough cause for bitterness on Her own.

<hr />

Vera to Roland

Buxton, 7 September 1915

I remember well enough the letter you complain of as 'icy & cynical'. I was feeling very bitter that afternoon, but why you should get the benefit of it I don't know. I am sorry; I always feel very repentant after sending anything like that. You are right that in such a case conversation is better than correspondence. Some things can be said quite easily which are better not written. The written word never quite hits the mark; it always implies so much more or so much less than you really mean. And there is of course a certain amount of what I might almost call 'anachronism' in a close correspondence in which each letter takes 2 or 3 days to come. I may come across something in a letter you have written in a 'perverse' mood which rouses me into icy & cynical remarks, and you may happen (as in this case) to get this outburst of frigidity just after you have sent me the most delightful letter in the world. The only remedy, I suppose, would be to write nothing either cynical or perverse. But all the same, I don't know that unadulterated 'ran sucrée' would suit either you or me. We can't help being ourselves – at any rate in letters!

Do these letters really mean so much? . . . For me too it means so much to hear at least something every day – 'only an empty envelope with nothing inside' rather than nothing at all. . .

Yes, we are more like our real selves in letters. I at any rate am so foolishly reserved & 'difficile' when I meet you, that it is a physical, let alone mental, impossibility to say & do the things I want to say & do. And afterwards, when You have gone away, and I think to myself that I may never get the chance to say & do those things again, I feel so angry with myself, and so impatient . . . . .

Mother says our entire intimacy is one of correspondence. I don't quite think that; there must have been *something* to start the correspondence and to inspire the keeping of it! But whenever we do meet it is never long enough to give us time to get used to each other properly . . . it is all so tantalising.

***

Roland to Vera

France, 10 September 1915

Yesterday I was so tired that I fell asleep and did not wake up again till after tea time. Hence you did not get even an empty envelope with nothing inside! I am so very sorry; and felt wretched when your letter came last night, out of the darkness as it always comes, and I read 'for there is always something to look forward to, and I know that . . . there will be a few minutes which will make the whole day worth while'. And those few minutes did not come.

I have been holding this pen in my hand and thinking, instead of writing, for several minutes. It is a habit that I must get out of, since there is no sign on the paper that I have been indulging in it and cogitative intermezzi of this kind are apt to lead to a some-what truncated and irrelevant epistle. I don't seem to be able to help myself, though. I wonder what I should say to you if you came along the trench now and in at the open doorway – I can imagine very well how you would step from the bright sun into the twilight, though I cannot see your face. I don't think I should say anything. I should probably feel rather like a very shy child at his first party; and just look at you; and you would look at me and through me with your 'wet' eyes (I do like that adjective of Clare's); and there would be a hopeless inadequacy about it all. I'm sure we should both forget that we had ever been so intimate in our letters. It does seem silly, though, doesn't it? When I have actually seen you intermittently for as long as 17 days, too!

***

Vera to Roland

Buxton, 8 September 1915

The Matron told me this morning that the Matron of 1 London General applied for my reference last night, so I suppose things may begin to move a little soon . . . I shall be sorry for many things to leave my present Hospital; I have liked the work as much as I ever could like that kind of work, and all the nurses seem fond of me & are in consequence ever so nice.

Vera to Roland

Buxton, 10 September 1915

What do you think of this for an 'agony' in the 'Times'? 'Lady, fiancé killed, will gladly marry officer totally blinded or otherwise incapacitated by the War.'

At first sight it is a little startling. Afterwards the tragedy of it dawns on you. The lady (probably more than a girl or she would have called herself 'young lady'; they always do) doubtless has no particular gift or qualification, and does not want to face the dreariness of an unoccupied & unattached old maidenhood. But the only person she loved is dead; all men are alike to her & it is a matter of indifference whom she marries, so she thinks she may as well marry someone who really needs her. The man, she thinks, being blind or maimed for life will not have much opportunity of falling in love with anyone & even if he does will not be able to say so. But he will need a perpetual nurse, & she if married to him can do more for him than an ordinary nurse & will perhaps find some relief for her sorrow in devoting her life to him. . . It is purely a business arrangement, with an element of self-sacrifice which redeems it from utter sordidness. Quite an idea, isn't it!

Roland to Vera

France, 11 September 1915

I have been rushing around since 4 a.m. this morning superintending the building of dug-outs, drawing up plans for the draining of
trenches, doing a little digging myself as a relaxation, and accidentally
coming upon dead Germans while looting timber from what was
once a German fire trench. This latter was captured by the French
not so long ago and is pitted with shell holes each big enough to
bury a horse or two in. The dug-outs have been nearly all blown in,
the wire entanglements are a wreck, and in among this chaos of
twisted iron and splintered timber and shapeless earth are the flesh-
less, blackened bones of simple men who poured out their red,
sweet wine of youth unknowing, for nothing more tangible than
Honour or their Country's Glory or another's Lust [for] Power. Let
him who thinks that War is a glorious thing, who loves to roll forth
stirring words of exhortation, invoking Honour and Praise and
Valour and Love of Country with as thoughtless and fervid a faith as
inspired the priests of Baal to call on their own slumbering deity, let
him but look at a little pile of sodden grey rags that cover half a skull
and a shin bone and what might have been Its ribs, or at this skele-
ton lying on its side, resting half crouching as it fell, supported by
one arm, perfect but that it is headless and with the tattered clothing still draped round it; and let him realise how grand & glorious a
thing it is to have distilled all Youth and Joy and Life into a foetid
heap of hideous putrescence. Who is there who has known & seen
who can say that Victory is worth the death of even one of these?

Excuse this morbid letter, but it is my mood of the present.

And now I really must go to sleep – even although it is four in
the afternoon!

———

Vera to Roland

Buxton, 11–12 September 1915

You aren't seriously thinking that the Army is to be your permanent career, are you? I am sure I need not ask that, for I know that

seriously you would never consider it. Why, the first part of that very same letter proves that you never could. A true soldier has no business to be affected by beauty or weather or sun or rain. Do you suppose a Napoleon or – Lord Kitchener would care whether the countries he ravaged were beautiful, or what sort of day he ravaged them on? You say that the choice is between the atrophy of your artistic side or the confinement of the adventurous & practical. I don't believe the alternative is as clearly defined as that, but suppose it is, do you really think there is any comparison between the man of thought & the man of action? The one is the pioneer & the other merely the imitator. The average person, the 'man in the street', is the man of action. The men of thought are few & far between but without them the men of action might as well not exist. You are one of the world's exceptions, & what is more you delight in that – in being different from other people. I can't really think you can deliberately contemplate sacrificing what makes you an exception for the sake of what would make you merely ordinary . . .

Of course, much as I always detested the Army before the War, I would rather have you as a soldier than not at all. At least, I think so . . . My own ideals are so entirely one with Unity, Non-Militarism, Internationalism that I should hate to think of someone I loved – perhaps too much, ranged on the opposite side to these. Although actually engaged in War you are not opposing but rather upholding them now, for as someone said 'This is a War against War.' . . .

Don't let the fact that you are successful as a soldier delude you. It is *because* you are an artist that you are successful thus . . . it would be just the same if you tried something else. The artist can do anything well. So, dearest artist, please be true to yourself & don't dream any more of slighting what most of all makes your existence worth while. . .

★ ★ ★ ★ ★

You know in one way I do sympathise extremely with your desire for military glory. For I do feel very much that I should love to be a successful nurse, & win the Military Cross (which is the only thing a nurse can get in the way of military decorations) myself, not so much for the honour's own sake as simply because it is *not* my own vocation, & makes a sort of Something Extra to what I know

I already possess. For the same reason your success as a soldier would delight me, just because it is something incongruous with your most real nature – something extra to what you already possess.

Sunday evening.

I have just reread your letter dated 10th, which I found when I came in a few hours ago. Dearest, because I am selfish enough to like getting a letter always, you mustn't get to look upon it as an additional duty added to your already heavy ones, or feel wretched just because I happened to mention how much it meant to me to get letters from you frequently. I don't even want you to write to me except when you really enjoy doing it.

Yes, what if I could suddenly appear in the trench & stand in the open door! I can just imagine how you would be rather pale, & tired, & would stand looking down at me with your sad eyes, & say nothing. 'Like a shy child' . . . . . Are you really shy of me? It is very strange too that I am so dreadfully shy of you! We neither of us seem to unbend, until perhaps it gets dark & we can't see one another properly, & seem to become more intangible. Yes, it is absurd that we should be so intimate in letters, & then when we are together that you should touch my hand almost as if you weren't doing right, & I even hesitate to meet your eyes with mine.

Roland to Vera

In the Trenches, France, 13 September 1915

I thought that after all an empty envelope *was* better than nothing.

Terribly busy at present and a letter is impossible yet.

This letter cannot reach you till after Wednesday 15th, when it will possibly be a case of Hinc illae lacrimae (let him that readeth understand). Expected but cannot tell for certain.

I will write & reassure you as soon as I can.

Meanwhile, all the love in the world.

Vera to Roland

Buxton, 14 September 1915

I could have wept this morning to think of you, my poor darling, in that charnel house of a trench . . . 'Of such is the glorious panoply of War.' And this is what you propose to make your trade? Never. It seems to me now that this War is scarcely for victory at all, for even if victory comes it will be at the cost of so much else, so many greater things, that it will be scarcely worth having. No, this War will only justify itself if it puts an end to all the horror & barbarism & retrogression of War for ever.

It has always been to me a thing to shudder at that the human body when it is done with is so difficult to get rid of – even by fire, which I suppose is the best way – in [an] unrepulsive fashion. It is not death itself which is the cause of dread; it is dissolution. I felt like that very much when I was nursing the man at the Hospital who died. His actual departing did not afflict me very much, but what did was the sight of his failing body before it happened. . . Sometimes in nightmare dreams I imagine what might happen to the physical being of someone I know & love – think perhaps of Edward's attractive face & tall form & dear long hands, & how they might lie unhonoured & untended in some No Man's Land in the Dardanelles – at the mercy of sun & rain & flies & birds of prey. I don't think you can really mean it when you say that your opinions differ as to whether it is really a pity to kill men on any sort of day. Were men brought into the world with toil & pain just for this?

Vera to Roland

Buxton, 17 September 1915

Yes, she read it this morning, & understood. I will try to wait & hope, which is the only thing left. There are some anxieties which even work cannot assuage. But thank you for not saying 'She must be shielded as long as she can.' I would rather know, & share your suspense, & if the dread is mine without the excitement, well, c'est la guerre, & this is Woman's part. Remember, she knows not the word 'forget'. Even Death cannot conquer some things, & over them 'War knows no power.'

I suppose by the time this gets to France I shall know – for better or for worse. Meanwhile, my whole thoughts are, as always, with what is so greatly, so terribly, dear.

> *'Till life & all take flight'* – & after –
> *'Never goodbye.'*

[Au Revoir, my dearest.]

Roland to Vera

In Billets, France, 18 September 1915

Everything exciting that was expected failed to come off after all. We expected an attack on the day I mentioned; they issued minute orders as to what was to be done when it came; parties went out to reconnoitre the Germans at night; we all slept not only in our clothing as always but hung round with revolvers, haversacks, etc. & ready for an alarm; but it never came. Only away on our left in the French area we could hear what is even at a distance the most terrifying thing on earth – the pounding of heavy guns, now fainter, now louder, but coalescing always into one dull, thundering roar. It lasted for three days and nights on end, lapsed for a little, and then went on again intermittently, growing fainter and fainter. At night the sky was lit with the flashes and flickered strangely with a yellow, restless, glow. As one of my men remarked, 'Someone's getting 'ell over there, sir!'

They say that we may be in for a little more excitement in a day or two's time, but personally I rather doubt it. In any case, if you do not hear from me even for a week or more, do not think that anything has happened. Whenever there are wars and rumours of wars of any kind, however innocent, it always means my being kept much too busy to write letters.

Meanwhile I am very glad to have a rest again. One of our officers is away and I have been doing his work as well as my own, and even without any rumours of attacks 12 days on end in trenches is rather trying to the nerves.

Roland to Vera

In Billets, France, 19 September 1915

Have just had a very delightful evening. We have got the Transport Officer of another battalion messing with us at present. He is a very charming man and rather a friend of mine, but his greatest asset is that he possesses a very good gramophone. This I insisted he should produce tonight. It did me a lot of good as mental refreshment. Among other records he had two that Edward used to play, Raff's Cavatina and Saint-Saens' Le Cygne. What a number of things have happened since the days when he used to condescend to fiddle at my Saturday afternoon Entertainments in the Schoolroom at Uppingham!

We are billeted in a different village this time, a little nearer the trenches and much more comfortable. These are to be our winter quarters when out of the trenches. That is, if we are still out here through the winter. The idea seems to be that the war will finish in a great smash up of some kind before the end of October. Personally I know nothing about it and don't much care. . .

There is certainly an appearance about things as of something being about to happen soon.

★ ★ ★ ★ ★

Monday morning.

Am writing in a wood – the same wood that I mentioned before – while the men are having their interval for dinner. I am feeling rather annoyed at being here at all really, as I very much wanted to go out riding with Adam. But it is my turn today. Yesterday morning, or rather from 9.30 a.m. till 5.0 p.m., we spent riding round the country reconnoitring roads and defences and villages in case we had to occupy them in event of an attack. It was

a glorious day and I have a special weakness for long white hedge-
less roads with Noah's Ark trees planted on each side.

You have written to me so many times, more than I have written to you lately that I will not try to answer any particular
letters... I am feeling at present excessively, dishearteningly commonplace. I must read your essay of a few days ago on Men of
Thought and Men of Action over again, to try to improve matters.
Attempted a poem this morning beginning 'Broken I came from
out the Ditch of Death', and produced some of the most appalling
rot.

Roland to Vera

France, 23 September 1915

I know nothing definite yet; but they say that all posts will be
stopped very soon.

Hinc illae lacrimae.

['Till life & all ...']

Vera to Roland

Buxton, 26 September 1915

I am sending this in case it should have a chance of reaching you
as a last word before all communication between us is cut off.

And if this word should be a 'Te moriturum saluto', perhaps it
will brighten the dark moments a little to think how you have
meant to Someone more than anything ever has or ever will.
That which you have done & been will not be wasted; what you
have striven for will not end in nothing, for as long as I live it will
be a part of me & I shall remember, always.

Yes, 'till life & all ...'

[Au Revoir.]

Roland to Vera

France, 28 September 1915

It is rather cruel to disturb people with false alarms. This last one has, it would seem, been as false as the former one of a few days back. There is still time for it to materialise; but that is improbable. Three is a lucky number, and the next may be a real one. I hope so. It depends always on what the other parts of the line – British & French – are doing. One can only wait.

We go into the trenches tomorrow.

Vera to Roland

Buxton, 1 October 1915

Oh Roland!

At the present moment that exclamation comprises every comment I have to make on the situation. 'Continuation of Allied Offensive' – I keep on reading, so I suppose you *are* in it now. But I felt so sure you were in all that awful weekend fighting . . .

When you are out there and know what is going on, it must be quite impossible to put yourself in the place of people here, who don't know & can't get news. You have no idea what it is like – or what these last few days have been to Mrs Leighton & me. Perhaps one day you will see the letters we have exchanged on the subject! For my part I have done nothing since Monday – when we first got the news of the great offensive & the victory – but watch the gate, or follow every telegraph boy that went in the direction of our house. We dared not think what the price of victory might be for us. From the accounts in the papers, one would think that every regiment out there had been in it. I suppose as a matter of fact the ones that were were in the minority. . .

Don't say you hope the next alarm will be real. I think the lives of some of those men who were in it will be spoilt for always by the memory of it, and many are deaf for life with the noise. Your short letter is very guarded. Let me know, as soon as you can get it past the Censor, all about it. Two men who used to be with

Edward at his preparatory school have been killed; one was a very great friend of his.

I am expecting to be called to London any day now. The wounded are beginning to come into England already & there will be a great rush soon.

Vera to Roland

Buxton, 2 October 1915

I have just found – & don't mean to part from – Edward's photograph of the last O.T.C. camp, taken just before War broke out. I love it – it is so very characteristic of the 'Three Musketeers'. There is Edward – absolutely immaculate & contentedly cheerful without being complacent, & Victor looking solemnly out upon the world from his meditative & rather spectatorish point of view. And there is you in the middle, looking somewhat unshaven & extremely untidy – hair brushed wildly back, shirt open at the neck, lips very firmly closed, eyes of such intentness & so very sad – for all the world like a desperate but undaunted poet! Not nearly as 'pretty' as Edward or Victor, but much more impressive. And as I was looking at it, it struck me that just so you might look, dear, when about to lead your men into action against overwhelming odds. And just because the idea occurred to me, I fell in love with this portrait of the dishevelled but picturesque person that was you, & mean to keep it by me.

Roland to Vera

In the Trenches, France, 7 October 1915

Dear Child,

I have waited to write to you for so long and have not been able to – ever since you sent me that sweetest of letters which was not after all a Te Moriturum Saluto. Although I have not answered them your letters of the last few days have meant perhaps more than usual. Everything is so very unsettled. We may be in the middle of an attack quite suddenly, with only a few hours' notice. My company has already been under orders to take a certain position at a certain time and then had the orders cancelled again a few hours later...

As to the present fighting you know more about it than I do: for you have newspapers & time to read them. We get only a few bare facts in telegrams ...

★ ★ ★ ★ ★

Good-night. I am just going to fire a few rifle grenades at the Boche. I'll let him have an extra one – from you.

Vera to Roland

Buxton, 7 October 1915

I could often have wept at the casualty lists that have kept coming in this week – so many officers and most of them so young too. Rudyard Kipling's son is among the 'Missing believed killed'. I always feel sorrier when they are the sons of intellectual & brilliant people. I don't why I should be, but somehow I always feel that they must mean even more to their parents than those of the more ordinary ones do to theirs...

Edward has been in London all week on a long leave – doing I don't quite know what, but among other things he wanted to see some lawyer about getting into the Artillery ... He is coming back here for the week-end & is bringing Thurlow with him... I have heard so much about him that I am very anxious to see what he is like. Probably too shy to address a word to me ...

Vera to Roland

Buxton, 9 October 1915

I believe Edward is really going...

Of course now the likelihood of his speedy departure has again turned up, pandemonium reigns in this harmonious household. Mother has a faculty I have often noticed in women who worry over trifles of being quite calm when things really matter, but Father is raging about, saying he will give up the business, the motor, the house, & do something which varies from having nothing more to do with any of us to shooting himself! ... I really cannot think why he should want to vent on us all the perturbation – for one can scarcely call such a selfish emotion grief – that Edward's departure causes him ... after all Mother is the one who has done everything for Edward & had all the troubles of his often troublesome existence; Father has only provided a little money which never meant depriving himself of anything ... Of course he can't waste his thoughts so much as to extend them often on someone who in comparison with Edward is so valueless and unimportant as I . . . . . since I am a woman and therefore a creature of an inferior grade to himself, my griefs & anxieties don't count in the same way, and if I were to have any great cause for sorrow, I think he would regard me with much the same sort of detachment & disinterested pity as I should look upon a devoted dog that had lost its master. I'm afraid that often even the dog gets more reverence than the poor 'play thing of man', in spite of all her higher education.

Vera to Roland

Buxton, 10 October 1915

It seems to be all true as far as anyone knows & Edward's departure some time next week is probable . . . . . I hate the idea of drafts. They never seem to have a proper chance to get initiated into the ways of the Front. Nearly all the casualties I have heard much about lately seem to have been among people who joined their regiment when it had already been out some time. The more I think of this War, the more terribly incongruous seems to me the contrast between the immense misfortune of the individual, & the calm ruthlessness with which hundreds of individuals are mown down at once by an impersonal gun. Postal Service,

A.S.C., R.A.M.C., Taxes, Hospitals etc – all perfectly organised simply to afford the greatest facility to the Science of Death – in its noble work of interrupting & nullifying all the other Sciences that make for life.

Thurlow is coming here to-night. He is twelfth on the list, and as two of the first ten may drop out, Edward thinks he has quite a respectable chance of going with him. Public opinion has made it a high & lofty virtue for us women to countenance the departure of such as these & you to regions where they will probably be slaughtered in a brutally degrading fashion in which we would never allow animals to be slaughtered. This, I suppose is 'the something elemental, something beautiful' that you find in War! To the saner mind it seems more like a reason for shutting up half the nation in a criminal lunatic asylum.

―――――――

Vera to Roland

Buxton, 11 October 1915

I really feel that the departure of Edward a few minutes ago is 'Farewell, a long farewell' this time . . . . .

★ ★ ★ ★ ★

I liked Thurlow so much. Whatever Edward's failings, I must say he has an admirable faculty for choosing his friends well. Mr Puckle remarked that to Father in the ages before the War. And *I* have good reason to realise & be glad of it, haven't I! . . .

But seeing Thurlow for a short time made me feel rather sad, for the nicer such people as he are, the more they serve to emphasize in some indirect way, the fact of your immense superiority over the very best of them! . . .

I read in some Women's Parish Magazine the other day 'Above all, let us never say anything to the dear men at the Front about our own affairs that would be likely to make them feel sad or trouble them in mind.' What do you think of that! Personally I think it is rather like treating 'the dear men at the Front' as children, which they certainly are not, I know that whatever I was & whatever I was doing, I should wish the people who wrote to me to treat me just as they did when talking to me & to keep the same attitude to me as when I was with them . . . . . But I do admit that I make you the victim of a temporary black mood rather too often.

More & more long casualty lists! And such a pathetic number of only sons, or cases where two brothers have been killed at the same time. I thought of them all this morning, & when I stood watching Edward, looking so charming & almost handsome, wave to me as the motor disappeared. But I didn't want a recurrence of yesterday's dismal thoughts. Instead I have been saying to myself ever since a verse out of Lawrence Binyon's dirge for the Fallen.

'They shall not grow old as we that are left grow old . . .'

Vera to Roland

Buxton, 16 October 1915

Just got my orders to go to 1st London General on Monday . . . I hear London is simply crowded out with wounded & all nurses are worked to the utmost.

The Zep. raid was pretty bad. One of them went right over my grandmother's house at Purley, and a lot of East Croydon was demolished . . .

Roland to Vera

In Billets, France, 18 October 1915

It is very much autumn this morning – frost and grey mist and dead leaves. I have just been inspecting trenches and gun emplacements, newly dug in the middle of an apple orchard. The trenches were floored with fallen apples that crunch as you walk along. I like Autumn. Un peu triste, perhaps: but so is everything that one really likes, n'est-ce pas?

You must be wondering what has become of me by now. Such a very long time without a murmur of any kind. I have been thinking how cruel it is of me to have left you letterless for so long.

A few words in the letter that has just come from your Mother, with the socks, hurt me. 'Sunday was a joyous day for Vera, your letter arrived, as, although you tell here there must be intervals in between, she worries.' And I do not realise this perhaps, and in the middle of my own work here I wake up suddenly and wonder what You are thinking. I am getting very absorbed in my little world here. It is the only way to stifle boredom and regrets. The war seems doomed to be everlasting and one might as well become interested in one's part if one is doomed to play it for so long. . .

. . . . . I have got to rush off now and teach people how to throw bombs. We go back to the trenches tomorrow.

Very much love, sweetest. Do you believe in telepathic letters?

Vera to Roland

St Gabriel's Hostel, Champion Hill,
London, 18 October 1915

Dearest –

I have just arrived here & done my unpacking. . . . .

We have to be at the Hospital at 7.0 for breakfast & as this place is at least a mile away from there & the only means of transport is a very intermittent bus, we shall have to get up at 5.45 every morning. . .

I hope you are all right. Nothing else matters if you are only that.

Au Revoir, my very dear. I will try & write to-morrow. And best of love – London – darkest London – sends you its love too & wishes – oh! so very much! – that it may soon see you again.

Vera to Roland

1st London General Hospital, 19 October 1915

I suppose I am really what the Sister would describe as 'getting into it quite nicely'. But of course I hate it. There is something so starved & dry about hospital nurses – as if they had had to force all the warmth out of themselves before they could be fit to be really good nurses. But personally I would rather suffer ever so much in my work than become indifferent to pain. . .

There are some pretty ghastly things in my ward. But I don't mind 'sights' one quarter as much as the general atmosphere of inhumanness (though this seems an incongruous word to use in connection with a hospital) that pervades everything. But of course I shall get used to it in time, although it seems as if I am going to get scarcely more time than you have for the things & people that really interest me. There is no provision made in these hospitals for any interests besides one's supposed interest in one's work.

_____

Vera to Roland

1st London General Hospital, 20 October 1915

To-day I have had a decidedly pleasant change into quite a different ward – where I believe it was originally intended I should be. The four Sisters – especially two of them – are delightful, and there is no other V.A.D. so I have heaps to do, which is the very best thing to prevent me from getting depressed. There are 60 beds in my ward, not all full yet as this part was only opened a fortnight ago. All are surgical cases – mostly very bad. Oh! I don't want you to get wounded now. I couldn't bear to think of you with one of these ghastly injuries such as I have to see more or less all the time.

_____

Vera to Roland

1st London General Hospital, 21 October 1915

The men being quite well apart from their wounds really makes it all the worse because they are so very conscious of the agony of having the wound dressed. I don't mind the general butcher's shop appearance, or holes in various parts of people that you could put your fist into, half so much as having to hold a head or a leg for the sister to dress it while the man moans & tries to squirm about. The orderlies won't do one or two of the dressings I have to help with – or rather, the Sisters won't have them, because they seem to be made sick so easily, & one of them who was holding a basin the other night fainted right on top of the patient.

Vera to Roland

1st London General Hospital, 22 October 1915

Don't get *too* absorbed in your little world over there – even if it makes things easier. It is my great object not to be absorbed in mine. There is so little time to be anything else that it will probably be hard – but nevertheless possible. After all the War *cannot* last for ever, and when it is over we shall be glad to be what we were born again – if we can only live till then – Life – oh! life! Isn't it strange how much we used to demand of the Universe, & now we ask only for what we took as a matter of course before – just to be allowed to live, to go on being.

Edward to Vera

Lichfield, 26 October 1915

We seem to be still no nearer getting out; 12 people from the *bottom* of the list went to the Dardanelles and another 3 to France last week. Being at the top of the list seems to mean nothing; it is all quite beyond my comprehension. I think the War Office must be mad. I went home last week end where the fast fading remnants of my cold caused Father the utmost disturbance; I really think he is too ridiculous for words . . . They are leaving the house about December 12th and going to the Grand, Brighton over Christmas and then going into rooms somewhere in that awful place, I suppose. We are moving from here the beginning of next week and going into huts at Penkridge near Stafford; it will be very boring but probably better than this place. . .

P.S. I attended a Court Martial for instructional purposes to-day. We all said 'swelp me Gawd' in great style.

Vera to Roland

1st London General Hospital, 30 October 1915

I went into Westminster Abbey for a few minutes. The evening service (which is now held in the afternoon because of Zeppelins) was going on. The music seemed to swell & thrill & lose itself in the great arches of the roof, and everything beneath the window was shadow, dimly lit by dusky gleams of sun. I thought of the last time I was in London – when you were here, & to my great astonishment found tears in my eyes when the dream faded. After all, it must be a great inspiration to be you – and such as you. I felt this afternoon that I would gladly work & fight & die, if I could only do one little bit towards saving this beauty from destruction. And that is what You are doing – & have been doing for seven long & weary months. If only you could have been there to-day – if anything could, it might have made you feel strong to face the dreary, dreary winter that has already begun.

Vera to Roland

1st London General Hospital, 31 October 1915

I seem to mind nothing now in the way of work. This morning, as I was sweeping our immense ward (one has to do a good deal of housemaid's work in the early morning before the actual nursing begins because of the usual incompetence of orderlies) I wondered to myself if I should ever be – what I have never yet been – really happy. But I wondered it more from force of habit than anything else. It certainly was not an expression of discontent, any more than it was the result of pleasure in my work. It is always so strange that when you are working you never think of all the inspiring thoughts that made you take up the work in the first instance. Before I was in hospital at all I thought that because I suffered myself I should feel it a grand thing to relieve the sufferings of other people. But now, when I am actually doing something which I know relieves someone's pain it is nothing but a matter of business. I may think lofty thoughts about the whole thing before or after but never at the time. At least, almost never. Sometimes some quite little thing makes me stop short all of a sudden and I feel a fierce desire to cry in the middle of whatever it is I am doing. I felt like it when a man asked me to wash him to-night & then told me I reminded him so much of a sister of his, only she was fair. It is always some absurd little thing like that. And those lines of Rupert Brooke's are always coming into my head as I look at the rows of poor permanently shattered people on either side of the long ward –

> 'These cast the world away, poured out the red
> Sweet wine of youth, gave up the years to be
> Of work and joy.'

Roland to Vera

France, 3 November 1915

'Occasionally I wonder if the person I am writing to is really there –'

He has certainly not shown himself very much lately, has he? It seems so long since I wrote to you last – I have never yet addressed a letter to Camberwell in fact. I can scarcely realise that you are there, there in a world of long wards and silent footed nurses and bitter, clean smells and an appalling whiteness in everything. I wonder if your metamorphosis has been as complete as my own. I feel a barbarian, a wild man of the woods, stiff, narrowed, practical, an incipient martinet perhaps – not at all the kind of person who would be associated with prizes on Speech Day, or poetry, or dilettante classicism. I wonder what the Dons of Merton would say to me now, or if I could ever waste my time on Demosthenes again. One should go to Oxford first and see the world afterwards: when one has looked from the mountain top it is hard to stay contentedly in the valley.

Have been very busy lately as Adjutant, during the absence of the latter. It is a job I like very much; but it doesn't give you much time for anything else. Hence in part my extreme busy-ness. I haven't had time to write to anyone for ages, and have in fact left Mother letterless for a whole month, and other people more so. It is late & I am very sleepy. We go back into the trenches tomorrow.

Edward to Vera

Penkridge Bank Camp, Stafford, 7 November 1915

We arrived here – the biggest camp I 'nave ever seen, about 4 miles W of Rugely on the top of hills about 700 ft – yesterday. We are much better off than in camp at Lichfield – 4 officers in a little wooden hut with a stove in it. Nobody has the least idea about the future.

Vera to Roland

1st London General Hospital, 7 November 1915

Of course you don't really deserve a letter. Sometimes, when after a particularly grey and monotonous day, I wish for a letter from you to cheer me up, and don't get it, I feel almost angry – though more with life in general than with you. With you I never can be *quite* angry. For the more chill and depressed I feel myself in these dreary November days, the more sorry I feel for you beginning to face the acute misery of the winter after the already long strain of these many months. When at 6.0 in the morning the rain is beating pitilessly against the windows and I have to go out into it to begin a day which promises nothing pleasant, I feel that after all I should not mind very much if only the thought of you right in it out there didn't haunt me all day. Rain always depresses me; still more rain where there are dead. And I am always thinking of Lyndall's words 'How terrible it must be when the rain falls down on you.' . . .

I have only one wish in life now and that is for the ending of the War. I wonder how much really all you have seen and done has changed you. Personally, after seeing some of the dreadful things I have to see here, I feel I shall never be the same person again, and wonder if, when the War does end, I shall have forgotten how to laugh. The other day I did involuntarily laugh at something & it felt quite strange. Some of the things in our ward are so horrible that it seems as if no merciful dispensation of the Universe could allow them and one's consciousness to exist at the same time. One day last week I came away from a really terrible amputation dressing I had been assisting at − it was the first after the operation − with my hands covered with blood and my mind full of a passionate fury at the wickedness of war, and I wished I had never been born. . .

I am just going back to duty. To-day is visiting day, and the parents of a boy of 20 who looks and behaves like 16 are coming all the way from South Wales to see him. He has lost one eye, had his head trepanned and has fourteen other wounds, and they haven't seen him since he went to the front. He is the most battered little object you ever saw. I dread watching them see him for the first time.

Roland to Vera

In the Trenches, France, 8 November 1915

It is getting more wintry over here now. At least the trenches are colder and wetter, which is much the same thing. I have an incipient cold myself and so perhaps notice it. But I am getting various winter garments sent out and shall be all right.

On Wednesday I am going off to the 1st Somerset Light Infantry, to be attached to them for a short time. . . I don't know yet how long I shall be there, probably about 10 days. I expect that a Regular Battalion will be rather a change.

I have to go and mess about with bombs now.

———————

Vera to Roland
                    1st London General Hospital, 8 November 1915

Most estimable, practical, unexceptional Adjutant,

I suppose I ought to congratulate you on the attainment of the position, even temporally. But I don't know that I do. I suppose also I ought to thank you for your letter, since apparently one has to be grateful now-a-days for being allowed to know you are alive. But all the same, my first impulse was to tear that letter into small shreds, since it appeared to me very much like an epistolary expression of the Quiet Voice, only with indications of an ever greater sense of personal infallibility than the Quiet Voice used to contain. My second impulse was to write an answer with a sting in it which would have touched even Roland Leighton (modern style). But I can't do that. One cannot be angry with people at the Front – a fact which I sometimes think they take advantage of – and so when I read 'We go back into the trenches to-morrow,' I literally dare not write you the kind of letter you perhaps deserve, for thinking that the world might end for you on that discordant note. . .

But I won't write more on this subject. In any case it is no use, and I shall probably cry if I do, which must never be done, for there is so much both personal & impersonal to cry for here that one might weep for ever and yet not shed enough tears to wash away the pitiableness of it all.

★ ★ ★ ★ ★

Yes, it must be queer for someone who knows me as I really am to imagine me being very serious and official in a hospital. Especially as the traditional imagination of a hospital, which you seem to share, is really hardly correct at all. Certainly my ward is so long and narrow that the vista of beds seen from one door to the other makes one quite dizzy. But in a surgical ward the nurses hardly occupy the silent-footed, gliding rôle which they always do in story-books & on the stage. For one thing there is too much work to be done in a great hurry. For another, the mixture of gramophones and people shouting or groaning after an operation relieves you of the necessity of being quiet as to your footsteps, for it drowns everything else. One does not often have to play the bedside Angel of Mercy of sentimental story illustrations. I certainly once spent some time beside a rather attractive young man when he was coming round after an operation, and while he was in great agony held his hand for twenty minutes, but it has only happened once. I agree with you in disliking an unusual whiteness; it is too acute a reminder of Death. But ours is rather mitigated by scarlet blankets, which are folded and hung over the foot of each bed...

I suppose there is no chance of your getting leave again soon? Everyone in your regiment seems to be getting it, & you to be doing their work. But perhaps you are not keen to leave even for a few days a sensible business-like life where one doesn't have to bother about little things like Poetry or Art or dilletante classicism?

Vera to Roland

Lowestoft, 14 November 1915

You will be surprised to see that I am here. I am a little surprised myself, as circumstances sent me here very speedily. On Friday evening for some unknown reason I suddenly felt very faint while on duty – an absurd thing I have never done in my life before – & was walked off in a semi-collapsed state & fussed over by Sisters. I said I was alright & implored them to let me go back on duty; however they wouldn't let me do that or even return to the hostel in the wind & rain but sent me to bed at the hospital, where I was kept till 11.30 yesterday morning to see the doctor. They supposed there might be something wrong with my heart but he tested it and said it was alright only I must have a rest at once, so I was told to go off for a long week end, & to go somewhere, it didn't matter where, that afternoon. Earlier in the week I had written to Mrs

Leighton & mentioned that I got occasional one-day-and-night leaves, and when I got down yesterday I found a very opportune letter from her asking me to come to Lowestoft if I got a leave some time soon. . .

Mrs Leighton met me at the station with a rather evident pleasure . . . She & Clare seemed quite interested in my uniform and examined it & made me talk about the Hospital for ages. They seemed rather surprised to hear about the nature of wounds & that such a thing as a clean or even moderately painless wound does not exist.

After the others had gone to bed Mrs Leighton & I sat up till 2.0, discussing you. I think you would have been mystified & a little astonished at some of the conclusions we came to. . .

The family asks me to inform you that they are contemplating leaving this house next Friday, probably for two months or more, and going somewhere near London. They are letting it to two officers who want it for something to do with defence purposes.

Roland to Vera

France, 17 November 1915

Am still with the Somersets – in the trenches at present. It is quite a holiday really. There is very little for me to do, and everyone here is very charming. There is a great difference between a Regular officer and a Territorial. I wish in a way that I had gone into the Regular, but of course that involves being tied by the heels after the war.

The weather is getting colder & colder every day. We have had snow all yesterday and today. It is quite Canadian in appearance now.

I expect I shall be recalled to my Battn. tomorrow or the next day. I shall be rather sorry to go back in a way. I haven't had a letter from you for a long time, it seems, and you haven't had one from me either. Do I seem very much a phantom in the void to you? I must. You seem to me rather like [a] character in a book or someone whom one has dreamt of & never seen. I suppose there exists

such a place as Lowestoft and that there once was a person called
Vera Brittain who came down there with me.

Roland to Vera

France, 21 November 1915

I am still with the Somerset L.I. [Light Infantry] and hear today
that I am to stop here until Dec. 10th (a month in all)... I got one
letter from you a day or two ago addressed to me here, & finding
it somewhat of an enigma presume that there is some correspondence for me waiting with my own Battn. I shall try to ride over
there to collect it tomorrow, if I can. I gather that you must have
been down to Heather Cliff but shall probably be enlightened by
your former letters.

Roland to Vera

France, 22 November 1915

Dearest,
    I do deserve it, every word of it and every sting of it. 'Most
estimable, practical, unexceptional Adjutant ...'
    Oh, damn!
    I have been a perfect beast, a conceited, selfish, self-satisfied
beast. Just because I can claim to live half my time in a trench (in
very slight, temporary, and much exaggerated discomfort) and
might possibly get hit by something in the process, I have felt
myself justified in forgetting everything and everybody except
my own Infallible Majesty. And instead of calling it selfishness
pure and simple I call it 'a metamorphosis', and expect in consequence consideration and letters which can go unanswered. No, I
don't deserve to get any letters at all – only to be ignored as completely as I have ignored you – and Mother.
    I got your letter as soon as I arrived at H[ébuterne] this after-
noon and it made me so furious with myself that I left the rest

lying on the table and rode straight back again. I don't think I have ever been so angry or despised myself so much. I feel as if I hardly dare write to you at all. And to make it worse I have given up any chance of getting any leave before Christmas in order to be with this Battn. for a month instead of only a week.

Oh, damn!

Vera to Roland

1st London General Hospital, 25 November 1915

I had a letter from your Mother yesterday to say they are at Keymer, seven miles out of Brighton. This is delightfully convenient for me as [my] family is leaving Buxton and going to Brighton on Dec. 10th, so I shall be able to see your & my people on the same leave. It is really quite worth while going to Brighton for my half-days, as we are not far from Victoria here, and the journey only takes about an hour.

Roland to Vera

France, 26 November 1915

Just a short letter before I go to bed. The Battalion is back in the trenches now and I am writing in the dugout that I share with the doctor. It is very comfortable (possessing among other things an easy chair, stove, an oil lamp, a table complete with tablecloth) and I am feeling pleasantly tired but not actually sleepy. Through the door I can see little mounds of snow that are the parapets of trenches, a short stretch of railway line, and a very brilliant full moon. I wonder what you are doing. Asleep, I hope – or sitting in front of a fire in blue and white striped pyjamas? I should so like to see you in blue and white pyjamas. You are always very correctly dressed when I find you; and usually somewhere near a railway station, n'est-ce pas? I once saw you in a dressing gown with your hair down your back playing an accompaniment for Edward in the Buxton drawing room. Do you remember?

. . . . . I am often regretful that you should be at the Hospital after all. I picture you as getting up at the same too early hour every morning, to go out into a cold world and to a still colder and monotonous routine of fretful patients and sanguinary dressings and imperious sisters . . . . . and then late to bed, to begin all over again tomorrow. It all seems such a waste of Youth, such a desecration of all that is born for Poetry & Beauty. And if one does not even get a letter occasionally from someone who despite his shortcomings perhaps understands & sympathises it must make it all the worse . . . . . until one may possibly wonder whether it would not have been better never to have met him at all or at any rate until afterwards. I sometimes wish for your sake that it had happened that way.

Vera to Roland

1st London General Hospital, 27 November 1915

Your letter of the 22nd was brought into my ward this morning, & when I read it, it nearly made me — even me — cry. And I wished then that I hadn't written quite as I did. Not that, I must confess, I didn't mean every word I wrote. I am often unkind to people in general, but I never have any temptation to be unnecessarily cruel to someone whom I love as I love you. And I am never quite sure whether it is not possible to have a love that suffers *too* long and is *too* kind, but perhaps it would have been better to have thought the things and not written them. Oh! I don't know. I was so very angry that day. And now I am so sorry — not exactly that I was angry, but that I have really hurt you. I can't tell you how much I wanted to see you after I had read your letter. If only you had taken the other letters with you, instead of leaving them on the table at H[ébuterne] I think you might have found things in them that would have made the sting of the other less sharp.

I am sorry your leave is not to come at present, yet, if you don't in the meantime 'get hit by something' (what a cruel little wretch that small phrase of yours makes me feel!) it will probably be better as far as I am concerned, for you to have it in a month or so's time rather than now. If you came now, the most you could see me would be in my 3 hours a day off-duty time, and possibly one day's leave, granted me as a *great* concession by the Matron. But we are allowed a fortnight's holiday in six months besides our day a month & half-day a week, and after 3 months, which I shall have had by the end of the year, I shall have the right to ask for a week of my fortnight . . . . . Oh! don't 'get hit by something' in the meantime! When I think how all my world would go down into the abyss . . . . .

Roland to Vera

France, 27 November 1915

I hope now to get leave about December 31st. Will you be on night duty then?

    Very much love, dear.

Roland to Vera

France, 28 November 1915

I have just been out for a walk behind the trenches to get warm. It is very cold, and unless you keep moving about your feet soon become more like ice than feet. The men have begun to get 'trench feet' (commonly called frostbite, though the doctor says it isn't the same thing exactly) from standing still on sentry duty at night. They ought to be much better off than last year, though, to judge from the grandmotherly care lavished on them by the powers that be. Personally I like cold weather very much, provided I can move about enough to keep warm: and I am one of the fortunate persons who don't get troubled with chilblains. It is an advantage to be on the fat side in this weather, I imagine!

I don't think that when one can still admire sunsets one has altogether lost the personality of pre-war days. I have been look-ing at a bloodred bar of sky creeping down behind the snow, and wondering whether any of the men in the trenches on the oppo-site hill were watching it too and thinking as I was what a waste of Life it is to spend it in a ditch.

★ ★ ★ ★ ★

Midnight
In Bed (of a kind)

I have just come back from going round the trenches with the C.O. Everything is very quiet tonight, with the stillness of frost. There were a few heavy trench mortars bursting with a 'crump' farther down the line, but otherwise nothing but silence and whiteness. . . . .

It will feel like coming to another planet to come back to England, or rather to certain people in England. My leave, of course, is not definite at all yet and may not even come off for some long time. But I have hopes; and anticipation is very sweet, and better often, one thinks, than the realisation. It was so last time, I remember.

Very much love, sweetest,
Goodnight.

———————

Roland to Vera

France, 30 November 1915

Your very sweet letter nearly made me cry too. It reminded me of how much I had really deserved the former one. No, it would not have been better to have thought the things and not written them: though they did hurt me, perhaps more than you thought they would. But it was very good for my Infallible Majesty; and you are very adorable when you are angry.

★ ★ ★ ★ ★

You would be very amused if you could see me now. The snow has melted and rain taken its place, with the result that the trenches are half full of liquid mud, suddenly-thawed traverses have fallen and blocked the way with earth and sandbags, and everyone is wading around in what the Ordnance Stores describe as 'boots, gum, thigh'. I am wearing some now, and came into the dug-out a moment or two ago looking like a peripatetic ball of mud, which proceeded to peel off various outer garments, shake some superfluous mud on to the floor, and sit down to write a letter. My top half is now more or less normal, but I am a sticky mess all down below. One cannot help feeling a child's pleasure in getting muddy, though; and apart from the difficulties of locomotion I enjoy myself thoroughly.

★ ★ ★ ★ ★

Do you really want to send me a Christmas present, or can you leave it till I come back on leave? The most charming present would be just a letter from you – and, if you like, a book. Please do not send me anything of the 'Winter Comforts for our Troops' variety – though I cannot picture you doing so! If your Mother would like to send me another pair of those extra large socks she sent a little time ago they would be very useful for wearing in my gum boots.

With which domestic detail I will go off to dinner.

Vera to Roland

1st London General Hospital, 1 December 1915

This is just a hasty note (as I wanted on receiving them to write at once) to tell you that I am going on night duty to-morrow till about Feb. 1st. This includes your leave, but it is just possible (though by no means certain) that I might be allowed a day or two off for that. . . Will you let me know as soon as you can *definitely* when your leave will be – as the earlier I ask the Matron the better chance I shall have of getting some . . . . . If I am unsuccessful you'll come up to London once or twice in the mornings, won't you? Luckily Brighton is an easy journey . . . . .

Apart from the difficulties of leave I don't mind night duty at all. I never was one, as you know, to mind being up in the night. And it is at least a change from the appalling monotony of things.

I shan't have to sweep, or do very many dressings. Night work is more supervision than actual toil. You sit in the ward – usually the only one on duty – & go on rounds about every ½ hr or hr. In between, when the ward is in a normal condition, you have time to read, and write letters – and *read* them! Of course, all the exciting things happen at night, like convoys coming, or Zeppelin raids, or people dying or going mad. But on the whole it is comparatively restful & I have been getting physically so weary just lately that I am glad of it.

Roland to Vera

In Billets, France, 2 December 1915
6.20 p.m.

Am just about to have a bath, & am writing this while my servant heats the water in a large biscuit tin. I am sitting surrounded by five tins of toffee, each of a different variety, which I have just bought at the canteen. I have a childish love of toffee and thought I would lay in a good stock.

I spent all the morning at a Court Martial as prosecutor. Not a very nice job, as it was a capital crime and the two men concerned were only damned fools after all. But the president seemed an indulgent sort of person, and I think they will escape being shot. They really quite deserve it, though, from the point of view of cold justice. . .

. . . . . The bath is ready now. (Quite an event in its way; though it does sound silly to make a fuss about a bath, doesn't it?)

Very much love, dear child.

Vera to Roland

1st London General Hospital, 3 December 1915

I hear Edward is fairly desperate now as he has had a final disappointment – 4 officers of the original 11th, including Thurlow, have been sent to the front, and he is left the only officer of the 11th, without any of his friends. This is through no fault of his own & there are even rumours that his name has been sent up for promotion & he is to be given some special work to do. But he is very sick with life, & I don't wonder.

Roland to Vera

France, 3 December 1915

You seem to have spent most of your time at Lowestoft discussing me & my general goings on. I should very much like to know what conclusions you & Mother did come to. You say that I should have been 'mystified and a little astonished' if I had overheard you. I wonder whether you ultimately decided that I *was* a somewhat fickle and superficial person. I shouldn't be at all surprised, you know . . . . . Well, after all, your real love was just a character in a book, n'est-ce pas? And She whom you took to Lowestoft the first time was simply a flesh and blood approximation to Lyndall? Is this true – or, rather, do *you* think it is true? It is quite possible to love an ideal crystallised in a person, and the person because of the ideal: and who shall say whether it is not perhaps better in the end? Though it must be very trying to be the incarnation of an ideal – very trying. Apropos of which I may remark that the unfortunate Olive Schreiner is too often made responsible for things over which she had no control whatever. Also that when one does not yet know one's own self, there will still be several persons who will profess an exhaustive knowledge of it & undertake intimate diagnoses from an entirely hypothetical basis . . . . . All of which sounds, and is, just a little bit bad tempered.

Good night, Phantom.

Vera to Roland

1st London General Hospital, 4 December 1915

No. You haven't lost the personality of Pre-War days. Roland Leighton's is at its deepest an individuality founded on a rock, and – 'War knows no power'. He had only forgotten Himself a little, and was yielding the substance to the shadow – giving up his real Majesty for a phantom he mistakenly thought more majestic than the actuality. But he has remembered now. The last few letters are a proof of that.

Was anticipation really sweeter than realization – last time? And why? And on who or what does the remark cast a reflection? With whom or what lay the fault? And yet you wrote just after, 'Was it not worth all the pain . . .'

At any rate, dear, the realization must be *better* than the anticipation, this time. And since the hours of our meeting – yours & mine – are likely to be even briefer than the brief ones of last time, they must make up in sweetness for what they lack in duration. Must – and shall.

Roland to Vera

France, 5 December 1915

I have just come back from a ride with the C.O. in the course of which my horse stumbled jumping a ditch and landed me ingloriously in the mud! Which was annoying and somewhat dirty.

You would never guess where I was yesterday evening. In a cinema, of all places! The A.S.C. run one in this village – in a barn, with seats, electric light, two performances nightly and a change of programme every day. It is quite civilised for a village only 4 miles from the trenches, n'est-ce pas?

We go back to trenches on Tuesday & I shall be in the 'confortable' dug-out that you envy again for a few days – till Friday or Saturday I expect, when I shall probably get orders to return to my own Regiment. The aforesaid dugout is not really to be coveted altogether, though: it leaks when it rains and my bed was such a pool that last time I had to sleep with the Doctor in his lower bunk, very much à la sardine.

Good night, dear. I suppose that to you nowadays it ought to be Good morning rather.

Vera to Roland

1st London General Hospital, 6 December 1915

It seems quite queer to think that (if you're not 'hit by something' in the meantime – oh! that expression does haunt me so!) I can really count the days till I see you. Do you remember our somewhat embarrassed meeting at St Pancras? I wonder what it will be like this time – where & when! And I shall probably be in the abominable uniform (which your mother nevertheless said she liked) and you'll wonder what sort of an object you've picked up, & how you or anybody else could ever possibly have thought she looked nice . . . . .

I am just going out into a sunny windy morning after rain. I do love my morning till 12.30 off-duty time. I never realised how lovely mornings are until I had been up at night.

Vera to Roland

1st London General Hospital, 7 December 1915

Circumstances forced me into speaking about my leave this morning, and I am actually really & truly going to get a week's leave at the same time as you get yours – a most splendid & unexpected piece of luck. How it happened was that this morning Matron sent for four other V.A.Ds & I and told us we were due for a week's leave, to begin to-morrow . . . This information caused me great dismay as I knew if I had a week now I would not get even a day in 3 weeks' time when you come. So I asked Matron if I could speak to her afterwards & then just stated briefly how matters were. I expected expostulation & certainly no suggestion of

special leave, but to my utter surprise she smiled sweetly at me &
said 'Certainly, nurse, I'll postpone your leave.' . . . I can't think why
the Powers that Be are so nice to me – unless it be that I have
rather better manners than most of the V.A.Ds here, who have no
conception of discipline and include some of the most impolite &
tactless people I have ever met.

To think that I can *really* look forward now to the end of this
month! If only you are safe till then! And it will be all the time this
time, instead of 3½ over-crowded days filled with railway-jour-
neys. I don't know whether I shall stay with my people or yours –
half & half I suppose, but from the point of view of seeing you it
really doesn't make much difference since they are going to be so
close. . .

★ ★ ★ ★ ★

Life seems quite irradiated now when I think of the sweet
hours that may be ahead – when I shall see once more 'the things
I strive to capture in vain', while the eyes you have perhaps forgotten will again make you think of Lyndall's.

Edward to Vera

> *Brocton Camp, Stafford, 9 December 1915*

Thurlow has gone to the 10th Bn. which is very annoying especially as they are in the Ypres Salient.

Roland to Vera

> *France, 9 December 1915*

I was recalled to my own Regt. unexpectedly suddenly yesterday
morning and am now in the trenches with them. Very wet and
muddy, and many of the communication trenches are quite
impassable. Three men were killed the other day by a dug-out
falling in on top of them and one man was drowned in a sump
hole. The whole of one's world, at least one's visible and palpable

world, is mud in various stages of solidity or stickiness. But the
men all take it as a joke and are splendidly cheerful. One consolation is that the German trenches seem to be, if anything, worse
than ours.

Roland to Vera

France, 13 December 1915

Shall be home on leave for week from 24th Dec–31st. Land
Christmas Day.

R.

Vera to Roland

1st London General, 15 December 1915

I would like to write you a specially nice letter to-night, because
I expect this will be the one I promised you should have for
Christmas – that is, if posts are delayed as much as we have been
warned they will be. It would be nicer still, perhaps, if I were not
a little disquieted by vague rumours that are going round here of
a big movement impending on the Western front, and a conse-
quent cancelling of all leaves in the near future. . . This is such a
wretched War – so abundant in disappointments & postpone-
ments & annoyances as well as more tremendous things, – that I
should scarcely be surprised to hear that everything I was looking
forward to, which temporally make life worth living, is not to
come off . . . . .

I have just had my December night-off, and have had a most
delightful time. I went down to the Grand Hotel at Brighton,
which I had never seen before. Fortunately lack of sleep does not
make me sleepy, and I thoroughly enjoyed yesterday, which was
made still better by most glorious weather. The war of course is
much in evidence down there, but not so much in its sadder
aspects, such as I see here. At Brighton there is more of the social

side of the War, if one can so express it. The Grand Hotel possessed an abundance of honeymoon couples and slightly wounded officers, and officers belonging to the various battalions stationed down there. It was delightful to take off my uniform and get into some decent clothes, & wrap myself up in my beloved fur coat & feel really warm for the first time for weeks.

But the most momentous part of the whole proceeding is that our respective parents have actually managed to meet at last! When Mother heard I was coming she wrote to your Mother & asked her & your father to tea . . . Mother looked very sweet, and I felt overshadowed & chastened, but Mrs Leighton seemed a good deal more interested in Father . . . he and Mrs Leighton contributed most of the conversation during the afternoon, with great vivacity; Father didn't even seem to mind when she criticised his beloved Edward in quite her usual style. She told Father she thought Edward inherited his lack of comprehension of women from him, and accused him of not being very interested in anything else but money! He didn't appear to mind even this . . .

. . . I was actually quiet for once & instead of talking sat opposite Mrs Leighton, and watched *your* sweetest expression coming & going on her face as she smiled. . .

The rain is pouring down on the hut roof, – & I wonder if it is pouring down on you too, amid your cold & mud & tumbled-down dug-outs. I am just longing to see you, with a chance of being clean & dry at last, sitting with me in a comfortable room before a nice warm hotel fire. . .

Is it an absurdity to wish you a merry Christmas, in the midst of sodden trenches, & cold & damp & misery? It seems so – with the enemy only comparatively a few yards away, and the Dead sleeping beside you & behind you & beneath your feet – the Dead who perhaps were struggling bravely in spite of cold & suffering, to create a gay spirit for Christmas time – this time last year . . . . . Yes, to wish you a happy Christmas would certainly be absurd. But I suppose the British soldier, who can go with songs to his death (or with even better than songs, like the Genius who called out 'Early doors, sixpence!' in the attack on Loos) can conjure up a spirit of gaiety at Christmas time. . .

Well then, a Merry Christmas! Perhaps soon after you get this you will be here again to answer it in person, in a better way than with pen & ink. And perhaps – not. But somehow I feel the end is not destined to be here and now. We have *not* fulfilled ourselves – and 'Someday we shall live our roseate poem through' . . . . .

Au Revoir, dearest.

Vera to Roland

1st London General, 17 December 1915

I went to Matron this morning and have now officially been given my leave at the same time as yours. Also I have actually been allowed to take it from 25th–1st, instead of 26th, as I expected. So I go on night-duty for Christmas Eve, and go down to Brighton on Christmas Day. I may not actually see you on Christmas Day, n'est-ce pas? For you will be dead tired & after all it is only fair that your family should have you to themselves for a little, without being interrupted by an interloper . . . But it would have been very hard to do monotonous, sordid work at the Hospital while knowing that You were in England . . .

And shall I really see you again – and so soon? You will be here for my birthday. And it will be the anniversary of the week which contained New Year's Eve . . . and two unreal and wonderful days, and you standing alone in Trafalgar Square, and thinking of – well, what *were* you thinking of? When we were really both children still, and my connection with any hospital on earth was unthought of, and your departure for the Front merely the adventurous dream of some vaguely distant future date. And life was lived, at any rate for two days, in the Omar Khayamesque spirit of

> *'Unborn to-morrow & dead yesterday.*
> *Why fret about them if to-day be sweet?'*

But we are going to better that – even that – *this* time.

Au Revoir.

The 7th Worcesters celebrated Christmas on 20 December in billets at Courcelles. On the evening of 22 December they relieved the 4th Oxford and Bucks Regiment in trenches at Hébuterne. Roland's platoon had been ordered to repair the barbed wire in front of the trench, and Roland went ahead to inspect it and to see that all was safe before the rest of the wiring party followed. It was a moonlit night with the Germans only a hundred yards away, and he had no sooner reached the gap in the hedge in the concealed path leading to No Man's Land than he was shot and mortally wounded. He died at eleven o'clock on the night of 23 December at the Casualty Clearing Station at Louvencourt.

At the Grand Hotel, Brighton, on the morning of 26 December, Vera had just finished dressing when she was called to the telephone. She dashed joyously into the corridor believing that after so long she was again to hear Roland's voice. But it was his sister Clare, telephoning with the news of Roland's death.

Robert Leighton to Vera
25 February 1916, describing Roland's funeral
at Louvencourt on 26 December 1915

At the funeral, the chief mourners were Col. Harman, Col. Barling, Captain Sheridan and Captain Adam . . . Men could not be spared from the trenches to form a firing party, but in other respects it was a military field funeral, very solemn, very simple, very beautiful. The mourners were all impressed by the sudden breaking forth of the sun as they followed the coffin out of the church and along the road to the cemetery. The acolyte who carried the censer was a picturesque figure. Incense was wafted into the grave. Holy water was sprinkled . . .

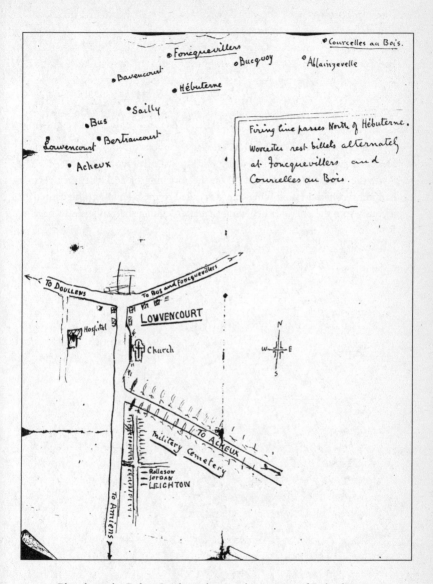

Plan drawn by Robert Leighton showing the situation of Roland's grave

Roland's last communication to Vera; and end of her last letter to him,
17 December 1915

1. *Vera and Edward Brittain at Melrose, Buxton, circa 1914.*

2. *Edward (back row, left) and Roland Leighton (front row, left) at the Uppingham School OTC Camp, Summer 1913.*

3. Roland Leighton, circa 1913.

4. Roland (left) and Victor Richardson (right) outside The Lodge, Uppingham, Summer 1914.

5. *Roland, 1915.*

6. *A photograph taken by Roland of two of his fellow officers outside their hut, Ploegsteert Wood, 1915.*

7. *Edward, 1915.*

8. *Vera as a V.A.D. nurse and Edward at Buxton, 1915.*

9. *Edward (foreground) with other officers, Brocton Camp, 1916.*

10. Victor Richardson as a schoolboy, circa 1912.

11. Victor Richardson, 1916.

12. Geoffrey Thurlow as a schoolboy, circa 1912.

13. Geoffrey in uniform, 1916.

14. Edith Brittain (left) and Edward (right) leave Buckingham Palace in November 1916 after Edward's investiture with the Military Cross.

15. *Vera and patients at the First London General Hospital, Camberwell, circa 1916.*

16. *The original manuscript of Vera's poem, 'To My Brother', inscribed on the flyleaf of a copy of the poetry anthology, The Muse in Arms. It was sent to Edward in Italy in the summer of 1918 but, tragically, arrived after his death in action. The poem commemorated Edward's courage on the first day of the Battle of the Somme.*

17. *Vera in the early 1920s.*

Good-bye, sweet friend . . .
. . . hand in hand, just as we used to do,
We too shall live our passionate poem through
On God's serene to-morrow.
— ROLAND LEIGHTON, 'Goodbye'

Perhaps some day the sun will shine again,
And I shall see that still the skies are blue,
And feel once more I do not live in vain,
Although bereft of You.
— VERA BRITTAIN, 'Perhaps–'

Vera returned to the 1st London General on 3 January 1916. Nursing proved an intolerable strain while her grief for Roland was still so raw, and in these early months of her bereavement she was to rely heavily on the support of Victor, who, having recovered from his dangerous illness, was assigned to light duties at the Woolwich Arsenal. The friendship of Geoffrey Thurlow, shortly to be back in England recovering from the slight wounds and shell shock he had received at Ypres, was also to become increasingly important to her. And from Edward, though soon to leave for France, Vera knew she could always derive solace and understanding.

Geoffrey Thurlow to Vera

In a farmhouse, France, 8 January [1916]

Dear Miss Brittain,

Please pardon me for writing to you. I am very very sorry: may you be helped through this terrible time. There are times, I know, when letters are but empty things and I cannot write.

Yours sincerely,

Geoffrey R. Y. Thurlow

Victor Richardson to Vera

Lessness Park Camp, Abbey Wood, Kent,
8 January 1916

Dear Vera,

May I come and see you on Wednesday afternoon? I suggest this next Wednesday, because I am on guard at one of the Arsenal entrances during the week, and as it is not an important position I could leave my coadjutor in charge for the afternoon, and dis-appear – without leave. Moreover I don't know when I shall have another opportunity – probably not for three or four weeks, and possibly not at all as I hope to join our drafting unit at Cambridge in about that time. My hopes in this direction are being raised by the application of Conscription to Home Service Territorials. The War Office are quite capable of refusing one as a volunteer and taking one as a conscript!

Of course if you do not feel inclined to see people I shall quite understand. If I do not hear from you I shall assume this to be the case. Otherwise I could be in Camberwell soon after 2–30.

Yours sincerely

Victor Richardson

Edward to Vera

Stafford, 9 January 1916

Thank you very much indeed for your letter and all the addenda and the letter from Captain Adam which, as you say, is abundant proof that Roland in war as in peace took every duty and burden upon his shoulders whenever possible and was never found too tired or unready to do somebody else's work as well as his own. I believe Captain Adam was really very friendly with him as they used to go riding together and Roland occasionally mentioned him in letters. . .

Tah has sent me rather a nice letter from old Puckle written to us jointly. I shall not mention you when I answer it, but Tah thinks it would be best not to write anything about Roland in the School Mag. but just to send the editor 'Violets' to put in and then 'let him that readeth understand' if he can, including Puckle.

Vera to Edward

1st London General Hospital, 10 January 1916

I enclose the copy of a letter written by the Chaplain who was with Roland, in answer to mine. He must be a very nice man – and to be called 'dear Sister' by a priest quite revives my interest in nursing again. As you see, he does not tell us much more, not having been with Roland after 4.15, but we shall doubtless know a good deal when he has made enquiries. But it seems more than probable he went out of life without knowing it. He would almost certainly have sent some message had he known – and to have received some message to inspire the long dreary years ahead would of course have made it easier for us. And in view of the fact that he said he would wish to know himself if he were dying, I cannot help feeling sorry if they did not tell him; I feel it was in a way deceiving him to let him give all he had without being able to take to himself the credit of having done so – without being conscious of his own heroism in making the supreme sacrifice. Being what he was, he would have liked to have realised what he was doing, and he would not have been afraid. I always think those words describing Lyndall's death – 'The old strong soul gathered itself together for the last time; it knew where it stood' – picture the ideal, conscious passing of a Splendid Soul.

And yet – he would perhaps have suffered exceedingly if he had fully realised all he would never have any more – if he had known he would never see sunset and dawn again, never go back to his Mother and Uppingham and 'Life and Love and –' me. As it was he must just have gone to sleep, glad to be at rest after the weariness of 4 months in the trenches in the worst possible weather, thinking he would wake to the light of day next morning, possibly seeing dreamily in his mind (as one does in quiet after long stress) scenes of the past at school, or at home when he was a child, or with me in later years, & probably rejoicing that he was wounded at last, as he always meant to be, & thinking he would have a long happy time at home, seeing much of the people he loved. To us it is heart-breaking to think he thought all this, and they knew it could not be but never told him, yet if, as the Chaplain suggests, there were medical reasons for not doing so right up to the end, they were of course right. . .

In my mind I have lived through his death so many times that now it has really happened it seems scarcely any different from the many other occasions in which the only difference was that it was not an actual fact. In fact I don't believe even now that I have felt such an utter desperation of renouncement as I did the first time he went to the front. I think my subconscious self must have told me then that I should not have him for long, in spite of my apparent belief, originated I suppose by my wish, that I should. . .

I am afraid I go about my work here very mechanically, although the priest's letter suddenly gave it a momentary glamour. I get long dreary moods in which there seems to be no point in anything, and I am conscious of no particular desire in any direction whatever, and there seems to be no future at all. And when the beauty of sunrise at the end of night-duty, or a glimpse of very pure sky behind bare tree-branches takes me for a minute out of myself, I get sudden shocks which shake me to the very depths, of realization that of all these things he loved so he is no longer conscious. At least we do not know that he is – & there is such an immense gulf between being conscious of them & not being so. And then, although I have often wished I was dead, it seems so unfair that I should be left to enjoy these things & he not. And I feel as if I am taking an unfair advantage of him, and can never enjoy them again, because he can't. . .

I seem to be writing to you in the *kind* of way I used to write to him. It is so strange not to write to him any more. . .

★ ★ ★ ★ ★

If only the War spares you & I, we will make of Him something that the world will never forget.

Vera to Edward

1st London General Hospital, 14 January 1916

It is a very important budget I am sending you to-night. Not only am I returning you his photograph, but I enclose a great deal else of more interest still – things which to me are a realisation sufficient to enrich all life for ever more.

But to explain these enclosures I must first tell you what happened yesterday. I was suddenly presented with another night – Thursday – off-duty, it being the usual date for the person who happened to be in my present ward, so yesterday morning I tore off to Brighton, had lunch at the Dudley and (needless to remark) immediately after went over to Keymer, where I stayed till 9.0. I

14. Edith Brittain (left) and Edward (right) leave Buckingham Palace in November 1916 after Edward's investiture with the Military Cross.

15. *Vera and patients at the First London General Hospital, Camberwell, circa 1916.*

16. *The original manuscript of Vera's poem, 'To My Brother', inscribed on the flyleaf of a copy of the poetry anthology, The Muse in Arms. It was sent to Edward in Italy in the summer of 1918 but, tragically, arrived after his death in action. The poem commemorated Edward's courage on the first day of the Battle of the Somme.*

17. *Vera in the early 1920s.*

FIVE

8 JANUARY 1916 – 17 SEPTEMBER 1916

Good-bye, sweet friend . . .
. . . hand in hand, just as we used to do,
We too shall live our passionate poem through
On God's serene to-morrow.
                    – ROLAND LEIGHTON, 'Goodbye'

Perhaps some day the sun will shine again,
    And I shall see that still the skies are blue,
And feel once more I do not live in vain,
    Although bereft of You.
                    – VERA BRITTAIN, 'Perhaps–'

Vera returned to the 1st London General on 3 January 1916. Nursing proved an intolerable strain while her grief for Roland was still so raw, and in these early months of her bereavement she was to rely heavily on the support of Victor, who, having recovered from his dangerous illness, was assigned to light duties at the Woolwich Arsenal. The friendship of Geoffrey Thurlow, shortly to be back in England recovering from the slight wounds and shell shock he had received at Ypres, was also to become increasingly important to her. And from Edward, though soon to leave for France, Vera knew she could always derive solace and understanding.

Geoffrey Thurlow to Vera

In a farmhouse, France, 8 January [1916]

Dear Miss Brittain,

Please pardon me for writing to you. I am very very sorry: may you be helped through this terrible time. There are times, I know, when letters are but empty things and I cannot write.

Yours sincerely,

Geoffrey R. Y. Thurlow

Victor Richardson to Vera

Lessness Park Camp, Abbey Wood, Kent,
8 January 1916

Dear Vera,

May I come and see you on Wednesday afternoon? I suggest this next Wednesday, because I am on guard at one of the Arsenal entrances during the week, and as it is not an important position I could leave my coadjutor in charge for the afternoon, and disappear – without leave. Moreover I don't know when I shall have another opportunity – probably not for three or four weeks, and possibly not at all as I hope to join our drafting unit at Cambridge in about that time. My hopes in this direction are being raised by the application of Conscription to Home Service Territorials. The War Office are quite capable of refusing one as a volunteer and taking one as a conscript!

Of course if you do not feel inclined to see people I shall quite understand. If I do not hear from you I shall assume this to be the case. Otherwise I could be in Camberwell soon after 2–30.

Yours sincerely

Victor Richardson

———————

Edward to Vera

Stafford, 9 January 1916

Thank you very much indeed for your letter and all the addenda and the letter from Captain Adam which, as you say, is abundant proof that Roland in war as in peace took every duty and burden upon his shoulders whenever possible and was never found too tired or unready to do somebody else's work as well as his own. I believe Captain Adam was really very friendly with him as they used to go riding together and Roland occasionally mentioned him in letters. . .

Tah has sent me rather a nice letter from old Puckle written to us jointly. I shall not mention you when I answer it, but Tah thinks it would be best not to write anything about Roland in the School Mag. but just to send the editor 'Violets' to put in and then 'let him that readeth understand' if he can, including Puckle.

———————

Vera to Edward

1st London General Hospital, 10 January 1916

I enclose the copy of a letter written by the Chaplain who was with Roland, in answer to mine. He must be a very nice man – and to be called 'dear Sister' by a priest quite revives my interest in nursing again. As you see, he does not tell us much more, not having been with Roland after 4.15, but we shall doubtless know a good deal when he has made enquiries. But it seems more than probable he went out of life without knowing it. He would almost certainly have sent some message had he known – and to have received some message to inspire the long dreary years ahead would of course have made it easier for us. And in view of the fact that he said he would wish to know himself if he were dying, I cannot help feeling sorry if they did not tell him; I feel it was in a way deceiving him to let him give all he had without being able to take to himself the credit of having done so – without being conscious of his own heroism in making the supreme sacrifice. Being what he was, he would have liked to have realised what he was doing, and he would not have been afraid. I always think those words describing Lyndall's death – 'The old strong soul gathered itself together for the last time; it knew where it stood' – picture the ideal, conscious passing of a Splendid Soul.

And yet – he would perhaps have suffered exceedingly if he had fully realised all he would never have any more – if he had known he would never see sunset and dawn again, never go back to his Mother and Uppingham and 'Life and Love and –' me. As it was he must just have gone to sleep, glad to be at rest after the weariness of 4 months in the trenches in the worst possible weather, thinking he would wake to the light of day next morning, possibly seeing dreamily in his mind (as one does in quiet after long stress) scenes of the past at school, or at home when he was a child, or with me in later years, & probably rejoicing that he was wounded at last, as he always meant to be, & thinking he would have a long happy time at home, seeing much of the people he loved. To us it is heart-breaking to think he thought all this, and they knew it could not be but never told him, yet if, as the Chaplain suggests, there were medical reasons for not doing so right up to the end, they were of course right...

In my mind I have lived through his death so many times that now it has really happened it seems scarcely any different from the many other occasions in which the only difference was that it was not an actual fact. In fact I don't believe even now that I have felt such an utter desperation of renouncement as I did the first time he went to the front. I think my subconscious self must have told me then that I should not have him for long, in spite of my apparent belief, originated I suppose by my wish, that I should...

I am afraid I go about my work here very mechanically, although the priest's letter suddenly gave it a momentary glamour. I get long dreary moods in which there seems to be no point in anything, and I am conscious of no particular desire in any direction whatever, and there seems to be no future at all. And when the beauty of sunrise at the end of night-duty, or a glimpse of very pure sky behind bare tree-branches takes me for a minute out of myself, I get sudden shocks which shake me to the very depths, of realization that of all these things he loved so he is no longer conscious. At least we do not know that he is − & there is such an immense gulf between being conscious of them & not being so. And then, although I have often wished I was dead, it seems so unfair that I should be left to enjoy these things & he not. And I feel as if I am taking an unfair advantage of him, and can never enjoy them again, because he can't...

I seem to be writing to you in the *kind* of way I used to write to him. It is so strange not to write to him any more...

★ ★ ★ ★ ★

If only the War spares you & I, we will make of Him something that the world will never forget.

───────────

Vera to Edward

1st London General Hospital, 14 January 1916

It is a very important budget I am sending you to-night. Not only am I returning you his photograph, but I enclose a great deal else of more interest still − things which to me are a realisation sufficient to enrich all life for ever more.

But to explain these enclosures I must first tell you what happened yesterday. I was suddenly presented with another night − Thursday − off-duty, it being the usual date for the person who happened to be in my present ward, so yesterday morning I tore off to Brighton, had lunch at the Dudley and (needless to remark) immediately after went over to Keymer, where I stayed till 9.0. I

arrived at a very opportune though very awful moment. All
Roland's things had just been sent back from the front through
Cox's; they had just opened them and they were all lying on the
floor. I had no idea before of the after-results of an officer's death,
or what the returned kit, of which so much has been written in
the papers, really meant. It was terrible. Mrs Leighton and Clare
were both crying as bitterly as on the day we heard of His death,
and Mr Leighton with his usual instinct was taking all the things
everybody else wanted & putting them where nobody could ever
find them. (His doings always seem to me to supply the slight element of humour which makes tragedy so much more tragic.)
There were His clothes – the clothes in which He came home
from the front last time – another set rather less worn, and under-
clothing and accessories of various descriptions. Everything was
damp & worn and simply caked with mud. And I was glad that
neither you nor Victor nor anyone else who may some day go to
the front was there to see. If you had been you would have been
overwhelmed by the horror of war without its glory. For though
he had only worn the things when living, the smell of those
clothes was the smell of graveyards & the Dead. The mud of
France which covered them was not ordinary mud; it had not the
usual clean pure smell of earth, but it was as though it were satu-
rated with dead bodies – dead that had been dead a long, long
time. All the sepulchres and catacombs of Rome could not make
me realise mortality and decay and corruption as vividly as did
the smell of those clothes. I know now what he meant when he
used to write of 'this refuse-heap of a country' or 'a trench that is
nothing but a charnel-house'. And the wonder is, not that he
temporally lost the extremest refinements of his personality as Mrs
Leighton says he did, but that he ever kept any of it at all – let
alone nearly the whole. He was more marvellous than even I
ever dreamed. There was his cap, bent in and shapeless out of
recognition – the soft cap he wore rakishly on the back of his
head – with the badge coated thickly with mud. He must have
fallen on top of it, or perhaps one of the people who fetched him
in trampled on it. The clothes he was wearing when wounded
were those in which he came home last time. We discovered
that the bullet was an expanding one. The hole where it went in

in front – well below where the belt would have been, just beside the right-hand bottom pocket of the tunic – was almost microscopic, but at the back, almost exactly where his back bone would have been, there was quite a large rent. The under things he was wearing at the time have evidently had to be destroyed, but they sent back a khaki waistcoat or vest (whatever that garment is you wear immediately below your tunic in cold weather) which was dark and stiff with blood, and a pair of khaki breeches also in the same state, which had been slit open at the top by someone in a great hurry – probably the Doctor in haste to get at the wound, or perhaps even by one of the men. Even the tabs of his braces were blood-stained too. He must have fallen on his back as in every case the back of his clothes was much more stained & muddy than the front.

The charnel-house smell seemed to grow stronger and stronger till it pervaded the room and obliterated everything else. Finally Mrs Leighton said 'Robert, take those clothes away into the kitchen, and don't let me see them again; I must either burn or bury them. They smell of Death; they are not Roland, they even seem to detract from his memory & spoil his glamour. I won't have any more to do with them.' And indeed one could never imagine those things the same as those in which he had lived & walked. One couldn't believe anyone alive had been in them at all. No, they were not Him. So Mr Leighton took them away; they are going to keep only that blood-stained vest he was wounded in, if it can be sterilized, as I think it can – and his Sam Browne belt. After the clothes had gone we opened the window wide & felt better, but it was a long time before the smell and even the taste of them went away.

. . . Even all the little things had the same faint smell, and were damp & mouldy. The only things untouched by damp or mud or mould were my photograph, kept carefully in an envelope, and his leather cigarette case, with a few cigarettes, a tiny photo of his Mother & George Meredith & the three little snapshots Miss Bervon took of us, inside. He must have had those things always with him, and the warmth of his body overruled the damp & decay of everything. There was his haversack crammed full of letters – he seemed to keep all he received. I found the rest of mine, and also several of yours, which I return in this. I seized them at once; I thought you would like them because they had been close to him, and also Mr Leighton has a habit of regarding every-body's letters to Roland as public property, much the same as Father regards yours to other people. He would be quite capable of reading mine; I saw him carefully engrossed in some of Mrs Leighton's, much to her dismay, and he was handling one of Victor's in a suspicious manner. Mrs Leighton is going to return Victor's letters to him, and I gave Mother three of hers back last night. There were letters from officers of the Norfolks, from Minnie Bennett at Uppingham, & one or two very pathetic & grateful epistles from the Mothers of Tommies, thanking him for his sympathy over their sons' deaths & his careful record of details, & hoping he would come safely through. There were letters from Tommies too – Norfolks & invalided Worcesters – letters intimate and affectionate but always respectful, almost reverential, at the same time. Mrs Leighton remarked almost with awe how very openly one has to live at the Front, when any moment one's most private personal belongings become the property of one's nearest relations & friends. . .

Then there was the box of cigarettes you gave him recently – opened & sampled but not much used – the socks Mother knit-ted him, the pen & pipe and book I gave him, and your present 'A Tall Ship'. Among his letters were one or two envelopes addressed to Mrs Leighton & me, having no letters inside. And there was one which interested me very much; it was from the same Father Purdie who has written to me lately. The one we found was writ-ten in the summer, before he came home on leave; it is about contributions & details for the 'Catholic Journal', and shows him to have [been] a confessed & acknowledged Roman Catholic all that time ago. But he never said anything to us about it when he was home. How reserved he was about some things! It reminds me of the small incident at Maldon of his showing you his foun-tain pen & not telling you it was from me. But I think he imagined I should have disapproved of his Roman Catholicism.

But, most important of all, a Book, a private exercise book, came back in his haversack containing some poems of his own, in various stages of completeness, mostly written in pencil, beside which even 'Violets' does not stand out as the height of his achievement. Some of the poems, like 'Triolet' & 'Lines on a Picture by Herbert Schmaltz', we already know. But the others, apparently, he has never shown anybody. There are seven of them. They are mostly love-lyrics – and I read them with a queer inward exultation over what his death has revealed. He was always reserved – less so in letters than in himself, but until I read these poems I think I never quite realised – I copied them all out. I don't think any were meant to be in their finished state, and transcription with some was quite difficult, there were so many substitutions & alternative expressions...

'Hédauville' is perhaps the most wonderful of all the poems. And it was his last – it must have been written only about a month before he died. And I wonder if he was prophetic in that – and I wonder quite what he meant. Oh! there are such millions of things I want to ask him – now.

But I feel immensely triumphant – exalted; I could not cry over those poems. How could I, being *I*! – Can you, being not I, but you? For in them 'He, being dead, yet speaketh' and after all, the words I quoted in his Rupert Brooke are still true –

> 'We have built a house that is not for Time's throwing
> We have gained a peace unshaken by pain for ever
> War knows no power.'

I feel, now that I have read these poems which only Death was allowed to reveal, a worthier, nobler, loftier person, both now and forever.

* * * * *

...I had tea with Victor on Wednesday. Of course we talked of Roland the whole time. I am going to write to him directly and send him the Speech Day poem and that written at Ploegsteert – the latter especially because on Wednesday he was talking a great deal about what Roland said at Uppingham of death in War being his ideal. You can send Victor any of the other poems you think he would like – all, if he would understand them, otherwise just what you think he will understand.

* * * * *

I have brought back with me a little case containing a packet of letters, a packet of his, the pipe & fountain pen I gave him, the Rupert Brooke – much read, damp & mildewed – which I gave him in July, my own photograph, and a tablet of *the* soap – which Mrs Leighton says I am to use. And above all, a copy I made of the poems. I am so much richer than I ever was before. And I have brought also a little Worcestershire coat badge, taken from his clothes; I bought a silver chain for it this morning and had a link put on it, so that I can have it always round my neck. I am wearing it now.

Edward to Vera

Stafford, 16 January 1916

I don't know what Thurlow said to you but I thought it was rather nice of him to write as he has only met you once.

. . . It is clear, in my opinion, that Roland was not told he would probably die for medical reasons, as his death in considerably less than the 48 hours was apparently not expected at all and it rather looks as though there was more chance of recovery than we were led to believe at first, but that he took the wrong turning rather quickly. Of course so much is a matter of surmise as we cannot know all the little details.

Victor to Vera

Kent, 19 January 1916

Thank you very much indeed for your letter and for the poems. You say that I have a right to see them: I cannot quite see that; for they are too intimate for it to be a right, or indeed anything but a privilege for me to see them: they are yours, and yours alone. Therefore I thank you again and again. At the same time I am very glad that Mrs Leighton is going to edit them and have them published. Then those at Uppingham who matter, that is those who perceive, will be made to realise what they and England have lost. I say that the people who perceive are those that matter because He, although He was the most able scholar the School had possessed for at any rate many years, had very little use for the scholar as such, unless his knowledge gave him that Understanding that we were all urged to acquire in the Lesson read in Chapel at the beginning of every term.

I think it probable, at any rate possible, that Edward suggested that you should not send me the poems. He would be quite justified in assuming that I should not understand them for I am a very ordinary matter-of-fact person. . . But I should be cold indeed if I could not grasp the exquisite beauty of His work, although I could not perhaps give a literal translation of every word of it. After all I understood Him a little, though not completely, and those poems are part of His very Self. I can hear Him saying some of those lines in conversation – lines such as 'And daisies are truer than passion flowers' and 'Sweetest sceptic, we were made for living' and again '– the elemental dust of War' contrasted with 'And all the loathesome pettiness of peace' is a theme he often . . . discussed with me. All through the last part of his time at Uppingham he seemed to look and long for the stern reality of War and the elemental principles that War involves. He considered that in War lay our one hope of salvation as a Nation, War where all the things that do not matter are swept rudely aside and one gets down to the rock-bottom of the elementary facts of life. It was at times like these that I realise what a disappointment it was to him that his eyesight had prevented his entering the Navy. He loved to picture himself on his quarter-deck and seemed to revel in the awe and respect in which that is held: 'saluting the quarter-deck' seemed to mean, in fact, meant, to him something symbolical of all those virtues of Patriotism and Duty which he held most high. It was at times like these that he spoke of wishing to be 'found dead in a trench at dawn'. He always said that the form of burial he should most prefer would be for his body to be placed on a ship, and the ship set on fire and cast loose upon the sea. Perhaps that is what He meant by 'A Hell of Fire'. Yes the ideal conveyed in 'Ploegsteert' is only too familiar. You say 'Parts of them are on a level with, even perhaps beyond, Rupert Brooke'. Most true, and I think we all know why – His life was so much more beautiful. There can be no doubt that Rupert Brooke's personality must have been a singularly beautiful one, but to me at any rate his poems are tinged with a certain sensuousness that He never knew. Perhaps that is why there is none of Rupert Brooke's bitterness and cynicism in His poems. If we leave out these qualities 'Ploegsteert' reminds me very much of 'Peace' and 'The Dead' (second sonnet). . .

No wonder you felt exultant and triumphant when you found His poems: if ever you owed Him a debt you repaid it when you inspired Him to write them. And His life at Uppingham during His last term seemed, if possible, more beautiful than ever before. During the last fortnight of that term – how we both longed for it to end – I read the 'Story of an African Farm' for the first time: it seemed to be like a key to His character. Perhaps that is why I love it so.

Your letter made me feel and realise the horror of it all in a way I had never done before. I think it is very cruel to send home the clothes worn at the time: I can't see that it is necessary. I do not think that He was hit by a dum-dum bullet in the usually accepted sense, though of course He may have been: the truth is that all the most modern Small Arm Ammunition tends to flatten at close range owing to the pointed nose of the bullet: the bullet is thus shaped, not out of wanton cruelty, but to secure a flatter trajectory thereby bringing a larger section of enemy ground into the danger zone. The terrific velocity of the latest Ammunition is also responsible for the severe nature of wounds received at close range. I am afraid we are no better than the Huns in these ways.

There is one comfort: I do not think He can have suffered much. It is awful to think of Him saying 'Lying on this hillside for six days makes me stiff' but I think this would be the correct explanation. An operation on the back, and I imagine the wound itself, would cause stiffness – at least I found it so: it would be natural to wander and in doing so one goes over the things that happened most recently, and all sense of time vanishes: I think the feeling of stiffness would associate itself with these wanderings. I do not think that there can have been anything anticipatory in the remark.

His belongings, letters etc. must be a rare proof of his still rarer integrity. I think his receiving letters from Tommies both in the Norfolks and in the Worcesters is truly wonderful. I am sure it is unusual, and it speaks volumes for his excellence and efficiency as an officer – more than any written or spoken tribute could do. Mr Leighton sent me the letters I had written Him during the last few months. They are models of what letters should not be and so fearfully commonplace and full of 'shop' that I think I shall destroy them. I shall see what Edward says.

I expect a Medical Board next week, but shall not be able to go to the front for quite two or three months, as the War Office have devised an examination in everything under the Sun – quite new work to me for the most part – that has to be passed before going out.

I don't think we need to apologise to each other for writing long letters about Him. I find myself writing to you as if I had known you as well and as long as I did Him – and Edward too. You must not mind that. I was glad when I saw you on that terrible New Year's Eve that you called me Tar. It was as He would have liked if He had been there. It is a great help to me to write long letters like this about Him. It helps to remember things.

Yours very sincerely

Tar.

———————

Edward to Vera

Stafford, 21 January 1916

I can't tell you with what a sense of exultation I read your big letter and Roland's 7 poems; it is strange to think that he who was so wonderful before has become even more wonderful through them, because they reveal an enormous amount especially with regard to his love for you. . . I hope Mrs Leighton will have all his poems published fairly soon, and perhaps in years to come, if the fates allow, I may be able to write music worthy of them . . . I wonder if it would be possible to find out when he became a Roman Catholic and if he really acknowledged himself as such.

Thurlow, who is rather inclined to deprecate my lack of religion and open mind on the question of the nature of the deity, the resurrection etc., in a letter to me not long ago said that at the front God (as he calls it) seems to be much closer and that a definite belief is almost a necessity. Now I haven't the least idea how true that may be but owing to the circumstances I suppose it is a possibility, and so I wonder if it was that influence (partly perhaps) which induced Roland to a more open confession of religion.

Geoffrey to Edward

France, 22–23 January 1916
In my bed with a candle beside me.

Dear Edward,

Thank you very much for your long letter which came today and which I've read and reread: also for caring to tell me so much about him: although I never met him, I feel as tho' I know him well by what you have told me. Some day I must read 'The Story of an African Farm': there must be something beyond this life, this tragedy, and what it is we can but conjecture. But on this subject we will talk in another letter . . . Those verses must have spoken messages to Mrs Leighton your sister and yourself especially as you say he didn't realise the veil of the Unknown would be lifted for him so soon, and so left no message. Thank you for sending me the two you did: they are beautiful & I like them immensely tho' I'm afraid I cannot understand poetry as those of great intellect can. You must have come through very deep waters old man and life in a Brighton hotel at such a time would have been intolerable. I do hope Life has lost some of its sting for you now. . .

★ ★ ★ ★ ★

I can't raise much enthusiasm over the people here and, in my turn, also miss you. We could have such good times together too now were we in rest: but Fate has willed it otherwise: after this rest we shall face the music – for that I'm thankful you're not here. The Bn. is now overstrength in officers so unless anything unforeseen happens it doesn't seem as if we shall come together out here does it? Overhead my platoon are snoring, tossing restlessly about and coughing: it is a farrago with one or two brilliant flowers in it. We come to blows occasionally too so I'm not beloved of the multitude. Our training here is very like that in England and all next week we've got Bn. days to be followed by Brigade Days. But this is all compensated by the glorious tranquillity and secure feeling of this place. It is beautiful too but no one cares for ought save cards, whiskey and other things. This morning as Orderly Officer I had to take Early parade at 7. As I was walking down the path to the field I saw the most wonderful sunrise I've ever seen. It was almost dark and low down in the sky was a deep orange colour with purple bars across it and then deep masses of purple clouds as I looked higher up the sky. . . As it was quite dark the effect was wonderful. Turning round to the right I saw the full moon shining brilliantly with some lavender coloured blurry clouds below it: a patch of deep blue above, with a lonely star high up in it. I walked on and saw the black forms of the Co[mpan]y. And when I had given orders for parade I stood and watched the day come in – the orange turned slowly to bright yellow and then Light came.

But enough of this . . . I haven't half enough guts for modern warfare and Shaw who was absolutely fearless was hit by a sniper on Christmas Eve. He was the son of the Bishop of Buckingham, I think it was, and a topping chap. Why all the best men go West is an unfathomable mystery isn't it?

Could you send me a copy of 'L'Envoi', when you get time I should like one a lot. Well old man in 2 mins more it will be Sabbath and my eyes are revolting so I'll say goodnight & roll into bed – I wrote now so that I could get a quiet hour not amongst the smell of sizzling bacon or other cooking aromas!

Cheeryo.

Sunday morning
10.40

Have just come in from Church Parade which was humorous but it is hard to think of things celestial when just by your side there is a bevy of cooks of an amusing trait of character peeling and eating carrots! Also it was with the utmost difficulty we heard anything. The moon brought with her a frost last night and today there is brilliant sunshine which is most cheering.

Bentley & I go for runs every evening to keep fit. I've got a black and white striped shirt with black bags and look most ghoulish!

Have you ever read 'Miss Esperance and Mr Wycherly'? It is a charming book especially if you like children . . . Hope to get up a scratch game of soccer with the men this afternoon: wish we'd played Rugger at school as there are games here among the officers . . . Chigwell went back last Friday . . . How I wish we could have our School life over again . . .

Later 6.10 p.m.

Summoned enough courage to play soccer with some men this afternoon. We played 'sixes' and won 4–2. It was a glorious afternoon & topping playing. I do wish from a purely selfish point of view that you were here.

We as a nation seem to be bungling through pretty thoroughly at present don't we? The fuss made over Derby's men in the papers quite infuriates one out here.

Dinner is in preparation here and so the usual accompanying smells.

Have just been reading the programme of the School Concert:-

> *'But manfully do your own duty*
> *Tho' you never be known to Fame.'*

. . . This must be very boring to you so I will end with the wish that it will not be long before we see each other.

In Life, in Death,
Yours

Geoffrey R. Y. T.

I feel that this letter is very badly expressed but you know what I mean to say.

Vera to Edward

Tar says He always used to say that our one hope of salvation as a nation lay in a Great War, & if He had said this to me I should certainly have agreed with him. I do condemn War in theory most strongly, as I suppose everyone who is not a lunatic or a fanatic does, but there are some things worse than even War, & I believe even wholesale murder to be preferable to atrophy & effeteness. It is better to do active harm & definite wrong than just to drift and make no effort in any direction; Dante gives a more tragic Inferno to the souls who earned neither praise nor blame than even to Brutus & Judas. And when the War in question is a War *on* War, all the usual objections are changed into the opposite commendations. . .

Did Mother tell you that I am thinking of giving up this place when my six months are up, & possibly not going on with nursing any more? It is not just that, much as I have always hated nursing, I now detest it so much that I can scarcely do it well at all, as that I must have a month or two's freedom in which to think things out & reconstruct life. Life has been shattered into fragments even more than I thought – how much, I realise more & more every day. And I am beginning to realise, too, that my existence won't be of much use either to myself or anybody else till I have had time to pick the fragments up & reshape them again. Here I am just a mechanical vegetable with no time to think on anything but just go on feeling vaguely miserable with no energy behind & no light ahead. And everything is so exactly the same as it was before, which brings it all back so vividly; it seems unendurable that everything should be the same. Moreover I am beginning to feel I am not really necessary. The whole place swarms with V.A.Ds – it is the only thing most girls can do, & Devonshire House has so many it is always sending us people we don't in the least require. Not everyone can do as well, perhaps, as Stella & me, but they don't particularly want you to be as good as all that; there is no chance of promotion, no increase of pay *ever*, no seniority even over people who only came yesterday – a more hopeless cul-de-sac I never came across. Practically anyone can be moulded into a nurse good enough to serve the purpose. And I am beginning to feel that I am quite thrown away on a job anybody can do, instead of finding something in which my brains & education will be of some value. If nurses were urgently required I would say nothing, but there are too many, & since no amount of good work can make you into a Sister or into anything different from what you are to start with, as time goes on there will be too many still more. And since there are other things which, in order that the Country & the War can go on, it is necessary for women to do, would I not be better in one of these? Que dit-tu? Anyhow, I propose to have my holiday – which I really feel I need, – & look round. If Father & Mother bicker much more it may be really necessary to earn one's living, too – and as I have no longer marriage to look forward to as an ultimate fate, I am thrown on my beam ends again. A girl can do so much more from a purely practical point of view when a man shares her life & goes about with her; it is harder to do things alone. I don't propose to go back to college while the War lasts, or do other work than war-work. But since this war seems likely to be interminable, it seems it would be better to find something to do which if it does not further, at least does not hinder, as this does, my ultimate object in life. I want to discuss it when we meet.

We have been expecting Zeppelins all night – warned they were coming, lights very low etc. But nothing as yet (3.30 a.m.) has turned up. Still, now they have started again & can get to Kent, it is only a question of waiting for them, I suppose – and London will become the next most dangerous place to the Front. As they want the Arsenal, 10 to 1 they'll find their way here instead. Possibly a raid that blew up the whole place, one's self included, would be an easy answer to many problems. But I suppose it is a pity to die or want to as long as there is even one person left who desires one's life.

Victor to Vera

Kent, 26 January 1916

Thank you very much for your letter which has just come. I feel that I must answer it at once, if only to allay as far as I can the agony of grief that His servant's letter must have caused you. It is hardly necessary, I think, for me to say how deeply I feel for you and I fully realise what you must be suffering.

I may say, in the first place, that I did not believe for a moment anything that was suggested or implied in that letter with regard to the circumstances under which He met His death. But to make quite sure I described what happened to one of our subalterns who spent six months in the trenches as an N.C.O. with the Queen Victoria's Rifles, and who was himself employed as a sniper. What he told me coincided exactly with my own views on all essential points; these views I will now try to explain. In the first place the wire in front of the trenches has to be kept in good order under all circumstances. The fact that there was a bright moon early in the night would not prevent the enemy making an attack later on in the night, or at dawn; and there is always the chance that if the wire was down they might get through, especially as any weak spots would have been marked down in daylight. This view would almost certainly be held by the officer responsible for the defence of the sector – quite probably Col. Harman himself, especially as he says he was speaking with Roland 20 minutes before. On the other hand the men – that is if I understand their point of view, as I hope I do – would say 'it's a very bright night and the blighters have been very quiet lately: no fear of their doing anything. Leave well alone and don't go asking for trouble'. I don't mean they would actually say this, but it would be there subconsciously, and anything like the death of one they loved would bring it out, and they would probably be very bitter about it. Now we know that Col. Harman was very much attached to Roland, and moreover we know nothing to suggest that he was not a man of ordinary intelligence and common-sense. And I was always convinced that Roland's own extraordinary nous would bring him safely through – in fact I remember writing and telling His Mother so when He first went out. I think therefore that we may safely assume that the work had to be done that night. As to whether it was absolutely essential for Him to go out Himself is, I think, very doubtful... But He was always eager to do everything himself, however small, in order that it should be done thoroughly; and moreover His was not the nature to allow another man, especially an inferior, to run a risk that He would not take Himself. I have not the faintest doubt that this noble quality was chiefly responsible for the enormous influence he had with all ranks. I remember he told me at Liverpool Street that day that 'the men always know whether an officer is afraid or not. The man who doesn't care a damn they will follow anywhere. But the man who shows the slightest hesitation will never get his men to follow him at all'. I think it should fill us with unspeakable pride that He was worthy of the best traditions of the old Regular Army – the best and bravest in the whole World. I feel it would be better to rejoice than to regret. At least that is how He would wish it. If I go out, my one hope will be to be worthy of Him: it will be very hard indeed...

I find I have not half answered your letter, but I shall stop now as I want you to get this as soon as possible. If you would care to I think I could meet you again next Wednesday as I am still waiting for a Medical Board: in any case I am fairly certain to be still here all next week.

Vera to Edward

1st London General Hospital, 27 January 1916

I enclose this enlargement from the camp group. Don't you think it is very good? I do; it gives an excellent idea of all of you. Roland looks like a desperate poet; Victor is very much Sir Galahad gazing after the Holy Grail; and you are – just you, with a *very* slight touch of the bedside manner. Anyhow, I am glad the only photo of the Three Musketeers is worth having. I have sent a copy to Mrs Leighton, also to Victor.

I got two letters yesterday which, except in the sentiments they expressed, were a striking illustration in contrasts. One was from

Roland's servant; the other from a Captain Adshead who was a subaltern in the same company as Roland when they first went to the front. They seem to have been great friends, for although as far as I remember Roland never mentioned him, yet He took him a good deal into His confidence & showed him my photograph. Captain Adshead is engaged too, so perhaps that was the reason, & it is the reason also why he sympathises so much with me.

The servant's letter is very quaint & pathetic; I have at the moment sent it on to Mrs Leighton, but you shall see it when I get it back. He had been His servant ever since He joined the Worcesters, & had accompanied Him everywhere even to the VIIth Corps Headquarters & the Somersets. The man seems very much distressed & lost without Him. He says he loved Him dearly & that they were such good friends he feels he has lost a brother, & can't believe He is really gone but that He must be only away on long leave. He gives all the details of His death, but I knew them mostly before & the letter is valuable to me more as a tribute to Him than as a source of fresh information. He does say, though, that in his opinion Roland ought never to have risked going out in front of the line as there was bright moonlight that night & the Germans, who were only 100 yards away, must have been able to see Him with ease. That gives one a little light. Somehow it is all too like Roland in his more rash moods. One can believe that He had been safe so long & trusted in his own luck so entirely that He was beginning to trust it a little too much. And He should have been *so* careful that last day of all. Yet it is so like Him to have allowed recklessness to overcome prudence just the one time it would be fatal, & to be all the readier to take the risk just when it was greatest. . . The man also says He was hit by a sniper, which hardly tallies with the Colonel's statement that the Germans opened fire from some fixed rifles. Perhaps he thought we should mind more if we knew it was a sniper, though goodness knows why we should; one German bullet is as deadly as another. Certainly the vital position of the wound seems to suggest a sniper's careful aim rather than an accidental bullet. The servant says too that he 'must admit' that Roland was the most beloved officer in the whole regiment. This letter altogether is a rare tribute to an officer & His power of inspiring others' deep regard.

Captain Adshead's letter is long & perfectly charming. I will quote some of it to you. . . 'I was returning from leave when I heard the awful news – my thoughts at once were of you and his mother . . . I wish I had been with the battalion at the time for then I might have seen every detail and perhaps been able to tell you of every little thing that happened until he died. But I have enquired of several people including our medical officer, who got him away. From each I found out that he was cheery up to the last – he was as conscious as I am now. He said he was in no pain at all – only cold – and by and by he said he felt comfortable – and the doctor tells me that he certainly did not think he was going to die. He talked to everyone around him quite in the ordinary way. Then he was taken to the hospital and after several hours was operated upon & seemed to survive it well. What happened afterwards I cannot quite understand – it is a technical reason that I do not understand. As far as I can find out, he seemed comfortable but very weak – though perfectly conscious and still under the same impression that he was not badly hurt. And then it seems he passed away quite quickly & without word or warning of any kind . . . If only I had been here I might have been able to find out something or he might have given me some message for you. But I can find none at all. I hope you will take comfort when you know that his was not a lonely death – that all the officers & *men* felt it so keenly. Do not feel that he was lonely – & yet he must have been, for my last wish before I die would be to have my mother and my girl with me before I went.' . . .

I really think now we have found out pretty nearly all about His end that is to be gleaned. He obviously had not the slightest suspicion – and one can scarcely even blame the doctor for not telling Him as they appear to have been startled by what happened.

Edward's last leaves had been legion. But finally, after many delays and false alarms, he received his orders to go out to France to join the 11th Sherwood Foresters. On 10 February 1916, Vera and Mrs Brittain saw him off at Charing Cross.

Victor to Vera

Kent, 8 February 1916

I am glad for Edward's sake that he is going out now, as I think he wants to; but it is very difficult to be pleased that anyone one loves is going out there. I am afraid you must all be feeling terribly anxious. I do not of course know where he is going: I only hope he does not go to the Ypres salient or anywhere like that, though I believe he would sooner go there to the 10th than to his own unit. I suppose there is no chance of Salonika or Egypt.

I want to thank you again and again for your last letter: I have tried to answer it before, but I am an indifferent letter writer and this is the third attempt! I am sure you know what it must mean to me if I can be of any comfort or help to you at all. I feel that in a way it helps me to repay a little of the great debt I owe to Him. For He, as you say, would have been most grieved if He could have known what you must suffer on His account. And I somehow think that He would have thought me the right person to whom you could talk about Him.

Victor to Vera

Kent, 15 February 1916

I am wondering what battalion Edward has gone to. I know he wants to go to the 10th near Ypres because he says the Colonel of the 11th dislikes him... I seem to remember now that he told me his great friend from the 11th went to the 10th, and of course that would be quite enough to make him wish to go to them too.

... I don't think I have ever seen Edward so happy and cheerful since the War started, as he was last Wednesday. I had a very nice letter from your Mother on Saturday, and she said he went off in high spirits. I am so glad of that, because I am sure all that sort of thing is so absolutely essential in an officer out there. I always think that with Roland, the gaiety and geniality of His personality must have been almost as great an asset as His devotion and thoroughness. . . Mrs Leighton said when I went there the week before last, that it was very extraordinary that we three should have been such great friends, as we were all so unlike each other. I don't think I have ever realised the truth of this before. Another strange thing was that when we were all three together we often did not get on at all. It was the more strange because any two of us were linked more closely together by affection for the third. I am afraid I was largely to blame. Edward was always so much cleverer than I was, and I think I may have been a little jealous of him where Roland was concerned. . .

I hope you do not mind my writing like this about the three of us, but you know that our friendship is the most valued thing I have ever had, or ever will [have], and now that you are His representative it seems natural to talk to you about it.

Vera to Edward
                    1st London General Hospital, 16 February 1916

Mother has shown me the little note you wrote saying you were going into the trenches. It seems such a short time since you left Charing Cross, but it must seem ages to you, and you must feel so far away from us all. I used to be able to imagine Roland in the trenches quite well – but it seems quite absurd that you should be there, you whom I can remember in a brown holland overall, crying because I threw a dead moth behind the couch! I do hope you will find a little time one day soon to tell me what your first impression of the firing line was. I should like to compare it with His. He said He was not afraid – but I cannot really see how one can help being afraid, even if one cares little for life. And I don't think the fact that you have had a long time to think about and prepare for it can make very much difference when you do actually get there – it must be so very different from anything else one has ever seen or done. . .

I feel very lonely now you have gone; the days seem to drag more and to be longer than ever. I only wish my duty were as obvious as yours; one's duty is certainly the only thing left to do, but it is a little difficult when one is not quite sure what one's duty is.

―――――――

Edward to Vera
                11th Sherwood Foresters, B.E.F., France, 16 February 1916

...We took 54 hours only to get into the front line trenches from when we left England. We were rushed through the base in 24 hours and crawled slowly up the country by train and went 5 miles from railhead in a London motor bus and after some trouble found our Qr Mr [Quarter Master] who gave us something to eat and we set off for the trenches in an hour and a half. I was never more surprised at anything than I was at the trenches but of course I cannot tell you why. I am bound really to omit all the most interesting things and so I have asked Mother to send me a diary...

It is quite easy for me now to understand how Roland was killed; it was quite ordinary but just unlucky. Something rather similar happened to Vincent Jackson whose name you may have seen in the list as Missing Believed Killed, only in his case the circumstances were more tragic because it might have been alright if the Corporal who was with him had not lost his head. V-J was hit in the leg and the Corporal immediately started to carry him back to the trench instead of waiting a bit. Of course they were seen by the Germans, fired on, and V-J was hit again 2 or 3 times and also the Corporal was hit in the hand. He then dropped V-J because he said he couldn't hold him any longer and got back himself, but the Germans got Vincent Jackson and though many of the men think he is not dead, I'm afraid there is little chance of his being alive. Some say that the Germans showed a spade above their parapet shortly afterwards as though to imply that they had buried him, but it is all rather gruesome. Life has become extraordinarily cheap. That happened about 10 days before I arrived. V-J was a very decent fellow, a scholar of Oriel, and got on rather well with Thurlow in former days.

―――――――

Vera to Edward

1st London General Hospital, 19–20 February 1916

I received your most interesting letter written on the 16th this morning, which was quite quick; Roland's nearly always took longer. It quite thrilled me to read it; just as when I read His first letter from the trenches it made me wish desperately that I were a man and could train myself to play that 'Great Game with Death' – I wish it were *my* obvious duty to 'go and live in a ditch', as Roland called it. But you roused my interest and curiosity very much. I want immensely to know what it was about the trenches that surprised you so. Couldn't you write to me more fully & explicitly & not censor it yourself? I should imagine that censoring your own letters must make you almost over conscientious; I know it would me. Roland, I remember, when He wrote long explanatory letters, used to get them censored by someone else, and I don't remember anything ever being cut out. I want to know, too, exactly what it all looks like before you actually step into the trench. Is it just two rows of ditches & nothing more – or are there ruins & things about? And are there always a lot of shells & things bursting, like you see in Punch cartoons? I am glad you are going to keep a diary – it is what I always tried to make Him do, and never succeeded. For one thing I think He was always so confident He would be alive at the end of it all & then be able to tell us as much about it as He wished.

I wonder if you really take it as calmly as you seem to in your letter. Yes, life must seem quite a small thing after all – but in spite of everything, I don't think I want you to hold it cheap, or to forget all else you meant to do. *He* never lost sight of His original aims & though He was so fearless, I don't think He ever really held life cheap; He combined a great indifference to death with a passionate love of life. If life seems a little thing to you yourself, remember it is not so to other people, even though they may seem far away; I shall have little enough left if you 'follow where all is fled', and Victor said the other day that if the War took you as well as Roland, he would not have any desire left to live himself. I would like to think of you as never forgetting that one day the War will end and the things that used to matter will matter

again; even if you are not to see them I still think it is better to
remember, for otherwise your work & life is lived only for the
moment and not for all time. And as the effects of this War will be
for all time the people who are playing their part in it will play
that part for all time too, and to remember this seems to make
one's lot – whether it be life or work or horror or death – so
much more worth while.

20/2/16

Victor, to my great delight, has taken to writing me long letters
about you three. I am learning a good deal. Incidentally, he has
instituted himself my 'Father Confessor' as he always used to be
that to Roland, and wants me to write to him about things in
general whenever I feel specially lonely and depressed. I wonder
where you derived your talent for choosing friends. Not from
Father or Mother, certainly. Your capacity for choice is better than
mine; at any rate the most momentous people in my life seem to
have been selected for me by you, or through you.

_____

Victor to Vera

Kent, 21 February 1916

I have been thinking things over since I saw you, and I am more
firmly convinced than ever that you should give up nursing and
take up something that will give scope to your ability. . .

I am writing so soon after seeing you, because I have had time
to think the problem over, and I have become more firmly convinced than I was last night, that you have not been defeated. At
the same time I am sure that your own agony and feeling of desolation have brought out those more tender and human qualities
that you once delighted in suppressing. . . And again if you told
me that pride made you seek more congenial and satisfactory
work than nursing, I should believe you unhesitatingly. It has been
at times hard for me to stay here doing an old man's work. It is not
that I want to go to the trenches: it is merely pride. But few

people, except such specimens as my Colonel, would blame me for it. Why then should anyone blame you for wishing to give up nursing? We each wish to be more useful: that is all.

Vera to Edward

1st London General Hospital, 23 February 1916

I have just seen this casualty list in the 'Times', with the kind of shock that the expected gives one when it actually happens. When a cursory glance informed me that 10th Sherwood Foresters predominated in the list of regiments, I looked at once for one of the few names that I always think of when reading the Roll of Honour, and saw that Thurlow had been wounded – I suppose in the recent fighting at Ypres. I have almost loved him since his little letter to me after Roland died, and I can't tell you how anxiously I hope that he is not badly hurt and that his name won't appear in the same part of the list as Roland's did. Perhaps you know all about this already – it is a week since it happened; but news travels slowly at the front, I know. Roland never heard of Garrod's death till I told him. . .

[Colonel Harman] has told [Mrs Leighton] a little more about Roland but nothing that gives us any more personal knowledge of his last hours or makes things any better. Roland's death, as you said, was due to something quite usual but unlucky. They had just taken over some new, unfamiliar trenches & Capt. Adam's company had their time in the trenches the first 24 hours; they were the first 7th Worcesters to enter them. As you doubtless know by this time, after a battalion has been some time in the trenches, it appears they get to know the chief danger spots, either by experience or by information they receive from the Bn. they are relieving. Apparently the Germans are a very precise sort of enemy who get certain spots where there is likely to be activity settled in their minds, & fire at these spots at fixed times. . . Roland's death was caused partly by bad luck, partly by the negligence or carelessness of the relieving Bn. to inform the 7th Worcesters that this was a danger spot. . .

We have a lot of fresh information, too, about the actual wound itself. It was anything but a clean bullet wound straight through, as we have been thinking; it was a terrible affair. Col. Harman would not actually use the word 'explosive bullet' – I suppose it is against etiquette in some way or another but he did say that 'the bullet exploded.' His actual words were 'The bullet exploded inside him & literally blew out his back.' . . . The dressing of Roland's wound took 20 to 30 minutes but Capt. Sheridan, the doctor, knelt beside Him & did it as calmly & deliberately as if in Hospital; he hurried nothing & left nothing out. But he said when he saw the state He was in that no man with any humane feelings left could bear to handle Him at all unless He were rendered almost immune from feeling, so they gave Him a very large dose of morphia indeed – and as far as we are concerned the Roland we knew really died then . . .

He was taken to Louvencourt in a motor ambulance, but as He had not to be shaken at all, the motor had to go at a snail's pace. Even so, it was because the journey had so much exhausted Him that the op. could not be done at once; they say He was very white & weak from the very beginning & particularly so when He arrived at the Hospital. The operation when it did occur was very severe indeed – even more so than we thought – when I tell you that an ordinary operation for appendicitis takes 20 minutes you will realise what kind of a one this was, for it lasted 2 hrs and ¼ . . . when they opened His back, old hands at it as they were, Barling & Wilkinson simply looked at one another & gasped . . . they could not remember any wound quite so terrible. Under the surface the whole of his back was literally smashed to pulp, so that the different organs were barely recognisable . . .

This letter has been written in the V.A.D. sitting-room, at tea, at supper, & in bed, so please excuse repetitions & incoherencies. It is so cold to-night – how cold *you* must be. When you write please tell me all the sorts of dangers you are in apart from a charge – give me a list of what the actual & possible perils of the trenches are & the times you chiefly incur them.

———————

Edward to Vera

11th Sherwood Foresters, France, 27 February 1916

As it is usually too cold to write in the trenches to which we return to-night I am writing a short note now. By the way I want to keep the letters you send me and so I shall send them back to you just as Roland did in case I should lose them here. . . I was very interested in all the information which Colonel Harman was able to supply and it all seems very terrible, though a perfectly ordinary occurrence with regard to the way in which it happened. We do very much the same here in relieving trenches as most of the communication trenches are full of water and so we have to use emergency roads across the open when rifle and machine gun fire may open on us at any moment; there are many danger spots but they continually change and so we just take our chance; we shall be doing so to-night. Also when we are in the front line itself there are various danger places where the trench is open to enfilade fire . . . Ordinary risks of stray shots or ricochets off a sandbag or the chance of getting hit when you look over the parapet in the night time – you hardly ever do in the day time but use periscopes – are daily to be encountered. But far the most dangerous thing is going out on patrol in No Man's Land. You take bombs in case you should meet a hostile patrol, but you might be surrounded, you might be seen especially if you go very close to their line and anyhow Very lights are always being sent up and they make night into day so you have to keep down and quite still, and you might get almost on top of their listening post if you are not sure where it is. I was out with my Sergt. and 2 men last Monday night about midnight for about 1½ hours.

The trenches surprised me so much because they are not trenches but breastwork made almost entirely of sandbags in millions, not dug in at all, and there is consequently no real system of communication trenches and the supports are in billets under shell fire but hardly close enough to prevent the Germans getting the front line any time they attacked. . . [There] are ruins all about the trenches and many places knocked about for some miles back. I do not hold life cheap at all and it is hard to be sufficiently brave,

yet I have hardly ever felt really afraid. One has to keep up appear-
ances at all costs even if one is.

Victor to Vera

Kent, 27 February 1916

I saw from the casualty lists that the 10th Sherwoods had been
having a stiff time. I was very sorry to see that Thurlow had been
hit, but still hope that it is nothing serious. I never realised that
Edward was so fond of him, as he has never told me much about
him. Perhaps you will tell me more about him, and also how he is
getting on. Is he older than Edward or the same age? I wish I
knew him. I hope he does not get well enough in time to go back
for the great offensive. . .

As far as one can tell the Verdun offensive is intended to antic-
ipate and overthrow our own, as did the Galician offensive last
year. But this year we are ready. Is it too much to hope that our
sacrifices will not be made in vain?

Another thing: if you continue nursing till October, you will
have served your Country for close on a year and a half: you will
have spent a year of that time in a great London hospital. Anyone
who knows anything knows what that entails, and a woman who
will face that work for a year – the last nine months under the
most cruel circumstances possible – deserves everyone's respect
and gratitude.

Vera to Edward

1st London General Hospital, 27 February 1916

I have just been to see Thurlow at Fishmongers' Hall Hospital,
London Bridge. He is only very slightly wounded on the left side
of his face; fortunately his eyes, nose & mouth are quite
untouched. In fact he says he won't even have a scar left, and the
wound is healing with a depressing rapidity. The dressing was only

strapped, not even bandaged, on. But he was in bed, and says he had not even been allowed to walk to the bathroom until to-day, so I think he must be suffering from shock as well, although he says nothing about it. He did not look ill at all, only a little tired. He was apparently wounded in the bombardment, before all the trench fighting began. He thinks hardly any of his battalion are left now.

I don't know whether he was at all pleased to see me. We were both very shy – at any rate I know I was, and shyness always makes me speak quite lightly about things of which I think anything but lightly, and I think it makes him too. We might have been less shy had we been alone, but there was another officer there all the time, a school friend of his who had come to see him too, and it is always slightly embarrassing to carry on a conversation in the presence of a silent third person...

I only stayed with him about half-an-hour; he was very interesting to talk to and I like him very much, as you know, but I felt sure he would much rather talk to the school friend than to me, and visiting hours at a Hospital are of course limited. He thinks he will be off duty about another month, and of course doesn't know whether he will return to the 10th. He might get sent to the 11th just as much. If he is still at that hospital on Thursday I shall probably go with Mother to see him again.

I have still more to tell you about Roland – and in a way these last details are much more important than any we have heard. At least they are to us, as they tell us about the last moments of the real Roland, before the morphia blotted out more than half his personality. We heard this last because a day or two ago Captain Adam himself came home on leave and telegraphed to Mrs Leighton from Southampton, hoping she might be able to come up to London at once & meet him. Owing to work or something she was not able to go, but Mr Leighton was going up anyhow, and he met him.

It seems that on the fatal night a man rushed up to Captain Adam crying out 'Mr Leighton's hit, Sir, and it's serious.' Adam at once ran out and found Roland lying on His face on the ground, throwing his arms about violently but incapable of moving his lower body or his legs. Adam knelt beside him (bullets were flying around them all the time) and said 'It's alright, dear old fellow; where are you hit?' Roland said 'Is that you, Adam? They've got me in the stomach, and it's bad – it's bad.' Then Adam tried to lift Him & said 'Can you manage to put your arms round my neck, and help yourself up a little, if you can?' Roland did put His arms round Adam's neck, and with the sergeant supporting His legs they got Him down into the trench. Far from being in no pain He was writhing all the time in most intense agony, but He never even groaned. Then they gave Him the morphia – and you know the rest. He never spoke again before getting the morphia except to say once more 'They got me in the stomach, and it's bad.'

I don't know what you will feel about this story – this final story relating to the first part. I knew they must be keeping something back when they said He suffered *no* pain. It scarcely seemed possible. We know now that in those few minutes of sensible consciousness, he faced the Truth – faced the fact that He was wounded in a vital spot, faced agony, more than probably faced death itself. He got with a grim exactness the answer to the prayer-poem for 'a strong man's agony.' And it was as a strong man that He bore it, and we can say of Him after all that 'the old strong soul gathered itself for the last time; it knew where it stood.' . . .

Well, one of the things this final part of Roland's story has made me feel is that as long as the War lasts, unless you or anyone else should for some reason or other need me and me only really badly, I cannot lead any but an active life, even though it should last for five years. After all He has been through, after all you may go through, & Victor and others, I *cannot*, even with the best motives in the world, shut myself up behind scholastic walls & behave as if I were forgetting the War. No, it must be some form of active service, and if it implies discomforts, so much the better. I am beginning to feel that to leave nursing now would be defeat – and since He was unconquerable, the person He loved ought to be unconquerable too, n'est-ce pas? Nations may fall, & religions may fail, and there may be a Hereafter & there may not – but amid all these things, amid death & grief and disaster & danger, the mind of man is unconquerable, if it choose. So I am beginning to feel – vaguely & unwillingly, it is true – that to leave this hospital, even though I hate it, would be defeat. I am beginning to think I shall not leave it, except of course for one reason, & that is if I got the chance of War-work of any kind abroad, preferably France. Otherwise, if I don't get any chance, I ought to stick to it, let it cost me what it will. That's one thing that Roland's agony has made me feel. No one He loved must be unworthy of Him. . .

The other thing I feel is that if I ever in life have any great physical pain to bear, I shall bear it ten thousand times better for knowing that 'He was writhing in the most intense agony, but He never even groaned.'

Victor to Vera

Kent, 2 March 1916

I am sorry I cannot meet you on Sunday . . . as I am going home on leave to-morrow before going to Hythe on Monday for a Musketry and Lewis gun course . . .

I don't know if you have heard, but I have had a letter from my brother to say that Carey has been killed. He was a great friend of the Musketeers, especially of Edward's. I have of course written to Edward: it will be a terrible shock to him. It is strange how this War singles out the best, and leaves the others. Is it because the best are the bravest, or are the Fates jealous of them? Puckle made a speech about Carey and said he was an especial friend of Roland's. He also said that there were in the House at that time, several friendships he considered quite remarkable.

Your details from Capt. Adam about Roland came as a great shock to me. They could hardly have been more terrible, especially now that we know the real nature of the wound. Yet I cannot help feeling that those twenty minutes were the consummation of His whole life – that He had always lived in preparation for that ordeal.

Vera to Edward

1st London General Hospital, 5 March 1916

I have been to see Thurlow twice since I last wrote to you – Thursday afternoon with Mother and this afternoon by myself. I did not stay very long to-day, though, as his mother & sister turned up when I had been there about an hour, but on Thursday we stayed for tea. Both times I found him most interesting; we had quite long discussions and I think he has quite got over his shyness of me. I should not have gone again to-day but that when I said good-bye on Thursday he asked me to come again before he went, which is to-morrow. On Thursday & to-day he was up, sitting before a gas stove, with a green dressing gown on and a brown blanket over his knees. He seems to feel the cold a great deal, which must be owing to the shock, and also for the same reason his nerves are very bad, so he has been given two months sick leave. He has not to go to a convalescent home, so is going to his own home to-morrow.

But he said to-day that he would come up to town when he is able to walk about all right, and take me to a concert. I don't think he can dislike me, as he doesn't strike one as being the kind of person who would pretend to want to see someone he didn't.

Of course he doesn't want to go back a bit, but since he has to go, he's got the same feeling as he had before, that he wants to go out quickly and get it over. He says he finds the anticipation so much worse than the things themselves, whatever they are. He says he is not a bit of a success out there because he is so afraid of being afraid, and he hates the way all his men's eyes are fixed on him when anything big is on, partly to see how he will take it, partly because they are afraid of anything happening to him. He says he objects to War on principle, & is a non-militarist very strongly at heart. I think it was very brave of him to join almost at once as he did. . . It is easy to see he is suffering from shock; he looks rather a ghost now he is sitting up, talks even more jerkily than before, & works his fingers about nervously while he is talking. . .

I had a letter from Victor yesterday: he is going to Hythe for a month for a musketry course. After that he hopes to get a better chance of going to the front; the final facts about Roland have made him more anxious to go than ever. He tells me that Puckle made a speech to the House about Carey, and also brought in Roland. Among other things he said that Roland and Carey were friends when they were at school together, & that there were one or two very remarkable friendships in the House just about that time. The reference to the Three Musketeers is obvious.

Edward to Vera

France, 5th March 1916

I was extremely sorry to hear about Carey for though not brilliant in any way he was trustworthy and reliable and very straight as a friend should be; we were very friendly my last year but one at Uppingham, did a great deal of our work together, and – more important still – spent a lot of our spare time together. I remember well how often we used to play fives together on the Bath Courts (which you know) and on our own court in our quad. It is as you say that the best of Uppingham will soon be on its chapel walls. Promise me one thing – that, should I die also, you will nevertheless go down to Uppingham, preferably with Tah if it be that he may be allowed to live, but if not that you will go at all events, and see those chapel walls and the Lodge and the Upper VIth Class room where we all sat so often.

Vera to Edward

1st London General Hospital, 8 March 1916

Every time I see your writing on the envelope it gives me a sudden sense of relief – because life would be so little worth while if you went too.

Yes – I *will* go to Uppingham, either with you, or if it must be, without you, after the War. . .

I have just volunteered for foreign service, by the way. Yesterday a list was put up asking for names of Sisters & V.A.Ds who would volunteer for foreign service if required. So I put my name down; in fact the majority of us have. It does not in the least mean that we are likely to go soon; in fact there is no special point except to find out who will go if called upon. The first draft from here to include V.A.Ds since the War began has only just been informed that it may be required at some future date; there are only six V.A.Ds in this, and they the first who came here – and of course lots came after them and before me. They even may not go for ages so it doesn't seem likely that any of us will be called yet; of course it largely depends on how the War goes, and if – as is probably the case – there is to be a great deal of fighting on the Western front, they would not be able to spare us from here. But if the War goes on long enough I suppose we should be called up sometime within the next year; I wish, if the call comes for me, it could be to France, because I should like to be near you – and Roland. But of course it is equally likely to be to Egypt, or India or Salonika, or Malta or Alexandria – which would be interesting enough, but I would rather, if I move at all, be a little nearer to the actual fighting than I am here, and of course at those places one wouldn't be.

But if I escape Zeppelins at home, and torpedoes, enteric or dysentery abroad, I promise you to go to Uppingham on behalf of us all . . . And as I told you before you went out, if the War spares me, it will be my one aim to immortalise in a book the story of us four, with the friendship of the Three Musketeers playing so large a part . . . Just as you, if you come through, will immortalise it all in music. Oh! if it could only *end*! We are all so weary.

Geoffrey to Edward

Eversley, Buckhurst Hill, Essex, 10 March 1916

Your sister came in to see me last Sunday afternoon but when Mother and Bite turned up she went. Asked her to go to Queens Hall with me on Saturday . . . Yes! The Board seemed to think I was ill and gave me two months sick leave from March 1st. Nearly everyone in the village seems to express regret that I'm not minus an ear nose or eye – they're a cheery crowd. . . Isn't it beastly when you can't keep warm and have to shiver and shiver – you must have been cold too lately as it's absolutely bloody: often I think of you and my men, – all that remain – out there. Shouldn't think you get the wind up at all. Personally was an excellent washout as I got very alarmed once or twice. . . Have never been on a patrol but should think they're rotten kind of things to be on. Found it was very much a matter as to how you got on with your Co[mpan]y Cmdr whether you went out often – do you find that so? . . .

One wonders why it is that the men go on and the half men usually are left: there must be a reason for it . . .

Last Tuesday there was a memorial service to the Old Boys at School who have finished the fight and I cabbed over to it: it was jolly being back again at the School. But why should I talk of all these things when you are probably damned cold in the trenches. Heigho! In many ways I should have said 'some ways'! I'm longing to get back as nearly everyone I know is out there. . .

> *'Goodnight, sweet prince, goodnight:*
> *Till life and all take flight.*
> *Never goodbye.'*

Thine.

Gryt

Edward to Vera

In the Trenches, France, 15 March 1916

Thank you very much for your letter and for Ave atque Vale which is extraordinarily good. I was very interested to hear all about Thurlow and I am glad he is going to take you to a concert. We came in last night and one of our officers – Teahan – was hit in the face by a rifle bullet while we were relieving in a communication trench. He might lose the sight of an eye ... he is a Canadian and in this company.

Edward to Vera

France, 29 March–2 April 1916

We are now within about 20 miles of Roland and will soon be much nearer still. It is very strange that we should have done much the same as he did last year. Though we are now in a picturesque little white town some way back we shall be in the trenches again very soon. . .

★ ★ ★ ★ ★

Sunday April 2nd 1916

I was interrupted just then by the old French woman on whom we were billeted; she wanted to know how she could get compensation for damage done by some of our people last November. After a conversation carried on with considerable difficulty – though my French is improving – for about an hour and a half, I at last persuaded her to go having told her about a dozen times that what troops did last November did not affect my company and she would only get satisfaction through applying to the Mayor. . .

This place is about 2 miles from the line and fairly knocked about. The church has a very tall spire (or rather the French equivalent for spire) with a brass or gilded figure of the Virgin with the Child in her arms on the top. However a shell presumably passing very close or else partially striking the statue has knocked it over so that it now leans forward almost horizontal to the ground far below and is only held there by the metal flanges by which it was originally fixed on the top of the spire. The other part of the church has been shelled a good deal but of course they don't knock the spire or any tall chimney down as they are useful to range on. The hitting of the statue was probably a mistake or else a very good shot. As you pass underneath the great big statue leaning over the road a long way above it seems extraordinary that it doesn't fall. If it did or if the spire was hit I'm afraid there would be a lot of casualties as people are always walking about there; it is just the middle of a town...

The country is greatly improved about here compared to what it was further north, and I am glad that Roland should have this broad, well cultivated, undulating land, which is by nature very peaceful, as His home. The country is really beautiful in its own way and though it has a certain sameness in its numerous fields it is far different from that wearying land where He and I have both been before. I think you and Mrs Leighton will be glad as I am. The sun set last night in a red glow over Him as I looked from here, giving a sense of the most perfect and enduring peace in spite of war.

Of course the trenches are very different here – chalk for one thing, and many other things too: but it is far better.

Vera to Edward
1st London General Hospital, 30 March 1916

I went with Thurlow to a most delightful concert at Queen's Hall last Saturday. I enclose the programme in case you would like to see it; just throw it away if it makes you too homesick for the bygone days. There are times, I know, when in order to fight or work in this War, one must forget all the previous things apart from it that have been and may be again. But I think when one is strong enough to endure the memory it is better to remember for one's own sake.

I liked especially the Tschaikovsky symphony. Thurlow was very amusing – he made nothing but a few jerky remarks till we had tea at Fullers, and then gradually thawed until he began really to talk; we had tea from 5.0 to 6.30, so you can tell our conversation must have been quite interesting. He is very nice when he talks about Roland; he seems to have a natural tact and sensitiveness which prevents him from ever making a jarring remark, though I am sure he would not think he was tactful if you asked him if he was. He looks much better, but seems very depressed with himself as an officer; his complaint is the very opposite to mine – he has more responsibility than he cares about & says he never knows what to do. But I do like him; he is interesting, and has that quality of straightness & honourableness and reliableness which characterises all your friends.

Vera to Edward

1st London General Hospital, 6 April 1916

I have had a busy evening with the Standard and Daily Mail maps since your letter came. Then you are actually *south* of where Roland is & was? Surely on your way from the north you must have passed very near to Louvencourt indeed? . . .

I went down to Keymer yesterday afternoon; it was a good way for a half-day, but poor Mrs Leighton is ill & obliged to stay in bed for two or three weeks with a badly strained heart. The doctor says it is all the grief & worry she has been through lately, added to the fact that she has not given herself enough rest during the last eight years, has caused it. If she will rest for the next few weeks, he thinks it will be almost completely cured; if she doesn't, he won't answer for the consequences. I think the book about Him took it out of her almost more than anything else; fortunately she just managed to finish & send it off to Hodder & Stoughton before she broke down; it will come out about the beginning of May. She was fairly cheerful yesterday but, for her, slightly irritable. It is astonishing how that cottage loses its atmosphere when she is not about in it; one almost realises that things in it are neglected & dirty & dilapidated when she is not moving among them. . .

I am leaving here & going to the War Office, as Mother has probably told you; my job is not fixed up yet quite, but I went to the War Office last Saturday & interviewed a man there who seemed pleased with me and wrote me out a recommendation. . . I shall be very glad to leave the Hospital in many ways – especially as I am in a ward where there is nothing to do at all.

Vera to Edward

Summerhayes, Purley, Surrey, 12 April 1916

It is very strange to think of really leaving the Hospital next week, for these last six months have been so very very long that I can scarcely remember what life was like before then, and Hospital routine is a monotonous routine into which one gets very firmly and drearily rooted – I say drearily because you are never called upon to use your mind or your initiative and finally get into a way of working mechanically without giving your thoughts to what you are doing. It will be a relief to get away from it too; nursing, but not so much nursing as the Camberwell Hospital, has become a sort of Old Man of the Sea to me – a sort of burden on my back, and I have a superstitious feeling that Life will bring me nothing satisfactory – no opportunities or openings of any kind – until I can get away from it. Perhaps it is because it is so associated with the bitter side of the most tragic thing that ever has happened or ever will happen to us. Tragedy uplifts truly enough, I think – but not until you can forget the bitter & remember only the lofty side of it. And Camberwell is associated in my mind with all the bitter side – so much so that the longer I stay there the more unbalanced I seem to become, till I can see nothing in proportion, blame myself for what I don't deserve & not for what I do, & cannot see anything clearly. . . Of course if the War ends soon, nothing else matters, but if it doesn't I really think we shall in the end be having women in under Staff jobs, & such like. One never knows what may come in these days. Oh! how I should love to be at work in France in some capacity – except, of course, as a V.A.D.! I am longing to use *some* side of my mind now, even if it isn't the literary side, after having used none at all.

This afternoon I have been playing over the slow movement from Beethoven's No. 7 Sonata, & some of the Macdowell Sea Songs which you used to play. Whenever I sit down to the piano now I can always see you playing away, absolutely unconcerned by other people's requests to you to come out, or listen a moment! If you were to die I think I should have to give up music altogether, for there would be so many things I could never bear to hear or play – just as now I cannot bear to play L'Envoi, or the

'Liber scriptus proferitur' part of Verdi's Requiem, which for some reason or other I always connected with Roland's going to the front. . . You mean to me all that [Roland] meant and all that Victor means, rolled into one. . . When I think of Roland & you, I feel so proud to be so intimately associated with you both, and I feel so unworthy of the two of you. . . I wonder why His death had such a strengthening effect on you and such a weakening effect on me. Perhaps you needed sharpening – I don't think I did, I was sharp enough before. Mrs Leighton is always warning me that if I am ever to be a success as a writer I must fight against bitterness & cynicism, both in my writings and in myself. You know, if the war ends & doesn't sweep you away with everything else, I don't think I shall want to have much to do with anyone but you for a long time – except the Leightons, & perhaps Victor and Thurlow. I don't know why I include Thurlow – whom I know comparatively little, and I don't know why he interests me so much. Perhaps it is that incongruities always interest me – and to have the face of a leader of men strong almost to unscrupulousness combined with an almost entire absence of self-esteem, and an excessive reserve & nervy-ness & shyness, is certainly an incongruity. All the same, in spite of his self-depreciation, he gives one the impression of immense, though latent, possibilities. But you don't agree with this view, do you? I was much amused the other day because Victor expressed a desire to meet Thurlow, & in a letter to Thurlow I happened to mention this. I received a prompt reply in which he remarked that new people disturbed him and he was afraid he wasn't quite so keen to meet Victor as Victor appeared to be to meet him!! What it must have cost him in the way of effort to take me to that concert! One felt all the time that he must have studied the etiquette of it all beforehand & was trying hard to remember! However he was brave enough to hope to see me again soon.

...ot place, but one hears the most terrible accounts of the trenches owing to the excessively elementary notions ...ccupants in matters connected with hygiene etc.

German offensive does not seem to have extended ...as as yet, and we will hope that it will not do so. At ...e I see that the Germans claim to have repulsed a ...k North of the Somme.

...t be able to go home this week. . . I am at present in ...road piquet at South Farnbridge between Southend

------

...ra

France, 30 April 1916

...April 9th, 3 weeks ago to-day, . . . I bicycled from the ...h you must now know, through 4 villages . . . to the ...e Roland's grave is, going in a North Westerly direction ... It was a fine but dull evening . . . and about 6 o'clock ...ing up the hill from the valley south of the village. I ...n the small military cemetery quite suddenly before I ...in the village as it is at the southern end where 2 roads ...run together through the village. It is very small and the ...in neat rows all close together; I should think there are ...or 60 buried there; some are French but most are ...There were several men about looking at the graves and ...ne when I first came up where the officers' graves were ...ointed them out to me. . .

...d up along the path and stood in front of the grave . . . .k off my cap and prayed to whatever God there may be ...ght live to be worthy of the friendship of the man whose ...s before me . . . . . But I did not stay there long because it ...ry clear that He could not come back, and though it may ...He could see me looking at His grave, yet I did not feel ...was there.

Victor to Vera

Westcliff-on-Sea, 16 April 1916

I had the satisfaction of hearing from Hythe yesterday that I got a 1st Class so I am content as far as that is concerned . . .

We are all on detachment here, but I think all the subalterns are going to be sent to Burnham – two are going there to-morrow. The 70th are mainly East Surreys, but there are other oddments as well. Our own detachment is going to be a sort of dumping ground for the whole of the 8th Provisional Brigade – they will take all those of any use and send us their scourings. All this sort of thing is hardly the way to develop the soldierly spirit. . .

Before I went to Hythe I often used to feel that I didn't care whether I lived or died. Like you I had nothing to do, and like you I was intensely lonely. But that one month of hard work gave me quite a new zest for life, and I am sure that when you get to the War Office and are given useful work to do you will find just the same thing. . . I only wish that they would give me something useful to do . . . One can do nothing here.

Vera to Edward

1st London General Hospital, 19 April 1916

You may be surprised still to see the same old address after all – for in the end I have not left here, and am not leaving. Although everything was so nicely arranged for me to leave, I changed my mind and like the erratic weathercock I may seem but really am not, almost at the last moment agreed, as they wished, to stay. The reasons for so doing are rather hard to give – but you yourself well understand, I think, motives of sentiment and conscience, which are difficult to explain but impossible to disobey and keep one's self-respect and peace of mind. Roland was partly the cause – for I still seem to belong to Him just as much as when He was living, and though He is dead He still has more power over me than anyone who is alive. No sooner had I decided to leave here than the strong conviction came over me, quite against my reason, that somewhere He was living still, & knew and disapproved. The conviction grew stronger & stronger until I could not read His letters or quote His poems or favourite quotations, especially that one on Patriotism, without inwardly reproaching myself for leaving what was hard. . .

The first two people on this Hospital's foreign service list have just been ordered to France, so it looks as if they are beginning to draw from here at last. That makes me all the more content that I am not going away from here, as though I don't in the least imagine I should enjoy foreign service or underestimate its hardships, monotony & loneliness, I should have felt ashamed to think I had given up the work just when the chance it holds of going abroad was emphasized. Unless anything unforeseen occurs my opportunity probably won't come for some months – but if the present rather cheery estimates of the length of the War that one hears on all sides are at all correct, it is bound to come in the end. . .

Of course, when I go abroad from here, I am just as likely – perhaps more so – to go to the East as to France. I only wish that, if I am fated to be sent to the other side of Europe. I could first make a pilgrimage to His grave, as you have done. I feel that if only I could see that

> *'Corner of a foreign field*
> *Which is for ever England'*

for me, I should not mind what happened, and should be strengthened & inspired to face a lonely life without interest or hope in itself. Do you think the Germans will ever get through to Louvencourt & ravage it before we have a chance to see His grave?

Next Sunday is Easter-Day. I think perhaps one may celebrate even more than one could last year, the Resurrection of England – an England purged of much pettiness through the closeness of her acquaintance in these days with Life and Death.

Vera to Edward

South

I have been unintelligent
measles . . . This is one of the
brought here in a motor a
experience to be a patient in
into a general ward & treated

The worst of this kind of
time to think; I can't read
haven't sufficient energy to
think about Roland and pict
over & over again.

Victor to Vera

I was intensely sorry to hear th
as although they are not at all s
after, and take care of yourself v
you feel very unwell and depres
much that it is very hard for yo
hope yours is only a slight attack,
sick leave will be very necessary

I can't deny that I was sorry to
the hospital, because I am so con
intellect for you to be there, as v
have to put up with. But of course
you really should know me better
to criticise you for taking what you
After all you must be the best jud
opinion is of much value.

I don't think you need worry y
although I know that it is hard not to.
he is probably very busy, especially a
trenches. I am glad that he is not in the

---

is that a very
state of those
of their late

The lates
South of A
the same ti
British atta

I shall n
charge of a
and Maldo

Edward to V

On Sunda
town, wh
place whe
all the wa
I was cor
came upo
was quite
meet and
graves ar
about 5c
English. .
I asked o
and he p
I walk
And I to
that I m
grave w
was so v
be that
that He

Geoffrey to Edward

Essex, 2 May 1916

I am jolly glad to hear that you are on a month's course . . . I went to my Medical Board at Warley yesterday at 11 and had rather an amusing time. An orderly shewed me into a waiting room so I began reading 'The Telegraph'. Suddenly the door opened and a R.A.M.C. Col came in 'Hullo. One of the lateweekenders what!'

'Good morning Sir.'

'I'm awfully sorry: thought you were one of my doctors. What are you here for – a board. Well! Come along & let's see what we can do for you.' We then went into another room.

'What's your name. Oh yes. Sit down please. Where were you hit? Had a bad time there didn't you? How long were you out? (Enter a Captn RAMC who sat down by his side.) Feel all right now?' 'Quite, I replied, with exception of buzzing row in my ears.'

'Oh yes you had shell shock a bit. Lost any weight? (To which I replied I hadn't the faintest idea!) Played golf or Tennis. Yes on Sat, Sir. Feel tired after it. Yes Sir. Do you think you are fit for active service: Yes Sir.

Then he began writing – 'We find that he is still somewhat debilitated and would be benefited (He paused here and turned to the Captn: How do you spell benefited: Well anyhow you've begun to write it so you must go on – he was writing duplicate – and I'll see what it looks like!) by a further month's leave.'

At this I was somewhat staggered 'Yes. Get about as much as you can. That'll be all Mr Thurlow. Good morning.'

★ ★ ★ ★ ★

Well old man, please don't think I've been trying to work more leave for I've not, tho' many people do. Have been on the flog round the last week especially & have had a bit of a head. C'est tout.

Sorry for giving you all these absurd details but he was rather a delightful man.

Whom do you think I met in Leicester Square a few days ago. – dear old Forster . . . . . he has been at Nice 3 months having developed lung trouble. Naturally he went into all his disgusting symptoms in detail!

To turn to other subjects. Wish you were here now as the country is simply beautiful: all the freshness of Spring is evident everywhere and walking thro' the forest with the bright green of beeches & silver birch standing out in contrast to sombre holly is a joy.

Vera to Edward

South Western Hospital, Stockwell, 4 May 1916

This time I really am in some doubt as to where you are. It is of course almost impossible to find out when I am shut up here without a map (or anything else) but when I get home I will try to discover. But cannot you revert to the method of putting dots under the letters, which I never fail to make out, even if Mother can't grasp it? You must remember that, as you have always known, my bump of locality is sadly deficient & that I have none of your talent for following with exactitude maps, directions, & points of the compass...

I really have not had at all a bad time here, though a fever hospital in one of the slummiest parts of London, with a ward-window looking on to a coal heap, does not suggest entertainment. But after the first two or three days, I felt much less ill & much less depressed; & the very ugly V.A.D. in the other bed turned out after all quite interesting to talk to...

I had a very brief note from Thurlow the other day in which in his usual abrupt way he informed me that the result of his board was 'Duty at 13th'...

The excitements in Ireland seem to be causing some little ferments and fears of invasion on the East Coast; Victor at any rate has been sent to take charge of a road-picket between Southend and Maldon, & doesn't know how long this thrilling method of defending la patrie will last. But I should think it had more possibilities of excitement – at any rate of false alarms – than walking round the Arsenal.

I am very glad to feel that you are in safety for three weeks – especially as that very fact may have possibilities, but I think I know what you feel about sharing the risks and discomforts of your own battalion. The former I suppose are increasing as this is the season when things are done, but the latter must be getting less now that the warmer weather is coming.

Vera to Edward

Sunny Bank, Macclesfield, 6 May 1916

I think it is more than probable that I shall get sent abroad quite soon after I get back to the Hospital as when I called at the Hostel yesterday to fetch my clothes the Sister in charge there told me that the Powers that be are asking for more names (they have already had some) of people from our Hospital to go abroad and she thinks it is very probable that they will go on asking until they have got everyone from 1 L.G.H. who volunteered. I was of course among these, as everybody with any spirit was, as I think I told you before. I have no great enthusiasm either to go or stay - except to go to France - as one can't feel wildly interested in any new departure concerned with work one dislikes anyhow, but since I am going sometime I would rather it were soon than late, a feeling you well know, as it is most unsatisfactory to be always wondering when one is going & where. Of course if I were lucky I might get to France, 'the land of all my loves' – or most of them, but it is just as likely to be somewhere in the East. So I hope you get leave fairly soon as I don't want to be sent off without seeing you; of course I mayn't go for months but it is probable that I shall. If there was great hurry I might even be recalled from leave, but [I] don't think that very likely. . .

Mother had a letter from Thurlow this morning in which he says he has another month's extension of leave, so if you can only get your leave when you think you may, you will see him after all. At his 'board' they asked him if he thought he was fit for active service & he said yes. Then they told him another month would do him no harm and he was to go about as much as ever he could. He says he feels a fraud but that it is not his fault as he gave them no list of symptoms hoping for more leave. If he is as obviously highly strung as he was when I last saw him I think the board is very sensible. I should think he is the kind of person who suffers more than anybody at the front. I wonder if you mind its horrors & trials as much as he does. I expect you do, but being calmer in your nerves and more confident of your own powers, you can bear it better. . . We have asked him to stay here for a day or two before I go south again, but expect he is sure to refuse, though I would like him to come.

Victor to Vera

Shoeburyness, 11 May 1916

I wonder if you really will be going overseas soon: I hope so for your sake if you really wish to go, and I suppose you do. My own chances of going are now considerably less than ever, if possible. We came here – 3 Officers & 250 men – on Monday at less than 24 hours notice, and I think we shall be here till the end of the War, as most of the men are National Reservists and the work is of a nature that suits them – guards and fatigues etc. As far as I can make out the War Office wanted to discharge all those who had not volunteered for Foreign Service and were liable for it under the Military Service Act; but they found that they could not spare them from this Home Service work, such as it is. Of course we are very comfortable here, and it is a very soft job, but I expect I shall make yet another attempt to go overseas. If you manage to go I shall feel a bigger 'skrimshanker' than ever; so I should not mind if you had to stay in England.

Victor to Edward

Shoeburyness, 18 May 1916

My dear Edward,
    You have written me many very beautiful letters in the course of our friendship, but never one quite so beautiful as this last one: it is quite sufficiently proof to me that you have not deteriorated

Victor to Vera

Westcliff-on-Sea, 16 April 1916

I had the satisfaction of hearing from Hythe yesterday that I got a
1st Class so I am content as far as that is concerned . . .

We are all on detachment here, but I think all the subalterns are
going to be sent to Burnham – two are going there to-morrow.
The 70th are mainly East Surreys, but there are other oddments as
well. Our own detachment is going to be a sort of dumping
ground for the whole of the 8th Provisional Brigade – they will
take all those of any use and send us their scourings. All this sort
of thing is hardly the way to develop the soldierly spirit. . .

Before I went to Hythe I often used to feel that I didn't care
whether I lived or died. Like you I had nothing to do, and like you
I was intensely lonely. But that one month of hard work gave me
quite a new zest for life, and I am sure that when you get to the
War Office and are given useful work to do you will find just the
same thing. . . I only wish that they would give me something
useful to do . . . One can do nothing here.

Vera to Edward

1st London General Hospital, 19 April 1916

You may be surprised still to see the same old address after all – for
in the end I have not left here, and am not leaving. Although
everything was so nicely arranged for me to leave, I changed my
mind and like the erratic weathercock I may seem but really am
not, almost at the last moment agreed, as they wished, to stay. The
reasons for so doing are rather hard to give – but you yourself well
understand, I think, motives of sentiment and conscience, which
are difficult to explain but impossible to disobey and keep one's
self-respect and peace of mind. Roland was partly the cause – for
I still seem to belong to Him just as much as when He was living,
and though He is dead He still has more power over me than
anyone who is alive. No sooner had I decided to leave here than
the strong conviction came over me, quite against my reason, that

somewhere He was living still, & knew and disapproved. The conviction grew stronger & stronger until I could not read His letters or quote His poems or favourite quotations, especially that one on Patriotism, without inwardly reproaching myself for leaving what was hard. . .

The first two people on this Hospital's foreign service list have just been ordered to France, so it looks as if they are beginning to draw from here at last. That makes me all the more content that I am not going away from here, as though I don't in the least imagine I should enjoy foreign service or underestimate its hardships, monotony & loneliness, I should have felt ashamed to think I had given up the work just when the chance it holds of going abroad was emphasized. Unless anything unforeseen occurs my opportunity probably won't come for some months – but if the present rather cheery estimates of the length of the War that one hears on all sides are at all correct, it is bound to come in the end. . .

Of course, when I go abroad from here, I am just as likely – perhaps more so – to go to the East as to France. I only wish that, if I am fated to be sent to the other side of Europe. I could first make a pilgrimage to His grave, as you have done. I feel that if only I could see that

> *'Corner of a foreign field*
> *Which is for ever England'*

for me, I should not mind what happened, and should be strengthened & inspired to face a lonely life without interest or hope in itself. Do you think the Germans will ever get through to Louvencourt & ravage it before we have a chance to see His grave?

Next Sunday is Easter-Day. I think perhaps one may celebrate even more than one could last year, the Resurrection of England – an England purged of much pettiness through the closeness of her acquaintance in these days with Life and Death.

———————

Vera to Edward

> *South Western Hospital, Stockwell, 27 April 1916*

I have been unintelligent enough to get an attack of German measles ...This is one of the numerous London fever hospitals; I was brought here in a motor ambulance . . . It is quite an interesting experience to be a patient in a hospital though I have not been put into a general ward & treated like a pauper, as I expected to be...

The worst of this kind of situation is that one has such a long time to think; I can't read for long as it hurts my eyes, and I haven't sufficient energy to write very much, so I lie here and think about Roland and picture to myself the details of His death over & over again.

Victor to Vera

> *Westcliff-on-Sea, 28 April 1916*

I was intensely sorry to hear that you have got German measles, as although they are not at all serious if you are properly looked after, and take care of yourself when you get up, they must make you feel very unwell and depressed; and you have had to suffer so much that it is very hard for you to be ill at the same time... I hope yours is only a slight attack, and I am sure that the fortnight's sick leave will be very necessary and good for you.

I can't deny that I was sorry to hear that you were staying on at the hospital, because I am so convinced that it is a waste of your intellect for you to be there, as well as on account of what you have to put up with. But of course I don't know your reasons, and you really should know me better than to think I should presume to criticise you for taking what you consider to be the best course. After all you must be the best judge of that, and no one else's opinion is of much value.

I don't think you need worry yourself unduly about Edward, although I know that it is hard not to. If he is still running a company he is probably very busy, especially as they have taken over strange trenches. I am glad that he is not in the Lens–Arras sector, as not only is that a very hot place, but one hears the most terrible accounts of the state of those trenches owing to the excessively elementary notions of their late occupants in matters connected with hygiene etc.

The latest German offensive does not seem to have extended South of Arras as yet, and we will hope that it will not do so. At the same time I see that the Germans claim to have repulsed a British attack North of the Somme.

I shall not be able to go home this week. . . I am at present in charge of a road piquet at South Farnbridge between Southend and Maldon.

Edward to Vera

France, 30 April 1916

On Sunday April 9th, 3 weeks ago to-day, . . . I bicycled from the town, which you must now know, through 4 villages . . . to the place where Roland's grave is, going in a North Westerly direction all the way. It was a fine but dull evening . . . and about 6 o'clock I was coming up the hill from the valley south of the village. I came upon the small military cemetery quite suddenly before I was quite in the village as it is at the southern end where 2 roads meet and run together through the village. It is very small and the graves are in neat rows all close together; I should think there are about 50 or 60 buried there; some are French but most are English. . .There were several men about looking at the graves and I asked one when I first came up where the officers' graves were and he pointed them out to me. . .

I walked up along the path and stood in front of the grave . . . . . And I took off my cap and prayed to whatever God there may be that I might live to be worthy of the friendship of the man whose grave was before me . . . . . But I did not stay there long because it was so very clear that He could not come back, and though it may be that He could see me looking at His grave, yet I did not feel that He was there.

Geoffrey to Edward

Essex, 2 May 1916

I am jolly glad to hear that you are on a month's course . . . I went to my Medical Board at Warley yesterday at 11 and had rather an amusing time. An orderly shewed me into a waiting room so I began reading 'The Telegraph'. Suddenly the door opened and a R.A.M.C. Col came in 'Hullo. One of the lateweekenders what!'

'Good morning Sir.'

'I'm awfully sorry: thought you were one of my doctors. What are you here for – a board. Well! Come along & let's see what we can do for you.' We then went into another room.

'What's your name. Oh yes. Sit down please. Where were you hit? Had a bad time there didn't you? How long were you out? (Enter a Captn RAMC who sat down by his side.) Feel all right now?' 'Quite, I replied, with exception of buzzing row in my ears.'

'Oh yes you had shell shock a bit. Lost any weight? (To which I replied I hadn't the faintest idea!) Played golf or Tennis. Yes on Sat, Sir. Feel tired after it. Yes Sir. Do you think you are fit for active service: Yes Sir.

Then he began writing – 'We find that he is still somewhat debilitated and would be benefited (He paused here and turned to the Captn: How do you spell benefited: Well anyhow you've begun to write it so you must go on – he was writing duplicate - and I'll see what it looks like!) by a further month's leave.'

At this I was somewhat staggered 'Yes. Get about as much as you can. That'll be all Mr Thurlow. Good morning.'

★ ★ ★ ★ ★

Well old man, please don't think I've been trying to work more leave for I've not, tho' many people do. Have been on the flog round the last week especially & have had a bit of a head. C'est tout.

Sorry for giving you all these absurd details but he was rather a delightful man.

Whom do you think I met in Leicester Square a few days ago. – dear old Forster . . . . . he has been at Nice 3 months having developed lung trouble. Naturally he went into all his disgusting symptoms in detail!

To turn to other subjects. Wish you were here now as the country is simply beautiful: all the freshness of Spring is evident everywhere and walking thro' the forest with the bright green of beeches & silver birch standing out in contrast to sombre holly is a joy.

Vera to Edward

South Western Hospital, Stockwell, 4 May 1916

This time I really am in some doubt as to where you are. It is of course almost impossible to find out when I am shut up here without a map (or anything else) but when I get home I will try to discover. But cannot you revert to the method of putting dots under the letters, which I never fail to make out, even if Mother can't grasp it? You must remember that, as you have always known, my bump of locality is sadly deficient & that I have none of your talent for following with exactitude maps, directions, & points of the compass. . .

I really have not had at all a bad time here, though a fever hospital in one of the slummiest parts of London, with a ward-window looking on to a coal heap, does not suggest entertainment. But after the first two or three days, I felt much less ill & much less depressed; & the very ugly V.A.D. in the other bed turned out after all quite interesting to talk to. . .

I had a very brief note from Thurlow the other day in which in his usual abrupt way he informed me that the result of his board was 'Duty at 13th'. . .

The excitements in Ireland seem to be causing some little ferments and fears of invasion on the East Coast; Victor at any rate has been sent to take charge of a road-picket between Southend and Maldon, & doesn't know how long this thrilling method of defending la patrie will last. But I should think it had more possibilities of excitement – at any rate of false alarms – than walking round the Arsenal.

I am very glad to feel that you are in safety for three weeks – especially as that very fact may have possibilities, but I think I know what you feel about sharing the risks and discomforts of your own battalion. The former I suppose are increasing as this is the season when things are done, but the latter must be getting less now that the warmer weather is coming.

Vera to Edward

Sunny Bank, Macclesfield, 6 May 1916

I think it is more than probable that I shall get sent abroad quite soon after I get back to the Hospital as when I called at the Hostel yesterday to fetch my clothes the Sister in charge there told me that the Powers that be are asking for more names (they have already had some) of people from our Hospital to go abroad and she thinks it is very probable that they will go on asking until they have got everyone from 1 L.G.H. who volunteered. I was of course among these, as everybody with any spirit was, as I think I told you before. I have no great enthusiasm either to go or stay – except to go to France – as one can't feel wildly interested in any new departure concerned with work one dislikes anyhow, but since I am going sometime I would rather it were soon than late, a feeling you well know, as it is most unsatisfactory to be always wondering when one is going & where. Of course if I were lucky I might get to France, 'the land of all my loves' – or most of them, but it is just as likely to be somewhere in the East. So I hope you get leave fairly soon as I don't want to be sent off without seeing you; of course I mayn't go for months but it is probable that I shall. If there was great hurry I might even be recalled from leave, but [I] don't think that very likely...

Mother had a letter from Thurlow this morning in which he says he has another month's extension of leave, so if you can only get your leave when you think you may, you will see him after all. At his 'board' they asked him if he thought he was fit for active service & he said yes. Then they told him another month would do him no harm and he was to go about as much as ever he could. He says he feels a fraud but that it is not his fault as he gave them no list of symptoms hoping for more leave. If he is as obviously highly strung as he was when I last saw him I think the board is very sensible. I should think he is the kind of person who suffers more than anybody at the front. I wonder if you mind its horrors & trials as much as he does. I expect you do, but being calmer in your nerves and more confident of your own powers, you can bear it better... We have asked him to stay here for a day or two before I go south again, but expect he is sure to refuse, though I would like him to come.

Victor to Vera

Shoeburyness, 11 May 1916

I wonder if you really will be going overseas soon: I hope so for your sake if you really wish to go, and I suppose you do. My own chances of going are now considerably less than ever, if possible. We came here − 3 Officers & 250 men − on Monday at less than 24 hours notice, and I think we shall be here till the end of the War, as most of the men are National Reservists and the work is of a nature that suits them − guards and fatigues etc. As far as I can make out the War Office wanted to discharge all those who had not volunteered for Foreign Service and were liable for it under the Military Service Act; but they found that they could not spare them from this Home Service work, such as it is. Of course we are very comfortable here, and it is a very soft job, but I expect I shall make yet another attempt to go overseas. If you manage to go I shall feel a bigger 'skrimshanker' than ever; so I should not mind if you had to stay in England.

Victor to Edward

Shoeburyness, 18 May 1916

My dear Edward,
    You have written me many very beautiful letters in the course of our friendship, but never one quite so beautiful as this last one: it is quite sufficiently proof to me that you have not deteriorated

literarily through being out there; and I very much doubt whether you have musically:– if you find it hardly possible to compose just now, is it surprising? And I am convinced that this is only temporary and superficial, and will not outlast the War in any case. One thing I am fairly sure of, and that is the Leightons, when they see you – as I hope we all shall very soon – will say in their delightful frank way how much you have improved since you went out. The reason why your last letter was so beautiful was because it was so very human. And after all to be human is better, and greater, and more beautiful than anything else.

Of course I am not going to believe that you have deteriorated morally: you only think you have. The truth is, you and I – as I have only just got to realise – are idealists. You will say that is a pretty strange sort of thing for a cynical, cold-blooded person like myself to say. But it is really true, I am convinced. And idealists are fore-doomed to fail – that is why, I suppose, I have always been inclined to despise them for unpractical fools. I suppose our ideal is Roland. He did not fail, but He probably thought He did. Yet I doubt if one man in a thousand achieves His spotless purity, His wonderful old-world chivalry, or His love of Country in the abstract. In the words of the Bible 'Such things are too great and excellent for me: I cannot attain unto them' – at least that is how I feel, and I rather think you do too. But I doubt if you or I have ever done very much that would be considered very wrong if considered by the standard of the World. I hope you will not think me inconsistent for calling myself an idealist: I have not said that I approve of idealism; but one cannot help what one is by nature and temperament, whether one admires it or not...

. . . Again I don't think many people – apart from the very Low Church party of our own English Church, and I never have paid much heed to such people & I don't suppose you have – really think that this War is a punishment for the sins of those who have suffered in it and through it. To me, at any rate, such an idea is absolutely unthinkable. Surely the Allies are God's instrument by which He will remove that spirit and doctrine which is the cause of such Wars as this one. Did not Christ, 'the all-powerful but yet meek, gentle, peace-loving, beneficent God', Himself say that He came to bring 'not peace, but a sword'. If

Germany should win, not only would the rest of the World be faced with material ruin, but the whole Christian principle by which things are more or less governed in civilised Europe would be overthrown. Such a state of things is unthinkable. . . God will – using the Allies as His instrument – prevent it from coming to pass.

———————

Vera to Edith Brittain

1st London General Hospital, 19 May 1916

[*Boy of my Heart*] is really fine . . . I had no idea she could do anything so good . . . Of course I come in a good deal; I wonder what you will think of me. She hasn't given me a sense of humour – though perhaps under the circumstances that is hardly necessary . . . she said she had wanted to keep me a kind of dream figure all through . . . Edward comes in a lot, nearly as much as I; she has made him, contrary to my expectation, a most charming & attractive figure; & she has portrayed quite accurately his formality & slight stiffness without being in the least unkind to him. Victor comes in in a conversation she has with him about Roland and me at Speech Day.

———————

Vera to Edward

1st London General Hospital, 31 May 1916

Ever since your leave was cancelled I have been making efforts to write to you but have never succeeded until now. Last night after lights-out I sat at the window & thought about you for ages. I had just been studying your photograph; photographs that are like people are quite heartrending when those people are far away and in danger. The Leightons are deeply disappointed you did not come. They expected you all the week-end and were just going to wire to me to enquire what had occurred when my p.c. to them arrived.

Victor & I had supper at the Trocadero on Sunday night. He

was in one of his excitable moods & almost forgot to salute in his anxiety to know what the news of you was. Your letter which I received on Saturday came rather too late in the day to enable me to telegraph to him. . . He somewhat surprised me by a very decided announcement that he intends after the War (in which apparently he still has very little chance of ever taking a more active part than at present) to go into the church. . .

I don't know what you think about these things but I do know that when you went to the front your opinions were altering rapidly and my own commonsense would tell me that what you have done & seen there must have changed them rapidly still more, even if I had not gathered as much from what Tar & Thurlow say about your letters. . . Why do you not write to me about these things? I don't know much about Thurlow, but I am certain that, just for the moment, I could understand your troubles & difficulties better than the temporally orthodox Tar. And what is more, though it may be a little difficult for you to realise, I have not only long passed the date when I realised I could never be orthodox again, but I have seen more of the horrors of War than he has. He has been near death, I know, but he hasn't seen men with mutilations such as I have, though he may have heard a lot about them; I must admit that when, as I am doing at present, I have to deal with men who have only half a face left & the other side bashed in out of recognition, or part of their skull torn away, or both feet off, or an arm blown off at the shoulder, & all these done only a few days ago, it makes me begin to question the existence of a merciful God just as Tar says you do. . .

. . . War is an immense Purgation – 'the washing out' as the Master of the Temple said recently, 'of the sins of the world in streams of innocent blood'. Of course it is all terrible for individuals, who are sacrificed in apparently disregarded numbers, tortured & made mad, & seemingly lost sight of in the Great Immensity, but one can only hope that in some Hereafter these, & those who lost them, will one day realise the Whole and see what it all meant, & understand their own part in it. . . Perhaps the Great Force we call God means us & our Allies to be the special instruments of its progress & knew we should only be worthy to be this after the tremendous ordeal we are going through now. And perhaps we are not only making ourselves worthy but are preparing a double work – that of making an end to War at the same time. For 'they that live by the sword shall perish by the sword' and so War could only be abolished by War itself.

Victor to Vera

Shoeburyness, 3 June 1916

I am delighted to hear that Edward is really home at last, and I am looking forward to Wednesday intensely. You say you wonder whether I shall be glad or sorry to hear that you are going overseas: you may well wonder – I do not know myself. I suppose I am glad – I know how glad and proud He would be, and I know that your own dearest wish is to go to France. In the same way I was glad when Edward went – in just the same way – except that perhaps I shan't be quite so anxious in your case unless you are sent to some unhealthy spot in the East. But I hope you won't think me very selfish if I confess to remembering that I shall be the last and only one left: you see I shall feel very lonely sometimes. I know it is unmilitary of me to say so; but it is a little difficult to keep up one's militarist pretences sometimes – at least I find it so.

However I heard this morning that after the end of this month I shall be sent to our draft-finding unit: it seems almost too good to be true after six months working for it in vain. As it is the Colonel of the 70th Prov. Batt. opposed it strongly, but Col. Hodgson seems to have been too many for him. So I may not be so very much behind you after all!

Victor to Vera

South Army Bombing School, Ingatestone, 11 June 1916

We English are really the most extraordinary as well as the finest race on earth: I had the most delightful evening with Edward on

Thursday – four precious hours together. Yet of those four hours we literally spent the first two in breaking the ice. We each felt we had a very great deal to say, and yet we did not know how to say it. I suppose the Army is like a freezing mixture. One shuts one-self up from people, and when one comes among people to whom one may speak what one really feels one either can say nothing at all or else one gives utterance to a heap of conventional shibboleths in which one does not believe. It actually seems easier to write to you and Edward than to talk to you. . .

Edward's typically immaculate attire delighted me on Thursday as much as Roland's disregard for such trivialities did when He was home. It may sound childish but in Edward's case I regard such things as the outward and visible sign of the inward spiritual grace. It would almost grieve me to see Edward untidy: I should begin to think that something was wrong with him.

Edward told me what he said he told you about things at the Front. . . I think there is no doubt that he feels the terror and horror of it all most acutely. I am more than ever convinced that it is worse for him than it was for Roland. Edward entirely lacks any primitive warring side to his character, such as Roland possessed. One feels with Edward that he is sustained by Duty alone. I do not think that the heroic and glorious side of War appeals to him as it did to Roland, and I think that this makes it much harder for him. . . Both Edward and Roland found the trenches boring, but compare what Roland wrote to me just a year ago before He went to the Somme with what Edward said on Thursday. After speaking of the dullness of the trenches Roland wrote something like this:– 'I hear we are going to Ypres: I hope it may be true. Better the clash of blades than this monotonous existence'. Edward just said very quietly, and almost irrelevantly 'The thought of those lines of trenches gives me a sick feeling in the stomach'.

Vera to Edward

1st London General Hospital, 11 June 1916

I am afraid you must have had rather a bad crossing last Friday or Saturday. I was thinking hard about you & the probable condition of the sea during a hail-storm on Friday evening, which thundered on to our corrugated iron roof so that you could scarcely hear yourself speak. And then at 7.0 a large Canadian convoy straight from Ypres – no intermediate hospital in France – came in, and we had seven of them in our ward, so for the rest of the evening I had not much time to think of anything at all. Our ward is almost entirely Canadian now; they seem to be getting it pretty badly in what the newspapers are already beginning to describe as the Third Battle of Ypres...

I had a queerly vivid dream last night; I thought that Tah and I suddenly got a letter each in Roland's handwriting; in the dream we knew he was dead just as we do in everyday life. I opened mine with the very strange kind of feeling that one would have if such a thing happened actually. In the letter he said it was all a mistake that he was dead, and that he was really a prisoner in Germany but so badly maimed that he would never be able to get back again. I felt a sudden overwhelming feeling of relief to think he was after all alive under any circumstances whatever, and I gazed & gazed at the familiar handwriting on both Tah's letters & mine, marvelling that it was really his, and as I gazed at it, it seemed gradually to change & become more & more different, till finally it was not like his at all but more like Captain Adshead's. It was a curious dream.

We had a memorial service for Kitchener in our little chapel at 6.30 yesterday morning: really rather picturesque with nurses, orderlies & wounded men.

Victor to Vera

> Southern Army Bombing School,
> Ingatestone, 13 June 1916

I am glad Edward seemed cheerful when you saw him. When he came down here he was obviously and only too naturally depressed at the thought of going back. He did not give me any details of the horrible things he must have seen, but he conveyed the atmosphere of horror to me without that. It was I think as much the way he said things as the things themselves. I'm sure Edward has nothing of the primitive man in him, and I am afraid I haven't either. I hate War bitterly as I have always hated it. I have tried to make myself a militarist, but my militarism is only skin deep: I am sorry to say I cannot honestly pretend that it is otherwise.

Apart from that I think we discussed the War more from a military than a personal point of view. We did not have a real theological discussion, but Edward says he still does believe in a Resurrection. I don't think he has altered at all really, but perhaps he is a little more inclined to be cynical than he once was.

Vera to Edward

> 1st London General Hospital, 15 June 1916

We have suddenly become very busy here, and are expecting still more large convoys. In consequence all leave has been stopped until further notice – a thing which has never happened while I have been here, busy as we have sometimes been. So it is very lucky you came when you did, as I certainly should have got no leave now. Our own ward is quite full – chiefly with Canadians. Even off-duty times are apt to get curtailed; one is even liable to miss them altogether. Some of our cases are very bad indeed and we are in for a busy morning to-morrow with six operations.

Edward to Vera

France, 26 June 1916

Dearest Vera,

The papers are getting rather more interesting, but I have only time to say adieu.

EHB

_____

Vera to Edward

1st London General, 28 June 1916

I believe I heard the guns *here* a day or two ago. What a clamour must be going on! One anxiety is more than enough; & sometimes I feel quite glad that Roland is lying where the guns cannot disturb Him however loudly they thunder & He cannot any more hear the noise they make.

_____

Vera to Edith Brittain

1st London General, 1 July 1916

The news in the paper – which was got at 4.0 this afternoon – is quite self-evident, so I needn't say more about it. London was wildly excited & the papers selling madly. Of course you remember that Edward is at Albert & it is all around there that the papers say the fighting is fiercest – Montaubon – Fricourt – Mametz– I have been expecting this for days as when he was here he told me that the Great Offensive was to begin there & of the part his own regiment had to play in the attack ... please be sure to wire to me at *once* anything you may hear about him – don't think you could tell me better in a letter whatever it is. Naturally I am very anxious indeed & I want to know anything you may hear as soon as you hear it. In great haste.

Early on the morning of 1 July 1916, Edward led the first wave of the attack of his company in the great British offensive that was to go down in history as one of the most terrible days of slaughter in the annals of the British Army: the first day of the Battle of the Somme. While his company was waiting to go over, the wounded from an earlier part of the attack began to crowd into the trenches. Then part of the regiment in front began to retreat, throwing Edward's men into a panic. He had to return to the trenches twice to exhort them to follow him over the parapet. About ninety yards along No-Man's-Land, Edward was hit by a bullet through his thigh. He fell down and crawled into a shell hole. Soon afterwards a shell burst close to him and a splinter from it went through his left arm. The pain was so great that for the first time he lost his nerve and cried out. After about an hour and a half, he noticed that the machine-gun fire was slackening, and started a horrifying crawl back through the dead and wounded to the safety of the British trenches.

Edward to Vera

France, 1 July 1916

Dear Vera,

I was wounded in the action this morning in left arm and right thigh not seriously. Hope to come to England. Don't worry.

Edward

Victor to Vera

4th Batt. The Royal Sussex Regt., Purfleet, 2 July 1916

Thank you very much for your letter. It is very good of you to say that you enjoy our occasional evenings in Town. I am afraid I must have seemed rather unsympathetic on Monday. I did not mean to be, but it seems to me that I do not understand you as well as I ought. Perhaps some day I shall be less slow and get to know you better. I could tell from one or two things you said the other night that you have summed me up remarkably well. . .

So far the hardest fighting seems to have been North and South of Albert – round Hébuterne and Fricourt – rather than actually opposite Albert itself. You must be finding the suspense too terrible for words – there is nothing on earth so bad as waiting from day to day knowing that the dearest person in the world is in such awful peril. I had a farewell note from Edward on Thursday written on the leaf of a notebook.

'... I am so busy that I have only time for material things. And so I must bid you a long long adieu.' By the way this note was written on page 106 of the book: 106 is one of my lucky numbers – my only one as far as I know. Let's hope it is a good omen.

Geoffrey to Vera

France, 4 July 1916

Dear Vera,

Please excuse my audacity in addressing you in this way instead of the stiff and formidable alternative 'Miss Brittain' – Mrs Brittain once said that you had no objection to it – also for me writing, but I've been thinking about you all more than usual lately and know what a trying time you must be having. May Edward be as well looked after as I was out there – thus I can wish him nothing better.

Vera to Edith Brittain

1st London General, 5 July 1916

I hope they will send him to England soon; I expect they will but we hear hundreds, & probably thousands of them, are waiting to come across as there are so many the boats cannot take them quick enough. He might even come to-day as the large number of officers we were expecting yesterday did not arrive ...

I think we are very lucky, his wounds in those places are not likely to be at all dangerous though they may be painful & long in healing. At any rate he is out of it for some time . . . It would be funny if he turned up here. I only wish he would . . . At last I can get a decent night's rest which I haven't had since the battle began although we get so tired.

By coincidence Edward was sent to the 1st London General. On 5 July, a fellow VAD rushed into Vera's ward to tell her that Edward had been in the convoy of wounded officers who had arrived during the night. After receiving permission from her Matron to visit him, Vera hurried to Edward's bedside. He was struggling to eat breakfast with only one hand, his left arm was stiff and bandaged, but he appeared happy and relieved. Edward would remain in the hospital for three weeks before beginning a prolonged period of convalescent leave.

Vera to Edith Brittain

1st London General, 21 July 1916

[Edward] is leaving the Hospital on Monday as the further treatment he requires cannot be obtained here . . . The doctor has promised to get Edward 3 months leave, which is very pleasant, & then of course there will probably be light duty after that. . . We don't know what to do to get through the work & I often have to go without off-duty times. We have got the Hospital absolutely full to overflowing now, and yesterday we were actually told that somehow or other we have got to find 520 more beds! That will make us nearly 3000; I don't know how we are going to do it, but the orderlies' barrack room is being turned into a ward . . . & every available inch of ground is being covered with tents – tents in the middle of Camberwell . . . our meals get cut short, & we get so tired we don't know where to put ourselves.

Geoffrey to Vera

France, 13 August 1916

Thanks very much for your long letter which I got yesterday by the same post as one from Mrs Brittain who rather amused me by saying that if she had had a chance of saying goodbye 'it might have included a kiss & in my mind's eye I can see your face!!' Well of all objectionable habits I think kissing is the worst. . .

No! Edward hasn't said anything about his arm, but he wouldn't no matter how bad. I'm awfully sorry to hear about it and only hope it will get well quicker than the usual neuritis which takes a long time doesn't it? Also that he won't have to come out here again.

———

Edward to Vera

14 Oxford Terrace, London, 24 August 1916

Father . . . brought up with him a letter from France addressed to me which mentions the following:–

To/ 2Lt. E. H. Brittain
(regiment etc)
The G.O.C. congratulates you on being awarded the Military Cross by the Commander in Chief.

———

Vera to Edith Brittain

1st London General, 25 August 1916

Isn't it unspeakably splendid about Edward's Military Cross! And how like him to send you a postcard, when anybody else would have wired; he takes it with the utmost placidity . . . he was wearing it to-day . . . other officers turn round & look at him, & he never appears to notice it. . . He says he will undoubtedly get promotion now – though what does it matter if you are a 2nd Lieutenant all your days, when you are an M.C.!

Geoffrey to Vera

France, 28 August 1916

A hasty line to thank you for your letter which I got this morning . . . . . (This dugout is full of weird insects which descend from the ceiling with a flop and settle on your hair, paper etc. – in fact anywhere) . . .

Well! For many things life is rather delightful here. When you see potatoes & cabbages growing well on the parados it seems singularly out of keeping with the rest. Machine guns are jolly active here at nights. Just outside our Coy HQs are two graves of French soldiers and further down one of a 'soldat allemand'.

. . . Expect Edward would prefer you to go to France wouldn't he? Please don't let him write until he is more or less all right. He said in his last card that in a few days he would write at 'Immense Length'. Well! Much as I'd like that he's not to do it.

(Another insect descends with a flop.)

Yesterday it rained on and off and we got slightly damp.

Just got the news that Roumania has come in on our side which is quite cheery. Please excuse this disjointed note but where I might be Interesting I am forbidden.

Geoffrey to Edward

France, 29 August 1916

I am sitting in a dark dugout, writing this with aid from a guttering candle. My fatigue men have gone away while it rains – Lander just came in to say that it has stopped so I shall have to carry on.

It has just started again so we can go on for a bit. Well! I had only time to send off a p.c. saying how damn glad I am that you've got the Military Cross – always thought you would do something great. If you are well enough I wish you would over-come your innate modesty & let me know all about it – please excuse my inquisitiveness but one likes to know how etc etc. That is one thing I've always longed for & shall long in vain, for I haven't much courage. Yesterday afternoon some whizzbangs arrived about 50 yds away which absolutely put the wind up me. At Ypres we used to watch them going to Hellfire Corner about same distance with almost joy. Still such is life. We shall be moving up shortly & I'm not looking forward to it much as am a bit off colour. Summer is over I think and rain has come. There is another strafe going on to the right a bit seem to be getting quite offensive.

It is rather delightful to find cabbage & potatoes growing wild on some parts of parados in front line trenches don't you think?

(Day has arrived from Sappers so must stop once again!)

★ ★ ★ ★ ★

Much later 6.15.

After Day came our new Padre who stayed a long time so hence this interval. . . (Really the amount of these little black beetles which flop down from the ceiling is unending.)

There has just arrived a magnificent storm: masses of black clouds, vivid lightning & great rolls of thunder. Nowadays one is reminded of 'So all day long the noise of battle rolled, Among the mountains to the northern sea. etc' When you were here didn't you yearn sometimes to see the sea again. It seems so clean when compared to land. . . How is Victor Richardson? Please remember me to him when you see him again. . .

Him that thou knowest thine

G.R.Y.T.

P.S. I was asked to Toby's 21st dinner a few days ago & sat next to a perfect twit who insisted on [calling] me 'old darling.'

'Pass the salt will you please, old darling etc etc' in drawled out tones. Really such people shouldn't exist!

Vera to Edith Brittain

1st London General Hospital, 1 September 1916

The two people going on the hospital-ship are off to-morrow; I expect it will be my turn soon. . . It is quite possible that I may be ordered abroad without being told definitely where I am going – the two who are going on the hospital-ship haven't the least idea where it is going . . . It would be rather thrilling to arrive some-where or other at night after a long voyage & say to one another 'Where (literally) in the *world is* this?'

––––––––––

Geoffrey to Edward

France, 5 September 1916

I have just come in from a voyage inland a few miles in a lorry and ambulance to get a bath & now once more we are clad and sane. This morning I was sent on a fatigue up to the village and when I got there I flogged round trying to find anyone who wanted me – of course the RE guide was absent & having interviewed members of the different Coys RE I made a strategic move home to find out the whole affair was a washout. Lander & Wilmot made two similar fruitless trips last night in torrents of rain. We came only yesterday & I'm not sorry as tho' there was nothing to write home about the Huns were worrying – never knew what they would do next from oilcans, aerial torpedoes, crumps whizz bangs to say nothing about gas alarms etc. Yesterday when he started crumping in particular round about Coy HQ's Lander who was sleeping peacefully in them, on the arrival of 2nd crump suddenly woke up & bolted down the sap near them where Wilmot & I were – I was trying to sleep after a night on tour . . . The scene of desolation in the dugout afterwards, caused by his flight was most amusing. Everything scattered all over the place – a perfect havoc. And above all it was pouring with rain & he had . . . no boots on for some reason. It reminded me of a rat, suddenly startled, bolting from its hole! . . .

I always was more or less windy but now I'm far worse than I was at Ypres: think the idea of going to England & returning a 'new man' is rot! Still the only excuse I had was that I felt a bit seedy: hope next time I shall be a little stouter. Poor old Wilmot has just had a brother killed . . .

. . . Hope for your sakes too that Vera doesn't go abroad – it would be pretty dire for Mr & Mrs Brittain with both of you away. . .

Well old man, I'm sorry this is so full of This & That. Do hope you are being less bothered with your arm nerves.

Edward to Vera

Sandgate, 17 September 1916

I am sorry but I know you wanted it and foreign service is the highest service. I shall arrive at Charing Cross just before noon to-morrow and I hope if possible that you may be able to meet me and tell me where you are going.

Beginning of the letter Vera wrote Edward about Roland's effects

SIX

19 SEPTEMBER 1916 – 19 DECEMBER 1916

I found in you a holy place apart . . .
Where mending broken bodies slowly healed
My broken heart.

> — VERA BRITTAIN,
> 'Epitaph on my Days in Hospital'

Your battle-wounds are scars upon my heart,
Received when in that grand and tragic 'show'
You played your part . . .

> — VERA BRITTAIN, 'To My Brother
> (In Memory of July 1st, 1916)'

Geoffrey to Edward

France, 19 September 1916

Many congratulations on your 2nd pip – knew it couldn't be long in arriving. No! I shall remain as I am for ever. To start with no one in the 10th knows one now: also I'm not the slightest use out here – far too windy etc: so that I shall never get promotion – don't particularly wish for it either. I think you are far too modest about your own self, old man, and even if you did not realise at the time about the Bn's right flank what matter? . . . Rather wish in a way that we were doing the stunt – to get things over, but there is time yet. Anticipation is usually worse than realisation what! We are on the move again so will be brief. . . Where we are the Hun usually uses many & varied mortars which are bloody things. It's been raining like hell here the last two days & working parties get a bit tedious . . . Rumour now that we are going to Abbeville for 'intensive training' for a month which means –! Eh bien. Whatever turns up hope I don't make an ass of myself: wish you could infuse some of your quiet delightful self confidence into me, old man! . . .

Well! In an hour or so we are moving – the Lord knows where!
Thine

Gryt

Geoffrey to Vera

France, 21 September 1916

I was jolly glad to have a long letter from Edward the day before yesterday and to hear that he is going strong. Victor Richardson also sent me a note by the same post saying that he looked to go to the East shortly: shouldn't have thought that he would have been passed fit. Things have altered here a bit and we were to have gone over the top a few days ago but it has now been washed out pro tem. Now we are trekking about just behind the line and in about a fortnight's time I expect things will happen. But Life is so uncertain out here now that we are here today & gone tomorrow.

We had some amusement here when we came in last night as there was little room for us as we were an extra Bn in the town. Luckily I got my men into a barn which was fairly clean and after some gesticulation and pigeon French I got some clean straw for them. Can't think why the French farmers have [no] idea of sanitation or drainage. I next met 3 of our officers engaged in an animated conversation with an extraordinary Curé: very tall, gaunt, unkempt, unshaven, unwashed – a revolting sight: he seemed to object to us coming into his house as a Highland regiment had just left after it had smashed most of his crockery and left the rooms quite filthy. Anyhow he was at length appeased and we took possession. Shall be moving again shortly probably tomorrow. Rain has been falling and the roads are quite liquified.

Well! all these domestic details will be boring to you.

Vera had been informed that she was to be posted to Malta. She was among a contingent of VADs who set sail on the *Britannic* on 24 September for a two-week voyage.

Vera to Edward

HM Hospital Ship Britannic, 23 September 1916

We left Waterloo (where by the way I felt very wretched as there were so many instructions & such a crowd & so much to do & such a general air of departure) at 12.30, arriving at Southampton at 2.10. . . We sailed down the Solent just as the sun was setting; it was a glorious evening with a smooth blue sea & the sun making a golden track which seemed to stretch from us to the fast disappearing mainland. . . Ships with searchlights are all about us in the dim distance – 10.15 now. There is a large life-belt – a new kind, of *waistcoat* shape, attached to each bed.

Geoffrey to Vera

France, 29 September 1916

Edward's letter yesterday told me that you were sailing on the 24th so I expect you will have been in Malta some time before this note reaches you...

Tho' we are some way behind the line sounds of a great battle can be distinctly heard. We are doing very intensive training it may be for a few days or a week or two, who knows? And then up into the breach again. Our previous attack was washed out at 11th hour & we came here... Everyone here who used to be in A Coy has heard about Edward on July 1st and are very bucked.

The village here is long & straggling and strange to say clean. My billet is at an estaminet on the crossroads & I often sit & watch the men outside filling the water carts or taking the horses down to the pond to water.

... This afternoon we were suddenly attacked on bayonet parade (Officers & NCO's only) by 4 valiant little Frenchmen ages from 4–6 each carrying a long stick with an apple attached to its end. When within 20 yds they opened fire by dropping the sticks behind their heads & then swishing them forward quickly & enroute the apple shot off but didn't hit its mark! They were jolly little men but one was a lunatic I think. However we laughed at them till we wept!

(The horses troop back to the transport lines.) Some of our officers have seen the new 'tanks' but I haven't yet. I hope I do so before we leave this place.

———

Edward to Vera

8 Oakwood Court, Kensington, London,
5 October 1916

The night of the day you left London (Oct. 23rd) the Zepps. dropped 4 bombs at Purley somewhere up that hill where we walked one afternoon when I was still bad only about 600yds. from the house but it did no damage. A foolish woman came out into the road and therefore received some shrapnel in one eye from one of our own guns but otherwise there was no damage except windows and a pillar box. . .

The next piece of news is that on the Monday after you left a wild telegram from Tah announced that he was going to France. I met him in town, helped him with all his shopping (and you can imagine he needed some help – it was an awful business as he didn't like most things and knew nothing about anything; occasionally he would suddenly take a violent dislike to a most necessary article of clothing and refuse to have it until I had wasted about ½ hr. conjuring up an imaginary situation in which he couldn't possibly do without the thing in question) and then stayed the night at Brighton. He had leave till Thursday (20th) and in that afternoon I got a wire from him to say that he was leaving Ch.X. at 7.5 pm. that night. I went to see him off and met his father and Miss Dennant on the platform, but no Tah ever turned up and I have heard nothing of him since and don't know whether he is in France or England but probably the former. He is joining the 10th Bn. Rifle Brigade, than which he might do much worse. I came here on Monday and as there is no servant till to-morrow night, though we have a char. till 5.30 pm, Mother and I do all the washing up at night and I made scrambled eggs in my pyjamas this morning (I mean while wearing my pjs.). It is awfully decent here only we are short of one person and her name is Vera – but that is unavoidable: with outspread hands one exclaims 'C'est la guerre – et que voulez-vous?'

Vera to Edward

Imtarfa Hospital, Malta, 10 October 1916

The day before we landed at Malta, 16 of us, self included, were quite suddenly seized with some variety or other of fever, but whether dysentery, malaria, enteritis or some other species no one seems to know . . . I am very much better now and my temperature is down to normal again . . . Everyone here is very busy trying to trace the origin of our disease so as to find out exactly what *is* the matter with us . . . We have had quite 12 doctors in here, sometimes five at once. Three of them are lady doctors, all very charming too, in khaki tussore coats & skirts, dark blue ties & solar topees. I am quite tired of giving my name (& wish it was Jones so that I didn't have to spell it every time), my age, my detachment number, particulars of what I had to eat lately, etc etc. They have taken blood tests of various kinds . . .

Vera to Edward

Malta, 15 October 1916

The chief disadvantages of Malta, as I can see already – though I like it ever so much better than I expected to – are 1. Flies 2. Lack of water 3. Glare of the sun. The third disadvantage of course can easily be mitigated, as, as soon as I leave here, I shall go into Valetta, where one can buy almost everything, & not expensively, and get a pair of green glasses! And if this is not enough I can always buy a solar topee . . . . .

Vera to Edward

Malta, 20 October 1916

Just received my 1st mail since arriving here . . . Oh! the glory of the mail! You who have never been further than France have no idea of it. I have just got 9 letters in all – ranging in dates from Sept. 28th (from Geoffrey in France before he knew I was coming here) to Oct. 9th (also from Geoffrey in France). You & he, by the way, are the only people who tell me anything coherently, so *do* write often, & don't imagine that other people have told me everything, because they never have. . . Only *you* give me any idea of how Victor went to France – which I am very astonished about; I had no idea his affairs were thus trembling on the brink. I haven't heard from him at all, but suppose he had no time . . . Promise me faithfully this one thing. If anything important (not necessarily only *the* most important thing of all, but just anything important) happens to either you, Geoffrey or Victor, will you cable to me at once? . . . For you have no idea what one feels out here when one realises it is Oct. 20th & the last one heard of anyone was Oct. 9th. . . It gives me a queer feeling to read Geoffrey's letter of Oct. 9th, & remembering that (quoting him) 'out here we are here to-day & gone to-morrow', to think that he has had time to die a thousand deaths between then & to-day.

Geoffrey to Edward

France, 20 October 1916

Just a note: we are now scuttling down South again: I say South meaning further south than we were!

Life here is an enigma and when all was ready we were suddenly transported as the stunt was off & here we are in an old town the belfry of which was built in 1150 odd and there is a quaint old castle. . .

I had a letter from Univ. last night which simply exuded Oxford and recalled many a pleasant evening two years ago about this time. Do you remember the delightful days in O.T.C. when you fell in with New Coll. & I with Univ. each totally oblivious of the other's existence what!

Edward to Vera

London, 21 October 1916

The arm is doing v. well though it is not quite right but I am quite fit for light duty. I applied for a board 10 days ago but as usual have heard nothing so far and the present leave is supposed to be up on Monday next. . . Geoffrey still seems to be existing but every time he writes he seems to expect the attack soon but if that goes on much longer the weather will soon make attacks impossible. . .

Tah is in great form judging by a letter from him last Sunday; he thinks the 9th K.R.R. [King's Royal Rifles], his brigade, and his division are the best of their kind that God ever made. Discipline and general management seem to please him greatly and, as he is apparently in a fairly quiet part 'some miles North of where Roland was' – probably near Arras, he is doing well at present. We all write conciliatory letters to Mr Richardson and Miss Dennant in turns and so try to prevent 65 Wilbury Avenue turning into an imitation graveyard...

I had an awfully good time at Uppingham a fortnight ago, and met several of the old people who seemed to be glad to see me. The House has got a very decent captain at present – of course he was only quite a small boy when I left – and the whole place seems to be doing well in spite of the War.

Geoffrey to Vera

France, 22–23 October 1916

Edward seems to 'find life hard' with most of the people out here he knows: I know the feeling well but I do hope he remains in England for a very long time tho' the war doesn't seem to be in its final stage yet by a long way, despite the opinions of some arm-chaired people at home.

Our stunt was suddenly washed out at the 11th hour and we are now settling a little farther South. Our present billet is in some charming scenery; a village in a valley surrounded by wooded hills with the many varied autumn tints on the trees and as the Sun has been brilliant yesterday & today the whole place is beautiful... But our time here is limited alas and we shall go on in motor buses, so soon we shall be in War again and shall be able to look back on our brief stay here with pleasure. And I think we may see again the town with the hanging figure from the Church which Edward knows so well.

All I hope is that I don't fail – for I must confess I'm a bit of a coward to use a strong word: not so much for myself but for the men under me am I afraid. Still let's hope for the best!

(Lunch is ready so must stop. Once again am I Mess President & can't enthuse over it much!)

Monday

We had a cold interesting ride here: if only people could have seen the miles & miles of motor lorries they would cease their complaints about the Army. All the men being packed into the lorries we set off and passed thro' the most charming country I've seen here yet. It grew colder as the sun went in and during the halts at odd intervals the A.S.C. [Army Service Corps] man told me all his life history which was both amusing and interesting – he came out in Aug 1914 & had some exciting times in a usually monotonous existence. As we were leaving a main road – it was dark – the road turned to the right at right angles and we saw red and other lights which looked like a hospital train but in reality it was the front part of the Convoy & I looked back & saw more lights twinkling away to the rear for miles. It was a fairy like sight.

———

Edward to Vera

London, 28 October 1916

I knew you would be troubled by flies though they might not be so bad this time of year but I expect you can imagine what it was like in Gallipoli in the summer; my experience about water supply is that outside England there never is enough water, and so I suppose we are exceptionally well off in that direction: presumably that is why no other nation washes and baths itself as much as we do. . .

In spite of my having informed the War Office on Oct. 13th that my leave ended on the 23rd they have taken no notice so far and so I have been on unofficial leave since Monday. The arm is very much better and I am not likely to get any more leave though I shall probably have a month on light duty. I don't think I want any more leave really as it is awfully boring in some ways living here with Mother and Father though of course it is London that makes it possible at all; there is nobody to talk to properly, nothing to discuss or take pleasure in, or realisation of what is good or bad etc. in books or music or anything – but you know yourself well enough what it is. Mother always agrees with everything I say in criticism and has an appallingly complete absence of artistic sense or appreciation whenever we go to a theatre or concert, while Father is something awful; he visits Harrods about twice a day on an average, does absolutely nix, and indulges in the usual trite and pessimistic speculations about the war, and will insist on asking me if I think the Russians or the Roumanians or somebody will do this, that, or the other. Most frightfully boring! With you and Tah and Geoffrey all abroad there is absolutely nobody for me at all. Capt. Watts, Gustard, and most of the others who were wounded about the same time as I was are with the 3rd Bn. at Sunderland (Durham), and so I expect to go there any time. Brocton seems to have become a training Reserve centre and only the stay-at-homes with the permanent jobs are there. All those who are just waiting to go out again seem to be at Sunderland which is rather awful – 261½ miles from London, nearly 7 hours and nearly a £2 fare so when once I am there there I shall stop, except for a possible long leave, until I go back to France. I believe I told you that I have had my photo taken, unknown to Mother who thinks it is unlucky: I am expecting them any day now – the proofs were very good, and for the first time in my life I was quite pleased at my own appearance ...

I finished the second volume of Sinister Street a few days ago – it is about the finest book there has ever been written, and it is such a pleasure for an author to say just what he means even if the language necessitated is slightly coarse, instead of continually beating about the bush as so many do.

———

Victor to Vera

Billets, France, 31 October 1916

You may or may not be interested to hear that I have done the unlucky thing, and transferred – been transferred that is – to the 9th K.R.R.C. [King's Royal Rifle Corps] – I left England six days after you did. If there is anything in your superstition that it is unlucky to transfer, I am in the words of the Prophets most decidedly 'for it'. In other words by all the laws of compensation I shall most certainly have to pay for the excellent time I have had since joining the 9th R.R.R. When I joined them with three others from the 4th R. Sussex they were recovering from two highly successful 'shows' on the Somme. I did two tours in the trenches with them, and we were then withdrawn for a proper rest. We are now resting & only doing three hours' work a day. It is perfectly delightful to be in a Battalion where officers are treated as such, and not as N.C.O.'s or private schoolboys, and where everything is properly run. We have quite a number of Regular officers & N.C.O.'s and I expect that accounts for it. The 9th K.R.R. were a unit of the First Hundred Thousand and a truly splendid lot. I shall never have another word to say against the New Army.

When we were in the line we were not so very far North of where Roland was, and it must have been just the same sort of thing that He experienced. I suppose it becomes boring after a time, but being so new I thoroughly enjoyed it. It is not half so bad as one is always led to believe – and of course one never appreciates the good side of it all till one has seen it. . . It was very quiet & without much excitement. We did not get any heavy shells at all till the last day when a couple of 5.9s amused themselves at our expense for about half-an-hour, but without doing any damage. Whizz-Bangs – about which one has heard so much – are perfectly harmless in a trench, as the trajectory is so flat that it is nearly impossible for them to land in a trench. There is practically no rifle or machine gun fire & what there is appears to be unaimed – fixed rifles & swinging traverses for the most. There is a lot of trench mortar work & also varied bombs, but one can generally see these things coming which renders them fairly harmless. The trenches are wonderfully clean even in bad weather & the dugouts very comfortable, though some people might dislike their earthy smell. Altogether life out here is very enjoyable & a welcome change from England. Of course a 'show' is a different business altogether. . .

I thought the above notes on trench life might possibly inter-est you. I have so far come across nothing more gruesome than a few very dead Frenchmen in No Man's Land, so cannot give you very thrilling descriptions. The thing one appreciates in the life here more than anything else is the truly charming spirit of good fellowship & freedom from pettiness that prevails everywhere.

Uppingham has just had another rude awakening. Did Edward ever tell you of Bunce? He had a rotten time & was everyone's butt owing to his athletic incapacity. Some time ago his C.O. described him as the life and soul of the Battalion – Puckle scowled when I refused to admit surprise. Now he has been killed out here by falling on a bomb during practice to save the lives of his men. His C.O. wrote 'He was a born leader of men.' Really I am beginning to agree with the Rifleman who when some dear old lady said 'What a terrible War it is,' replied 'Yes Mum, but better than no War.'

Geoffrey to Edward

France, 3 November 1916

Well! We had a pretty rotten time this last time up & had some casualties. We got in yesterday morning about 9, having been relieved at 8 the previous night. I never did feel so done up in my life. We got in a bit of a mess going out as the whole Coy went back over top en masse instead of by platoons & they were shelling a bit. So I plunged boldly on with all the men I could get hold of & when I halted for a bit was surprised to find Wilmot & the rest of Coy almost behind: on we slipped & fell over a waste of mud & it was almost the last straw when I fell over over on top of a mule long dead & got covered with – well you know what. However later on about 2 miles I slipped into a crump hole & got filthier than ever. (There is a topping sandy cat here which insists on walking over the paper & playing with me!)

Well! We staggered on & on and then found that our guide to the new camp had been on in advance with Daniel so Wilmot & I told him to wait for B & D Coy to come on & then went to the

'Walking Wounded' place & got some tea & bread – Wilmot then saw the M.O. & got a lift home on the score of bad feet. The trenches were frightfully muddy so much so that men got stuck for hours on end before they could be dug out – unlike the liquid mud at Ypres.

Geoffrey to Vera

France, 3 November 1916

I quite agree about one's friends: abroad they mean far more to one than at peace in England & after the War people will be more sincere I think than before... I should love to see Malta and all its reminiscences of the Past and glorious colourings tho' the heat must be appalling. Yes! I love Rupert Brooke & took him up with some of the other verses which Edward gave me, to the trenches the last time but owing to wet, mud and squashed cake in my pack, which, the cake, seemed to permeate everything my edition is somewhat dilapidated now tho' the dearer for that. We had a fairly bad time of it & when relieved at 8 one night we didn't get back here until 9 the next morning so you can understand how far we came... To start with the entire Coy got out to go back over the top at the same time instead of by platoons at intervals & the Huns started shelling so I got on & took all the available men & went on which was the only thing to be done, feeling very 'windy'. Well! I had been over the land by day & as there were no landmarks, by night it was difficult to find the way so we plunged on splashing thro mud & crump holes. I halted & heard Wilmot's voice behind & found almost the entire Coy. following: later we came across Daniel & we all egged on. The trenches were full of sticky mud & some men got in for 16 hrs without being able to get out. We got up the hill & finally got on duckboards & by this time we were rolling along asleep for the most part – however with much effort we struggled into camp – 10 miles is a long way to come after a tour in trenches don't you think?

Well! This morning I spent in spring cleaning & as I had fallen flat twice I was literally covered with mud from head to foot! Also my servant got hit so have been showing my new laddie how to carry on – but these domestic details must be horribly boring.

Vera to Edward

St George's Hospital, Malta, 4 November 1916

It seems queer still to think of Victor at the front. I don't wonder he thinks his regiment a marvel after what he has been used to; any form of active service must be quite a godsend after the P.Bs [Provisional Battalions] & the old women there that he has been used to. . .

I like this hospital immensely & cannot say anything good enough about the Matron & Assistant M. There are the fewest possible conventions & the greatest possible freedom; all the rules are so sensible that no one dreams of breaking them. As for the nonsense about V.A.Ds being unable to be left on duty without a Sister no one thinks anything of it here; if they did the Sisters couldn't get off duty as often there is only one to each block. It is a frequent occurrence to have charge of anything between 50 & 100 patients for a whole afternoon or evening & sometimes for a whole day when the Sister has a day off. Our block has five wards with 14 patients in each; there is only one Sister – & another V.A.D. & me there. It's a task taking all their temperatures & pulses morning & evening; they all have medicines too, 3 times a day, sometimes two or three different kinds, which I have to give. They are all malarias & eye wounds & diseases. It makes me laugh to think how in some wards at the 1st London I wasn't allowed to give a single medicine.

Edward to Vera

London, 5–7 November 1916

I will most certainly send you a cable if anything of the least importance happens to Tah or Geoffrey . . . I don't know if Father has forgiven you for going to Malta but he never says anything about it now if he hasn't because he knows my opinion on the subject . . .

Nov: 7th

Such a lot of things seem to have occupied me that this had been a bit out of it for 2 days. Had a letter from W.O. [War Office] this morning telling me to report my address to Hqrs. London District, Home Guards, Whitehall and that I should have medical board 'shortly', after which I must proceed at once (in italics) to the 3rd Battalion at Sunderland, so I expect I shall go about the end of this week or beginning of next. . .

A week ago to-day (31st) I went down to Keymer and had a very interesting day. Various people are writing to Mrs L. via Hodder and Stoughton with ref. to Boy of my Heart. One was a girl whose fiancé was killed after being in France a week and who thought he was just like Roland. Another was an officer of the delightful name of Gerald Wynne Rushton who first wrote some weeks ago, saying that he was badly wounded and was going to have a serious operation and if it turned out badly and he was dying she must come and see him (in Dublin if you please) before he died. He has however got over the operation and now wants to meet Mrs Leighton, but his glamour has rather disappeared since he enclosed a very rotten poem of his in his last letter. Another is a Flying Officer who writes in the handwriting and style of a man of 50 but is really 19. His name is Reginald Lowndes but he always signs himself Reg. . . . In his letters he explains what an awful sinner he is which he says is due to being badly brought up and having a very worldly mother; he is pleased to think that he and Roland would have been great friends and he seems to admire him very much and Mrs Leighton. At Keymer we had a fine time with the usual food difficulties; as we could only get 3 eggs for supper I made scrambled eggs on a sort of spirit stove with great success.

Vera to Edward

Malta, 10 November 1916

I am glad you were still on leave when you last wrote, though I understand absolutely that you will not mind when it comes to an end; somehow, though it is due to you, you feel impatient at being unoccupied when everyone is doing so much & all the people you care about are abroad. Yes I know just what it is like in the flat; now perhaps you realise what I had to put up with for two years, & not even in London, but in Buxton. Mother used to tell you I was 'difficult' & 'discontented' & 'trying' & you really used to think there was a good deal in what they said, but now – do you wonder? The only variation of the present life was that Father instead of going to Harrods, used to sit in front of a blazing fire & smoke till the room became unendurable, & instead of talking about the War used to talk about the weather! It was awful too to be working for an exam alone, & want to discuss the books one was reading, & the things one hoped to achieve, & get other opinions about them – there was no-one, no one! Only Mother to remark that she hated the sound of the word 'exam'. I think I might quite well say with Roland 'I am always lonely – mentally.' For after that there was only the nine months at Oxford, & then – hospitals. In all the five years I have described, I have never really been able to see much of you – never, for any consecutive period.

Geoffrey to Edward

France, 12 November 1916

Well! I saw that an account of our doings I was in was in Nov 8th Times tho' we didn't actually take the trench mentioned. I was sent on in advance. Next morning I went up again to look round tho' this time we were in a trench in which the Boshe had been before. Had to go over the top for 100yds down the ridge in full view of Boshe (my first guides lost their way so had to start all over again with new ones).

Once again we have to eat so more anon!

6.oo pm

To resume after chasing around seeing that Mess stuff arrived
from Canteen & all surplus stuff packed ready to move off
tomorrow. Heigho. It's a busy life. Well! Boshe sniped us going
down & after I had looked round – the trench was full of
departed Huns ghastly sights – but you know all about such.
Somehow in daylight they looked far worse than at night. I was
almost ill on the spot for such things affect all our family that way.
Going back Huns sniped harder & got my guide in shoulder but
he cheered up at prospects of blighty in front of him. We were
haring along in the mud for dear life! This time up I was disgustingly windy chiefly owing to having to stay in one rotten
little bay as the trench had been closed by our heavies prior to
our inhabitation: also the Boshe crumped us pretty heavily. I was
quite glad to get back alright – Coming across that Sunken Road
again we had a narrow shave as just before we got to it suddenly
a shell burst – we couldn't hear it coming about 2 yards to our
right & how on earth we got out without anyone being hit I
cannot think. . .

This afternoon I borrowed Lefroy's horse & rode into the city
with the Tower – it was quite decent being there again & there are
one or two quite decent shops there now – as far as shops go in
this part of the world.

Yesterday afternoon Wilmot & I passed about a yard away from
the Prince of Wales who trots around here quite a lot: he looks an
awful babe.

———

Vera to Edward

Malta, 13 November 1916

One's work [here] is less rigid, less mechanical & stereotyped,
though one has much more responsibility, & it matters a great deal
more whether one does things well or badly than it did in
England. There there was always someone or other watching you
so closely that if you did anything wrong they would pounce on

you & do it themselves; here there is no one to watch how you are doing things, & if you do them wrong only the result will show... This makes you much more careful & therefore much more sure of yourself. I feel the personality that was crushed & oppressed out of me at Camberwell returning by leaps & bounds. Geoffrey was right about that place; there was an atmosphere about it that was deadly & I ought to have left it long before I did, especially after last Christmas (though I am glad I didn't for the sake of July 1st & after).

———————

Edward to Vera

London, 16 November 1916

You may already know that there has been another big show against the German original front line N. of Thiepval against which all of our attempts on July 1st were unsuccessful. We have now taken St. Pierre Divion and the famous impregnable Beaumont Hamel, but I am afraid casualties must have been heavy. I am also much afraid that Geoffrey may have been in it and possibly Tah too if he was moved down but we don't know anything yet.

———————

Victor to Vera

Billets, France, 18 November 1916

Thank you so much for your letter. I was delighted to get it and to find that you had not forgotten my existence which is rather what one expects on Active Service. One soon learns that people are remembered in 9 cases out of 10 so long as they are actually present. Afterwards – no. It is inevitable that it should be so.

I am very glad to hear you are feeling better & are not as worried by the climate as you expected to be. I hope by now that you are quite well, though it is a great pity you are brought so much in contact with Infectious Diseases. I think they are fairly harmless when you are well yourself, but if you are run down it is rather different. . .

As you might expect I only just managed to get out at all. 36 names were sent in from our Battn. In response to an urgent call from Eastern Command & I was last but one on the list – they don't encourage people who want to go, in the T.F., as they always regard France as a penal settlement. I was told I was to be attached with 14 others to the 10th R.B.'s. When I got to the Base I was told I was to be attached with 3 others to the 9th K.R.R. When we arrived we were told we were to be transferred. . . . I really could not stand a Territorial crowd again. I daresay they fight as well as any one else, but they are so hopelessly ignorant when it comes to doing things in the right way. . .

I am thinking of trying for a permanent commission in the Regulars. What do you think about it? The only objection I can see to it is the pay, and after the War one will, I should think, be able to live on one's pay in most regiments, though probably not in the Rifles. I think I should try to get into the Indian Army after the War if by any chance I am still alive then, as the pay would be higher and the life more interesting as there generally seems to be a certain amount happening on the frontier. . .

I am afraid I can't really agree with what you & Thurlow say about 'catching up' Edward by coming out here. I don't think I shall change at all out here. After all Edward did not change at all until July 1st when . . . he became 10 years older. Before I came out I hoped that being out here would turn me into a normal person. I no longer entertain any such hopes. A 'do' on the grand scale may have that effect on me, but it is really hardly worth while being changed for an odd five minutes. Perhaps you do not agree?

I hope Thurlow will not get hit again. I expect he has been in this latest show which seems to be about the biggest thing the British have done. If we can only keep the Somme wound open during the Winter, it should prove of the greatest assistance to us in the Spring.

———————

Geoffrey to Vera

France, 18 November 1916

Since my last letter much has happened – we have been to the War again and the weather treated us abominably: however our Bde did well taking an important Hun trench – we didn't go over the top but had to clean up and hang on to the trench. Luckily we had no officer casualties tho' there were many among the men. But as our no. of officers is at present the irreducible minimum perhaps this accounts for it. . .

This village has an interesting old castle and church and is a thoroughly delightful place. Our billets are luxurious and to find oneself in a bed once again is perfect bliss; the people too cannot do enough for us. How long we remain here I cannot tell.

But enough of self. Edward sent me one of his delightful letters a few days ago & he says he is taking a course of Homer to revive himself – I envy him as my little Latin & less Greek won't allow me to do the same tho' I know what he enjoys from a few lines done at Chigwell, painfully and slowly looking up each word etc. It seems rotten having to return to Sunderland, away up there in exile, as the fares to London are enormous. Still, hope the W.O. has forgotten his existence. Do you know if he has been decorated yet (A wee kitten is frightfully interested in my pen & makes frequent dabs at it!) at Buckingham Palace?

(Wilmot wants me to sew up his new cap as he has removed the flap!) Yesterday we went into a large town with a glorious cathedral, by motor lorry, and spent most of our time shopping new boots puttees caps etc: if this goes on our accounts at Cox will fast ebb out. However the shops there were perfectly priceless and we thoroughly enjoyed ourselves!

Once more we are talking about ourselves. Haven't heard from Victor Richardson for some time: hope he is all right.

Vera to Edward

Malta, 28 November 1916

I had no idea until you told me that there had been anything in the nature of a 'show' about the middle of November. Our vague little communiqués are worded just the same whether they are about a great advance or the haphazard capture of a few prisoners in a small village, and as I think I have told you, we have no newspaper for news. I have asked Mother to send me the daily edition of the Times describing any event of importance like the sinking of the Britannic, the British Advance, or the death of Francis Joseph, as the Weekly Times, which I have chiefly for the casualty lists, only summarizes. . .

Isn't it dreadful the way hospital ships are being torpedoed; I should think even the Germans will find it hard to explain away four in a fortnight. I suppose since they cannot shake our supremacy at sea they are wreaking their vengeance on the only kind of ship which is known not even to attempt to defend itself. We are all very sad at the fate of the poor gorgeous Britannic; it seems impossible to imagine those beautiful saloons & state cabins at the bottom of the sea. We are wondering what is the fate of some of the nice people we met on board but we hear that some of the Sisters are coming here to recover from the shock & partly to wait till the Powers that Be decide what to do with them; so I suppose we shall hear all about it. The Germans, as you probably know, had threatened her, and now that she *is* sunk I suppose there is no harm in telling you that we had a very narrow escape ourselves; we were chased through the Archipelago by a submarine & for some time were in considerable danger though fortunately for our peace of mind we did not know it at the time. . . We only thought we were going rather fast for a region supposedly difficult to navigate, but as we always went very fast it did not impress us much. Isn't it extraordinary that both the ships which brought us here should have suffered the same fate!

———

Edward to Vera

> *Cleadon Hutments, near Sunderland,*
> *29–30 November 1916*

Wasn't it rotten that the Britannic would be sunk like that though nearly everyone was saved? A lucky escape for you. The night before last (27th–28th) we had Zepps, again for the first time for six or seven weeks; they came to the NE coast not far from here and E. coast of Norfolk; one was brought down and we distinctly saw another brought down about 20 miles S of us near Hartlepool. We had a warning and all lights were put out and the men 'stood to' in their huts. One of the sergeant-majors was the first to see the Zepp. which was well caught by searchlights and you could see the flash of shells bursting around it though it was too far off to hear. Suddenly it caught fire at one end, the fire spread lighting up the whole sky, and amidst the cheers of the Cleadon detachment, the ball of fire fell (as we afterwards heard) into the sea.

> *November 30th*

Lawks! Fancy being 21. How ridiculously old!

———————

Geoffrey to Edward

> *France, 5 December 1916*

Hope the Investiture by the King won't prove a very terrible ordeal. Personally I would loathe it but it matters not as I shall never get a Military Cross ... Hope you are managing to keep dry and warm now? I should love the place for the sake of its bleakness and the sea but I suppose you soon get weary of it all. . .

There are selfish moments when I long to have you here – we could have such topping rides together in the afternoons and the country is great here and in parts forcibly reminiscent of the fir forests in England. And then in the evenings it would be a joy to have you here, but it is better really that you aren't. (Vera says

Victor Richardson loves war and says 'Any war is better than no war' etc. Well! If he is not a hypocrite I admire him and wish I had his martial temperament!)

Well! I hope Fate may bring us together again some day: that we should be back at Oxford again seems too much to hope.

Sorry this letter is so dull tonight. Everything seems awry and words won't come as I want them to.

Victor to Vera

France, 6 December 1916

You seem to think that I have become a quite horrible individual. Perhaps that is so, but I don't think you quite understand the way I look at things. To start with you are quite right when you speak of coming out here as a release from imprisonment. It is. I wouldn't be back in England for worlds. . . I was perfectly wretched until I did get out here.

It is quite awful to feel the silent contempt of those whom one regards as one's dearest friends. Perhaps I am over sensitive: I cannot help that. . .

After all if I stopped to consider the deeper meaning and significance of these things my life would be one long misery. And it is the same, I am sure, with every man who thinks. Take a man in the prime of life killed by a stray bullet as many often happen. Consider all the anxieties of his upbringing – all that the trained product has cost materially and spiritually. Reflect that in one minute's time one may be just the same – blotted out for eternity. Why! one simply can't afford to let one's mind dwell on these things. One could not carry on.

You will be surprised to hear what has depressed me more than anything else – the Crucifixes one occasionally sees standing in desolate shell-swept areas. The horror of the one intensifies a hundredfold that of the other, and the image of the tortured Christ strikes one as an appalling monument to the Personification of Utter Failure.

As regards suitability for this kind of War – very few men are suitable & I most certainly am not. But one has to strive to become suitable – and very few indeed fail entirely in this respect. One has to try therefore to convince oneself – and if possible other people – that one is at any rate a decent imitation of a soldier.

Geoffrey to Vera

France, 7 December 1916

Do you know Tosti's 'Goodbye'? The gramophone is playing it now – I love it. We have 'La Cygne' which Edward plays and used to play to us at Sandgate – often yearn for those days again. Mrs Bendon sent me a note today & wanted to know if there was any chance of my getting leave at Christmas – the fatuous people at home who mainly ask this question in letter after letter (Orders just arrive.) make me furious as there isn't the slightest chance of leave for months yet as I am still 2 from the bottom of the list! Eh bien. We are keeping our Christmas here on the 12th as on Christmas day itself we shall be elsewhere - who knows where? Expect we shall leave a few days after and it will be a long farewell to civilization and its luxuries. Still I suppose all good things come to an end some time or another but our priceless little mess with its high carved oak chairs & round oak table with wonderfully carved foxes for legs: our sheeted beds: the peaceful village with the railway running alongside and beyond the railway the swirling Somme: all these with the fir woods will be a pleasant dream in the future. There is a quaint old town crier here who comes round from time to time beating a large drum and then chanting much French. At present as our Lewis Gun Officer is on leave, I'm doing his job and find it awfully interesting and have got a fairly intelligent set of men to instruct. The great advantage of the job is that I get a horse for route marches and any other time I want it. Never shall I forget Edward & myself setting forth in great splendour from some stables in Folkestone, to have our first riding lesson: and my horse bolting with me causing a realistic John Gilpin effect: the Canadian Tommy who restored my hat &

handkerchief which had floated away, without the vestige of a smile on his face always has my admiration.

In those days we often used to sit on the beach at the end of the garden and look at the waves tumbling in over each other. Such things only a small portion of mankind seem to appreciate and are looked on by the majority as extraordinary people. Mrs Brittain sent me a topping photo of him done in the same way as my last ones at the Army & Navy Stores. It is an excellent likeness of him (Enter Daniel again and Wilmot!) tho' he looks much older. I shall send mine home before we leave here but you will have had one before now. He seems to be having a frightfully cold time up at Sunderland and I do hope he stays in England for a long time. Fate seems to have decreed that we shall not serve together again for a long time. . . On Christmas Day – 12th here – the men are having an enormous feed which will make most of them ill I think. A concert is to be held afterwards which should be amusing at least. (Dinner so yet another interruption.) . . .

8.40

The first night we were in this village at the station end of it, my jolly old thing who owned the billet suddenly burst out with 'Oh but Monsieur you are so lovable.' I fled up stairs to hide my embarrassment (don't know how this word is spelt).

Had quite a strafe with my present landlady who objected to me using my rubber bath in my bedroom as she said that the water 'washed away the ceiling below' – which was perhaps poetical licence on her part – and all the time she had a priceless bathroom with an English shaped bath in it and two huge coppers in which to boil lashings of water – but the French don't understand the desire to wash.

Well! Please excuse this dull letter but nothing has happened here of interest lately except a bomb accident the day before yesterday which gave Blighters to six men.

Vera to Edith Brittain

Malta, 12 December 1916

I do wonder if I shall ever see [Edward] again; it is very hard that we should be the generation to suffer the War, though I suppose it is very splendid too, & is making us better & wiser & deeper men & women (at any rate some of us . . . . .) than our ancestors ever were or our descendants ever will be. It seems to me that the War will make a big division of 'before' & 'after' in the history of the World, almost if not quite as big as the 'B.C.' & 'A.D.' division made by the birth of Christ . . . We are all very excited about the Fall of the Government, and very glad, as it is bound to make a change in the prosecution of the War, & it could hardly be a change for the worse! We are anxiously waiting for details.

Geoffrey to Vera

France, 15 December 1916

Well! We left our village of peace early in the morning. . . We marched away to a village five miles away and the snow over the fields and on the trees looked topping. Altogether the effect was rather Napoleonic. After 4 hours on the train – which were quite cool – we detrained and I was detailed to take charge of the unloading party. We got the Lewis Gun limbers out and had the bodies of the cart fixed on.to the wheels and then got the stores out quickly. After that we found billets and got warm.

The next day after parade in the morning I rode over to an Officers Ordnance place (Post just come in! Cheers! parcel & several letters) to get some kind of rain coat but their stock had run out so I went over again yesterday afternoon, but again the new stock hadn't arrived. . .

After tea we went to the 'Very Lights' a concert party of — Div. which was excellent. The stage was draped with dark green & white in stripes and the pierrots were in dark green with white bobs.

'A Long long Trail' sung behind the curtain opened the show & it had a most pleasing effect. The dancing & everything else was topping but perhaps this was due to the fact that there was a stringband as opposed to the ordinary blare without violins etc. The man who was Columbine danced perfectly & was a jolly good impersonator. Our Div. lady is hopeless always mincing about & very gawky, grinning inanely the while! In fact our 'Duds' are hopeless where compared with the Very Lights . . . Soon even this place will be 'long ago & far away'!

There is a jolly little kid here called Michain with an enormous head & solemn large blue eyes and a full moon face if I may describe it thus. His surprise at hearing our gramophone was too funny for words. Must go off to Quartermaster now to get a canteen and see about Ammunition for Lewis Guns. . .

Later. 3.15 p.m.

. . . Haven't heard from Victor Richardson for a long time expect he is as busy as ever and one who likes war must do far more work than his more peace loving brethren.

I wish his mantle might fall on my shoulders.

(Wee child has just entered so I gave him two chocolate biscuits which pleased him.)

Vera to Edward

Malta, 16 December 1916

There are so many things I wonder if I shall ever do. More than anything I wonder if I shall ever see you again. In England Mother says the War is expected to last *five* years more. I should think we should all be dead by then – from exhaustion, if nothing else.

It's the anniversary of Roland's death in a week; I am so glad I am here – a place He never knew, & where I never knew Him – rather than at Keymer or at the 1st London, which would be full of the unhappy memories of this time last year. It doesn't seem a year ago – & yet so much much more.

Geoffrey to Edward

France, 16 December 1916

Well! We have parades in morning here and usually the afternoon off but I expect we shall be moving up very soon. There is an officers Ordnance a few miles away & this afternoon I went over for the 4th time to try to get some kind of Waterproof coat as my trench coat is quite hopeless now & would be too costly to have it done up. Well! The stores were in but not unpacked so am going again tomorrow to see if any better luck! Went with Lander who did nothing but talk about his promotion & why he ought to have 3 pips up! Such conversation is naturally boring . . . . .

After tea we had priceless baths at the Divisional baths & when clean went to the 'Duds' our Div. Concert Party. They are jolly good but not so good as the 'Very Lights' which belonged to [the] Div. we relieved.

———

Edward to Vera

Cleadon Hutments, near Sunderland,
19 December 1916

I came up to town on Tuesday the 16th, went to Buckingham Palace on the 17th at 10.30 am. Mother came with me in the taxi from home and I dropped her just outside the gates and drove in alone; I ascended a wide staircase and deposited my hat and stick in a sort of cloak room, keeping my gloves (your gloves), went up more stairs, was asked by an old boy in a frock coat what I was to receive, was then directed to another old boy who verified my name etc and told me to stand on one side of the room – a large room with portraits of royal personages round the walls. There were 3 C.M.G.'s, about 12 D.S.O.'s and about 30 M.C.'s so it was a fairly small investiture. We were instructed what to do by a Colonel who I believe is the King's special private secretary and then the show started. One by one we walked into an adjoining room about 6 paces – halt – left turn – bow – 2 paces forward – King pins on cross – shake hands – pace back – bow – right turn and slope off by another door. The various acts were not read out, but the Colonel just called out 'Receive the C.M.G.' etc. Colonel so-and-so. The King spoke to a few of us including me; he said 'I hope you have quite recovered from your wound', to which I replied 'Very nearly thank you, Sir', and then went out with the cross in my pocket in a case. I met Mother just outside and we went off towards Victoria thinking we had quite escaped all the photographers, but unfortunately one beast from the Daily Mirror saw us and took us, but luckily it does not seem to have come out well as it has not been in the paper of which I am glad as it is rather bad form to have your photo in a ½ d rag if avoidable. That evening I went down to Folkestone because Watts and a fellow named Hutchings – a lieutenant (regular) whom I met here and got to like very much – were going to the front the next morning. I talked to Watts till nearly 1 o'clock that night and Hutchings arrived by the leave train in the morning and I saw him for an hour. I felt their going awfully because I had quite enjoyed life up here while they were here, but now it has become intolerably boring. I had to come back here on the Friday night (15th) because they would not extend my investiture leave, and so I hadn't time to do much shopping. . .

You may be interested to hear that I am taking a regular commission for various reasons: e.g. at the end of the war I couldn't be sent away and told I wasn't wanted any longer perhaps before I was prepared to go and perhaps just at the wrong time of year for going to Oxford, but could send in my papers in my own time, but nevertheless should have the right to do so just as soon as a temporary officer if I did want to go at once; also there is more standing attached to a regular commission and it might be of considerable assistance to me in getting into the Civil Service. Anyhow it is clear that I should still be making a living of a sort while I was looking round to see what was to be done and should not have to live on Father which would be so objectionable after all this time. Of course it is also conceivable that circumstances might almost compel me to stay on in the Army after the war, though I have no desire to do so, and in that case it would be far better for me to take a regular commission now; I have already lost over 2 years seniority; why lose more? Of course if I do this I shall retain my temporary rank as lieutenant and shall probably continue to serve with a service battalion. However . . . I am soon going to apply to go to Grantham on a short machine gun course as I want to know more about those most important weapons. I also want to get away from this desolate and boring place for a time . . . After that I shall be about ready to go out again.

Dearest, I know it is just a year, and you are thinking of Him and His terrible death, and of what might have been, even as I am too. This year has, I think, made him seem very far off but yet all the more unforgettable. His life was like a guiding star which left this firmament when he died and went to some other one where it still shines as brightly, but so far away. I know you will in a way live through last year's tragedy again but may it bring still greater hopes for 'the last and brightest Easter day' which you and I can barely conceive let alone understand, when

> *'We too shall live our passionate poem through*
> *On God's serene to-morrow'.*

How happy I would be to see you meet again!

———————

Ploegsteert, May 1915.

Love have I known + dawn - and gold of day-time
And winds and songs, and all the joys that are,
Known once, and as a child that tires with play-time
Leaped from them to the elemental dust of War.

I have [struck out] blood + death, ... that has [struck out] to cease.
And ... ... but ... to cease.
I am sickened, with ... love that only lives for lending,
And all the loathsome pettiness of Peace.

Give me, Good God of Battles, a field of death,
(A Hell of fire;) a strong man's agony.

(* The bracketed words were scribbled out [something]
also evidently intended as a substitute for them.)

*Roland's 'Ploegsteert', as transcribed by Vera and sent to Edward,
14 January 1916*

SEVEN

26 DECEMBER 1916 – 11 JUNE 1917

I spoke with you but seldom, yet there lay
Some nameless glamour in your written word . . .

So now I ponder, since your day is done,
Ere dawn was past, on all you meant to me . . .
— VERA BRITTAIN, 'In Memoriam: G.R.Y.T.
(Killed in Action, April 23rd, 1917)'

I am so tired.
. . . all I loved the best
Is gone, and every good that I desired
Passes away . . .
I am so tired.
— VERA BRITTAIN, 'Sic Transit—
(V.R., Died of Wounds, 2nd
London General Hospital,
Chelsea, June 9th, 1917)'

Victor to Vera

France, 26 December 1916

You asked what we think out here about the sinking of hospital ships in the Mediterranean. In the first place I am afraid we don't think very much about it at all – it is not brought home to us as it is to you. I think we are all rather apt out here to concentrate our attention on the Western front. In the second place some of us are a little apt to criticise the Navy, but I plead not guilty to this charge myself. By the way one of the boats I travelled on when I took that draft out in July – the Queen – was sunk in the Channel raid a month or two ago.

I expect to be going on the Coy Commander's Course at 3rd Army School shortly. I am very glad as it is a very thorough Course, and ought to make me tolerably efficient from the technical point of view. But I am afraid nothing will ever make me a good soldier, owing to my being one of those unfortunate beings who are cursed with a temperament. Of course I get on alright as things are with us at present, but I have not yet seen War. I am perpetually haunted by the fear of not coming up to scratch in an emergency. I tell you it is a positive curse to have a temperament out here. The ideal thing to be is a typical Englishman. And the curse is trebled if you are also impetuous and excitable as I now realise I am and always have been. . .

We came out of trenches on the anniversary of the day on which He was mortally wounded. That afternoon was the most glorious sunset I have seen out here. Only a coincidence of course, but it appealed to me. I have felt His loss more in the last three months than ever before. I feel that He would have been able to banish all my doubts and fears for the future.

Vera to Edward

Malta, 29 December 1916

I thought Christmas time would make me very sad but it really has not after all, as it is impossible to do anything but enter into the spirit of things here. Everyone is so friendly & so free, & everyone seems determined to make up for the lack of home advantages by taking an extra amount of trouble. Then of course the weather, which is very bright & warm & full of colour without being too hot, adds greatly to everything. . . I remember on New Year's Eve last year sitting in the chill dimness of that little room at Keymer and miserably wondering how I was ever going to get to the next New Year's Eve, & what it would be like. But I don't think anything I imagined came anywhere near the mark, & I certainly had no presentiment of all the big things that would happen in between.

This afternoon a cable came from Mother & Father wishing me many happy returns; wasn't it sweet of them! At first it gave me quite a fright as I had been so busy all day that I had quite forgotten it was my birthday at all, & I immediately jumped to the conclusion that either Geoffrey was dead or you had gone back to the front. However I just remembered before I opened it.

Geoffrey to Edward

France, 30 December 1916

At present there is an animated game of bridge going on at this somewhat small table so concentration is a trifle difficult! Well! We have left civilization for some time and when the Bn. went up this last time I was left behind in charge of details which was lucky as the Bn. had a rotten time owing to hard frost and much wet – tho' the numbers of trench feet have been remarkably few – 3 in fact. I had to appear on parade each morning to drill untrained men who are dumped when the Bn. moves up. On the first afternoon I went for a ride with Jacques – am awfully glad we learnt to sit on a horse together down at Folkestone – wonder if those days will ever come again let's hope so – & the next afternoon I went into a village you know quite well to get some canteen stuff for the Mess. And yesterday afternoon we were rushing around getting the camp ready for the Bn. when it came [in]. Got our Mess a priceless dinner & put out their valises & hot water bottles in them . . . At 12 pm. an order came in for me to be at — Camp to collect stragglers at 7 am. Well! I arose at 5.30 & there was a heavy wind & driving rain . . . Got in about 7.30 and was damned glad to get brekker – once again I'm Mess president. The weather lately has been wet here. Really War begins to lose its glamour after a bit don't you think?!

Geoffrey to Vera

France, 30 December 1916

Well! We moved away from Civilization in two days and then spent Christmas Day in moving camp to half a mile away. When the Bn moved up I was 'dumped' i.e. left behind in charge of the 'Details' here.

In the mornings at 9 I had to saunter about on parade while the untrained men were being drilled. The first afternoon Jacques & I went for a ride to discover good roads for transport and at one spot on the left of the road we saw green grass growing. All else is churned up mud here at present! The next afternoon I went into a village, thro' which Edward has passed I'm sure, and bought quantities of stuff for our Messes as once again I'm Mess President. The last day was spent in allotting the huts to the Company Quartermaster Sergts & in getting ready for the arrival of the Bn. Really I'm getting quite domesticated! Put out all our C. Coy officers' valises & put hot water bottles in to air them and made things look as cosy as possible: had a good meal ready for them when they came in about 9.30–10 drenched thro' and war-worn. . . At 12 pm a message came round that I was to go to — and be there at 7 am. to collect & bring in stragglers. So I arose at 5.30 with the wind whistling outside and rain splashing down & set out on the Doctor's horse. It was rather eerie as I hadn't the faintest idea of the way and the horse kept on seeing vain things. However having found 10 men lying on top of many pairs of skwelching thigh boots I got them out & we trickled slowly homewards. . . Really I'm far too sympathetic with the men to be any earthly use as an officer. To get on well you usually want to be absolutely selfish & heartless – of course there are exceptions. We shall be a long time I think this time up. I only hope that I may be given strength both of mind & body – if Fate wills it – to last.

———————

Vera to Edward

Malta, 3 January 1917

Do you remember how I always used to tell you that when He & I met, right up to the very last, we never could think of anything to say? Wouldn't it be difficult to know what to say if one met again after being separated by the greatest gulf of all. And as you say, He's so unforgettable, even though He belongs, as it were, to another life in which both you & I happened to live as well. I can see you now teasing Him about 'The Quiet Voice', and I remember very distinctly how I cried one day just after He had gone to the front when I was looking in one of your drawers for something or other & came across a letter from Him to you signed 'Sometime An Ancient Majesty', & another signed 'Monseigneur'; I remember it made me think of the time we might have had all together at college. Sometimes I feel very weary of this life – specially when I recall such small incidents – & wonder if this age-long War will leave *anything* worth having behind it at all. If not, may it not leave us either! . . .

It seems rather curious that on the night of Dec. 23rd I was kneeling by my bed in the dark thinking about Him & that night last year when suddenly just before 11.0 at the very hour of His death the whole sky was suddenly lighted up & everything outside became queerly & startlingly visible. At first I thought it was just lightning, which is very frequent at night here, but when the light remained & did not flash away again I felt quite uncanny & afraid & hid my face in my hands for two or three minutes. When I looked up again the light had gone; I went to the window but could see nothing at all to account for the sudden brilliant glow. A day or two after I heard that there had been a most extraordinary shooting-star which had lit up the whole sky for two or three minutes before it had fallen to earth. Shooting stars also are common here, or rather, there is so much less atmosphere between us & the stars than there is in England that we can see them much more clearly; but this was quite an extraordinary star; of course they never light up the sky like that one did. (Someone suggested it was the Star of Bethlehem fallen to earth because it could no longer shine in the dark horror of War.) Just coincidence of course, but strange from my point of view that it should have happened at that hour. I remember one day last winter how Clare pointed out to me a star, which shone very brightly among the others & said 'Wouldn't it be strange if that star were Roland'.....

Edward to Vera

Cleadon Hutments, near Sunderland, 4 January 1917

Most of the 11th Bn. who were wounded on July 1st have just gone or are just going back again; I got another month light duty a week ago to-day and so expect to be passed fit for general service in about 3 weeks and to go out again sometime next month just like last year. I am afraid there will be some very big show this spring and summer as I think we shall make every possible attempt to break through; if we do so and are not hampered by the weather the war ought to be pretty well ended this year, but I think there is still a great sacrifice of life to be made yet, and, as you say, we may never see one another again...

Over Xmas and New Year everyone was on the alert up here and all along the coast because there was some information that the Huns might make a raid on the coast; the artillery and machine gunners had to 'stand to' at 5 am. every morning, but nothing has come of it and normal conditions are on again.

Vera to Edward

Malta, 12 January 1917

Mother sent me out the 'Times' with Roland's 'In Memoriam' notice in it; the Leightons sent it too. Though I would never say so to them, I am afraid I don't like it very much, for I don't think He would have liked it; I can't exactly say why, unless I can express what I mean by saying He wouldn't have cared for anything so adjectival. I always remember the night He spent with me in Buxton 2 years ago next March just before He first went to the front, & how He said to me 'I do hope if I am killed no one will put that I was the "dearly beloved" son of anyone in the paper.' If I am alive next December it will be my turn & I will put one in myself 'in proud & undying memory' certainly, but more of the quieter kind I think He would have appreciated. What do you think yourself?

I have always meant to tell you but until now have forgotten, that one of the chief reasons why I am so fond of St. George's is that when you stand just below the Sisters' quarters (this hospital is at the bottom of a hill) the road leading downhill over the rocks from the next hospital, St. Andrew's, seems to unfold itself like a ribbon, & reminds me more than any road I have ever seen of

> 'The sunshine on the long white road
> That ribboned down the hill . . . .'

Somehow this road seems to link up Buxton & France & Malta, & gives me the feeling that I have been destined to stand upon it from the beginning of time. . .

The other night a great event took place – namely I had a bath, the first proper one I have had since coming here, bad as it may sound. Formerly we had just a little hip bath (one between 6) & if we wanted hot water we had to fetch it ourselves in cans from boilers in the back yard (the boilers only hold enough for about 12 people). But now three bath tents have been put up & we can all have a bath twice a week; there is a tap with *real* hot water, worked by a geyser on a primus. (You have to keep on constantly getting out of the bath to pump the primus, which would other-wise go out, but what of that!) As the mechanism is somewhat complicated, an orderly prepares our baths for us, and on windy nights it is very amusing to see people clad in nightgowns & great coats with hair streaming over their shoulders standing out-side the tents waiting their turn for the baths, and making frantic efforts to prevent all their garments from blowing round their necks!

Edward to Vera

Cleadon Hutments, 14 January 1917

I expect you know that Tah is at the 3rd Army School throughout January and has the courtesy title of Captain while he is there and has to wear Captain's badges; it is a most curious thing and I have never heard of an instance of it before. . . I am fed up with this place. I have been waiting to be put on that Lewis Gun Course at Grantham for 3 weeks and nothing has happened yet. . .

Geoffrey to Vera

France, 18 January 1917

The weather has been wet here lately – we arrived from the line about 3 days ago: we shall only be here about a week and then up once again. This village is dull – a long line of houses on either side of the road: low lying, it is usually swathed in mist: but the town with the Leaning Figure is near and Wilmot & I got a lift in to it yesterday. There are more shops in it than there were in the early days of last August when I was dumped with 7 others beside a small stream in which we bathed every day. Last night was cold and this morning all the mud and drabness of the place was covered with snow. This afternoon I went on a tour of exploration to find a place for a range but could only find one place, a quarry, and that useless, as men work there all day. I must say the country looked topping: everything snow white & clean. . . Over the road outside there flows an endless stream of traffic, limbers, lorries, red cross ambulances, infantry marching up and marching back, all day long.

Geoffrey to Edward

France, 24 January 1917

The weather here is fine and frightfully cold at present – hope it abates before we go up next time or there will be some bad feet. We shan't be here much longer...

I'm beginning to feel as tho' I don't care a damn about this Bn. It is rather difficult to keep up an everlasting enthusiasm but I grow more & more convinced that I shall end my days as a 2nd Lt: I wish for the School's sake only that it might be otherwise.

Vera to Edward

Malta, 25 January 1917

You ask me how long I mean to stay in Malta; well, as you know, we sign on for 6 months at a time, & I think it more than likely that when Stella & I have done our first 6 months, which is in two months time, we shall sign on again for another 6. They are making it more & more difficult & disadvantageous for us to resign now, & one can only leave by resigning & joining up again, to be sent goodness knows where. I can't possibly do anything else but nurse till the war is over; even if I meant to do nothing (which I certainly do not) I think it very unlikely under the present more energetic system of government that either I or anyone else would be able to do nothing for long. Since I am in for nursing I may as well do it not only in its highest form (which foreign service is) but in a place where I am happy... I think if one has to be in hospital it is better to be far away from home; it is very unsettling to be able to go home or to friends' houses & then have to go back on duty just as you are getting into the home atmosphere; it makes you hate hospital so much more, & then you never get interested in the hospital because you have so many interests outside.

... in the end I realise that the only person I really mind about not seeing for a long time is yourself, & I am afraid that by coming back to England in April I shouldn't be much nearer seeing you than I am here, except for a possible three or four days leave, which when I remember your last leave, I have often thought is worse than nothing. I feel sometimes that I don't want to see you again until I know that you are safe & I can go on seeing you for a long time, comprenez-vous this feeling? And as far as Malta is concerned I should feel a funk to go away just before the heat (when there are of course always more patients) when other people have to stay & face it, working harder than in the cold weather because so many people try & leave before summer comes.

Edward to Vera

Cleadon Hutments, 4 February 1917

I think I told you before that I was due for a medical board on Jan: 28th but I have not had it yet. New orders have been given to the medical staff here that all young officers who can possibly be passed fit are to be got out to France again before the end of this month. Consequently I am sure to be passed for General Service when I do get my board, but in the meantime I have heard a rumour that I am going to be sent on the Drill etc. Course at Chelsea. It is a very good course - everything done the way the Guards do it – and generally lasts nearly 3 weeks. For many things I should be quite glad to get away from here, but it is so awfully boring living at home. On the last sick leave of mine I could hardly live out the 10 days I had there because Mother and Father got on my nerves so awfully, and I seem to know so few decent people in town. . .

I had a letter from an innkeeper in Burton-on-Trent the other day saying that a certain Corporal Speed in my company had an illegitimate child by a Miss Jordan who is the innkeeper's ward, and was not paying for its upkeep. Under such circumstances a man's pay is compulsorily stopped to the extent of 4d a day as I expect you know. I interviewed the Corporal who is a very decent boy not yet 19 and found that he was quite willing to marry the girl but couldn't get his parents' consent and didn't want to quarrel with them and sort of get cut out of any inheritance there might be etc. Of course he cannot go out to France until he is 19 and I explained to him and he clearly understood where his duty lay, especially in the event of his being killed, because his parents will allow the marriage after the war. Speed wrote to his father again for consent on Friday and got a negative answer, and so asked me to write to him this morning which I did. You can imagine it was difficult not to overstep the limit to which the company commander of his son's company might reasonably be expected to go, and it took some time but it was quite good in the end. Probably some more facts will come out when he answers but at present it seems to be a case of the obstinate, pig-headed father trying to avoid the consequences of his son's temerity. It is the old, old story, as old as the hills, but these things take up a Company Commander's time.

Do you know, dear child, that women are a great problem to me. I meet very few, of those I dislike almost all, and I don't think I understand any of them. Of course I am speaking of girls of about my own age. Most other officers of my age seem to know any number of fairly decent girls; now and then of course they seem to get hold of a rotten one and sometimes even a prostitute, but I never seem to meet any. Can you throw any light on the matter and do you think I shall ever meet the right one because at present I can't conceive the possibility? I don't usually speak from recesses of the heart as I am to-day to you – perhaps it would be better if I did – and I don't know why I should this sleepy Sunday afternoon especially as I am writing in the mess instead of in my room as I do usually, but there is no accounting for moods. Having a totally inadequate father and mother it is of great advantage to me to talk to you sometimes although you are miles away over the sea. It is not the desire to be just like other people that makes me talk about women, because I always knew that I should not be quite ordinary in many ways, but I am inclined to think that my lack of knowledge of women is partly due to an incomplete upbringing. . . All love to you – a woman whom I do at least half understand –

Geoffrey to Edward

France, 27 January 1917

A short note: at present we are sitting in a dugout. Brilliant frosty morning: much aerial activity: one Boshe brought down quite near here. A bit of a strafe on during the night & we were so pricelessly warm here that I was positive we should have to stand to or something equally beastly. However we didn't have to so slumbered fitfully on. Well! Tonight we go up farther & après cela! Really nowadays I am absolutely one appalling mass of wind, and it's sometimes hard to believe the famous song, 'what's the use of worrying it never was worth while'. . . Wish I could get on that course that Victor Richardson is on but no chance at present as Wilmot will be the next.

Geoffrey to Edward

France, 8 February 1917

Hope you are keeping warm & fit. At present we are unexpectedly waiting – & I hope I don't make an idiot of myself in any way . . . 'Thus conscience doth make cowards of us all' as Hamlet says. Wish I had more of Victor Richardson's martial spirit.

   Well To our next meeting
   Here or in the Hereafter
     Cheeryo –

Gryt

Geoffrey to Vera

France, 15 February 1917

We have just had the new pattern helmet issued to us: – another pause as 2 letters came back from the Orderly Room uncensored – the latest men from England make me feel ill the yarns they spin about their own martyrdoms here is the limit. . . Just before I went up last time letters came from Edward & Mr & Mrs Brittain people are awfully good the way they write to us don't you think? Well! They told me that you had signed for another 6 months and I think it is the best thing to do especially as you say you would probably only see Edward a very short time in England. . .

Weather here has been quite cold but today a thaw has set in and the sky is cloudless: everything seems quite like Spring. Yes! Those cigarettes you sent me are simply topping – in fact the best I've ever met yet but please don't send me any more as however cheap they must be costly. It was awfully good of you to send them and I should not have hesitated to tell you point blank if I disliked them – really the number of wouldbe affable hypocritical fools one meets in the army only tends to make one blunter than ever. Daniel has just come back from the course Edward went to when he was in this part of the world: we have had a pleasant change while he has been away: abominably selfish & conceited & in consequence a good officer. But perhaps the last remark is a bit too strong! I like 'Hédauville November 1915' immensely – the more I read of His the more I wish I could have met Him. The Trio must have been strangely unlike individually in a great many things I should think. Haven't heard from Victor Richardson for a long time now: hope he is going strong. . .

We had a lively time up in the line this last time and were in an extra 2 days which tho' it sounds a paltry period in reality seemed an eternity. Our leave is being worked disgustingly and at present I am 4th on [the] list & I suppose leave will be stopped soon. Still there are others in worse cases than mine! Mother has been very seedy for some time past and that is the chief reason why I yearn for leave.

Edward to Vera

Cleadon Hutments, 18 February 1917

I had a medical board on Feb. 7th and was very surprised to get another month's home service; the same afternoon I got orders to

take a draft of 70 men to France and left at 7.30 pm. We stopped at several places to pick up other drafts and arrived at Folkestone without changing at 7 am. on Thursday the 8th. The men were put in the rest camp – 59 of the best houses on the front have been commandeered for this purpose – and I went to the Burlington for a bath and breakfast; later I went to see the Bendons but they were out. We crossed about 3 pm. that afternoon closely escorted by destroyers and went to the rest camp at Boulogne that night; it was awfully cold because it was one of the coldest nights of this winter and the camp is right on top of the hill behind the town. We left there the next afternoon and crawled by train to Calais where after a 4 mile march in the snow I handed them over at the Base Depot. I then returned to Boulogne by the night Paris express which took 2½ hours to do the 23 miles and eventually got to a Hotel about 3 am, got up at 9.45 and caught the morning boat which got me back in town at 4 on Saturday. . .
I think it is certainly as well that you have signed on for another 6 months as the sea seems to be anything but safe at present; even in the Channel they have to be very careful and are always coming across mines. . .

We are getting a lot of impossible people up here just now from Cadet Schools; I am unlucky enough to have 2 of them sharing this room with me. I changed my room just before I took that draft because I couldn't stand a very saintly person who would spend hours studying the bible and our fatuous prayer book and because there was a refreshingly aesthetic fellow in here (he is rather a bad character in many ways but is *really* in love with an actress); unfortunately he went back to France while I was away and so I find I have jumped from the frying pan.

––––––––––

Victor to Vera

France, 18 February 1917

I hear from Edward that he has got another month's home service. It's rather bad luck on him, but it may give us some chance of meeting when I get home. I expect he will get back in time to be in at the death, and I hope we shall neither of us come down at the last fence. I really think it all ought to be over – I mean the serious business – by the end of the Summer. At any rate Sir Douglas Haig is very confident, and we are all looking forward to the next few months.

I haven't heard from Thurlow for ages. Have you any news of him? I think he must still be on the Somme, as I met Karpeles of the Lodge who is in the Trench Mortars in his Division, when I was at the base & he said they were down there. I am still in the same old place, or one of them.

I am afraid I haven't any other news. Do you still like Malta as much as ever?

I also met Stuart Smith of the Lodge at the Base. He agreed with me that Edward has completely altered since July 1st. I believe you always thought so too.

Vera to Edward

Malta, 20 February 1917

You & I are not only aesthetic but ascetic – at any rate in regard to sex. Or perhaps, since 'ascetic' implies rather a lack of emotion, it would be more correct to say exclusive – Geoffrey is very much this, and Victor, & Roland was. What I mean by this is, that so many people are attracted by the opposite sex simply because it *is* the opposite sex – the average officer & the average 'nice girl' demand, I am sure, little else but this. But where you & I are concerned, sex by itself doesn't interest us unless it is united with brains & personality; in fact we rather think of the latter first, & the person's sex afterwards. This is quite enough to put you off the average 'nice girl', who would neither give you what you want nor make the effort herself to try & understand you when other men, who can give her what *she* wants, are so much easier to understand. . . . I think very probably that older women will appeal to you much more than younger ones, as they do to me. This means that you will probably have to wait a good many years before you find anyone you could wish to marry, but I don't think this need worry you, for there is plenty of time, & very often people who wait get something well worth waiting for.

. . . I think the old saw about young women being so much older than young men for their age has always been very untrue & since the War is more so than ever. Women 'grow up' in a certain sense (that of finishing their education just when they ought to begin it) much sooner than men, & so get a sort of superficial 'grown-upness' due to mixing with people & going out in a way that the boy of the same age doesn't. But in the things that really count it is the boy who is grown-up; he has had responsibilities which under the present benighted system of educating women she has never had the fringe of – especially if he is at a Public School. The boy of eighteen or nineteen has probably – and since the War certainly, had to cope with questions of morality & immorality whose seriousness would astound her if she understood it, and deal with subjects of whose very existence she is probably ignorant. Of course a man doesn't mind the superficiality of inexperience if all he asks of her is her sex – but you, as you said before, are different, & won't be satisfied until you meet with someone very exceptional, or else someone who has learnt things 'with suffering and through time'. Exceptional as I was, I don't think the I of the days before I had loved & lost Roland would satisfy the You of to-day.

I don't think it's a question of upbringing at all. Our upbringing would have been incomplete in far more than this if we hadn't dealt with it ourselves & supplied a great deal that it would otherwise have lacked. But of course it may be true that Father's very Early Victorian attitude towards women may unconsciously have influenced & even reproduced itself in you a little – I have noticed occasionally a slight suspicion of patronage in your dealings with women; I don't really think this is because you think their sex inferior so much as you realise their inferiority (as it probably is) to you in personality & brain. I, conversely, feel the same with many men! But it is necessary to be rather more careful in dealing with women, as if a man patronises a woman she always thinks it is because of her sex, whereas if a woman patronises a man, he (if he is acute enough to notice it, which he generally isn't) never puts it down to *his*!

. . . It is such a wild stormy night & the sea is beating the rocks like anything. On this island, the land seems to shrink as one knows it better, & the miles & miles of sea between here & home to get longer & longer – though I can still write to you across them! But one begins to understand a little the significance of the Revelation – 'And there was no more sea.' For here sea is the very symbol of separation.

Geoffrey to Edward

France, 25 February 1917

Where we go after this is a conundrum some say forward: others, backward. This village is most peaceful and tonight is strangely quiet save for a distant bumping of guns and an occasional mowl of a cat.

The posts have been very erratic just lately. Haven't heard from Victor Richardson for a long time now. This afternoon we had a Soccer match Officers v. Sergts which was amusing We won 6–3. But our latest arrivals are most of them more than odd. Have come to conclusion that one gets a frightful snob in the Army. At times like these when we are not in the line I wish you were here. Well! The night is far spent & I will turn into bed: sleep well.

Edward to Vera

Roker, 27 February 1917

Last Saturday we had a regimental cross country run in which I ran for my old company – C company. We had teams of 20 men from each of the 7 companies and the race was about 5 to 5½ miles. C company won by a substantial margin; I came in 4th and we also got the 2nd and 6th places and 19 out of our 20 got in within 15 minutes of the winner which they had to do in order to count; I can scarcely be considered anything else but fit for active service after that; I seem to have surprised a lot of people who had no idea that I could run... I think there is a good deal being done in France just now especially on the Somme; judging by the papers we seem to have complete ascendancy though I don't suppose things go as smoothly as they make out; I think it is quite likely that Bapaume will fall in a month or two·... There is a new order out now (I forget if I told you last week) that all wounded or sick officers on leaving hospital will go to convalescent homes until fit to rejoin their units; the reason is that so many wounded officers have too gay a time in the West End when on sick leave and don't get better quickly enough, but being wounded will certainly not have some of the attractions which it had previously.

Geoffrey to Vera

France, 1 March 1917

I have just come in after billeting for the Bn. I was sent on in advance this morning and had a delightful ride. Seems quite springlike here and as I left – I was reminded of your last letter and tho' not actually the same place the verse is applicable: 'The sunshine on the long white road That ribboned down the hill'.

When Horace had carried me to the top of the hill I turned round & saw far below me a gang of Hun prisoners working: beyond the peaceful village which we are leaving tomorrow & then standing outlined in blue mist – [a] Church. I went on over a hill & vale thro 2 charming villages and then arrived here leaving Horace to philosophise in a stable while I went round looking at billets: afraid the officers won't think much of their billets tomorrow as there is only room for half of them.

The peasantry here is delightful & the funny old thing here insisted on me going to warm myself before the fire a moment ago & then extricating all my family history which was rather amusing. The Interpreter who came with me is a jolly old boy too & keeps one in fits of laughter.

Victor to Vera

France, 4 March 1917

Your letter came just before I set out on a working party. We were working about 300 yards from Fritz on top with bullets from fixed rifles & machine guns whistling about – a beautiful moonlight night, but I found it too dark for reading letters all the same. You will hardly believe it, but I almost enjoy bullets whistling round me nowadays – I regard it as excellent nerve training for the Push, and as a recent article in the Times said with reference to the French victories at Verdun the infantry must be 'trained in body, mind, and spirit'. Another example of what I mean – in ordinary times I would always go out of my way to avoid seeing a street accident. The other day I saw one of our planes 'brought down in flames' and actually went to investigate for myself. You can imagine what I saw when I got there & T won't describe it. Thank God the pilot was dead before I arrived, but it was the worst thing I have seen out here or anywhere else. Still this is the 'training of the spirit' or perhaps of the 'mind' – it is always hard to tell where one begins and the other ends.

I think on the whole I agree with what you say about belief in dogmas, yet one is told that [without] faith there is no salvation. In that case my chances of a future life are not worth very much. However I haven't time now to worry too much over these things. Worry only lessens morale. I suppose I must in the words of Blake – or was it Cromwell? – brought up to date 'Trust in God and keep close to the barrage'. By the way you will be pleased to hear that I have given up the idea of going into the Church, unless anything very unexpected happens.

The day after your letter came my C.O. recommended me for a permanent commission in the 60th.

Edward to Vera

School of Musketry, Strensall, near York, 19 March 1917

I came on this Musketry and Lewis Gun course on March 6th and it lasts till March 30th. It is *the* musketry course in the North of

England and ranks only 2nd to Hythe. Consequently I haven't had a minute to myself since I came and therefore no time for letters. It took me over 2 hours this evening after a full day's work to copy in the rough notes I took during the day. It is really very hard work indeed especially as I was very backward in musketry – a most boring subject – before I came, and I must do pretty well on the course. . . We are 5 miles from York (beautiful organ in the Cathedral) but I have my motor bike here. If I don't go to France at the end of the Course I shall return to Sunderland . . . There is some excitement about just now; Bapaume and Péronne fell on Saturday and yesterday respectively. It is quite likely that Geoffrey may be in the show somewhere. But it is anything but a disorderly retreat as you will know, in fact I think the Huns have considerably upset our plans for the offensive by retiring a bit too soon. The question of road-making and transport of guns and personnel of all kinds is of the utmost importance and I don't know if we were quite ready for it. The 11th Bn. were up to a week or so ago still in the Ypres district . . . There are a few decent people out of the 80 or so officers on this course but not many. One in particular a regular before the war in the 2nd Lancashire Fusiliers who has been through the Retreat, the Marne, the Aisne (wounded), the second battle of Ypres and first gas attack, and had about 3 months of the Somme, been wounded 3 times altogether (he refuses to wear any wound stripes) and is still a subaltern is very decent and most amusing; he will be going out again soon.

Vera to Edward

Malta, 21 March 1917

I am not any longer in the surgical block I told you about as I have been put on night duty for a month, & have gone to the eye & malaria block where I first started life at this hospital. . . . I have to go round every four hours doing eyes, which keeps me quite wakeful. At first I felt horribly responsible at being in sole charge of so many people, but now I have got used to it, especially as none of them are really very ill. The first night I was on there was a terrific wind & thunder & lightning all night. It was most eerie going round in a blustering darkness with a hurricane lamp which occasionally blew out, with thunder crashing around. . . .

We have just heard of the taking of Bapaume & Péronne – surely a great triumph. . . . From all accounts there don't seem many casualties, or even to have been much of a fight. One can hardly believe it possible after the sanguinary struggles for a few yards; it almost seems as if there must be some ruse at the back of it on the part of the enemy. It seems extraordinary too that Kut, after all the struggles to reach it, should fall to us so easily in the end – to say nothing of Baghdad.

One hesitates, after so often having seen our national optimism weighed in the balance & found wanting, to accept the favourable interpretations of these events which one finds expressed in some of the papers. What is the meaning of it all, do you think?

Victor to Vera

France, 24 March 1917

My dear Vera,

Mrs Leighton has just sent me Rhymes of a Red Cross Man. They are indeed excellent, but their vivid realism is oppressive – at least I find it so just now. With regard to 'Pilgrims' it is true in part. It is true that none of us would wish those we love to do other than 'smile and be happy again'. But none of us wish to die. The 9th/60th is probably one of the finest battalions in France, and the Division, when the Divisions were placed in 4 categories after the Somme Battle, shared 1st place in the 1st category with the Guards. Nevertheless I venture to say that there is not one officer, warrant officer, N.C.O., or rifleman who looks on death as 'The Splendid Release'. That is the phrase of 'a Red Cross Man' and not of a member of a fighting unit.

I often wonder why we are all here. Mainly I think, as far as I am concerned, to prevent the repetition in England of what happened in Belgium in August 1914. Still more perhaps because one's friends are here. Perhaps too, 'heroism in the abstract' has a share in it all. But the attitude of 90% of the British Expeditionary Force is summed up in the words of two songs, the first a marching song to the tune of Auld Lang Syne that the little old men have been heard to sing:

> *'We're here because*
> *We're here because*
> *We're here because*
> *We're here.'*

The second is a song from one of the revues – what country but 'our dear, far, forgetting land' could produce such music at such a time? –

> *'I'm here and you're here*
> *So what do we care.'*

No 'we ain't no bloomin' 'eroes'. And I think it's just as well. . . .

'Punch' some time ago had an essay in the 'Watch Dogs' Series on 'a little word of six letters' which epitomises the Army's view of the War. If taken literally it is, alas, no exaggeration – it is a shorter word than sanguinary – and figuratively it really expresses the whole situation, but my one fear in case of my safe return is that I may be perpetually uttering it in the drawing room.

The situation as far as we are concerned is at present only slightly changed, but I hope that on the day of the hunt it will alter considerably. You speak of being anxious about Geoffrey Thurlow. At the present moment I would gladly change places with him. He is probably 'well away and over the country' by now, and open warfare has none of the terrors of breaking new ground.

Edward doesn't seem to enjoy his Musketry Course. Just as I did he is taking it far too seriously. I can't define exactly how he has changed since July 1st. In that one day I think he aged ten years. I wonder if I shall be the same: I don't think so somehow or other, but it is quite impossible to say.

I can quite understand your desire to wander further. I am a restless spirit myself – in fact you yourself once accused me of being a rolling stone.

Well, Vera, I may not write again – one can never tell – and so, as Edward wrote to me, 'it is time to take a long long adieu'.

Ever yours

Tah

Geoffrey to Vera

France, 25 March 1917

Don't you often speculate on what lies beyond the gate of Death? The after life must be particularly interesting. No chance of getting leave & Mother seems to be quite unwell: it is rotten being away from home when anyone isn't well. Haven't heard from Victor Richardson for a long long time – hope he is still going strong. . .

Well! Our Bn. has been trekking about France a good deal lately & I've been billeting officer – a thankless but **strenu**ous task as directly the Bn. is in off you go to another **village** and repeat the process. At the place where we halted a few **days** I was made Town Major & quite enjoyed the work. . . Called one lane after Chigwell 'Chigwell Lane' and hope that if any who have been at Chigwell pass by that way they may be reminded of better days. We have marched away 2 days and yesterday at the end we had a jolly old road fatigue!

Tonight I walked home with Wilmot who is in a convalescent home near here. It has been a brilliant day with a fresh wind: we passed along between fields, some green and some with bright red earth recently plowed: and then came to a large forest. The wind made a delightful rustling in the trees & had it not have been for the distant continual bumping of guns War might not have existed.

Geoffrey to Edward

France, 25 March 1917

Sorry I've not written before but we have been nomads for some time past & I've been billeting officer. Need hardly tell you how much running around there is in that office as you know more about it than I do. Then when we arrived at the last place it wanted a temp. Town Major & I got the job & having rigged up a topping little office had name plates printed for all the streets, maps drawn, billet lists made out & half billets numbered with billet plates – I had to leave with the Bn to come wandering back again – decidedly feeling as if things were just beginning to look well. A Corps Brigadier rolled in day before we left & congratulated me on 'Excellent work done.' but what avail is that! Anyhow here we are & have had one day of peace. Tomorrow being Sunday we are almost certain to move...

Bright sunshine all day & quite Spring like. Only wished for some things that you were here as so few people seem to appreciate Nature even out here. I had a letter by same post from Vera who seems to be going strong.....

Edward to Vera

Roker, Sunderland, 27 March 1917

I came back from Strensall in a hurry on Sunday night; somebody had the wind up about invasion or something of the sort or else it was a big practice show, but at all events all courses were broken up and everyone had to return to his unit with all speed. I got here about 10.30 pm. and found the battalion standing to etc., but normal conditions were resumed last night. I expect to be sent back to Strensall in a day or two; we only had 5 days more to go but of course all the exams. were to be done and unless we have them we cannot be classified or given certificates. It was rather a rotten place altogether and after stewing in the very dry bones of musketry for 3 weeks I feel as though I had lost touch with literature of all kinds and am unable to be interesting or interested in anything that really matters. . . I was passed GS [fit for General Service] in York a week ago yesterday and so it is quite likely that I may return to France any time now; I will send you a wire as I promised when I get orders to report at Folkestone. Nearly all of the more decent people here have been sent to France while I have been away and so I have really very little interest in this place at present; there are 3 very indifferent specimens in this billet with me. Much to my annoyance and also to his, Hutchings, who is now fit for light duty, has been sent to the Machine Gun Corps at Grantham instead of back here; he had done a lot of Machine Gun work before and so they have just seconded him without asking him if he wants to go there or not: of course he doesn't. The War Office is really one of the most annoying institutions in some ways; they almost seem to try their hardest to separate people who don't want to be separated. I feel quite certain that there is one battalion in France to which I shall not go, and that is the 10th, because Geoffrey is there. My papers for a regular commission have gone in at last now that I am GS though I expect I shall have to wait some time before I am gazetted. I must stop and read a little Swinburne as an antidote to that awful musketry and then have a bath – a commodity which I have been unable to enjoy for 10 days. For some things I don't think I shall mind very much going back to France; sometimes it is rather rotten to think what other people, especially one's friends, are doing and suffering, and to be almost entirely out of it oneself.

Vera to Edward

Malta, 2–3 April 1917

Three of our Sisters have just been ordered to transfer to Salonika. I wish they would send some of us. . . I would volunteer like a shot. Not because the city of malaria & mosquitoes & air-raids & odours suggests many attractions, but because this wandering, unsettled, indefinite sort of life makes one yearn to taste as much as one can of what the War has placed within human experience. Apart from the prospect of nearness to you & Geoffrey & Victor,

& in spite of the many inducements to a speedy departure from this life at Salonika, I believe I would rather go to Salonika than to France. France one can, & is practically sure, to go to after the War, but I don't suppose anyone would go to Salonika except on business! That preference of mine is no rash whim, but a well-considered statement, since here one gets to know a good deal about Salonika & all it implies, & penetrates the veil, half of dread, half of romance, which shrouds it in the minds of most people in England...

Have you read the report of the Commission on the Dardanelles? It makes very tragical reading, but it is extraordinarily interesting in conjunction with the colour & romance of Masefield's 'Gallipoli'. The latter makes you feel, in spite of the condemnatory language of the report, & the sense one has all through that the campaign was an utter failure with nothing in its result large enough to justify it, that it must have been a very fine & wonderful thing to have been one of that small Army that fought so gallantly for such a forlorn hope. Since Roland had to die, & to die wounded in cold blood instead of in the heat & excitement of an action, I have often wondered whether really I would not have been glad for him to have been at Gallipoli, as he so nearly went. He was such a person for a forlorn hope. And nothing more could have happened to him than to be dead. We might then not have known the place of his grave, but after all that doesn't matter much. I cannot see that one gets more satisfaction out of a wooden cross on a mound of grass than out of an unknown gully or ravine on the Gallipoli peninsula...

April 3rd

My mail was depressing to-day; as well as your news about being passed fit there was a letter from Father in the usual strain – German retirement at the wrong time for us and therefore anything but an advantage (of course you say this too & I always suspected it) – Russia internally rotten & likely to sue for a separate peace – conditions dreadful at home – end no nearer in sight etc etc. This sort of letter is so much more depressing out here than at home; for it is long before you get another to remove the impression. Victor too sends me a letter half cynical, half hope-lessly resigned; apparently he was on the verge of an attack, for he spoke of perhaps never writing to me again, & says – as you said to him before July 1st – that it is time to say a long long adieu. This too leaves me anxiously & very sadly wondering how long it will be before I hear any more of him & what it will be when I do. I think I would rather have had an attitude of open resent-ment & rebellion in the face of death than this sort of stifled bitterness. . .

Had a delightfully vigorous & colourful letter from Geoffrey – though he longs for leave.

Vera to Edward

Malta, 5 April 1917

Mosquitoes are beginning to be a pest; they fly around the bunk at night & sing me to sleep by day, by reason of which I wake to find a swollen hand or a disfigured face. Fleas & other still more unmentionable unmentionables are rampant just now & not likely to become any less so. The mess has just had to be pulled down because the latter variety were found mixed up with the structural arrangements; while the notice board has had to be thoroughly cleansed & disinfected because the fleas had made themselves a happy home behind the notices.

Rumours are rampant that we may soon be very busy, and off-duty times etc are all being carefully arranged with a view to that prospect. I only hope we are.

Edward to Vera

No 1 School of Instruction, Brocton Camp,
Stafford, 8 April 1917

You will be surprised to see that I have been sent on another course instead of going back to France. I only came back from

Strensall to Sunderland last Monday and on Wednesday had orders to come here which I did yesterday; the course lasts 8 weeks which means that I shall not be in France till about the 15th of June – nearly a year since I left. I am not altogether pleased about it because I have been GS [fit for General Service] for 3 weeks now and I ought really to be back. . . This is a general course for officers who already command companies or are likely to command one next time they go out to France so it may be quite useful; it is almost entirely devoted to the tactics of open warfare and trench warfare is hardly going to be considered at all. . . I heard from Geoffrey about 10 days ago and from Tah last Thursday; both seem to be quite alright and Tah gets more humorous every letter he writes.

Vera to Edward

Malta, 10 April 1917

It is just over 6 months now since we landed here. Sometimes I get quite homesick – though never for long at a time – & very fed up with Malta. It is gloriously romantic on moonlight nights, & in the evening & the early morning, but has a certain hard brightness in broad daylight which makes you long for the grey skies & half-tones & soft shadows of your own country. One longs too for permanent relationships, like one's own people & one's lasting friends; here everyone you come in contact with, whether patients, M.O.s or fellow-nurses are so much 'ships that pass in the night'. I wish something or other would bring you, if only for a few hours, to this little dumping-ground of the nations.

Geoffrey to Vera

France, 16 April 1917

Thanks awfully for your jolly long letter of the 3rd. We are now sitting in a rough shelter in the Hun's old second line weather wet and coolish. I was awfully glad to hear from you again: also from Edward that he had been sent on Senior Officers Course at Brocton: I was on it when warned for front again last July: so he ought to be there almost two months. . . No! I am not a 'brave soul' in fact as Shakespeare says 'the valiant never taste of death but one' I am one of the cowards 'who died many times before their death'. . . Yes! Life out here does make one appreciably older but I think when the war is over Edward will regain some of his former 'youth' again.

I can only hope Victor Richardson is now in England. In a day or so I may be in the same predicament as he was when he wrote to you. . . I often yearn to see the sea again it is so refreshingly clean when compared to the squalor of the army: and Edward & I had two delightful months with the Bendons, and these seem to stand out as a patch of sunlight to the rest of one's army life.

Well! You will now accuse me of being despondent & melancholy. Perhaps I am but a perpetual fear goes with me that I fail at the critical moment – for in truth I am no soldier.

Anyhow let's hope for the best. . .

Do you remember the Queens Hall concert we went to together? Often have thought what an outsider you must have thought me when I arrived late, but I had only just come down from Lincoln where I had been staying with my sister who teaches there, and the trains were all late.

Vera to Geoffrey

Malta, 16 April 1917

You are really a good correspondent; Mother says you are 'most faithful' to her too. Not like Victor, whose letters are few & far between, & very short when they do come. To me, at any rate, he conveys most by what he leaves unsaid. I have been rather anxious about him this last week, for last time I heard of his whereabouts he was at Arras, & I feel sure he must have been in the great battle – which at present we here only know of as an immense Fact, shorn of all its details. I hope you didn't get into even the fringe of it.

I have been off-duty for a day or two with a bad throat & general malaise, but am back again to-night. I am beginning to be glad that I came out when I did, and not straight into the kind of weather that is just beginning. The nights are still quite cool but the days are getting very hot . . . The sirocco is blowing to-night in a hateful way, rushing down the stone verandah, & making the doors & shutters creak & groan. To me this particular wind always seems fraught with sinister things; it hides the stars, so that the night is as black as ink, & makes the men peevish & sends their temperatures up.

Vera to Edward

Malta, 17 April 1917

I have to keep on writing letters, because the vague bits of news from France that filter through to us make me so anxious to receive them. From the long list of names that appear in the telegrams there seems to be a vast battle going on along the whole of our front & the French one too, but it is very difficult to make out at all what is happening. *Is* Geoffrey anywhere in the Bapaume direction? The longer the War goes on, the more one's concern in the whole immense business seems to centre itself upon the few beings still left that one cares about, & the less upon the general issue of the struggle. One's personal interest wears one's patriotism rather threadbare by this time. After all, it is a garment one has had to wear for a very long time, so there's not much wonder if it is beginning to get a little shabby!

Geoffrey to Edward

France, 18–20 April 1917

. . . by time you get this we shall have either won thro' or failed. We have been bivouacing now for over a week & the cold & rain don't tend to make the men fit so I hope they will be all right. It is rather depressing to watch the Huns levelling to the ground a pretty little village seen thro' trees beyond the river. Such wanton destruction seems a sin but I suppose we do the same.

Well! If this be the final test goodbye. Wish I had more trust in myself. Please remember me to Mr & Mrs Brittain.

Thine.

Gryt

Later 20th

We moved [back] a bit last night & are now down in deep dugouts for a day & a bit & then we move again and In haste to get this posted. . .

'Pray for my soul. More things are wrought by prayer than this world knows of.'

Hoping to see you sometime in the future.

Thine.

Gryt

Edward to Vera

Telegram, London, 18 April 1917

Victor dangerously wounded serious

Brittain

Vera to Edith Brittain

Malta, 20 April 1917

There really does not seem much point in writing anything until I hear further news of Victor, for I cannot think of anything else . . . I knew he was destined for some great action, even as I knew beforehand about Edward, for only about a week ago I had a most pathetic letter from him – a virtual farewell. It is dreadful to be so far away & all among strangers. . .

Well, I won't make any more comments. Victor, as you know, has always been so much a survival to me of a part of Roland that it [is] unnecessary to lay any stress on his immense value for me – Poor Edward! What a bad time the Three Musketeers have had!

––––––––––

Geoffrey to Vera

France, 20 April 1917

I have had a note from Edward today to say that Victor Richardson is at Rouen and badly wounded. Awfully sorry & I can only hope he will soon get over it and that by time you get this you will have had better news of him. It was a very brief note from Edward and yet terribly concise.

After tea tonight wanting to be alone – we came back last night for a day or two & then we go up for a stunt – I walked out along a high embankment and everything was fresh and cool quite in contrast to the heated atmosphere of our dugout.

As I looked westward I saw just below me in front of the embankment the battered outline of Hun trenches with 2 long straggling communication trenches winding away into some shell torn trees: the setting sun reflected in the water at the bottom of many crump holes making them look masses of gold. Over this derelict plain a thin line of men going back to billets in a large town, which stood outlined against a pale yellow sky with dark purple clouds low down in the sky: over to the right tall trees astride a river also looking gold in the last rays of the sun and beyond the river more ruined houses from which occasionally flashed a large gun.

Well! It was all quite beautiful & I wish Edward could have been with me if it were any other place than this. I walked on along the line broken in many places by shell holes until I came to a gap where a large bridge had been blown up over the river which swirled along in a yellow torrent below: along the bank a line of pack mules carrying up ammunition & they were reflected in the quieter side of the river.

Everything seems very vague but none the less certain here & I only hope I don't fail at the critical moment as truly I am a horrible coward: wish I could do well especially for the School's sake. I think you would love Chigwell – everything is so peaceful there. Often have we watched the many splendours of the Sunset from the School field. But all this will be boring you.

> *'War knows no power safe shall be my going*
> *Safe tho' all safety's lost, safe where men fall*
> *And if these poor limbs die, safest of all.'*

Rupert Brooke is great and his faith also great.
  If Destiny is willing I will write later
    In haste

                G.R.Y.T.

Edward to Vera

                          Telegram, London, 22 April 1917

Eyesight probably gone may live

                Edward Brittain

Edward to Vera

                          London, 22 April 1917

It is not known yet whether Victor will die or not, but his left eye was removed in France and the specialist who saw him thinks it is almost certain that the sight of his right eye has gone too. He was brought into the 2nd London General, Chelsea – only about 2 miles from here – on Thursday afternoon, 19th. We don't know exactly when he was hit but I should think it must have been close to our parapet when attacking on April 9th. The bullet – probably Machine gun – went in just behind the left eye and went very slightly upwards but not I'm afraid enough to clear the right eye; the bullet is not yet out though very close to the right edge of the temple; it is expected that it will work through of its own accord. I came up from Stafford on Friday night and saw Victor twice yesterday; he has never really recovered consciousness at all yet but I think he was just sensible that I was there and was just able to say 'yes' when the sister asked him if he knew who it was. The eye that has been removed and all the upper part of the face is covered with bandages and is much swollen though the swelling was rather less when I saw him again in the evening. He was asleep then and a good deal of blood had just come down the nose which was probably a good thing; the breathing was quite regular. The right eye was closed but when the sister lifted the eyelid it seemed to me that the eye had no sight at all. We are told that he may remain in his present condition for a week. I don't think he will die suddenly but of course the brain must be injured and it depends upon how bad the injury is. I am inclined to think it would be better that he should die; I would far rather die myself than lose all that we have most dearly loved, but I think we hardly bargained for this. Sight is really a more precious gift than life. If he should live I know that you and I and Mrs Leighton can help enormously and there is music, but as you know his people are quite inadequate for him under such circumstances. A permanent injury to the brain must of course also be considered. He was brought down to Rouen on Wednesday April 11th and was there a week I think in No 8 General where I was. I am just going to meet Mr Richardson at Victoria and we shall see Tah again this afternoon. I have to go back to Stafford to-night.

Later

There is much better news. . . . the Matron of the 2nd London telephoned to say that Victor was conscious and so Mother and I went down at once. He was much better and recognised my voice; I asked him how he was and he said 'Right as rain' and he caught hold of my hand and said 'You haven't been long'. (The sister had asked him before if he would like to see me.) Then I said 'Your Father is coming to see you in an hour or two'. Then he made the most hopeful remark of all saying 'What's the betting he's late'. Of course you know that Mr Richardson is invariably late and so that shows how much better Tah is. He also told me to sit down and so I sat down on the bed. Mother went off to Victoria to meet Mr Richardson's train and he came along as soon as possible but Tah had dozed off again [by] then. He also has a slight wound in the right arm. Mr Richardson told me that he had just had a letter from Tah's Colonel whose name is Porter, in which he said the battalion was attacking a redoubt called 'the Harp' just East of Arras; they took the first line and then came under heavy Machine Gun fire. Victor who was leading his platoon was hit in the arm but took his coat off had the wound bandaged and went on; it was at the 2nd German line that he got the bullet through his head and the Colonel himself gave him morphia because he was in pain. The Colonel in his letter after saying that he hopes he will not lose his sight 'because sight is so much more valuable than life' also says 'You have good reason to be proud of him . . . he did his best and it was a good best too. I have sent his name in for the Military Cross and have no doubt that he will get it.'

Mr Richardson and I went again this afternoon and he recognised both of us by our voices. When the sister asked him who was speaking he said 'It's Dad'. I read the board by the side of his bed and it said that there was probably no vision in the remaining eye and the optic nerve was severed. 'When asked in a moment of consciousness if he could see anything with his right eye he said that he could see nothing at all.' I suppose it is possible that something might be done by an operation but I am afraid it is not very likely. Unless he has a bad relapse I think he will live. . . I don't think Tah realises yet that he is blind. As he lies on his bed with bandages round his left eye and head and the right eyelid closed, he looks just like a picture of the Christ – the familiar expression generally shown on the Cross.

If only that right eye might have its sight!
Ever yours

Edward

We haven't had any more news from Geoffrey since my last letter.

Vera to Edward

Malta, 23 April 1917

My own dearest Edward

Your letter of the 8th has just arrived but contains no reference to the terrible news of the last day or two; it seems to be the only one that has come, so I suppose all my letters have missed the mail just when I wanted them most. It is dreadful to have to wait a week for details. That is the hardship of foreign service – not climate or distance so much as the separation by time & distance from anything that matters. But I am very glad to get your letter to know that you won't go out again till the middle of June. At the rate things are going now, matters may be very far advanced by then . . . . . Don't want to go any sooner. The Three Musketeers have suffered enough.

I am broken-hearted indeed about Victor. It is better to be anything than blind; I am not sure that it is not better to be dead. I suppose he is disfigured very much. His lovely eyes – I can't bear to think they will never any more look 'right into one's soul' as Mrs Leighton said they did. It is a terrible way to have bridged the gulf that lay between him & you – & Roland. I wish Roland were here to be with him & give him the strength he will so much need if he lives. I am very, very glad that you are in England still; now Roland is dead, no one else could help him in anything like the way you can. I would give anything to be there too, for I feel I owe him so much; I remember how good he was to me after Roland died, and how he comforted me that week-end of the Somme Battle when I was desperately anxious about you. So it is very hard to feel I can do nothing for him in return at the time of his greatest need. . . Anyhow. I know that you will make him

understand, better than any letter could, my indescribable sorrow
& regret – one can't call it pity, as pity is not a sufficiently rever-
ent feeling for one of those who 'so marvellously overcame'. If
there is anything I can do for him – anything at all – you will tell
me, won't you? It places all of us who cannot fight under a burden
of debt almost more than we can bear – to feel that we owe our
safety to the lives & sight & strength of such as you & Roland &
him. I feel I could never repay it enough, even if trying to meant
giving up practically all I ever meant to be or do. I feel as if
Roland's sad eyes were looking at me out of Eternity, imploring
me to try to give Victor some of the comfort He would have
given him if He had been here.

Captain J. W. Daniel to Edward

> *10th Sherwood Foresters,*
> *France, 26 April 1917*

You will have heard by this time, I expect, of the death of poor
Geoffrey Thurlow, & as you & he seemed such great pals – I feel
you will like to know how he lost his life. The hun had got us held
up & the leading battalions of the Brigade had failed to get their
objective. This battalion came up in close support thro' a very
heavy barrage, but managed to get into the trench – of which the
Boche still held a part. Our C.O. was wounded & taken prisoner
early in the fight so it fell to my lot to take over command of the
battalion. Everything was in a state of uncertainty, & as 'C' coy was
on the right flank – I sent a message to Geoffrey to push along the
trench & find out if possible what was happening on the right. The
trench was in a bad condition, & rather congested, so he got out on
the top. Unfortunately the Boche snipers were very active & he was
soon hit thro' the lungs. Everything was done to make him as
comfortable as possible, but he died lying on a stretcher about fifteen minutes later. We placed him in a shallow piece of trench &
the spot was marked, so he will be buried decently by our padre
as soon as he can reach the spot. His death is a great loss to the
battalion, & especially to 'C' coy; I have been his Company

commander since last August & I know how very popular he was with the officers & men – particularly with his Lewis Gunners . . . . . please accept my letter of consolation as an expression of my sympathetic feelings – as I know what it is to lose a pal.

We are out of the line now but don't expect to be in these decent billets for very long . . .

I must end now; the best of luck to you.

Yours very sincerely,

J. W. Daniel
Capt.

Vera to Edward

Malta, 27 April 1917

I can't think what has happened to my mails, as the last letter I received was yours written on April 8th.; they can't have been torpedoed or suppressed, as other people have got theirs all right. I am so longing to hear more details about Victor, whether he is soon likely to be out of danger & whether his eyesight can be saved. Some member of the family sent me a cable after yours to say 'Head wound improving. Recommended Military Cross.' It would be so splendid if he could get the latter – some small compensation for all that he has lost. He will indeed have bridged that gulf between you which made him so miserable; do you remember that evening when we all dined at the Coventry Restaurant & he would hardly speak because he felt the difference between you so acutely. I always thought he would rise to the occasion in the end; when nervous & sensitive people can once make up their minds to a thing they usually do it supremely well; the fear is only beforehand. I feel a little sad, perhaps, to think that Roland, the bravest of the brave, alone of you three has no decoration, & lies beneath His Cross instead of wearing it. But He would have been the last to grudge them to you, & after all His courage needed no guarantees.

. . . None of you have mentioned at all anything about [Victor's] reason being affected, so I am hoping it is not, though unfortunately it is a characteristic of so many head wounds, though sometimes only temporally. He will be very wonderful if he can live with a clear mind through meningitis & a dangerous wound in the head. Poor dear Tah! I am afraid the future will seem very long & blank to him, though perhaps freedom from the jarring sense of inequality with those he loves best will give him a peace which even the knowledge of his blindness cannot quite destroy. I do wish I could see & talk to him, but am afraid it is not likely yet (though in this world of vicissitudes anything may happen) as I have just signed on again to-day. Now that I have served so long I feel very unwilling to break my service even for a little time, as continuous service in these days, when so many people who started nursing got bored & left it off, is an honourable & in many ways an advantageous thing, & of course even the least little interval breaks it, spoiling one's record & cancelling the past. This doesn't necessarily mean that one can't come to England for a little time without breaking it. There may be ways & means in the future of managing that. . .

Don't be surprised if you should not hear from me for some time as it is quite possible that mails may be stopped, or at least temporally suppressed, especially from here homewards. Exciting things are happening fast now out here; of course I can't tell you what, but if you refer to either my last letter or last but one (I can't remember which) you may get some idea. They have not yet affected me individually but are bound to in the end. So don't be surprised at anything you hear (though not immediately). Of course don't alarm the family. As yet I can tell you nothing definite even if I were allowed. There is a great coming & going & stir, & the Island is wild with rumours, but the substantiation of them is so far only in its early stages. I am still on night duty; we offered to stay on to suit Matron's convenience, as with so many changes & everything so unsettled it is well to have no more moves to make than are absolutely necessary.

The news all over the world is too thrilling for words. After all it is a great thing to live in these tremendous times, dwarfing, as the 'Observer' says, everything that has ever preceded them.

The weather here is unusually cold for April in Malta, but the fleas are becoming rampant. One gets quite callous about them, although they are so annoying.

Vera to Geoffrey

Malta, 28 April 1917

I am waiting anxiously for any mails – which are much delayed – to hear all the details about Victor Richardson. I expect you know more than I do, as I have only had two or three cables. I absolutely cannot realise that if he dies – which from the last cable appears more likely than it did at first – he will probably be blind. . . . My last cable said he had been recommended for the Military Cross; I only hope he gets it & that if he does it will be some small compensation to him – if anything can compensate – for all that he has suffered & lost, to know that he bridged the gulf which he always felt existed between himself & Edward. I remember so well when once we three dined together soon after Edward got his M.C. that Victor would hardly speak at all because he felt the difference between them so acutely. We both teased him a good deal at the time about his apparent sulkiness & I expect we were rather unkind; I feel very sorry now that we did . . .

I wish I could get some leave & go to England; I am most anxious to see Victor, though I think I should find it very hard to know what to say by way of comfort to someone whose future must look so long & blank. I should love, too, to see Edward before he goes back – I was so overjoyed to hear he will be in England at least till the middle of June – but I think nothing is more unlikely than a chance of Blighty, especially as yesterday I signed on again. Now that I have done this for so long I feel unwilling to break my service even for a little time, as continuous service in these days when so many people got bored with nursing & left it off, has a certain amount of standing & is in many ways an advantageous thing in this branch of national affairs, & of course even one little interval spoils one's record . . . . .

I sent you some more of those cigarettes the other day . . .

Edward to Vera

Brocton Camp, Stafford, 30 April 1917

Dearest Vera –

I only heard this morning from Miss Thurlow that Geoffrey was killed in action on April 23rd – a week ago to-day – and I sent you a cable about noon. No details are known yet as his people only got the War office telegram on Saturday evening; I have been afraid for him for so long and yet now that he has gone it is so very hard – that prince among men with so fine an appreciation of all that was worth appreciating and so ideal a method of expression. . .

Always a splendid friend with a splendid heart and a man who won't be forgotten by you or me however long or short a time we may live. Dear child, there is no more to say; we have lost almost all there was to lose and what have we gained? Truly as you say has patriotism worn very very threadbare.

Victor seems to be much better; Mother will be able to tell you more about him than I can as she sees him every day. She says his voice has come back just as it was before and that he speaks quite sensibly though his memory is not yet very good. He has asked for me to come and see him again and I hope to get up next Saturday. He doesn't seem to realise that he is blind yet but thinks he has a bandage over his eyes; I am rather afraid of what may happen when he finds out. I will write again in a day or two as soon as I hear any more about Geoffrey. This is an unlucky place – I was here when Roland died of wounds, when Tah was blinded, and when Geoffrey was killed.

    Good-night, dear child,
       Your affectionate

Edward

Edward to Edith Brittain

Stafford, 3 May 1917

I have so often felt before that Geoffrey would go but it is very hard when it comes; he never cared for war or any form of militarism and I don't think he ever wished to die that way. But his standard of life approached so nearly in my opinion the ideal and he was so far removed from anything approaching worldliness that I am sure he will be quite alright. You know, this country will be awfully rotten after the war; when you consider my case only with regard to the officers with whom I have made a real friendship since the war began, you find that they have nearly all gone and the people who have got through for the most part are of a lower type altogether.

Vera to Edward

Malta, 4 May 1917

I don't know if this letter will surprise you very much, but after all I have decided not to stay here for another 6 months – chiefly because I *know* that for a time at any rate you need me more than anyone out here can possibly do, & I have always known that I would come from the ends of the earth if you needed me. If we were terribly busy here I might have to think twice, but we are anything but; life is all too pleasant out here, the climate & country glorious & very little work to do . . . . . As soon as the cable came saying that Geoffrey was killed, only a few hours after the one saying that Victor was hopelessly blind, I knew I must come home. It will be easier to explain when I see you, also – perhaps – to consult you about something I can't possibly discuss in a letter. . . Anyone – or no one – could take my place here, but I know that nobody else could take the place that I could fill just now at home. I hope you won't think badly of me & imagine this is just an excuse to get home, for since I intend to nurse till the end of the War I would rather do it with this unit than any, as I love the system & have made many good friends, and when I have done all I can at home shall make every effort to get back. But if I can't manage that I can easily go somewhere where I shall be quite as useful.

Of course, there is still a question of my resignation not being accepted, as I had signed on again before the cables came, & then resigned just after, but the Matron thinks I shall probably be allowed to go. I shall probably have cabled home definitely one way or the other before you get this letter. I hope to get back some time this month as I am coming overland, not so much because it is safer as because it is quicker & more sure; one may wait indefinitely for a boat in these days. . . . The overland journey takes anything from 4 to 18 days . . . Of course I shall be with a party of some kind, either medical or nursing service, as one is not allowed now to do that journey alone. My great object is to get back before you go to the Front again.

I can't tell you how I shall miss Geoffrey – I think he meant more to me than anyone after Roland & you. As for you I dare not think how lonely you must feel with him dead & Victor perhaps worse, for it makes me too impatient of the time that must elapse before I can see you – I mayn't even be able to start for two or three weeks.

Geoffrey & I had become very friendly indeed in letters of late, & used to write at least once a week . . . After Roland he was the straightest, soundest, most upright & idealistic person I have ever known. Often I have wondered what it would all lead to – & I suppose now I shall go on wondering to the end. It is another case of 'whom the Gods love'; the people we care for seem too splendid for this world, & so we lose them.

The very evening after your cables came to say that Geoffrey was killed I had a letter from him, within 3 days before his death, which was in all ways a farewell. It was the kind of letter I always hoped I should have had from Roland if He was to die, for it made you feel that Death could not conquer a person of such fine & courageous natures as They were, and that the Dead would never really go very far away from the people they loved. Strangely enough even before this letter came I did not feel that Geoffrey had gone so completely as I felt Roland had, & even now he does not seem to have gone very far away – of course his faith in a Hereafter was very strong.

Surely there must be *somewhere* in which the sweet loves & intimacies begun here may be continued, & the hearts broken by this War may be healed. It is all so hopeless otherwise ...

Goodnight my dear. I hope I shall see you not too long after [you] get this. Is it *still* possible to 'Rejoice, whatever anguish rend your heart', I wonder?

Vera to Edith Brittain

Malta, 4 May 1917

When your letter came saying how you wished I was in England to comfort Edward because of Victor, I felt rather mean in signing on again & being unable to be of use at home for 6 months at least, but when I got your cables saying that Geoffrey was killed, I knew that I must try to come home if possible, for I know that I can comfort him as no one else can. I am coming partly for your sake when he goes out again, partly because I may be of more help to Victor than any of you know, but chiefly for Edward, for I hope to get home before he goes out again ... Anyone – or no one – could take my place here, whereas nobody else could take my place with Edward or you or Victor, so after I had thought it out for a long time I felt you had the first claim. It is very difficult sometimes to know what is the right thing to do, but at least I know in this case that I am not making your need of me an excuse to go home, for since I intend to go on nursing till the War ends I would rather do it with this unit than anywhere; I love the system of this hospital, I have made many good friends ... I don't intend to leave the service for good, only for a little time; after which I shall join up again all being well ... I am coming overland, not so much because it is safer as because it is quicker & more sure; one may wait indefinitely for a boat in these days ...

I can't tell you how I shall miss Geoffrey – more I think than anyone after Roland & Edward. It seems terribly hard that Victor should be blinded & Geoffrey killed within a few weeks of each other; poor Edward must feel that there is no one left of his generation...

It is another case of 'whom the Gods love'; I feel as though all the people I love are too splendid to last & that is why I lose them...

Goodbye – I hope I shall see you not long after you get this. I feel I must try to be of some use to the living since I can't be of any use to the dead.

Vera to Edward

Malta, 6 May 1917

You say that you & I must make things worth while to Victor as his family is inadequate for dealing with the situation, & Mother says that in future days 'he must be our especial care'. I have thought a great deal about both your letters. No one could realise better than I our responsibility towards him – not only because of our love for him, but because of his love for us, & the love felt for him by the One we loved & lost. I am not sure that this doesn't apply more to me than to any of you. I at any rate know this, that I should be more glad than I can say to offer him a very close & life-long devotion if he would accept it, & I can't imagine that Roland, if He had known what was to be – if He knows – would be anything but glad too. Those two are beyond any aid of ours – They who have died; and the only way to repay even one little bit of the debt to Them is through the one who remains: 'Happiness' said Olive Schreiner 'is a great love and much serving.' For his sake – for all your sakes – there is nothing I would not do for him...

The Army is characteristically slow in its method of dealing with my attempt to get home. It has already taken a week & has not yet officially given me permission to go, although it cannot possibly refuse me when I only signed for 6 months & have already done nearly eight. Then when it gives me permission to go I have to ask for permission to go overland & quickly. They will take about a fortnight to decide this, & then probably play about with my passports for a month! All of which makes me very desperate when it is a question of time before you go, espec. as there is very little to do here. I forget if I told you in my last letter that I tried to get leave, rather than resign altogether – which they absolutely refused. It seems rather hard to refuse leave to a person who has served for nearly two years, had very little leave, & asked no favours – but such is the way of the Army. However perhaps it is just as well, as leave might not be long enough, and in any case I needn't be long without serving, as when I came out here they told me at the 1st London that if I came home they would be very glad to have me back. Part of the 1st London is still at Camberwell, but a large part has gone to France; I expect they would let me go to which ever I wish, so if they won't let me back here or there are reasons against my going back, I could certainly do that.

The journey home is difficult now & dangerous in parts. Pray for me to come through it safely & quickly for all your sakes. But should I not, & should I get done in on the way home, at least you know my motives for trying to come.

I dare not think much about Geoffrey. As I work there is a shadow over everything; I know it is there but I try not to think why it is there or to analyse it too much. Do you think it strange, I wonder, that while I loved – & love – Roland so much, I loved Geoffrey a little too? To me there always seemed to be something very much in common between them – though I suppose there always is something in common between 'whatsoever things are pure, whatsoever things are lovely, whatsoever things are of good report . . . . .' This something, whatever it was, seemed to express itself in their mutual love of Rupert Brooke, their mutual sense of the glory of the earth, in Geoffrey's love of Roland's poems. . . When I think of Roland & Geoffrey & Victor & you I am reminded of Carlyle's mourning in the 'French Revolution' over the loss of 'the eloquent, the young, the beautiful, the brave'. How better could you describe Them – Roland the eloquent, Geoffrey the beautiful, & all four of you so brave & so tragically young. (Victor's conduct on the Day was glorious – worthy of Roland & of his best self. I almost wept in reading of it – dear old Tah.) . . .

Strange that Geoffrey should die on exactly the same day as his beloved Rupert Brooke 2 years before. And the same day of the month as Roland.

Vera to W.H.K. Bervon, her uncle

Malta, 7 May 1917

... One might have surmised, but could not have anticipated, that everything that made the world worth while for Edward would be so suddenly wrecked; I can feel his need of me as strongly across all these miles as if he had actually expressed it, and as long as he is in this world his need of me will come before everything else; whether it ought to or not is beside the question. So you see how desperately anxious I am to get home before he goes back into the vortex that has robbed him of everything. . .

Edward to Vera

Stafford, 7 May 1917

I have heard from Capt. Daniel who was Geoffrey's company commander and Miss Thurlow has heard from Wilmot, whom I met when I was in the 13th, and from the Adjutant, but the accounts do not agree on all points. However this is roughly what happened. The battalion attacked on April 23rd through a heavy barrage and Geoffrey got through that alright. The C.O., Lt. Col. Gilbert whom I knew at the 13th as a Capt., was wounded and captured quite early and Daniel had to take over command of the battalion. This apparently left Geoffrey in command of C coy but I am not sure about this; he may have been in command of it before the attack started and he may not have been in command of it at all. Anyhow the attack was held up and nobody knew what was happening on the right where C coy was. Daniel sent a message to Geoffrey to push on and find out what was happening. He did so, presumably taking a number of men with him; the German trench, in which he was, was very congested and so he got out on the top and was soon hit in the left lung by a sniper. He was brought into the trench and put on a stretcher where he died in about ¼ of an hour. Daniel says that he did not suffer any pain and as death was probably caused by haemorrage (probably spelt wrong but according to the Greek) I believe there would only be a feeling [of] slight suffocation. The place was marked and 'he will be given a decent burial by our padre as soon as he can get up there'. Wilmot says that stretcher bearers were trying to bring them down to the dressing station through a heavy bombardment and that he died while they were carrying him. . .

Tah was told last Wednesday that he will probably never see again, but he is marvellously cheerful. I went up to town on Saturday and came back last night; I was with him quite a long time on Saturday evening and yesterday morning and afternoon. He is perfectly sensible in every way and I don't think there is the very least doubt that he will live. He said that the last few days had been rather bitter. He hasn't given up hope himself about his sight and occasionally says 'if I get better . . .'

Vera to Edward

Malta, 12 May 1917

I have at last got permission to resign & 'proceed to the United Kingdom' & now it is a case of wait, wait, wait, until the opportunity to do so comes. I may leave in one week, maybe two, maybe three; the chief point is to get back before you go, & as (D.V.) I hope not to be too long once I start, it would be all right even if I didn't go till the beginning of June, as you cannot go, can you, before June 15th? Should come even if you had gone, because of Tah, but I *must* see you. . .

The risk of course is great, but half the world at present are running greater ones daily & the issue may make it well worth while. The uncertainty about going & the suspense about things happening at home are hard to bear, but I shall count these as nothing if only I can reach you. . . I have written to the family about it so you can talk about it to them; don't let them worry; time enough for that if anything does happen. One only hopes for the best; 'the Gods are not angry forever', & perhaps for once they will be kind to those to whom they have been so cruel.

Edward to Vera

Stafford, 28 May 1917

Awfully glad you have got back alright. If I had had any idea that you would arrive so soon I would have made an effort to get leave last week end. I shall get home sometime on Friday evening – I don't know the train yet. You have arrived in time and it will be great to see you again. I expect you have seen Tah to-day.

Vera spent the ten days following her arrival back in England in constant attendance at Victor's bedside as he struggled to learn braille. His mental faculties appeared to be in no way impaired. On 8 June, however, there was a sudden change in his condition. In the middle of the night he experienced a miniature explosion in his head, and subsequently became very distressed and disoriented. By the time his family reached the hospital Victor had become delirious.

Lieutenant-Colonel H. Sharpe

2nd London General Hospital,
Chelsea, to Headquarters, London District,
9 June 1917

Regret to inform you that Lieut. Victor Richardson, 4th Royal Sussex Regt. attached 9/K.R.R. [King's Royal Rifles] died at this hospital this morning.

Cause of death: – G.S.W. [Gunshot wound] temporal region and both eyes blind. Cerebral abscess.

His relatives were notified and were present at death.

Edward to Vera

Roker, Sunderland, 11 June 1917

Dearest Vera –

I suppose it is better to have had such splendid friends as those three were rather than not to have had any particular friends at all, but yet, now that all are gone it seems that whatever was of value in life has all tumbled down like a house of cards. Yet in Tah's case I will not, I cannot say that I wished from the bottom of my heart that he should live; I have a horror of blindness, and if I were blinded myself I think I should wish to die. The idea of long years without the light of the sun and the glory of its setting and without the immortal lamp of life is so abhorrent to me – and the thought of that has been hanging over me these 2 months – that I cannot altogether deplore the opening of the gates of eternal rest to that Unconquerable Soul, although I loved him in a way that few men can love one another. I am so very glad that you were near and saw him so nearly at the end; in a way too I am glad not to have been there; it is good to remember the cheerfulness with which he faced the living of a new life fettered by the greatest misfortune known to men. Yes, I do say Thank God he didn't have to live it. We started alone, dear child, and here we are alone again: you find me changed, I expect, more than I find you; that is per-haps the way of Life. But we share a memory which is worth all the rest of the world, and the sun of that memory never sets. And you know that I love you, that I would do anything in the world in my power if you should ask it, and that I am your servant as well as your brother

Edward

20 Lonsdale Rd.,
Roker,
Sunderland.

11ᵗʰ June 1917.

Dearest Vera —

I suppose it is better to have had such splendid friends as these three were rather than not to have had any particular friends at all, but yet, now that all are gone it seems that whatever was of value in life has all tumbled down like a house of cards. Yet in Tah's case I will not, I cannot say that I wished from the bottom of my heart that he should live; I have a horror of blindness, and if I were blinded myself I think I should wish to die. The idea of long years without the light of the sun and the glory of its setting and without the immortal lamp of life is so abhorrent to me — and the thought of that has been hanging over me these 2 months — that I cannot altogether deplore the opening of the gates of eternal rest to that Unconquerable Soul, although I loved him in a way that few men can love one another. I am so very glad that you ⋯ not ⋯ ced ⋯ man.

⋯ you he didn't have to live it. We started alone, dear child, and here we are alone again : you find me changed, I expect, more than I find you ; that is perhaps the way of life. But we share a memory which is worth all the rest of the world, and the sun of that memory never sets. And you know that I love you, that I would do anything in the world in my power if you should ask it, and that I am your servant as well as your brother

Edward.

*Beginning and end of Edward's letter to Vera about the
loss of his three friends*

Everything seems very vague but
none the less certain here + I only hope
I don't fail at the critical moment as
really I am a horrible coward; wish
I could do well specially for the
School's sake. I think you would
love Chegwell — everything is so
peaceful [there]. Often have
watched the many splen[did]
the Sunset from the [Bell].
But all this will be boring
"War knows no power safe
Safe this all safely low...
Safe where men fail
And if these poor limits
Rupert Brooke is great
great. If destiny is willing
In haste
G.R.J.D.

changed since July 1st.
In that one day I think he aged
ten years. I wonder if I shall
be the same: I don't think so
somehow or other, but it is
quite impossible to say.
I can quite understand your
desire to wander further. I am
a restless spirit myself —
in fact you yourself once accused
me of being a rolling stone.
Well, Vera, I may not write
again — one can never tell — and
So, as Edward wrote to me "it is
time to take a long long adieu"

*Final pages of the farewell letters by Geoffrey (20 April 1917) and
Victor (24 March 1917) to Vera*

EIGHT

25 JUNE 1917 – 24 JUNE 1918

. . . I learnt that human mercy turns alike to friend or foe
When the darkest hour of all is creeping nigh . . .

I shall always see the vision of Love working amidst arms
In the ward wherein the wounded prisoners lay.
— VERA BRITTAIN, 'The German Ward
("Inter Arma Caritas")'

. . . . to the sunset land of Avalon
You and your music and your dreams are gone,
Not here, dear child, not here to be fulfilled.
— VERA BRITTAIN, 'Epitaph for Edward'

I walk alone, although the way is long,
And with gaunt briars and nettles overgrown;
Though little feet are frail, in purpose strong
I walk alone.
— ROLAND LEIGHTON, 'Roundel (Vera Speaks)'

Because you died, I shall not rest again. . .
— VERA BRITTAIN, 'Roundel ("Died of Wounds")'

And so, farewell. All our sweet songs are sung . . .
— ROLAND LEIGHTON, 'Vale'

Edward returned to France in the last week of June 1917. For Vera, numbly going about household chores in the flat at Oakwood Court, there appeared now to be only one course of action: to return to nursing overseas. In July she was interviewed once more at Devonshire House, and requested a posting to France so that she could be near Edward.

Edward to Vera

France, 25 June 1917

My valise is still lost but I thought I had better come on here yesterday so I left Boulogne about midday. As I have for the moment got a good servant I am quite alright as he was able to get me some blankets without any fleas and I managed to borrow a towel and such other things as I lack from other officers. That valise is an absolute mystery. I searched every possible place at Boulogne and got a message from Folkestone to say that nothing was known about it there. I suppose it will turn up sometime but it will be an awful thing if it doesn't as I shall probably not be able to claim anything like its true value.

Edward to Vera

France, 25 June 1917

Owing apparently to some foolish mistake of the War Office I am going to be sent to the 2nd Bn. instead of the 11th. . .

Toujours

Edward

Edward to Vera

France, 27 June 1917

I am now under orders and may go up to the 2nd Bn. at any time. If I don't like it I shall write to Major Hudson who is at present in command of the 11th ... and ask him to ask for me. That is the only way of effecting the change. I have been in Calais all morning ... and got a shirt, 2 collars, a towel, and 2 prs. socks at the Ordnance Stores. I shall be able to carry these things in my pack and shall be able to subsist on them for some time. My only real difficulty is that I have no revolver and I am not going to buy another one.

———————

Edward to Vera

France, 30 June 1917

I have arrived at the transport lines and shall be starting for the trenches in half an hour or so. The battalion is apparently just at the place where one would wish it wasn't, as the papers have not failed to mention the place every day for the last week or so. However you will observe that this is page 106. It is strange that I should have left the line a year ago less one day.

———————

Edward to Vera

France, 30 June 1917
A dug-out
8.45 p.m.

The unexpected has happened again and I am in for another July 1st. If it should be that 'Ere the sun swings his noonday sword' I must say goodbye to all of this – then good-bye. You know that, as I promised, I will try to come back if I am killed. It is all very sudden and it is bad luck that I am here in time, but still it must be. All the love there is in life or death to you, dear child.

Edward to Vera

Billets, France, 3 July 1917

It's alright. I am so sorry to have worried you. All the same we have had an awful time. When I reported my arrival on Saturday night having only left Étaples in the morning, I was told that I was to go up with the company and that they were going to attack in the early morning. The whole thing was a complete fiasco; first of all the guide which was to lead us to our position went wrong and lost the way completely. I must tell you that the battalion had never been in the section before and nobody knew the way at all. Then my company commander got lost and so there was only one other officer besides myself and he didn't know the way. The organisation of the whole thing was shocking as of course the position ought to have been reconnoitred before and it is obviously impossible for anyone who has never even seen the ground before to attack in the dark. After wandering through interminable trenches I eventually found myself with only five men in an unknown place at the time when our barrage opened. It was clearly no use attempting to do anything and so I found a small bit of trench and waited there till it got light. Then I found one of our front posts (there was no proper front line) and there we had to stop till we were relieved last night. As you can imagine we had a pretty rotten time altogether. I don't think that I and the other officer who reported with me ought to have been rushed into the show like that after a tiring 2 days travelling and not knowing the map etc etc. However we are likely to be out for a few days now and I may have an opportunity of getting to know the officers and men here.

Edward to Vera

France, 4 July 1917

We came back to a village about 7 miles behind the lines yesterday morning . . . We expect to be here for a few days. I am in command of A company at present but I don't expect I shall be for long. The C.O. said he was pleased with the way we carried on in the line. It is an awful nuisance not having my valise: I do hope you will be able to do something to find it at your end because I can do nothing at all now I am here. Will you please send me a copy of the contents of the valise as soon as possible because, if I hear nothing of it in another week or so, I shall have to start claiming for it.

Edward to Vera

Billets, France, 7 July 1917

I am getting on pretty well here now and like the N.C.O.'s and men of my company very much. At present I have only one officer who is very good in action but I don't care very much for him as a personality. I wonder if you will remember 2 wounded men of the 11th Bn. whom we met at Eastbourne that afternoon you came down – Ptes. Shaw and Mantle. Mantle is now my servant – an awfully nice boy (though he did omit to wake me in time yesterday). He remembers you alright and says he would like nothing better than to get a blighty and have you to nurse him.

Edward to Vera

11th Bn. Sherwood Foresters, France, 11 July 1917

It is just fine being back here again. I arrived yesterday afternoon and found the battalion out at rest. Everything is just the opposite to the 2nd Bn.: here everybody is glad to see me back and ready to lend me things because I've lost my valise. . . I was sent back to A coy. at once with Capt. Harrison in command – he was in the July 1st 1916 attack with the company and was just senior to me then. I am his second in command and there will be 4 other subalterns when they return from leave and courses. Two of the old company servants are still here including the officers' cook and yesterday my old servant Coy came up to see me: I am not taking him on again because he has got a good job on the Brigade Canteen and he is rather old and has done his full time in the trenches; I have got a young fellow named Barrett who is very smart. Col. Watson is back in command of the Bn. and seems very glad to see me and Major Hudson second in command. He by the way got the D.S.O. for the show on June 7th and so is now a D.S.O., M.C., Croix de Guerre and has never been touched, which is a bit of a record. . . I had hoped that my valise would be here but no such luck! I don't know what to do about it. Do you think an ad. in the Personal Column of the Times would be any use? Please thank Mother for the pair of socks but please don't send any more clothes out because I can't carry a thing more; it was a pretty big job getting here yesterday as it was. I have just this moment seen 3 of our observation balloons brought down by a Hun aeroplane in flames; all the men in them escaped in parachutes. As usual our aeroplanes arrived too late and the anti-aircraft guns were ineffective. The battalion will probably be out resting for some little time.

Edward to Vera

France, 15 July 1917

Thanks awfully for your letter; you know quite well really that long letters from you could never bore me. Don't do anything about my kit yet; as soon as you send me the complete list of contents of the valise I will put in a claim. Owing to its being summer I can carry on pretty well as I am at present except for a revolver and I don't know what to do about that. I have had an answer to messages sent to Folkestone and Boulogne and nothing has been heard of it. Please guard most carefully all the receipts on my file and also let me know if possible the amount I paid for some of the bigger things. It will probably be months before I get everything back again unless the old valise turns up and every single item will have to be bought in England as I cannot get leave to go down to the base to get it. Will you find out for me the price of a new valise much like my old one with straps and name and regiment painted on and also the price of a 3 fold sleeping bag. I'm afraid it is no use sending anything out until I tell you to buy the valise and send it because I have nowhere to put anything. I have to read cheap books (when I have time to read anything which isn't often) and then throw them away. It is alright to send provisions etc. because they go with the mess stuff . . . We are still out but kept awfully busy and it is very hot, the company commander seems to have to do all the work and have all the worry as well just now.

Edward to Vera

France, 17 July 1917

I have got various papers on which to write my claim but I don't know when I shall have time to write it all out as it will probably take about 2 hours as it has to be done in duplicate and I don't think I am likely to have 2 hours to myself for ever so long. I will try to send you the prices I am claiming for each article so that you will be able to make out an exact duplicate if necessary. The correct Army Form is o.1784 . . . Will you get me 2 pairs of pants, short (well above the knee), thin, Aertex preferred, and cheap as they won't be wanted for very long. We are wearing shorts in the hot weather when out of the line; they consist of service trousers cut down issued from the Stores here. Hence the request for pants. No time for more.

Edward to Vera

France, 27 July 1917

When you send the new valise you might include a bag of sundries – elastic bands, etc and also cleaning brushes etc. as before but please note that my valise must not weigh more than 50lbs including the things I have here which probably weigh 15lbs at least. . . .

About Tah's M.C. I am inclined to think that the War Office thought from Mr Richardson's letter that he wanted to be presented with it at once; just at the time George [V] was in France and has been very busy lately as you know. If Mr Richardson had said there was no hurry and that he would like to receive it from the King when an opportunity offered it would probably have been alright. The idea of making any difference about Territorials is past and gone and the M.C. is just as often posthumous as anything else if not more so. . .

In the Times Lit. Supplement of July 12th there is a long article about Robert Nichols who seems to be a poet of unusual merit; his works up to date complete are only 3/6 so you might like to get them; don't send me the book but I should like some of the best of them in my own book; those quoted in the article are excellent.

Edward to Vera

France, 29 July 1917

Your going to France or at least the probability of it is rather more sudden than I expected. I hope you will be able to let me know where you got to. If you should get to the C.C.S. [Casualty Clearing Station] in a fairly large town near here I might be able to see you frequently but you would be shelled at intervals; they started shelling the place a bit just after I had left it on Friday afternoon: I went to do some shopping, buying amongst other things a canvas bucket which leaks so badly that I can't use it. . . I may be able to write respectable letters before long; I feel more inclined towards it every day; I think it was July 1st and 2nd which upset me a bit.

On 3 August Vera joined a small draft of nurses who were being sent out to France to replenish the staff of a large military hospital. The next day, the third anniversary of the outbreak of war, she left Boulogne, bound for the 24th General Hospital at Étaples. This little fishing port lay upstream from the lively resort of Le Touquet Paris-Plage, along a spreading coast where sand dunes pushed back the sea.

Vera to Edith Brittain

> 24th General Hospital, Étaples,
> France, 5 August 1917

... I arrived here yesterday afternoon; the hospital is about a mile out of the town, on the side of a hill, in a large clearing surrounded on three sides by woods. It is all huts & tents; I am working in a hut & sleeping under canvas, only not in a tent but in a kind of canvas shanty, with boarded floor & corrugated iron roof ... The hospital is frantically busy & we were very much welcomed . . . You will be surprised to hear that at present I am nursing German prisoners. My ward is entirely reserved for the most acute German surgical cases; we have no cases but the very worst (26 beds) & a theatre is attached to the ward ... The majority are more or less dying; never, even at the 1st London during the Somme push, have I seen such dreadful wounds. Consequently they are all too ill to be aggressive, & one forgets that they are the enemy and can only remember that they are suffering human beings. My half-forgotten German comes in very useful, & the Sisters were so glad to know I understood it & could speak a little as half the time they don't know what the poor things want. It gives one a chance to live up to our Motto 'Inter Arma Caritas', but anyhow one can hardly feel bitter towards dying men. It is incongruous, though, to think of Edward in one part of France trying to kill the same people whom in another part of France I am trying to save. . . .

Well, Malta was an interesting experience of the world, but *this* is War. There is a great coming & going all day long – men marching from one place 'somewhere' in France to another, ambulances, transports etc passing all the time. One or two 'courses' for officers are quite near here, & there are lots of troops training. Everything of war that one can imagine is here, except actual fighting, & one can even hear the distant rumble of that at times; usually by day the noise of things passing along the wide straight country road which runs right through the hospital drowns the more distant sounds. It is an enormous hospital – twice as many beds as at the 1st London.

Edward to Vera

France, 5 August 1917

Very glad you have arrived over here alright; I can't think for the moment where No 24 is but I don't think it is in Boulogne itself; anyhow I hope it will be decent. We have not been in this show as you may have heard before you left England; we are still in the same place and are going further back to-morrow according to the latest information.

Edward to Vera

France, 7 August 1917

We are rushing about the country and I have been billeting for the battalion for 2 days; we are not changing our front as far as we know. Most of my kit has arrived but no valise and it is a regular problem to get it carried some in waterproof sheet and some in other people's valises. Weather much better and it is not at all bad for marching. Hope you are getting on alright.

Vera to W.H.K. Bervon, her uncle

24th General Hospital, France,
9 August 1917

I had a pretty rough crossing last Friday . . . On the 4th anniversary of our declaration of War I came here with 4 others. This hospital is at a place very much in the centre of things; it is known as 'the advanced clearing station' which means that when the clearing stations get full this whole place is used as one; it is the next stage. . . The work I do is heaps more advanced than I have done hitherto . . . Everyone was charming to us when we arrived; they are extremely busy because of the push & could do with us very well. . . About a third of the Sisters are regular Army; the Matron of course is, & without exception is quite the most delightful of the many matrons I have had dealings with, being a lady in every sense, tall & pretty with a charming manner & very young looking in spite of a South African ribbon. . .

You may perhaps have heard that I am nursing German prisoners. This hospital is delightfully cosmopolitan; we take both surgical & medical cases from the front & locally – nearly all from the former of course – of British officers & men, German prisoner officers & men, and Portuguese officers. My hut is known as the 'German Acute Surgical Ward'. There is a theatre attached to the ward where we have anything up to 18 or 20 operations a day. Half the things are kept in the theatre & I wander in & out to fetch things while the operations are going on, & nobody minds. I see all sorts of interesting things going on; the operations are mostly amputations, chests, abdominals & heads. Any bad operation case goes immediately into our ward. . . The hospital is frightfully busy all through . . . Malta changed my ideas about the amount an individual can be capable of & responsible for, but this changes them still more. Even in the 1st London after the Somme push I have never seen such bad wounds as these Germans have. . . It is hardly possible to feel any antipathy towards one's patients in practice however much one may in theory; they are far too ill & utterly dependent on one for that. . . Our own men are very good to them; they came in to see them & give them cigarettes & fetch them drinks. One German patient has a great affection for one of our orderlies who comes in to see him every evening.

. . . There is a great coming & going [along] the road all day long – troops, transports & ambulances going from one place to another 'somewhere in France'. At night it is full of glamour, with the glow of lighted huts & tents on either side & the transport lights coming out of the distance & disappearing into it again. Further up the road at the end of a wood below some sandhills is the Military Cemetery – a forest of wooden crosses stretching right down to the sea, and each long mound a mass of gay-coloured flowers – nasturtiums, marigolds & iceland poppies; it is one of the most impressive & beautiful sights I have ever seen. . .

Edward to Vera

France, 13 August 1917

Many thanks for your letters of the 7th and 9th. I think I know whereabouts you are though I don't really know the side towards the sea. I know you can get things in Paris Plage alright but I don't want anything now thanks except that accursed valise; if it does-n't come to-morrow I shall have to dump all those parcels with the surplus kit and the Lord alone knows if I shall ever see them again. It is very strange that you should be nursing Hun prisoners and it does show how absurd the whole thing is; I am afraid leave is entirely out [of] the question for the present; I am going to be very busy as I shall almost certainly have to command the coy. in the next show because, as you know, some people are always left behind and Harrison did the last show just before I came out. I shall probably not be able to write at all regularly after the next few days though I don't know for certain. . . Things are much more difficult than they used to be because nowadays you never know where you are in the line and it is neither open warfare nor trench warfare.

Edward to Vera

France, 14 August 1917

I am just going away for 3 days for a special course during which I shall be very busy. The amount of rain is terrible and is making the ground in an awful state. I may be able to write again when I get there. The valise has not arrived and so I have had to send nearly all my kit away.

Edward to Vera

France, 18 August 1917

I have just rejoined the battalion which is in the same place and am in to-night's orders to be acting Capt. pending the usual certification in the London Gazette . . . This course, from which we have just returned, has been all about our show and as I told you before, I shall be in command of the company; I expect it will be pretty rotten.

Edward to Vera

France, 22 August 1917

Many thanks for your letter of the 19th. The valise has arrived to-day and so I have got somewhere to put my things at last. I am not in any show at present and we have no clear details for the future . . .

Edward to Vera

France, 27 August 1917

Capt. B. is now in a small dug-out with our old friend wipers on the left front and though he has got the wind up because he is in command of the company and may have to go up to the line at any moment, all is well for the present. The company are unfortunately out in the open under bivouac sheets and as it rained like hell last night, what time I guided the platoon sergts. round with my lamp issuing out rum, and is still raining a lot and very cold, they are as comfortable as they might be.

Edward to Vera

'The Frontier', France, 31 August 1917

Arrived here about 2 am. this morning 3 parts asleep from a few hundred yards behind the line where we were very lucky as I didn't have a single man in the company hit though there were a fair number of shells about most of the time we were there. We had a thin time with the weather, as we went up the day you wrote last and all arrived soaked; personally my feet never got dry till we got back here. . . I discussed local leave with the Adjt. this afternoon and he said that after the show he would try to get me on the Company Commander's Lewis Gun course at Le Touquet – lasting a fortnight – which would suit us both pretty well.

Edward to Vera

France, 2 September 1917

We have now got a padre who is the last word in absurdity and so we had what I should call a fatuous church parade this morning rendered additionally humorous because somebody had lost all the hymn books; we stood there stolidly with beatific expressions on our faces while the bands played 4 or 5 verses and an amen for each hymn; those of us who were capable of remembering the words didn't dare to sing in a vast and conspicuous minority. The attitude of the Army towards religion is very odd.

Edward to Vera

France, 6 September 1917

I have just applied for 3 days local leave from Monday the 9th. I might get it and I might not. If I do I will call at the 24th General and ask to see you probably some time on Monday afternoon as it takes about 5 hours by train from here. This is just to give you a warning in case I should come but I know you will quite understand if I don't turn up.

Edward to Vera

France, 14 September 1917

I don't think you have ever told me the name of your sister. I suppose it is because of her chiefly that you don't like to be moved from the German ward; personally I think I prefer that you should be nursing our own men though of course the one is service as much as the other. It was awfully rotten that I couldn't get that 3 days leave – if they had arranged to give it me a day earlier it would have been alright as they would probably not have recalled me and I should not have been back to-night just in time to enter the front line. You will be interested to hear that the leave may be re-submitted at a later date – après la guerre perhaps!

Edward to Vera

France, 19 September 1917

I have been too busy to write and I shall be again [for] some days I expect. I am quite alright myself though I have had several casualties in the company and the end is not yet... Don't worry at all please, and you know that I will write whenever I can.

The very best of love

Edward

Vera to Edith Brittain

24th General, France, 25 September 1917

I have all the time been waiting & hoping for some news of what has happened to Edward in this push; I have been too anxious about him to write about anything else . . . . .

Here there has been the usual restless atmosphere of a great push – trains going backwards & forwards all day long bringing wounded from the line & taking reinforcements to it; convoys coming in all night, evacuations to England & bugles going all the time; busy wards & a great moving of Staff from one ward to another. Our prisoners have of course made the German ward very busy . . . . .

I wish you could see this hospital – though of course you would probably see nothing but a dusty sandy camp of huts & tents! But it has the nicest atmosphere of any I have been in yet, & I have never come across such a charming & pretty Matron either at my hospitals or anyone else's. I have never got on with the V.A.Ds so well anywhere before either . . .

Edward to Vera

France, 25 September 1917

We came out last night, though perhaps 'came out' scarcely expresses it; had about 50 casualties including 1 officer in the company – the best officer of course. I ought to have been slain myself heaps of times but I seem to be here still. Harrison has arrived back and it is quite a relief to hand the company over for a bit.

Edward to Vera

France, 2 October 1917

A line to tell you that I am alright. We were suddenly called upon to go up again and take over our former sector for another

4 days much to our disgust, but fortunately most of us are back again and for the moment well behind the line in the same place as we were at the end of July and beginning of August. I am expecting leave any day but I'm afraid I shall not be able to see you on the way as we now go by C[alais]. I haven't heard from you since I wrote last but I expect you are very busy owing to this continual pushing... Some time I will tell you all about what we have done in the 2nd half of September during which we only had 3½ days out of the line, which is heavy work for the salient when straffing.

Vera to Edith Brittain

24th General, France, 3 October 1917

Just a line to tell you that I have at last had a letter from Edward dated Sept. 25th to say that he has come safely out of the Strafe though his company seems to have suffered badly & he has lost his best officer. He tells me that he is going home on leave . . . . . I am very sad I am not there but of course I would not be in England now for long at a time for anything on earth . . . . .

Edward to Vera

France, 7 October 1917

I am awfully sorry you have been so worried. My leave seems to have been stopped for the present for some reason or other and also we are probably going up to Y[pres] again to-night to provide working-parties etc. which is as unexpected as it is objectionable; it is filthy weather, cold and pouring with rain and I have just caught a bad cold and so am not particularly pleased with life.

Edward to Vera

France, 10 October 1917

— That curious dash because a shell made me jump. This is rather a filthy place because it is so wet and our camouflaged tents are inclined to let water in. I think I am being cheated out of my leave because of the time I spent with the 2nd Bn. That time ought to count really but it looks as though it isn't going to because people are starting to go on leave who should come after me. We haven't had a mail for 3 days owing to our sudden move and so I expect there will be a letter from you when it does come. I am very glad you have written some more poems so as to make enough for a small volume; I will ask Mrs L[eighton] about it; I believe you were thinking of Erskine Macdonald before. By the way why haven't you sent me any of your new poems as you know I should like to have them?

Vera to Edith Brittain

24th General, France, 12 October 1917

Someday perhaps I will try to tell you what this first half of October has been like, for I cannot even attempt to describe it in a letter & of course we are still in the middle of things; the rush is by no means over yet – Three times this week we have taken in convoys & evacuated to England, & the fourth came into our ward all at the same time. Every day since this day last week has been one long doing of the impossible – or what seemed the impossible before you started. We have four of our twenty-five patients on the D.I.L. (dangerously ill list, which means their people can come over from England to see them) and any one of them would keep a nurse occupied all day but when there are only two of you for the whole lot you simply have to do the best you can. One does dressings from morning till night. I never knew anything approaching it in London, & certainly not in Malta. No one realises the meaning of emergencies who has not been in France. Nor does one know the meaning of 'bad cases' for they don't get to England in the state we see them here; they either die in France or else wait to get better before they are evacuated . . . . .

Edward to Vera

France, 12 October 1917

We are in another lot of wet tents surrounded by mud and it is very cold as usual; consequently our servants, with the customary incorrigibleness of the British soldier, are singing lustily and joyfully. A new draft has just arrived wet through and are sitting on wet ground under wet bivouac sheets. The next man due for leave has been out 16 months and the next dozen have been out 15 or 14, and the order has just come round that all men must wash their feet in hot water – presumably in the dixies in which tea is made or else in the canteens out of which they eat and drink as there is no other receptacle: I suppose the A.D.M.S. thinks we carry portable baths in the forward areas – and the Intelligence Officer has managed to procure us 2 bottles of whisky, the first we have had for quite 3 months, and the bombing officer – a gentleman of forgetful disposition about 7ft by 4 and clumsy in proportion and belonging to our company – has gone to the Field Cashier miles away and has probably got lost as he started about noon and it has now been dark an hour, and the C.O. has cursed most people during the day, and I observe that this tent is not as waterproof as it may have been once upon a time, and there is our old friend miserably holding on to the eastern slopes of the ridges from which he has been driven but still demanding our presence in this sorrowful land: of such is daily life.

Vera to Edith Brittain

24th General, France, 15 October 1917

I hope Edward's leave soon comes off as it would cheer Father considerably to see him. I am afraid it is no use looking for any signs of me for at least six months; the leave of the old people here is very much overdue & of course we have to take ours in rotation with them . . . . .

We are still in a great rush & taking convoys every day; I have had a heavy day although I have managed to get off this evening. I am at the moment sitting in an extremely cold bath hut (occasionally conversing with Sister Moulson who is doing the same thing in the next door bath room) waiting for the hot water to be turned on . . . you have to sit in the bathroom and wait as otherwise all the baths get taken.

This is going to be a dreadfully cold winter, & every day the rain teems down, very cold & heavy.

Edward to Vera

France, 24 October 1917

I will be a little more expansive to-day as we are a long way back from the line and I don't think it matters my telling you where-abouts we have been. When the Bn. went into the line last time I was left behind to be O.C. Details (about 150 NCO's and men); on the night of the 16th Lieut. J.W. Jackson of C coy. was killed; on the night of the 17th Capt. Whyatt commanding C coy – one of the original officers of the battalion, he joined 3 weeks before me in 1914 – was killed; on the morning of the 18th Lieut. Groves whom I mentioned to you the other day was badly wounded, 1 Sergt. and 3 men being killed by the same shell and Whittington who is also in A coy. went down with shell shock; as Clark was on leave this left Harrison by himself and only one officer in C coy, both companies being in the support line which, as you know, always gets the worst of the shelling. Consequently I got a message on the night of the 18th to go up the next morning which I did and joined Jack in a filthy bit of trench, nearly got killed the same night changing to another support line, spent the next day in a pill-box, the night in a sap and got out safely in the morning. Jack also got out safely. Of course we lost quite a lot of men: some of them had only just joined but we might have come off worse considering that we were in the most pronounced salient just E of Polygon Wood – one of the worst bits of the whole front during the whole war. . . I quite understand why you didn't write during the interval but, if possible, please don't do it again or else I shall not tell you when I am about to face anything unpleasant and then you will not be able to help me face it. . .

I must stop. We have at last a gramophone and a very fine song by a man named Sherrington – 'Sweet early violets'. Good-night.

———

Edward to Vera

France, 1 November 1917

I am too busy to write – been working all day without a stop – it is now 10:30 pm. Harrison went to-day probably for good and so I am OC coy again; there is an awful lot to do. We are still in the same place. Please write as often as possible; you have no idea how bitter life is at times – but I know you are almost as busy as I am.

———

Edward to Vera

France, 4 November 1917

It is awfully hard to command a company when you have a rotten memory like I have; I have to put every blooming little thing down or else I should be in a mess in a few hours. . . I tried to get 2 days or even 1 local leave but it wasn't really possible as Harrison went rather suddenly and is now struck off the strength and so, unless I make a mess of it which I suppose I shall do sooner or later when I have been sufficiently discouraged, I am to remain OC company. . .

If you don't get letters from me for a bit you will not be surprised nor will you stop writing to me when opportunity allows.

Vera to Edith Brittain

24th General, France, 12 November 1917

Father's letter about Edward going to Italy . . . arrived to-day. It is very hard that he should have missed his leave after you have waited all this time, & as for me, half the point of being in France seems to be gone, and I didn't realise until I heard he was going how much I had counted on & looked forward to seeing him walk up this road one day to see me. But I want you to try & not worry about him more because he is there, because whatever danger he meets with he could not possibly be in greater danger than he has been in the last few months, as anyone who knows what it is to be at Ypres for that length of time would tell you. And, apart from the disappointment of not seeing any of us, I think he will be very glad of the change; no one who has not been out here has any idea how fed up everyone is with France & with the same few miles of ground that have been solidly fought over for three years. There is a more sporting chance anywhere than here . . . . . If only I get the chance of going I will; not that it would be so much advantage now, as now that the whole Western front is under one command I expect people will be moved about from Italy to France & vice-versa just as they have from one part of France to another, & won't necessarily stay the whole time in either one or the other . . . . .

At the beginning of November, the 11th Sherwood Foresters had been posted to join the Allied reinforcements on the Italian Front in the Alps above Vicenza. Following the humiliating rout of the Italian army at Caporetto that October, in which the entire Italian war effort had almost disintegrated, the job of breaking the Austrian offensive had assumed a new and pressing importance.

Edward to Vera

British Expeditionary Force, Italy, 15 November 1917

This will of course be no surprise to you especially as you will have been some time without a letter from me. Please write Italy very plainly in your address to me. I am rather disappointed with this part of the country – we are close to where Vergil was supposed to be born and the city forms the adjective so often applied to him (even in Tennyson's ode to Vergil) – it is flat and not specially interesting apart from its novelty. We marched through the city yesterday – it is old, picturesque and rather sleepy with narrow streets and pungent smells; we have been accorded a most hearty reception all the way and have been presented with anything from bottles of so-called phiz. to manifestos issued by mayors of towns; flowers and postcards were the most frequent tributes. Some of the country we passed through was very fine; après la guerre finie there are several places where you and I might like to stay a while. At present we are in some difficulties with regard to getting what we want; we point to a word in a dictionary as a rule but shopping is a great difficulty. It is not especially cold here in fact rather warm in the daytime but it will probably be very cold nearer the line and most of my thick clothes etc. just missed me as we left before they came . . . Write at once.

Edward to Vera

Italy, 17 November 1917

I have got 5 officers now, one for each platoon and a second in command and so I am not so badly off though very busy still. We have got a very hard job to do here and during the next few weeks the uninitiated may think we have failed in it but I trust we shall not really have done so; everything is going to be very different to what we have been used to before.

Edward to Vera

Italy, 23 November 1917

I am very tired as we have been moving for several days and are at a little village at the foot of the hills; the mail doesn't often go out or come in so I don't know when this will go. We are quite alright though generally tired out but we have to go on again.

Edward to Edith Brittain

Italy, 4 December 1917

We are in the front line – a most extraordinary place – very quiet at present and very few shells . . . The Piave is very wide just here and so the Germans and the Austrians are a long way off. One of our chief difficulties is getting enough to eat and smoke . . .

Vera to Edith Brittain

24th General, France, 5 December 1917

The hospital is very heavy now – as heavy as when I came; the fighting is continuing very long this year, & the convoys keep coming down, two or three a night . . . Sometimes in the middle of the night we have to turn people out of bed & make them sleep on the floor to make room for the more seriously ill ones that have come down from the line. We have heaps of gassed cases at present who came in a day or two ago; there are 10 in this ward alone. I wish those people who write so glibly about this being a holy war & the orators who talk so much about going on no matter how long the War lasts & what it may mean, could see a case – to say nothing of 10 cases – of mustard gas in its early stages – could see the poor things burnt & blistered all over with great mustard coloured suppurating blisters, with blinded eyes – sometimes temporally, sometimes permanently – all sticky and stuck together, & always fighting for breath, with voices a mere whisper, saying that their throats are closing & they know they will choke. The only thing one can say is that such severe cases don't last long; either they die soon or else improve – usually the former; they certainly don't reach England in the state we have them here, & yet people persist in saying that God made War, when there are such inventions of the Devil about.

———————

Vera to Edith Brittain

24th General, France, 12 December 1917

Unless unforeseen & compelling circumstances arise I have no intention of ceasing to be a V.A.D. for some time to come, nor do I intend ever to do it in England again. In fact apart from the people in it, I have an intense distaste for England, nor do I think I am ever likely to settle permanently in it for any great length of time in my life. Now that I have seen a little of the world I have begun to realise how much more nearly every [other] country appeals to me.

———————

Edward to Vera

Italy, 12 December 1917

We are still in the line which is a much warmer spot than it was when we first arrived in fact we were quite heavily shelled yesterday and I had a man killed. We expect to go out very soon and hope to be out for Xmas. . . It has come on beastly wet and made the trenches in a most awful state. We are still using our little house as company HQ but we had a shell through one of the rooms yesterday – nobody was in it at the time but a lot of kit was destroyed and if I had been in the next room (where I was 10 mins. before) I should probably have been hit by a piece of the wall which got knocked out; I am having a fair-sized dug-out made but it isn't ready yet; the R.E. [Royal Engineers] are supposed to be making a deep one for us, but as usual they are so slow that we shall probably be at another part of the line before it is finished.

Edward to Vera

Italy, 17 December 1917

Many thanks for your letter of Nov. 21st. As soon as I have a moment I will try to answer some of the questions you have asked me but I am too busy to do more than scribble a line at present. We got out of the line alright and are in quite decent billets; I have just had 2 new drafts to the company which means a good deal of work and in addition to everything else I have to try to get up a concert for the men at Xmas. I am trying to read the Loom of Youth which is excellent but I am only progressing slowly at present: it is a bit exaggerated but otherwise a very reasonable portrayal of the public school. Victor would have liked it immensely as it very largely expresses his opinions.

Edward to Vera

Italy, 22 December 1917

I am so thankful for your letters – they are now as before the greatest help in the whole world . . . I don't know whether I am glad to be here or not – it sounds strange but it's quite true; I was glad to leave the unpleasant region we were in not far from you and the novelty was good for a time but yet in a way it is all the same because there is no known future and the end is not yet, though, on the face of things at present, there is perhaps more chance of return. Why do you want me to get married – a most improbable occurrence? Anyhow there will be no chance for a very long time. It is wonderful that you manage to write a play in spite of all your work: I never have time to do anything – scarcely time to write letters, but I suppose there is always that great difference between you and me – you are interested in your work and are naturally more energetic while I continually have to make myself interested in mine and I dream of things and never do them. It is partly the fault of the army itself; for one thing there is very little encouragement and it is very hard to do everything right – partly because different senior officers vary so enormously in their opinions about how a thing should be done – and also this sort of routine is so deadening; it is a life of thinking about little details the whole time and especially thinking about the right one at the right time; the brain must be essentially a machine of memory and after that the rule of life is expediency. It is very tiring and uninteresting. I can't get on with this because of a number of messages, orders, etc which are continually arriving . . . I am rather a grumbler.

Those 2 poems of Masefield's are very good and will go in the book when I have time to write them in. Poetry counteracts the deadening influence a good deal; I have Rupert Brooke alright and the manuscript volume. If you have a Swinburne with you will you send me one or two of the best choruses out of the Atalanta. I am reading the Loom of Youth in bits when I have time. It is very good and it is very true even if slightly exaggerated. The author, who I suppose is Gordon Caruthers in the book, seems to have been a little unfortunate in not finding a really satisfactory leader among his various house captains and friends and also was one of those people who are too secure in a position which is satisfactory enough to be in sympathy with anybody else, but he does seem to realise eventually that there are other things besides games; it is a pity he didn't seem to have anything to do with music. In other things he hits the nail on the head with remarkable precision notably perhaps when speaking about masters trying to get boys to appreciate the 'old men's poets' instead of showing the way to the more modern poets who better satisfy the ardour of youth. My experience is that the language and morals generally are not so blatant as he depicts them though what he says is very fairly reasonable.

We are only half in the mountains here; we face them and the Austrian sits on them; they look very beautiful at times, sometimes near sometimes far off, and there is generally snow on the higher ones. We have had a little snow here lately but it hasn't stayed. . .

We were all very short of anything to smoke until just lately when some cigarettes came for me from home; it is an absurd country for supplies though canteens are arriving now: I think the poorer people live entirely on polenta – a heavy, tasteless, fat, yellow cake which they make themselves and eat hot and an inferior species of vino which is rather bitter and rather too potent for the men who would drink it as though it was beer when they first got here. The servants are singing 'Hark the herald angels' and 'Good King Wenceslas' somewhat out of tune and raucously in the kitchen. One of my officers is such a useless idiot – can't do a thing right – continually gets the men's backs up – and is frightfully obsequious to me which is so annoying. Unfortunately there aren't any courses to send him on like there were in France. The gramophone returned last night with the spare kit from the base: great joy – Sweet Early Violets and Down in the Forest again. I wonder how long it will be before we have to dump it again.

. . . I wish I could see you again; it is so long since I did that we shouldn't be able to talk properly for about ½ hour. It seems so much more than 2 years ago since Roland was killed – tomorrow and Monday I will think of you whenever I can and our love for him may lessen the miles between us. What a long war this is! It seems wonderful to have lived so long through it when everyone else is dead.

Goodnight, dear dear child

Ever your

Edward

Edward to Vera

Italy, 31 December 1917

It has been a rotten year in many ways – Geoffrey and Tah dead and we've seen each other about a week all told: so there's a sob on the sea to-night. I don't seem to be able to write decently; so often I feel tired and fed up when I've done my ordinary work and so waste what little spare time I have; I wish I could manage to write to you more. I had quite an interesting talk with the CO the other day about the Battalion and some of its former and present officers; Fyldes is in hospital at present so the CO and I are the only officers who joined the Bn. in 1914.

Edward to Vera

Italy, 4 January 1918

It is very cold where we are on the top of a hill which you may know, as you know where we are from the papers, and everything freezes up; unfortunately the men are in bivouacs and a few in dug-outs and so it is rather rotten for them; we have a tiny hovel – the mess and kitchen are one and the floor is of earth. 3 of us sleep in one sort of attic above and the other 3 were sleeping in another one last night but nearly got blown out by the draft. However there is a fire and the gramophone still plays. . . I am not surprised to hear that it is a very cold winter in France. I have got my sheepskin now and so usually manage to keep fairly warm. About Nov. 25th we sent for cigarettes for the men hoping they would arrive by Xmas; 4500 arrived the night before last which enabled us to give 25 to each man. It was impossible to get cigarettes of any sort here until quite recently.

Vera to Edith Brittain

24th General, France, 10 January 1918

Conditions at home certainly seem very bad . . . Everyone is servantless, no one visits anyone else or goes away, & the food seems as hard to get hold of in other places as in London now. But do if you can try to carry on without being too despondent & make other people do the same, & for goodness sake don't talk about 'going down-hill', for the great fear in the Army & all its appurtenances out here is not that it will ever give up itself, but that the civil population at home will fail us by losing heart – & so of course morale – just at the most critical time. The most critical time is of course now, before America can really come in & the hardships of the winter are not yet over. . .

Here the cold is intense & to make matters worse our oil ration has temporally run out . . . . . The other morning I came off duty in a blizzard to find that the wind had blown open my window which I had left shut, & my whole room & bed were covered several inches in snow, just like outside . . .

Edward to Vera

Italy, 10 February 1918

Very glad to hear that Erskine Macdonald was so favourable in his criticism; it is certainly rather unusual – I should think – for him to half-finance a first volume of any sort. . . I am extremely busy again with all sorts of work chiefly range practices and difficulties connected with washing men and clothes. The most excellent system of giving a man clean underclothes every time he went to the baths which we had in France cannot apparently be done here. The present system is to have a Corps laundry; all kinds of units send clothing when asked to do so: the result is that the company has to have (say) 50 shirts, 45 pants, 55 socks, and 30 undervests collected. This of course leaves a lot of men without a change of certain garments; then at some time or other they will carefully return to you washed 35 shirts, 50 pants, 40 socks, and 20 undervests. At present we are doing some of the washing ourselves. A few people come over and drop bombs when the moon is favourable – otherwise there is not much war going on.

Edward to Vera

Italy, 19 February 1918

Nothing very exciting is happening here; we are now right under a mountain famous about 6 weeks ago and doing working parties.

The change of scenery is rather pleasant; it seems to me that it is the mountains and nothing else which have made Italy renowned for its beauty; anything more uninteresting than the Lombardy plain it would be hard to find...We are now having what will probably be the last spell of cold weather; the mountains had a lot of snow on them a day or two ago but it is disappearing rapidly now.

Edward to Vera

Italy, 4 March 1918

I haven't been very well since Wednesday 27th and came to hospital yesterday and am now much better. I think it is PUO or something of the sort much like what you had on leave. Unfortunately our M.O. [Medical Officer] is away on Rome leave and the temporary substitute is a rotten specimen – knows nothing at all; he only took my temperature in the mornings until I suggested its being taken in the evening too, and gave me quinine tablets and never dieted me at all. So my temp. was 102.5 yesterday morning and so he fortunately gave up the unequal struggle after 4 days and sent me to hospital... – anyhow they got my temp. down to normal this morning from 103 last night but of course that isn't for the ears of the family or else they will be taking the next train to Italy.

Edward to Vera

Italy, 9 March 1918

Many thanks for yours of the 1st. It was certainly a great pity about that leave; I wonder where we shall meet next time. I am much better and expect to leave hospital to-morrow; they are all very busy in my absence as there are only 2 officers on duty. My temperature has been quite down for 2 or 3 days in fact it is 97.6 to-night and I have been out for short strolls in the afternoon with a padre who is in my room; he is ancient but a much better padre than our own who I think I told you is an absurd specimen. Many thanks for your roundel and Vernède's poem. Have you any idea at all when the book is coming out?

There is a beautiful glimpse of the mountains through this window; the further ones are still covered with snow as it is rather cold still though it is supposed to be the last cold spell. I expect you will be very busy soon when the raiding season, which is now at its height, is over. We hear that the Hun is going to use a new kind of gas. The war here is for the moment as before.

———————

Edward to Vera

Italy, Easter Sunday 1918

I haven't heard from you for some time either but I don't expect to for some time as I can imagine you being most awfully busy. I won't talk about your push as you will have too much to do with it as it is but I am glad we have recaptured Albert if only for memory's sake; if the Hun cannot break our line, and I don't think he can, I should think that the end of the war is fairly near. We are in the line with snow all about us – a great change as it is very cold but we are just getting used to it. There have been wonderful sights to see – in parts it is quite like one or two places I saw in Switzerland – huge peaks covered with tall pine trees – marvellous roads with hairpin bends and everything solid rock where the snow lies until June... However I can't tell you as much about things as I would like. The company is quite well and quite enjoying the novelty at present. Early this morning we had a most extraordinary communion service about 300 yrd behind the front line behind a knoll – a most original performance. I am very busy as usual under the circumstances and expect to be more so quite soon.

———————

Edward to Vera

Italy, 19 March 1918

Whittington is hoping to go on leave soon and if he does is going to get married; he has been putting it off for most of the war, I think, and has now more or less naturally decided that the war isn't going to end...We have had an awful lot of trouble with the civilians on whom we are billeted; the places are very small farms for the most part, very dirty, and with an average of 6 to 10 small, screaming children in each: several families, some being refugees, live in each house. The day we got here 4 teaspoons disappeared and the next day most of the sugar ration went and then a knife and 3 plates and several cigarettes out of the room where I sleep. Consequently I sent for an interpreter this afternoon and there was a great wailing and chattering for about ¼ hour – one of the stolen articles made its appearance about every 5 minutes except 3 teaspoons and a knife for which we eventually accepted 9 lire; I was rather sorry to take money off them but there was nothing else to do if the business was going to be stopped and of course they get paid a little by the Government for every day we use the billet.

While the fighting on the Western Front continued unabated as Ludendorff maintained his attack, Vera received a letter from her father, informing her that her mother had suffered a complete breakdown and had entered a nursing home, and that it was Vera's duty to leave France immediately and return home to Kensington.

Vera to Edith Brittain

24th General, France, 31 March 1918

I have put in an application to be allowed to resign before the end of my contract, & as you know that is all I can do – Father appears to imagine that it rests with *me* whether I come home to-morrow or in 6 months . . . However, I am practically certain to be back within a month, so you need not worry any more as I can then reopen the flat & then you will soon probably be able to come back again. Father can quite well look after himself for another week or two; in fact it will do him a great deal of good, so you must make up your mind not to worry about him . . .

Edward to Vera

Italy, 10 April 1918

Judging by the news we get daily the worst of the show in France seems to be over and the main object has not been achieved; however I can imagine you to be so busy that you have no time for anything and I quite understand why you haven't written for some time. Do you know exactly what is wrong with Mother . . . if only she will rest I expect she will be alright in time. It will be impossible for you to come home now for several weeks at least however necessary it may be. Although we are lucky here to be out of the show in France we are getting a pretty rotten time with the weather – rain and snow continually and very poor accommodation. The night we arrived at this line of trenches I had 40 men sleeping out in the open and the rest in wet dugouts and it is by no means warm in this weather when you are nearly 4000 ft. up. Even now most of them are only in Italian bivouac sheets and it has snowed or rained almost without cessation for the last 24 hours. However they manage to get over it through being more or less used to it. We are in a log hut 10' x 6' and are highly delighted when the water does not come in much. It has a sort of gravel floor which is getting very wet to-day: we all mess in it and 3 of us sleep in it. Still the Austrian is quiet and has the wind up properly about us; we bagged 3 prisoners the other day – not my company unfortunately but Gibson's though we were out after him the same night.

It is most pathetic to think that the old places where we were 2 years ago are now in the hands of the Hun as also are the graves of many people we know. As far as I can tell Louvencourt is still behind our lines though fighting in Aveluy Wood doesn't sound far away. I was talking to a major who is attached to us yesterday about making some dugouts in a strong piece of ground and he was very particular about wire goggles being worn by men working or living there because of splinters caused by shells bursting on the stone 'because', he said, 'I can imagine nothing worse than being blind for the rest of your life'. It seemed rather strange that he should say that on the anniversary of the day on which Tah was blinded.

———

Edward to Vera

Italy, 26 April 1918

I sympathise with you very much at having to go back just now especially as nobody at home will understand that you particularly wanted to stay where you were. In one of her letters not long ago Mother said something about its being a good thing for you to come home as you disliked the work so much, but of course it was a bit easy to read between the lines. Naturally I realise that Mother is ill and not quite as usual but it is most annoying to read in her letters about her anxiety that you should arrive home before the Bosch gets to Calais etc. i.e. it doesn't matter a damn if they get to Calais or Boulogne as long as you get home first. Incidentally Mother and Father seem to have got it firmly into their heads that the Bosch is going to get the Channel Ports and that we are going to lose the war etc., not of course realising that the latter can never happen and the former would only be a nominal affair owing to the remarkable fact that we have got rather a good Navy. As a matter of fact we have done extraordinarily well in this Hun push as you will know yourself, the withdrawal East of Ypres being probably a master stroke. Either the Bosch or we had to do a big show and whoever did it stood to lose everything if he failed. We await the counter-offensive.

Vera arrived home at the end of April to find the London flat empty and
her father in a local hotel. She immediately brought her mother back to
Oakwood Court from a Mayfair nursing home, and took charge of the
household. But it was with a strong air of resentment that she tried to reac-
custom herself to the dull monotony of civilian life.

Edward to Vera

Italy, 12–13 May 1918

I receive alternately doleful and breathlessly breezy letters from
Mother and so I suppose she is rather better except on the occasions when she and Father have a tiff. Many thanks for the
slippers, brilliantine, and socks which arrived about 3 hours ago;
the books sound most promising: I was listening to somebody
eulogising Hugh Walpole in general and 'Fortitude' in particular
only the other day; if you remember 'the Dark Forest' annoyed me
rather because his beastly Russians were so terrified of whizz-
bangs. As you say the war is certainly looking up a bit. Reports
from various units clearly show many of the Bosch successes to
have been very 'Pyrrhic' especially as regards morale. However I
am preventing the mess cook from going to bed; he has to sleep
in the mess to counteract the ever-present tendency of the crockery, food etc. to disappear – this is a wonderful nation for
scrounging.

Edward to Vera

Italy, 20 May 1918

Last night I got a circular about the Uppingham War Memorial
asking for subscriptions etc. The intention is (1) To set up a sort
of memorial in the chapel with all the names of the people who
have been killed (2) To pull down the Lodge and make a new
large Hall bigger than the old Schoolroom on either the North
or East side of the quad. and to have a larger colonnade on the

remaining side, and (3) To assist with money people who would
have sent their sons to Uppingham had it not been for the war
especially sons of officers killed in the war preference being given
to O.U.'s.

---

*Receipt for Edward's donation to the Uppingham School War
Memorial, sent shortly before his death*

Edward to Vera

Italy, 30 May–3 June 1918

If the war goes on much longer nobody will go back to Oxford
in spite of the concessions; I often think I am too old now to go
back. I am getting terribly bored with what we are doing just
now –

3rd June 1918

– however I am now in hospital and oddly enough not so bored as before because it is rather a relief to be down in the foothills again and not to have anything to do for a change. It is just a form of PUO which everybody is having just now but fortunately not all at quite the same time. I shall be back again in a few days... I never know what you are going to decide on next but still I quite agree with your new point of view; it is better not to go to Oxford at all than to go and have a rotten time feeling that it was a mistake. After all Experience is a great form of instruction and it is not to be had to the same extent as now in ordinary times, whereas the full advantage of Oxford could only be had in those ordinary times. I should have thought you could have got out again to No 24 quite soon by getting the matron there to ask the 1st London to send you out to her as soon as you joined them, just in the same way as I could probably get Hudson to ask for me if I had to go home for a wound or anything after I was alright again. However I don't suppose they will keep you at home in any case when you do rejoin because you have now got so much more experience than the average individual. I rather think leave has been reopened while I have been away which is hopeful but of course I am about 20th on the list.

　　With much love
　　　Your affectionate

Edward

Vera to Edward

10 Oakwood Court, London W14, 4 June 1918

As a V.A.D. I must perforce join up in England as a sink-scrubber once more, & have always the limited scope of a permanent subordinate. As a W.A.A.C. [Women's Army Auxiliary Corps] officer I should have responsibility over women, which I [think] I'm worth, & am liable to be sent almost up to the firing line. This War is never going to end & V.A.D.ing leads nowhere, but a woman's commission might lead to some sort of official appointment après la guerre. Of course when I first joined there was no such thing as a woman officer but now her day is beginning to dawn. The case would be analogous to that of an R.A.M.C. [Royal Army Medical Corps] orderly who got [a] commission in the Infantry. Please give me your opinion which I value greatly. If you would rather think of me as a nurse I should prefer to remain one. Would Roland have liked me to wear khaki?

The novel is progressing but Mrs Leighton & I have decided it cannot be published till some time after the War as there's too much truth in it about things & people. If I published it now I should have to water down the plot & weaken the characters. Mrs Leighton says 'No, it's too good as it is to lose; write it as you thought it & hold it back.'

I have an idea [for] another which I could publish & shall begin when I've finished the other. In the second the hero will be taken from you, & I don't suppose you'd have me up for libel!

Vera to Edward

London, 5 June 1918

Wash out yesterday's letter; have been enquiring about W.A.A.C. officers & find they are not needed at all; there isn't even one vacancy in the whole Corps. I am really very glad, for whatever else I tried to be I know I should always be a nurse at heart, anyhow for the 'duration of the War'. And I know I am a good one; as for my career it is literature really; nothing else matters. As for nursing I love it now, & my uniform as well (espec. the indoor version), having, as Mrs Leighton says, 'earned the right to love them by suffering in them'. Rather a nice way of putting it, n'est-ce pas? Somehow no female figure in the whole of this War has such a glamour as a hospital nurse, or such dignity. No one else so much 'looks down into the depths', which is a privilege, as it means a corresponding ability to look up into the heights.

One somehow felt that if there were something else for which one was needed & to which one's abilities were better suited one ought to try & do it, but I am glad there isn't. After all, I repeat, I'm a good nurse, & even if there is less authority attached to it I would rather look after a ward of wounded Tommies than an Army of domestic servants. I should never love any motto so well as 'Inter Arma Caritas'.

At the beginning of the third week in June, the newspaper headlines were dominated by reports of an Austrian offensive on the Italian Front during which there had been heavy fighting. Edward had not written since 3 June, and as the days passed and no word came from him, Vera wandered restlessly round the Oakwood Court flat, barely able to conceal her fear. Edith Brittain was staying with her mother in Purley, and Vera and her father were just finishing tea on the afternoon of 22 June when they were interrupted by a sudden loud knock at the front door. Vera went to the door and received a telegram which she opened and read 'in a tearing anguish of suspense': 'Regret to inform you Captain E. H. Brittain M.C. killed in action Italy June 15th.'

At three o'clock on the morning of 15 June, the Austrians had launched a surprise attack with a heavy bombardment of the British front line along the bottom of the San Sisto Ridge. Five hours later, the enemy had penetrated the left flank of Edward's company and had begun to consolidate their positions. Edward had led his men in a counter-offensive and had regained the lost positions, but while keeping a lookout on the enemy, a short time later, he had reportedly been shot through the head by a sniper and had died instantaneously. He was buried in his blanket with four other officers in the small cemetery at Granezza, 4,000 feet up in the mountains.

Marie Leighton to Vera

Keymer, [?] June 1918

My dear, dear Vera,

What can I say to you? We were all laughing last evening – about 5.30 – when the telegram came and as I more than half expected one from Jack I never thought of Edward and felt no alarm – and that made the shock the worse – I never did anything after for the evening. Robert was here, too, as well as Evelyn, and, of course, Clare. There's no need for me to say that we all send deep and great sympathy. But as for me - I knew him so well, lately, and loved him so much! It's horrible. I think of his handsome dark head falling back – oh are you sure, quite sure? Isn't there any possibility of a mistake?

And you – oh, I turn my thoughts away as yet when they get anywhere near the subject of what it means to you.

Is your mother strong enough again to stand it? I must write her at Purley. Yes, I can see that it is a good thing that she is there. Thank Heaven at least that he died helping to get a victory. I had just posted a letter to him yesterday. He had come to mean so much that his going will make a lasting difference – a piece of one's life taken away, so that things can never be quite the same again. And there – the 'Three' are gone!

I feel too much blinded and choked to write more now. Tell your father – won't you – how much our hearts are with him?

Yours with love always,

Marie (Leighton)

Robert Leighton to Thomas Arthur Brittain
Keymer, 24 June 1918

My very dear friend,

You have not need, I am certain, to be assured of my deep and earnest sympathy with you. I who have passed through the same harrowing ordeal know only too well what it means to a father to be deprived thus abruptly of the son in whom his highest hopes and expectations have rested. However much we may have dreaded the coming of such a fatality to our dear Edward, the dread has always been tempered by a soothing faith that he would be spared to us and that his good fortune would follow him throughout the whole terrible war; and now that the cruel worst has happened it is very hard indeed to realise the awful truth that we shall never, never see him again. But with the anguish that is now in our hearts there is a proud consolation in knowing that he met his death gloriously in the hour of victory in one of the greatest and most decisive battles of this great war. He would not have us grieve. Let us then be brave, as our sons were brave; let us be thankful that it has been our privilege to give our sons to our country and to the cause for which they so nobly sacrificed their precious lives. It was all that we could do, you and I. We should either of us eagerly have given up his own life if by doing so his boy might live; but we could not make the choice and it only remains to us to bear our own burdens bravely and to make them lighter by the sweet and loving memory of the bright young lives that are gone.

I have heard no particulars beyond the announcement in Vera's telegram. It was good of her to let us know so promptly. Dear Vera. Not many women have suffered more than she has suffered in this war. I grieve for her and for her mother, as I grieve for you.

Believe me always

Yours most sincerely

Robert Leighton

"I, too, take leave of all I ever had."

Lieutenant Roland Aubrey Leighton 7th Worcesters.
(Died of wounds near Hébuterne., Dec. 23rd 1915)
Buried at Louvencourt.

Lieutenant Victor Richardson M.C. 9th K.R.R.C.
(Blinded at Vimy Ridge, April 9th 1917. Died
of wounds 2nd London Gen. Hosp. June 9th 1917.)
Buried at Hove.

Lieutenant Geoffrey Robert Youngman Thurlow, 10th Sherwood
Foresters
(Killed in action at Monchy-le-Preux,
April 23rd 1917.) Buried ?

Captain Edward Harold Brittain M.C. 11th Sherwood Foresters
(Killed in action leading his company in the
counter-attack in the Austrian offensive on
the Italian front, June 15th 1918.)
Buried at Granezza, Lusiania.

*Vera's inscription on the first page of a notebook in which she preserved items
memorialising Roland, Victor, Geoffrey and Edward*

NOTES

Page

12   **Beethoven Concerto:** Edward was a proficient violinist, and Vera would sometimes accompany him on the piano.

13   **Somerville:** Somerville College was one of four women's societies in Oxford, and famous for its academic excellence. It was founded in 1879 in a group of buildings on a piece of land between Walton Street and the Woodstock Road.

      Exhibition: Vera's exhibition was worth £20 a year.

14   **'The Story of an African Farm':** This novel by the South African writer and feminist, Olive Schreiner (1855–1920) was first published in 1883, and caused a sensation because of its advocacy of the emancipation of women. Lyndall is its idealistic, strong-willed, and ill-fated heroine.

      the Quiet Voice: Roland was teased by his friends for this mannerism, as Edward was for his 'bedside manner'.

15   **'Mill on the Floss':** This novel by George Eliot (1819–80) influenced Vera's thinking, especially in its delineation of Maggie Tulliver, the protagonist.

      'Earth has not anything . . .': First line of the sonnet 'Composed on Westminster Bridge' by William Wordsworth (1770–1850).

16   **'Forerunner':** One of a trilogy of philosophical novels by the Russian writer Dmitri Merezhkovsky (1865–1941) which appeared (1896–1905) under the general title *Christ and Anti-Christ*. They argue that Paganism and Christianity are two halves of a yet-to-be-revealed higher truth.

      'Woman & Labour': A pioneering feminist work by Olive Schreiner, published in 1911, which considers women's relationships to work, to war, and to men.

      'Robert Elsmere': A novel (1888) by Mrs Humphry Ward describing the spiritual struggles of an Anglican clergyman who loses faith in the Christian orthodoxy of his time.

17   **'Sallust before Sunrise':** This poem by Roland was apparently never completed.

      Omar Khayhamesque feeling: A reference to the central theme of *The Rubaiyat of Omar Khayyám*, the free translation by Edward Fitzgerald (1809–83) of quatrains by the twelfth-century Persian poet.

18   **'Raffles':** A play (1906) adapted by E. W. Hornung and E. W. Presbrey from Hornung's popular novel, *The Amateur Cracksman* (1899).

19   **Lowestoft:** The Leighton family lived at Heather Cliff at Lowestoft, on the Suffolk coast.

20   **'L'Envoi':** The second verse of Roland's poem reads, 'But our youth's paths once met;/And think not we forget/How great a brother's debt/To you is owed.'

      'a striving . . .': *The Story of an African Farm*, I, 10, and epigraph to II.

21   **Camp:** The Uppingham OTC Summer Camp at Aldershot.

27   **Lyndall's remarks:** *The Story of an African Farm*, II, 6.

      Edward is going to business: For a short time after war broke out, Edward accompanied his father to the family paper business, Brittains Ltd, near Leek in north Staffordshire.

28   **McKenzie:** Reverend H. W. McKenzie, headmaster of Uppingham, 1907–15.

29   **Kitchener:** Horatio Herbert, first Earl Kitchener of Khartoum and of Broome (1850–1916). Secretary of State for War, 1914.

30   **Ellinger:** Maurice Ellinger, Uppingham schoolfriend of Edward's.

31   **Olive Schreiner thinks differently:** In *Woman and Labour* Chapter VI.

33   **Miss Penrose:** Emily Penrose, principal of Somerville, 1907–26.

      Pass Mods.: Pass Moderations was the Oxford examination, usually taken at the end of the undergraduate's first year, that qualified the student to proceed with work for the BA course.

50   **'the eloquent, the young . . .':** From the passage lamenting the execution of Girondin deputies in *The French Revolution. A History* (1837) by Thomas Carlyle.

51   **you can get anything . . .:** *The Story of an African Farm*, II, 6.

      'gentlemen in England . . .': From Henry's impassioned exhortation to his troops before Agincourt, in Shakespeare's *Henry V*, IV, iii.

54   **his aunt:** Since the death of his mother three years earlier, Victor's aunt, Miss Dennant, had been a surrogate mother to him.

59   **'Only a turn of the head . . .':** The first words of Roland's 'L'Envoi'.

60   **'And you set out . . .':** From Roland's 'L'Envoi'.

64   **a certain order of minds:** *The Story of an African Farm*, II, 1.

66   **Censorship:** As a junior officer, Roland had the responsibility for censoring his men's letters. All ranks had occasional access to green envelopes which were used on the understanding that the contents

were of a private or family nature, and could only be opened by the base censor. In his letters to Vera, Roland employed a dot-code under the letters of certain words in order to give her a rough idea of his whereabouts.

72 **a large Hospital here:** The Devonshire Hospital in Buxton, established in 1858. It possesses the largest unsupported dome in the world and this dominates the Buxton skyline.

'The Echoes of Despair . . .': *The Story of an African Farm*, II, 2.

82 **Neuve Chapelle:** A surprise attack (10–13 March 1915) by the British brought initial success but little ultimate advantage; about 13,000 men were lost on each side.

83 **'Men must work . . .':** From *The Three Fishers* by Charles Kingsley (1819–75).

85 **2nd Lieut. Gladstone:** W. C. G. Gladstone (1885–1915), Liberal MP for Kilmarnock Burghs, and oldest grandson of the great Liberal prime minister.

86 **a vast wood:** Ploegsteert Wood (known colloquially among British troops as 'Plug Street Wood'), on the Franco-Belgian border.

87 **body of a dead soldier:** Seeing this corpse, and sending Vera violets plucked near it, inspired one of Roland's finest poems, 'Villanelle', originally called 'Violets'.

89 **second battle of Ypres:** The defence of Ypres (22 April to 25 May) cost 60,000 British lives, leaving Ypres and a reduced salient still in Allied hands.

92 **Unter den Linden:** The main thoroughfare of Berlin.

96 **my letters arrive . . .:** Roland's letters could take sometimes five or six days to reach England, while from England to France there was a quicker two-day service.

98 **poisonous gas:** The Germans had released cylinders of chlorine gas at Ypres.

intervention of America: Anti-British and pro-German sentiment in the United States had grown strongly enough to foster fears that she would enter the war in support of Germany.

the sinking of the *Lusitania*: The British liner *Lusitania* was torpedoed off southern Ireland by a German U-boat on 7 May 1915 with the loss of 1,198 lives. The ship was in fact carrying American munitions to Britain.

99 **Dardanelles:** The ill-fated Dardanelles offensive had begun in March 1915.

105 **A St John's Wood garden:** Roland had lived in St John's Wood, north London, as a child.

106 **anti-German fury:** The sinking of the *Lusitania* had provoked attacks

by mobs on German-owned premises in London and other cities over several days. This resulted in the extension of internment (14 May).

106 **fighting . . . north of Lille:** On 9 May an unsuccessful attack had been made by British troops 20 miles south of Ypres on the Aubers Ridge near Lille, resulting in great loss of life.

109 **War Sonnets of Rupert Brooke:** Rupert Brooke had died of blood poisoning in the Aegean on 23 April while sailing to the Dardanelles with the Royal Naval Division. *1914* his famous sonnet-cycle, was first published in December 1914 in *New Numbers* but was shortly to appear in book form (16 June 1915).

110 **German outrages:** Based on the flimsiest of uncorroborated evidence, German troops had been accused of 'Murder, lust and pillage' during the invasion of Belgium.

112 **'Sometimes such a sudden gladness . . .':** *The Story of an African Farm*, II, 11.

113 **Festubert:** The Battle of Festubert (15–25 May 1915) saw a further attempt by the British and French to break through German defences south of Aubers Ridge. Once again it failed, with heavy casualties.
'that immortal garland . . .': From *Areopagitica* by John Milton (1608–74).

115 **conscription:** The issue of conscription would become an increasingly pressing one as the year wore on. There was a wide gulf between the political parties on the subject, and many Conservatives believed that the Asquith Government would be incapable of such an act of compulsion. However, in August 1915 came the National Register which compelled every citizen between 16 and 65, male and female, to supply details of age, sex, and occupation. It also gave them the opportunity to state whether they were prepared to perform work of national importance. This was widely seen as a prelude to conscription. By October the Derby recruiting scheme had been introduced to ask every eligible man to attest to his willingness to accept military service when called upon to do so. This failed to produce the hoped-for rise in the numbers enlisting, and in January 1916 compulsory military service was introduced for single men between 18 and 41.
Lord Northcliffe's papers: *The Times*, *Daily Mail*, *Daily Mirror*, and *Evening News*.
Coalition Government: Asquith had formed a coalition government comprising Liberals, Conservatives, and Labour members in mid-May.
entrance of Italy: Italy entered the war in May 1915.

116 **Zeppelin raid:** The first Zeppelin raid on London occurred in the East End at the end of May 1915. Seven were killed and thirty-five injured.

117 **Sterndale-Bennett:** Robert Sterndale Bennett (1881–1963), grandson

of the Victorian composer Sir William Sterndale Bennett, and brother of the popular composer T. C. Sterndale Bennett, was Director of Music at Uppingham School 1908–1945.

The Prime Minister: Herbert Henry Asquith (1852–1928), Liberal prime minister, 1908–1916, had dissolved the Liberal Cabinet in mid-May.

118   **'gifts more rare than gold':** A misquotation of Rupert Brooke's 'The Dead' (*1914*, III), 'a rarer sort than gold'.

124   **the name of a man . . .:** Second Lieutenant Frank Helm of the 8th Manchester Regiment.

125   **sent down South . . .:** The 7th Worcesters started their journey south on 26–27 June by moving from their trenches north of Ploegsteert Wood to Bailleul; by the end of July they would be firmly established in the Somme country at Hébuterne.

126   **nursing:** Vera had started at the Devonshire Hospital as a VAD probationer. The VAD (Voluntary Aid Detachment) scheme had been established in 1910, under the auspices of the British Red Cross and the St Johns Ambulance Association, to assist the professional military nursing service in the event of an emergency. Within months of the outbreak of war the VAD organisation had begun to expand, and by 1916 would have 80,000 members, including cooks, ward maids, and motor drivers, as well as nursing auxiliaries.

130   **A Field Service postcard:** postcards used by soldiers containing printed formulas of communication (e.g., 'I am quite well'); words not needed could be crossed out.

132   **. . . who haven't got 'red hats':** i.e. are not permanent members of Headquarters Staff.

133   **Hinc illae lacrimae:** 'The cause of grief is now clear' (literally, 'Hence those tears'); quoted by Horace and Cicero from the *Andria* of Terence. Vera and Roland had agreed that he would use these words if he knew he was going into action.

134   **My uniform:** The starched blue and white uniform of an auxiliary VAD.

140   **Devonshire House:** The headquarters in Piccadilly, London of the Red Cross which administered VAD appointments.

145   **'a child whom a long day's play . . .':** *The Story of an African Farm*, II, 9.

152   **Your little Villanelle:** Roland had shown Vera his poem 'Violets' while on leave. In her diary Vera wrote that 'The poem was dated April 25th 1915, and was called 'Violets'. I remembered how on that day he had written me a letter – he was then in Ploegsteert Wood – enclosing some violets from the top of his dug-out which he just said he had picked for

me.' She read the poem and handed it back to him without a word of criticism, 'moved by its union of brilliance with personal love'. (*Chronicle of Youth, Vera Brittain's War Diary 1913–1917*, edited by Alan Bishop, Gollancz, 1981, 250–51.) 'Violets' is printed in *Testament of Youth*, 135.

Julian Grenfell: Grenfell (1888–1915), the eldest son of Lord Desborough wrote several poems, but is chiefly remembered for the much anthologised 'Into Battle' which he had sent home in a letter. Grenfell died of the wounds he had received at Ypres on 26 May, and the poem was published in *The Times* shortly after that.

153 **Tonius:** Edward's nickname for Roland (after Mark Antony) acknowledges him as leader of the Uppingham triumvirate.

156 **Like Waldo . . .:** In the final chapter of *The Story of an African Farm* the hero, Waldo, who is Lyndall's soulmate, sits in the sun rejoicing in life, and then dies.

158 **death of a cousin . . .:** Frank Marrable, Vera's second cousin, whom she had never met.

Oh damn, I know it: From 'The Old Vicarage, Grantchester' by Rupert Brooke.

159 **Nirvana ideal:** The absorption of the individual personality into the Supreme Spirit (a Buddhist concept).

'I shall remember . . .': Opening words of 'A Year and a Day' by Kathleen M. Coates.

161 **'For, hand in hand . . .':** Lines from Roland's poem 'Goodbye'.

163 **Clare:** Roland's younger sister Clare Leighton (1899–1989), later a distinguished woodcut artist.

165 **their red, sweet wine of youth . . .:** A reference to Rupert Brooke's 'The Dead' (*1914*, III). Roland's letter is a powerful and damning rejection of Brooke-style rhetoric. For a discussion of the significance of this letter, see Paul Berry and Mark Bostridge, *Vera Brittain: A Life*, Chatto & Windus (1995) 89.

167 **it will possibly be a case of . . .:** See note to 133 above.

168 **Were men brought into the world . . . ?:** This paraphrases, perhaps unconsciously, a powerful passage in Schreiner's *Woman and Labour* (see IV, 'Woman and War'), and also strikingly foreshadows Wilfred Owen's poem 'Futility'.

169 **'War knows no power':** From Rupert Brooke's 'Safety' (*1914*, I).

'Till life . . .': From 'Echoes: XLII' by W. E. Henley (1849–1903).

170 **Transport Officer, Adam:** Captain W. Adam had been a friend of Roland's from the beginning of his service in France.

Raff's Cavatina and Saint-Saens' Le Cygne: Popular pieces by Joseph Raff (1822–82) and Camille Saint-Saëns (1835–1921).

171 **'Te moriturum saluto':** 'I salute you who are about to die'; an

adaptation of the gladiators' greeting to the Emperor Claudius (10 BC–AD 54), 'Ave, Imperator, morituri te salutant'. Roland's warning turned out again to have been a false alarm; but for five days Vera was left in suspense that he might have been involved and killed in the Battle of Loos (25 September–14 October 1915) which was another enormous military failure with losses of 60,000 men.

174 **Rudyard Kipling's son:** In September 1915 Kipling's only son John, aged eighteen, was reported missing believed killed at the Battle of Loos. For years Kipling refused to accept John's death despite eyewitness reports by soldiers who had seen him lying dead in terrain so shell-blasted that it was understandable that his body had never been found.

176 **'Farewell . . .':** Beginning of a speech by Cardinal Wolsey in Shakespeare's *Henry VIII*. (IIIi).

Mr Puckle: Horace Puckle, housemaster of Roland, Edward, and Victor at The Lodge, Uppingham.

177 **Lawrence Binyon's dirge . . .:** 'For the Fallen' by Lawrence Binyon (1869–1943) first appeared in *The Times*, 21 September 1914. The quotation is the beginning of the fourth verse which would be inscribed on countless memorials after the war.

178 **The Hospital:** The 1st London General Hospital in Cormont Road, Camberwell, south-east London, had been commandeered from St Gabriel's College for Ladies, a teachers' training college. It was one of four Territorial General Hospitals established in London for war casualties. There were over 1000 beds, and, in July 1915, 122 trained and 90 untrained staff. Vera and other VADs lodged in a hostel on Champion Hill.

180 **leaving the house . . .:** The Brittains were leaving Buxton following Mr Brittain's early retirement from the paper business.

182 **'These cast the world away':** Lines (slightly misquoted) from the octave of Rupert Brooke's 'The Dead' (*1914*, III).

184 **'How terrible it must be . . .':** *The Story of an African Farm*, IIi.

196 **'War knows no power':** From Rupert Brooke's 'Safety' (*1914*, I).

201 **'Unborn to-morrow and dead yesterday':** *The Rubaiyat of Omar Khayyam*, stanza XXXVII.

202 **Col. Harman:** Later General Sir Anthony Harman (1872–1961).

208 **the Chaplain:** Father Albert Purdie, later headmaster of St Edmund's College, Ware.

209 **'The old strong soul . . .':** *The Story of an African Farm*, II, 1.

212 **George Meredith:** Well-known poet and novelist (1828–1909).

Miss Bervon: Florence Bervon, Vera's aunt, (1864–1936) the eldest sister of Mrs Brittain, and co-principal of St Monica's, Kingswood, Surrey, 1904–31.

214   **Hédauville:** Written by Roland at the time of his estrangement from Vera in November 1915, this poem is strangely ambiguous. Roland appears either to be prophesying his own death, or to be suggesting that his relationship with Vera is cooling and that she will find happiness elsewhere. For a fuller discussion of the poem's meaning, see Berry and Bostridge, 94–6.

214   **'He being dead . . .':** Hebrews II, 4.

   'We have built a house . . .': Beginning of sestet, Rupert Brooke's 'safety'.

216   **'And daisies . . .':** The first two phrases are from Roland's 'Hédauville' and 'Nachklang'; the final two from his 'Ploegsteert'.

   body placed on a ship: The funeral of a Germanic hero (see the conclusion of *Beowulf*).

221   **'Miss Esperance and Mr Wycherley':** *Miss Esperance and Mr Wycherley*, (1908) a novel by L. Allen Harker.

   Chigwell: Chigwell School in Essex, where Geoffrey had been a pupil, was founded in 1629 by the Archbishop of York. It is magnificently situated in 70 acres of playing fields and woodlands.

   Derby's men: Men conscripted into the army under the Derby recruiting scheme. See note to 115 above.

222   **Stella:** Stella Sharp, a friend of Vera's from her school days who was also a VAD at the 1st London General, and would accompany Vera to Malta.

236   **Verdun offensive:** On 21 February 1916 a 14-inch shell exploded in the Archbishop's Palace at Verdun; this marked the beginning of the furious German offensive which would continue until the end of June, shattering the French fighting spirit.

238   **'a strong man's agony':** Conclusion of Roland's 'Ploegsteert'.

239   **a letter from my brother:** Maurice Richardson, at Uppingham, kept his older brother informed of school news.

242   **Bite:** Nickname of one of Geoffrey's two sisters.

243   **Ave atque Vale:** This poem was not included in *Verses of a V.A.D.* (1918), but was probably the foundation of two poems that frame Vera's 1934 collection, *Poems of the War and After*.

244   **This place . . .:** Albert. The leaning Virgin and Child on top of the town's basilica became associated with a powerful mythology. One version of the myth was that the war would end when the statue fell. It remained hanging until April 1918, brought down by heavy British gunfire when Albert was given up to the Germans. By that date the Golden Virgin had been seen by hundreds of thousands of men on their way up the line to the Somme.

246   **the book about Him . . .:** *Boy of My Heart*, 'a record exact and faithful, both in large things and small, of the short years of a boy who

willingly and even joyously gave up his life and all its brilliant promise for the sake of his country', appeared anonymously in June 1916.

247 **Macdowell Sea Songs:** Edward MacDowell, American composer (1860–1908).

248 **Verdi's Requiem:** Guiseppe Verdi (1813–1901) wrote the great *Requiem* in honour of his compatriot, the novelist and poet Manzoni.

250 **Roland's favourite quotation on Patriotism:** 'It is not a song in the street and a wreath on a column and a flag flying from a window . . . It is a thing very holy and very terrible, like Life itself. It is a burden to be borne, a thing to labour for and to suffer for and to die for; a thing which gives no happiness and no pleasantness – but a hard life, an unknown grave, and the respect and bowed heads of those who follow.' (John Masefield)

250 **Corner of a foreign field . . .:** slightly misquoted from Rupert Brooke's 'The Soldier' (*1914*, V).

252 **. . . the town, which you must now know . . .:** Albert.

254 **excitements in Ireland:** The Germans had tried to land arms in Ireland, while in Dublin the Easter Rising of April 1916 had been suppressed.

255 **Macclesfield:** Mr and Mrs Brittain had taken a furnished house in Macclesfield, where Vera and Edward had lived as children, before deciding upon a final move.

257 **'Such things are too great . . .':** Psalm 139, 6.
'not peace but a sword': Matthew 10, 34.

260 **'they that live by the sword':** Matthew 26, 52.

262 **Third Battle of Ypres:** Vera was being a little premature. The British would not begin their offensive to drive north-east from Ypres to the Belgian coast until the second half of 1917.
Kitchener: On 5 June 1916 the HMS *Hampshire*, on which Lord Kitchener (1850–1916) had been travelling to Russia, struck a mine off the Orkneys and sank. Kitchener was drowned. The unexpected news of Kitchener's death was felt as an abrupt shock throughout Britain.

270 **'So all day long . . .':** From 'The Passing of Arthur' in *Idylls of the King* by Alfred, Lord Tennyson (1809–92).

277 **8 Oakwood Court:** The Brittains had moved to a block of mansion flats, off Kensington High Street. In April 1917 they would move again to 10 Oakwood Court, a larger flat in the same block.

279 **Valetta:** The administrative and commercial centre of Malta, situated on a peninsula between two deep harbours.

280 **Sinister Street:** A novel (1913–14) about Oxford University life by Compton Mackenzie (1883–1972). It had become a *succès de scandale* after the first volume was banned by the circulating libraries.

287   **This hospital:** Following her recovery from illness, Vera had moved in
      the last week of October to St George's Hospital, about two miles west
      of Valetta, just above St George's Bay.

290   **Prince of Wales:** Edward, Prince of Wales (1894–1972), later Edward
      VIII, was attached to the XIV Army Corps Staff, and made routine tours
      of the trenches.

291   **Another big show . . .:** Attacking from the same positions as on 1 July,
      British troops took Beaumont-Hamel in mid-November.

294   **The sinking of the Britannic:** The *Britannic*, the ship on which Vera
      had travelled out to Malta, struck a mine on 21 November 1916 while car-
      rying over a thousand wounded soldiers; about fifty people were drowned.
      Death of Francis Joseph: The aged Emperor of Austria, Francis
      Joseph (1830–1916) had died in November 1916.

297   **Tosti's 'Goodbye':** A song by Francesco Tosti (1846–1916).
      Mrs Bendon: Geoffrey and Edward had been billeted with the Bendon
      family while training at Sandgate on the Kent coast.
      John Gilpin effect: A reference to the headlong gallop of the hero of
      the well-known poem by William Cowper (1731–1800).

299   **'A Long long Trail':** A plangent music-hall song popular with the
      troops.
      Fall of the Government: Asquith's Coalition Government had
      resigned in December 1916, and Lloyd George had succeeded Asquith
      as prime minister.

312   **'The sunshine on the long white road . . .':** Opening lines of
      Roland's 'Hédauville'.

317   **'Thus conscience . . .':** Shakespeare, *Hamlet*, III i.56.

320   **Sir Douglas Haig:** General Sir Douglas Haig (1861–1928), comman-
      der in chief of British forces.

322   **'And there was no more sea':** Revelation 21, 1.

323   **Bapaume:** By late February 1917 the German command had surren-
      dered Bapaume without a struggle.

326   **Kut . . . Baghdad:** General Maude's forces had recaptured Kut on the
      northern bank of the Tigris in February 1917; and on 11 March 1917 his
      army entered Baghdad.
      Rhymes of a Red Cross man: *Rhymes of a Red Cross Man* by Robert
      Service (1874–1958), a stretcher-bearer in France and Flanders, was pub-
      lished in 1917.

331   **Report of the Commission on the Dardanelles:** Published in 1917,
      the report condemned the instigators of the Dardanelles expedition.
      'Gallipoli': By John Masefield (1878–1967). An almost mystical account
      of the campaign, suffused with chivalric values.
      Russia: The March 1917 Revolution, with the overthrow of the Tsar

and the imposition of a Provisional Government, had recently taken place. Russia would sue for separate peace with Germany when the Bolsheviks came to power, under the Treaty of Brest-Litovsk (1918).

334 **'The valiant never taste of death but once':** Shakespeare, *Julius Caesar*, II, ii, 30.

the great battle: The Battle of Arras (9–14 April 1917).

335 **sirocco:** A warm humid wind from the Sahara which blows across the Mediterranean in the winter.

336 **'More things are wrought by prayer . . .':** From Tennyson's 'The Passing of Arthur' in *Idylls of the King*.

342 **'so marvellously overcame':** From the last line of a poem Vera had sent to Edward: 'Ave atque Vale' by Norman Hugh Romanes.

344 **The news all over the world . . .':** Vera is responding primarily to the American declaration of war against Germany (6 April 1917); but also to such events as the beginning of the Russian revolution (6 March) and the Allied victory at Vimy Ridge (10 April).

348 **question of my resignation . . .:** Vera's resignation was accepted on this occasion, and she did not have to break her VAD contract.

'whom the Gods': 'Whom the gods love die young' (Plautus); quoted in Byron's *Don Juan*.

349 **'Rejoice, whatever anguish . . .':** A line from Owen Seaman's 'Lines written in King Albert's Book', a poem Vera had sent to Edward in January 1916.

350 **'Happiness is a great love . . .':** *The Story of an African Farm*, II, 12.

351 **'whatsoever things are lovely . . .':** Epistle to the Philippians, 4, 8.

352 **The battalion attacked . . .:** At Monchy-le-Preux, three miles south-east of Arras.

W.H.K. Bervon: William Bervon, 'Uncle Bill' (1872–1925), was Mrs Brittain's younger brother and Vera's favourite uncle, to whom on occasion she turned for advice and support. He worked as a banker in the City of London.

353 **'He will be given a decent burial . . .':** In fact after the fighting Geoffrey's body had disappeared, and was never found. He is, however, commemorated on three war memorials: at Chigwell School, University College, Oxford, and at the Faubourg d'Amiens cemetery where he is one of 2652 British soldiers commemorated on the Arras memorial.

354 This letter is preserved in Victor's file among the Army Service Records at the Public Record Office, WO 374/57378.

362 **Major Hudson:** Major Charles Hudson (1892–1959) DSO, MC, soon to be promoted to Lieutenant-Colonel. In the Twenties he became Chief Instructor at the Royal Military College, Sandhurst.

367 **George:** George V (1865–1936).

Robert Nichols: One of the most popular wartime poets, Nichols (1893–1944) had fought with the Royal Artillery on the Somme but had soon been invalided home with shell shock. He then went to America to lecture as part of the British Mission (Ministry of Information). *Ardours and Endurances* (1917) contained war poems dedicated to the memory of two friends killed at the Front, and quickly became a bestseller.

368   **'Inter Arma Caritas':** The Red Cross motto, 'Love amidst War'.

369   **Everything of war . . . except actual fighting:** Étaples was one of the British Expeditionary Force's base camps. Étaples Base, about a mile out of the town, provided hospitals, prisons, stores, railway yards, and port facilities as well as infantry depots through which, it has been estimated, more than a million officers and men had passed by September 1917, for regrouping and retraining on the way to the Front. At the far north of the camp was the Bull Ring, the infamous area of training grounds where troops were put through a harsh and demoralising course of training. **this show:** The Third Battle of Ypres.

374   **The name of your sister . . .:** Faith Moulson (born 1884) ('Hope Milroy' in *Testament of Youth*), a member of Queen Alexandra's Imperial Military Nursing Service.

375   **what has happened to Edward in this push:** Edward's company had been involved in the fighting around Passchendaele in September 1917.

377   **poems . . . for a small volume:** Vera's first book, published in August 1918 as *Verses of a V.A.D.* Erskine Macdonald, an alias for Galloway Kyle, was an unscrupulous publisher of amateur verse, who made profits out of unsuspecting authors. Macdonald was shown the typescript of the poems by Marie Leighton, and agreed to publish them after Mr Brittain offered him 'ten reams of antique printing paper' for no charge.

382   **the city . . .:** Mantua.

385   **The Loom of Youth:** A novel by Alec Waugh (1898–1961) which caused a sensation on its publication in 1917 because of its attack on public school education. The book criticises the public schools' worship of sport, and the stranglehold of classics on the curriculum, and also depicts homosexuality among the boys. *The Loom of Youth*'s attack upon a system that was providing officers for the Front was considered to be in poor taste. The preface by the Sandhurst historian Thomas Seccombe argues that the public school system was partly responsible for the war. **Swinburne . . . Atalanta:** *Atalanta in Calydon* (1865) by Algernon Swinburne (1837–1909). Edward had received the complete works of Swinburne among the presents for his twenty-first birthday.

387   **'a sob on the sea . . .':** From Roland's 'Triolet'.

388   **conditions at home . . .:** By early 1918 there were disturbances in

London and some provincial towns protesting against coal and food shortages. Coal rationing had been applied to London in October 1917, and queues for such basic commodities as sugar, butter, tea, and meat were a common sight at this time.

389   **a mountain famous . . .:** On 17 February 1918 the battalion had arrived at Possagno, a village at the foot of the mountains between Monte Grappa and Monte Tomba.

390   **PUO:** Pyrexia (fever) of unknown origin.

391   **Vernède's poem:** The patriotic *War Poems* of Robert Vernède (1875–1917) had been published in 1917.

393   **The worst of the show in France:** This refers to Ludendorff's great offensive in March 1918 in attacking the southern part of the British sector on the Western Front. By the end of the month the Germans had advanced 40 miles and taken 1,200 square miles of territory; but they had also overrun territory that the previous year they had gone to great lengths to abandon, and they had sustained casualties of 250,000 men. It was clear strategically that they could not win the war.

395   **Hugh Walpole:** Novelist (1884–1941). *The Dark Forest* (1916) and *Fortitude* (1913) were among his fiction.
      the Uppingham War Memorial: Four hundred and forty-seven names of Uppinghamians killed in the war would eventually be inscribed on this memorial.

398   **The novel . . . idea [for] another:** 'The Pawn of Fate', Vera's first attempt to write a novel based on her war experiences, combined a melodramatic plot with a fictionalised Faith Moulson against the background of 24 General Hospital at Étaples; it was never completed. The proposed second novel, with Edward as protagonist, foundered almost immediately, presumably as a result of his death.

400   **Jack:** Mrs Leighton's brother.
      Evelyn: Evelyn Leighton (died 1967), Roland's younger brother. Trained as a cadet at Osborne and Dartmouth Naval Colleges, he later became a captain in the Royal Navy.

SELECT BIBLIOGRAPHY

Berry, Paul, and Alan Bishop, eds. *Testament of a Generation: The Journalism of Vera Brittain and Winifred Holtby*. London: Virago, 1985.

Berry, Paul, and Mark Bostridge. *Vera Brittain: A Life*. London: Chatto & Windus, 1995; Pimlico, 1996.

Brittain, Vera. *Verses of a V.A.D.*, London: Erskine MacDonald, 1918. Facsimile edition, with Introduction by Paul Berry and Mark Bostridge: London: Imperial War Museum, 1995.

—— *Testament of Youth, An Autobiographical Study of the Years 1900–1925*. London: Gollancz, 1933; New York: Macmillan, 1933; London: Virago, 1978; London: Fontana, 1979.

—— *Poems of the War and After*. London: Gollancz, 1934; New York: Macmillan, 1934.

—— *Chronicle of Youth: War Diary 1913–1917*, ed Alan Bishop with Terry Smart. London: Gollancz, 1981; New York: Morrow, 1982; London: Fontana, 1982.

Brooke, Rupert. *1914 & Other Poems*. London: Sidgwick & Jackson, 1915. *The Collected Poems*. London: Sidgwick and Jackson, 1915. *Poetical Works*, ed G. Keynes. London: Faber and Faber, 1970.

Gorham, Deborah. *Vera Brittain: A Feminist Life*. Oxford: Blackwell, 1996.

Leighton, Clare. *Tempestuous Petticoat: The Story of an Invincible Victorian*. London: Gollancz, 1947.

Leighton, Marie. *Boy of My Heart* (published anonymously). London: Hodder & Stoughton, 1916.

Leighton, Roland. *Poems*. Privately published: David Leighton, 1981.

Mackenzie, Compton. *Sinister Street*. London: Martin Secker, 1913; Harmondsworth: Penguin, 1960.

Masefield, John. *Gallipoli*. London: Heinemann, 1916.

Nichols, Robert. *Ardours and Endurances*. London: Chatto and Windus, 1917.

Parker, Peter. *The Old Lie. The Great War and the Public School Ethos*. London: Constable, 1987.

Schreiner, Olive. *The Story of an African Farm*. London: Hutchison, 1883 (as by Ralph Iron); Harmondsworth: Penguin, 1939.

—— *Woman and Labour*. London: T. Fisher Unwin, 1911; London: Virago, 1978.

Tylee, Clare M. *The Great War and Women's Consciousness*. London: Macmillan, 1990.

Walpole, Hugh. *Fortitude*. London: Martin Secker, 1913.

—— *The Dark Forest*. London: Secker, 1916.

Waugh, Alec. *The Loom of Youth*. London: Grant Richards, 1917; Harmondsworth: Penguin, 1941.

INDEX

The addition of 'n' indicates that relevant information, keyed to that page-number, will be found in the Notes.

www.virago.co.uk

virago

To find out more about Virago authors, visit:
www.virago.co.uk

Visit the Virago website for:

- Exclusive features and interviews with authors, including Margaret Atwood, Maya Angelou, Sarah Waters and Nina Bawden

- News of author events and forthcoming titles

- Competitions

- Exclusive signed copies

- Discounts on new publications

- Book-group guides

- Free extracts from a wide range of titles

PLUS: subscribe to our free monthly newsletter